MW00447101

Prentice Hall

Drive Right

UPDATED TENTH EDITION

Authors
Margaret L. Johnson
Owen Crabb
Arthur A. Opfer
Randall R. Thiel

Consulting Author
Frederik R. Mottola

Boston, Massachusetts
Upper Saddle River, New Jersey

About the Authors

Margaret L. Johnson is a former supervisor of Driver, Consumer, and Health Education at Glenbrook North High School, Northbrook, Illinois. She was also an instructor of Traffic Safety and Driver Education at Northeastern Illinois University in Chicago.

Owen Crabb is a former Driver Education Specialist with the Maryland State Department of Education. He has also assisted several states in developing driver education programs.

Arthur A. Opfer has taught driver education at both the high school and college levels. He is a former Regional Traffic Coordinator for the Superintendent of Public Instruction at Educational Service District 105, Yakima, Washington.

Randall R. Thiel is Education Consultant for the Alcohol-Traffic Safety Program for the Wisconsin Department of Public Instruction. He has taught driver education at the high school level and has been involved in teacher preparation programs at universities in Texas, Pennsylvania, and Indiana.

Frederik R. Mottola is Professor Emeritus of Public Health at Southern Connecticut State University and Executive Director of Driver Behavior Institute. He is the creator of the Zone Control System of Space Management and Reference Point Visualizations. He is a consultant and educator for traffic safety education programs for teachers, students, and drivers on local, national, and international levels.

PEARSON
Prentice Hall

ISBN 013-131607-9 (hardcover)
5 6 7 8 9 10 10 09 08 07
ISBN 013-131610-9 (softcover)
3 4 5 6 7 8 9 10 10 09 08 07

Consultants and Reviewers

Consultants

Leon Butorac
Former Traffic Safety Teacher
Auburn High School
Auburn, Washington

Jerry L. Gaines
Driver Education Coordinator
Palos Verdes Peninsula Unified School District
Palos Verdes Estates, California

Terry Kline
Assistant Professor
Traffic Safety Institute
Eastern Kentucky University
Richmond, Kentucky

Gregory Schitkovitz
Teacher, Driver Education
Glenbrook North High School
Northbrook, Illinois

Elizabeth A. Weaver
Driver Education Specialist
Department of Education
Boise, Idaho

Reviewers

Barbara E. Brody
Coordinator, Driver Education Improvement Program
Minnesota Highway Safety Center
St. Cloud State University
St. Cloud, Minnesota

Paul Cram
Teacher, Driver Education
Washington High School
Washington, Illinois

Alex Hansen
Department Chair, Traffic Safety Education
Lakes High School,
Clover Park School District
Lakewood, Washington

Sally Ann Holland
Instructor/Owner
Drivers Edge
Glenburn, Maine

David J. Holloway
Teacher, Driver Education
Windsor High School
Windsor, Vermont

James M. Lewis
Department Chair, Driver Education
Simi Valley High School
Simi Valley, California

Edward McEvoy
Department Chair, Driver Education
Hempstead High School
Dubuque, Iowa

William G. Robbins, Sr.
Instructor/Owner
Rocky Mountain Driving Academy
Lakewood, Colorado

Major Thompson
Department Chair, Driver Education
Fayette County Community School
Fayettville, Georgia

C.E. Welch
Department Chair,
Driver Education
Southeast High School
Springfield, Illinois

Contents

Unit 2
Controlling Your Vehicle *88*

Unit 3

Driving in Different Environments *172*

Unit 4

Being a Responsible Driver *288*

Unit 1

The Driving Task

CHAPTER 1
You Are the Driver

You Are the Driver!

Imagine you have just received your driver's license. You've worked hard to get this far, and now it's time to celebrate. Your driving privilege is one of the things that makes this moment possible. Beyond this moment, driving will play an important part in your life. How important do you think it is to maintain a good driving record?

This chapter introduces you to driving and the responsibilities that go along with it. You will also learn how driver education and driver's licensing programs can help you become a responsible, low-risk driver.

Go Online
PHSchool.com
For: Chapter 1 online activities
Visit: PHSchool.com
Web Code: cak-9999

1.1
You Are Part of the System

Objectives

1. Describe the three parts of the highway transportation system (HTS).
2. Tell how the HTS is regulated.

You are about to take a driver education course, apply for your driver's license, and join the millions of others who share our country's roads. If you grow to meet this challenge, you will have a lifetime filled with many new opportunities. Your key to this exciting future will be your ability to master the new skills needed to manage the conflicts and risks associated with driving.

In everyday life, there are many types of conflicts and risks. But, the main **risk** in driving is the possibility of having a conflict that results in a collision.

The Highway Transportation System

When you drive, you will become part of a massive system called the **highway transportation system,** or HTS. The HTS has three parts: people, vehicles, and roadways. The purpose of the HTS is to move people and cargo from one place to another in a safe, efficient, and economical manner.

Of all transportation systems, the HTS is the most complex. It has the greatest variety of users, including drivers, passengers, motorcyclists, bicyclists, and pedestrians. The HTS has a wide range of roadways from simple rural lanes to complex multilane urban roads and expressways.

People

The people who use the HTS by walking, driving, or riding are called *roadway users.* Roadway users vary greatly in their ability to use the system.

While most individuals consistently drive in a safe, low-risk, responsible manner, others do not. Drivers with good skills sometimes operate their vehicles when they are overly distracted, tired, ill, or impaired by alcohol. To protect yourself and others in these situations, you will have to be the one to take responsibility for avoiding trouble.

Vehicles

Think about the wide range of vehicles that use the HTS. Mopeds and motorcycles are small and have little protection. At the other extreme is the tractor-semitrailer weighing tons. In between are cars, vans, small trucks, buses, campers, farm vehicles, and construction equipment. During this course, you will be called on to develop special skills to lower risk and avoid conflicts when interacting with these vehicles.

Roadways

Roadways of the HTS vary from dirt lanes to complex multilane expressways. Common conditions such as rain, nighttime, or rough pavement, can become major problems. It is up to you to maintain control of your vehicle at all times and in all conditions.

The highway transportation system consists of a complex mix of people, vehicles, and roadways.

Regulating the HTS

Drivers who operate their vehicles in a responsible, low-risk manner are the most important part in the HTS. To make sure this happens, all states grant individuals the privilege of driving on their roads by issuing them a driver's license. By passing a licensing exam, you agree to obey traffic laws in exchange for the privilege of operating a motor vehicle on public roads.

Many federal, state, and local government agencies help regulate the HTS. The federal government has established the National Highway Safety Act with a set of traffic-safety guidelines. Federal, state and local governments in turn enforce these national guidelines:

- Laws are passed to make up the **vehicle code.**
- Enforcement agencies assure that laws are obeyed.
- Motor vehicle departments set rules to assure that driver and vehicle standards are met.
- Courts decide whether drivers charged with violating the laws are guilty or innocent.
- Highway traffic engineers plan, build, and maintain the complex system of roadways.

Review It

1. What are the parts and purpose of the HTS?
2. How is the HTS regulated?

1.2 Your Driving Task

Objectives

1. Explain how social, physical, and mental skills work together in your driving task.
2. Name the four steps in the IPDE Process.

The **driving task** includes all the social, physical, and mental skills required to drive. To perform the driving task with low-risk results, you must develop habits for

- using knowledge and visual skills, as shown in the picture
- obeying traffic laws
- judging time and space
- anticipating how your car will respond under normal and emergency conditions

Social Skills

Like other social tasks, driving requires you to interact successfully with people. If you are a courteous driver, you not only obey traffic laws, but you make an extra effort to work with other drivers. Without courtesy and cooperation, low-risk driving is impossible.

All drivers bring their own problems and skill levels to your shared driving world. A big part of your driving task will be applying your social skills to these types of situations so that everyone avoids conflicts.

Physical Skills

You must learn the physical skills of driving so well that they become natural habits. Then you can focus your attention on the social and mental tasks of driving. Beginning drivers often need to concentrate heavily on the physical skills of driving. After extended practice, these drivers acquire the ability to control their vehicle. They can then focus their attention on the social and mental aspects of driving.

Mental Skills

Safe, low-risk driving is primarily a mental task that involves decision making. Physical skills are minor when compared to the necessary decision-making skills.

The IPDE Process

The **IPDE Process** is a process of seeing, thinking, and responding. The four steps of this process are pictured on the opposite page.

- **Identify** important information in the ongoing driving scene.
- **Predict** when and where possible points of conflict will develop.
- **Decide** when, where, and how to communicate, adjust speed, and/or change position to avoid conflict.

Mental and visual skills are critical to your driving task.

Identify the oncoming car, turn signal, and driveway.

Predict that your path of travel and the oncoming vehicle's path of travel will conflict.

Decide to slow or stop.

Execute speed reduction decision by taking foot off accelerator and gently braking.

- **Execute** the right action(s) to prevent conflict.

Two other systems will help you use the IPDE Process. The **Smith System** is an organized method designed to help drivers develop good seeing habits. In addition, the **Zone Control System** is a method for managing the space around your vehicle. These systems will help you apply the IPDE Process for effective, low-risk driving.

Once you have mastered the IPDE Process, you will be able to drive in a way that reduces conflicts. This ability, called **defensive driving,** lowers the risk of conflict by protecting you and others from dangerous driving situations.

Review It

1. How does the driving task require a blend of social, mental, and physical skills?
2. What are the four steps in the IPDE Process?

1.3

Your Driving Responsibilities

Objectives

1. Explain how your attitude will affect your driving.
2. List some examples of HTS breakdowns.
3. Describe several major causes of collisions.
4. Explain how drivers can help protect our environment.

When you earn your first driver's license, the state you live in will extend you the privilege to drive. Driving is a privilege—not a right. The driving privilege is based on the assumption that you will be a responsible traffic citizen and obey all traffic laws. Driving also is a major responsibility. If you assume it and respect it, you will enjoy a lifelong adventure of safe, low-risk, low-stress driving. If you do not handle this responsibility, you have the power to ruin your life and the lives of others.

Attitude

Your attitude toward life and driving affects your willingness to learn and to effectively use safe-driving habits. For many, reckless driving is a way of getting attention. What they don't realize is that they are getting noticed in a negative way.

Road rage shows an extremely negative attitude toward driving. The driver who is in a rage is likely to do anything. Your best defense is to put distance between yourself and the enraged driver. Don't challenge an enraged driver. Instead, give way. Be extremely cautious at intersections because some drivers simply refuse to obey red traffic lights. In extreme situations, alert police if possible.

Other drivers drive in a responsible low-risk way day after day, year after year. They know their low-risk driving eventually will gain them respect. Getting quick attention is easy. Earning respect over the long haul takes time and effort.

Your attitude will guide you as you manage your relationships with others. There will be times when others will try to get you to do things you normally would not do. They will push you to drive in a way you shouldn't. Saying no—especially to a friend as shown in the picture—isn't easy.

You Are the Driver!

How can you use these techniques to say "no"?

- Ask questions.
- State the problem.
- State the consequences.
- Suggest alternatives.
- Leave and encourage others to join you.

Breakdowns in the HTS

A breakdown in the HTS occurs when any part of the system does not work well. Traffic tie-ups and collisions are two examples of HTS breakdowns. Your ability to drive responsibly will be the major factor in helping you avoid being part of these breakdowns.

A **collision** occurs when a vehicle conflicts with and hits another object. Collisions are a major cause of injury and death.

Collision or Accident?

Collision is a more accurate term than *accident.* Why? Because *accident* implies that something just happens by chance. In reality, almost every collision is the product of a predictable cause. The drunk driver hit the pole. The speeding driver ran off the road. The careless driver didn't wear a safety belt or tuned a radio at the wrong time and hit a tree.

Over the years our national driving record has steadily improved. This is the result of an ongoing highway safety effort involving engineering, enforcement, and education. Still we should not be lulled into a false sense of security. Check the chart on this page and compare your chance of dying in a car crash versus other events.

Causes of Collisions Of all the possible causes of collisions, driver error is by far the most common. Frequent errors include breaking various laws, not slowing in adverse weather conditions, and operating a defective vehicle. Other serious driver errors are

- following another vehicle too closely
- driving too fast for conditions
- not wearing safety belts
- driving after drinking or using drugs
- driving while very tired

Like most complex events, traffic collisions usually have more than one cause. For example, a vehicle skids off a slippery turn and collides into a tree. The initial report might list the cause as driving too fast for conditions. But a close inspection might reveal that the road was abnormally slick and the tires on the vehicle were very smooth. The slick roadway and the smooth tires added to the problem. Even though the primary cause of the collision was driving too fast, you must know all the factors involved to really understand why the collision happened. If you had been the driver in this collision, what aspects could you have controlled?

Causes of Death The chart on the next page compares traffic collisions with other major causes of death for young people. Why is driving such a high-risk activity? Lack of experience is a major factor for this poor driving record. Other factors include increased exposure to night driving, increased risk taking, susceptibility to peer pressure, and mixing drinking and driving.

Does this mean all young drivers are bad? Absolutely not! All drivers can learn to apply the principles of responsible low-risk driving with good results.

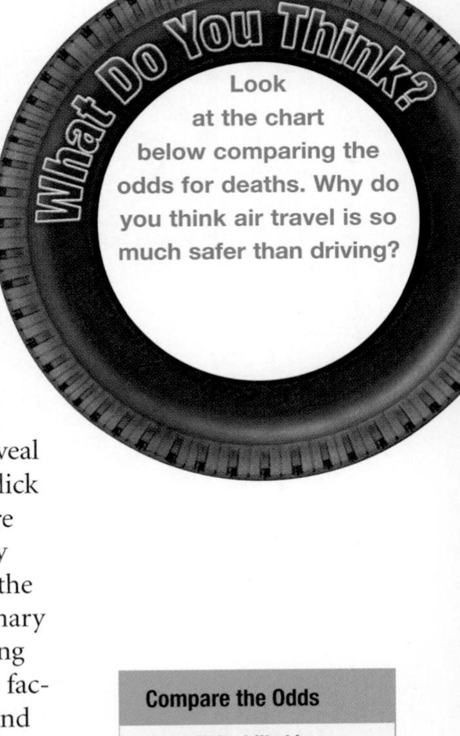

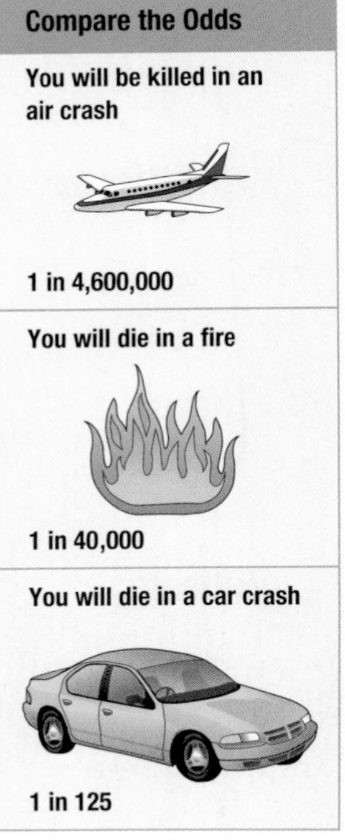

Driving a car is still the most dangerous way to travel.

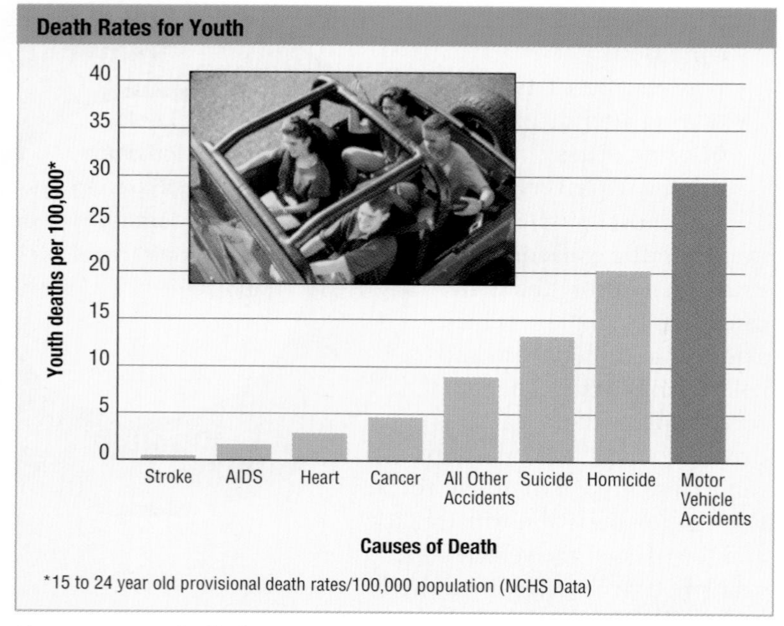

More young people die from vehicle collisions than from any other single cause.

Social and Economic Loss Collisions have tremendous social and economic effects. Traffic collisions cost our nation billions of dollars each year in property damage, time away from work and school, medical fees, and insurance premiums. The cost of mental anguish and physical suffering simply cannot be measured.

Other Responsibilities

In addition to driving, all drivers have additional responsibilities. These include financial and environmental responsibilities.

Financial Responsibility

As a driver, you are responsible for your share of driving-related costs. Vehicle-related costs include fuel as well as maintaining and insuring your car. You also are financially responsible by law for any damage or injuries that you cause.

Environmental Responsibility

Our nation's demand for transportation has created many threats to our environment, including

- air pollution
- water pollution
- chemical spills
- land pollution through thoughtless disposal of vehicle-related products

How can transportation-related environmental problems be managed? All drivers should act responsibly by

- buying and maintaining fuel-efficient vehicles
- using fuel-efficient driving habits
- recycling used materials
- reducing driving through car pools and the use of public transportation when possible
- working for strong national, state, and local policies that encourage the use of energy-efficient driving

Review It

1. How do attitudes affect driving?
2. What are some examples of breakdowns in the HTS?
3. What are the three major causes of collisions?
4. What are some actions drivers can take to protect our environment?

1.4

Your Driver's License

Objectives

1. Explain how a graduated driver licensing program can help you drive more safely.
2. List some of the main concepts stressed in a quality driver education program.

Once you start driving, everyone will want you to become a safe driver. Your family will support you. Your friends will encourage you. Government and private industry will try to help you through licensing and education programs. Still, driving is one of the most dangerous activities you will ever do. For young people, the risk is even higher. Look at the graph on this page to see just how deadly driving can be.

Why is the highway death rate among teens so high? Most of the time, young drivers simply make mistakes from inexperience. *Forty-one percent of the young people who were killed in these collisions died in single-car collisions.*

Licensing Process

The purpose of a comprehensive driver licensing program is to make sure only safe drivers are allowed on public roads. Most licensing programs require applicants to take written, physical, and driving exams.

Graduated Driver Licensing

Structured practice-driving time for new drivers works. As you ride with other drivers, you pick up some good and bad driving habits.

To help young drivers adjust to driving, many states have a **graduated driver licensing program**, which requires young drivers to progress through a series of licensing stages. Typically these programs have three stages.

Learner's Permit Stage Supervised conditions include

- The learner receives a permit to drive when supervised by an adult, licensed driver.
- The permit must be held for a minimum period of violation-

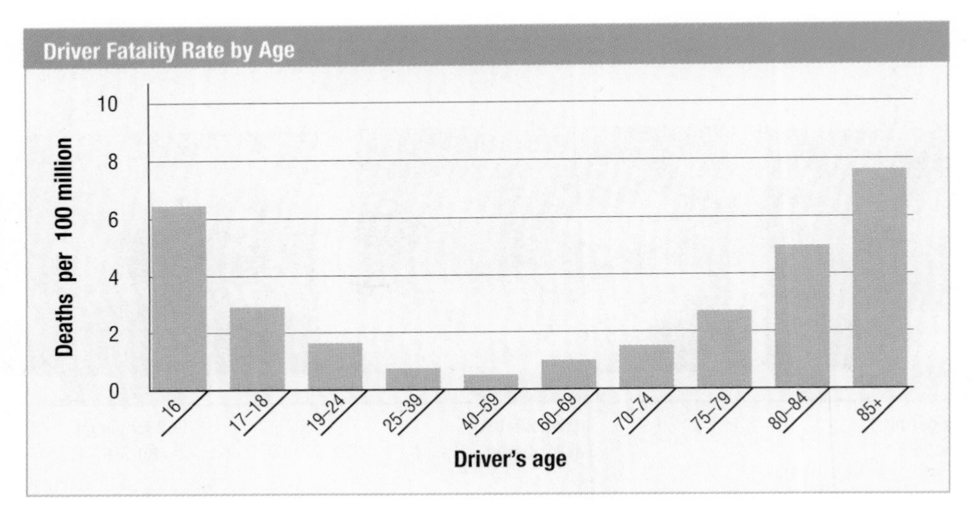

The main reason that the death rate for 16-year-old drivers is so high is lack of driving experience.

free and collision-free driving (usually six months).

- Safety belts must be worn by all occupants.
- Other licensed drivers, such as family members, may be asked to provide a minimum number of hours of practice driving.

Intermediate License Stage The learner drives under the following restrictions during this stage:

- The learner must have successfully completed the learner's permit stage and an approved driver education course.
- Supervised driving may be continued to meet the required hours.
- Safety belts must be worn by all occupants.
- Night driving, especially late night driving, is restricted.
- Passengers can be limited in age and/or number.
- The intermediate license must be held for six months or more of collision-free and violation-free driving. If the learner has a violation or collision, the intermediate license "clock" is set back to zero.
- Penalties for violations are increased. Many times violators are required to go to traffic school.

Full-Privilege License Stage To graduate to this full unrestricted license stage, the learner must

- successfully complete the intermediate stage violation-free and collision-free
- in some states, complete an advanced driver education course

Do these graduated driver licensing programs work? Yes! In New Zealand, Australia, Canada, and

Graduated driver licensing programs have three basic stages.

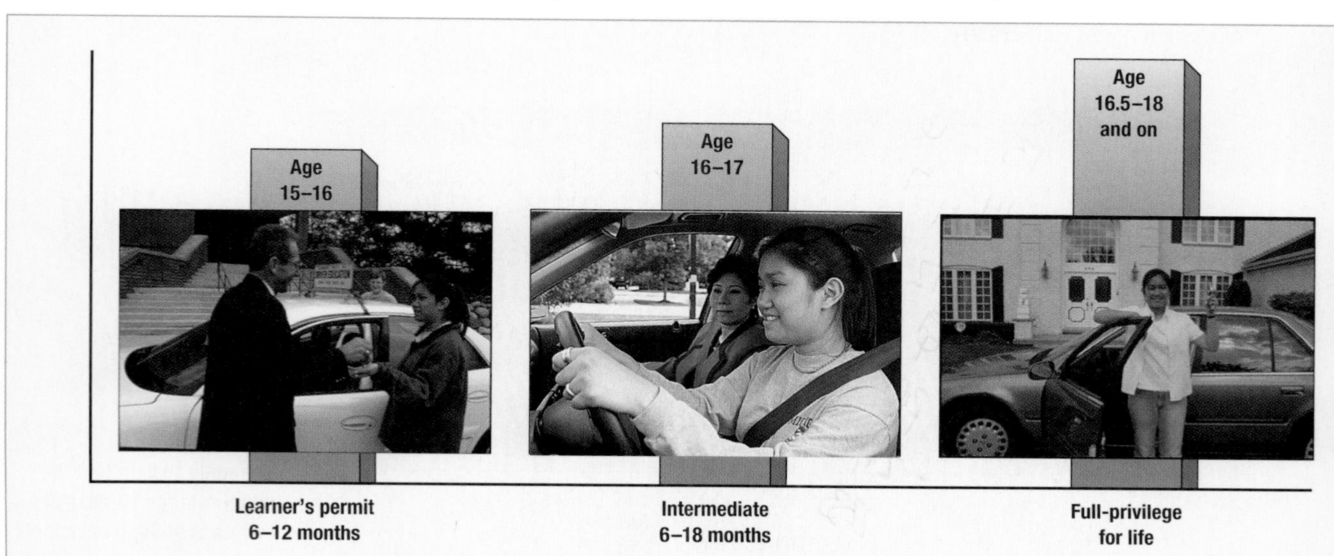

more recently in the United States, they have demonstrated their worth.

Even if your state does not have a formal program, you can follow the stages of these graduated licensing programs to obtain similar results. Just remember that good drivers never stop learning.

Organ Donor Program

You may indicate your desire to be an organ donor by filling out an organ donation declaration on your driver's license or by signing an organ donor card. Remember that the most important step in considering organ donation is informing your family and other loved ones of your decision. This will ensure that your wishes are carried out.

Implied Consent Programs

In most states you may be asked to sign a statement when you get your driver's license saying that you agree to take an alcohol test on request. If you refuse to take the test, you will lose your driver's license.

EARLY DRIVER EDUCATION Dr. Amos E. Neyhart taught one of the first high school driver education courses in 1933. He taught the course free, in his own car. Dr. Neyhart explained that before his class was offered, people learned to drive from the people who sold cars. They would teach how to start, steer, and stop. But once the buyer got moving and steering, the salespeople would jump out!

Driver Education and Your License

As you begin this course, you probably are thinking of the advantages of your new driver's license. You should be equally interested in learning the skills you need to become a responsible, low-risk driver. The driving situation shown here and on the next page is an example of a lesson to be learned.

You Are the Driver!
What would you predict might be around the curve?

You Are the Driver!
Would you be ready to avoid these hikers?

You will have a wide range of classroom and on-road experiences in this course. Under the professional guidance of an instructor, you will learn the skills and develop the habits needed to become a low-risk driver.

Be sure to include night driving and bad weather in your supervised driving experiences.

Your Beginning

The *Drive Right* program is your start toward becoming a responsible low-risk driver. The course you are about to take is based in part on the following key concepts

- Driving is a mental decision-making process. In this program, you will learn how to use the IPDE Process to become a responsible low-risk driver.
- Your driving will be greatly influenced by your attitude.
- Safety belts and other restraints must be used at all times.
- The statistics arguing against drinking and driving should convince you to never drink and drive.

Once you pass your driver education program, you should take at least one year to ease into full-time driving responsibilities. After you have driven well under a wide variety of road and traffic situations, you can start to think of yourself as an accomplished new driver.

A Continuous Process

This driver education course will help start you on your personal lifetime driving adventure. It cannot teach you about everything you will encounter when driving. As long as you drive, you will need to use and improve your skills in a systematic way. Good drivers never stop learning.

Review It

1. How can a graduated driver licensing program help you?
2. What are the key concepts in a quality driver education program?

Chapter 1
Review

Reviewing Chapter Objectives

1. You Are Part of the System

1. What are the three parts of the highway transportation system (HTS)? (4)
2. How is the HTS regulated? (5)

2. Your Driving Task

3. How do social, physical, and mental skills work together in your driving task? (6)
4. What are the four steps in the IPDE Process? (6–7)

3. Your Driving Responsibilities

5. How will your attitude affect your driving? (8)
6. What are some examples of HTS breakdowns? (9)
7. What are the major causes of collisions? (9)
8. How can drivers help protect our environment? (10)

4. Your Driver's License

9. How can a graduated driver licensing program help you drive more safely? (11–12)
10. What are some of the main concepts stressed in a quality driver education program? (13–14)

Projects

Individuals

Investigate Research to find more information about the National Highway Safety Act. When was this law passed? What are the major features of the law? Write a short report to summarize your findings. Discuss your findings with the class.

Interview Interview three drivers. Choose one driver who has been driving for less than two years, one driver who has been driving for between five and ten years, and one who has been driving for more than ten years. Ask these drivers if they feel they have developed any bad driving habits. After the interview, decide what the driver can do to overcome each bad habit mentioned. Discuss your findings with your classmates.

Groups

Brainstorm As a group, list all the possible factors you can think of that may lead to risks in driving. When your list is complete, categorize each risk according to whether or not the driver can control the risk. Then put the risks in order from most to least dangerous. Compare your results with those of the other groups in your class.

Observe Traffic As a group, observe the drivers in your school parking lot as they arrive at or leave school for the day. Rate the drivers on a scale of 1 to 5. Drivers rated as 1's show a low-risk, defensive attitude toward driving; 5's show a high-risk, negative attitude. List the reasons, based on the drivers' behaviors, for each score you assign. Discuss your group's findings with your class.

Chapter 1
Review

Chapter Test

Check Your Knowledge

Multiple Choice Copy the number of each sentence below on a sheet of paper. Choose the letter of the answer that best completes the statement or answers the question.

1. Which of the following is part of the highway transportation system (HTS)?
(a) vehicles (c) people
(b) roadways (d) all of these

2. Safe, low-risk driving is primarily a _____ task.
(a) physical (c) social
(b) mental (d) none of the above

3. If you drive in a low-risk way, you will
(a) get the attention you want.
(b) gain others' respect.
(c) improve your ability to compete.
(d) be able to maneuver easily.

4. Graduated driver licensing programs
(a) usually are completed in three licensing stages.
(b) are conducted worldwide.
(c) have resulted in fewer collisions among young drivers.
(d) all of the above

Completion Copy the number of each sentence below. After each number, write the word or words that complete the sentence correctly.

5. The four steps of the IPDE Process are identify, predict, _____, and execute.

6. Drive _____ by protecting yourself and others from dangerous and unexpected situations.

7. When applied to driving, the term _____ means the possibility of having a conflict that results in a collision.

8. The _____ is made up of people, vehicles, and roadways.

Review Vocabulary

Copy the number of each definition in list A. Match the definition in list A with the term it defines in list B.

List A

9. federal and state laws that regulate the HTS
10. contact between two or more objects, as when two vehicles hit each other
11. organized method designed to help drivers develop good seeing habits
12. method for managing the space around your vehicle
13. program requiring young drivers to progress through a series of licensing stages
14. all the skills—social, physical, and mental—required to drive

List B

a. Zone Control System
b. graduated driver licensing program
c. Smith System
d. vehicle code
e. driving task
f. collision

Think Critically

Write a paragraph to answer each question.

1. What are your responsibilities as a participant in the highway transportation system (HTS)?
2. Why do you think the death rate for drivers and passengers is higher among teens than other age groups?

Chapter 1 Review

Decision Making

1. What part of the HTS is most important in keeping this a low-risk driving situation?

2. The IPDE Process is an ongoing process used to avoid conflicts. How can you apply it to this situation?

3. This car buyer is checking various new car fuel economy ratings. How does this decision help or hurt the environment?

4. This driver is receiving supervised instruction from his father. How can this instruction help him become a safer driver?

Pico
Pico

CHAPTER 2
Signs, Signals, and Roadway Markings

You Are the Driver!

Imagine that you are driving on the street shown here. The red traffic light is about to turn green. Are you in the best lane to continue straight? Will you have to stop for other vehicles that plan to turn? How might pedestrians create a problem for you?

Safe, organized driving would be a lot more difficult without signs, signals, and roadway markings. To be a safe and responsible driver, you must know what signs, signals, and roadway markings mean. This chapter discusses these controls and how to respond to them properly.

For: Chapter 2 online activities
Visit: PHSchool.com
Web Code: cak-9999

2.1 Traffic Signs

Objectives

1. State the meaning of the eight shapes and eight colors used for traffic signs.
2. Describe the actions to take at STOP, YIELD, and speed limit signs.
3. List five situations where warning signs might be used.
4. Explain how guide signs and international signs help you when driving.

You will see hundreds of different traffic signs as you drive. While traffic signs serve many purposes, each traffic sign has a specific shape and color.

Shapes and Colors

Note the eight sign shapes and eight sign colors shown on the opposite page. Each sign shape and color has a special meaning. By knowing the meanings of these shapes and colors, you can get valuable information from a sign—even at a distance.

Each traffic sign has a specific purpose. A **regulatory sign,** such as a STOP sign, controls traffic. A **warning sign,** including a signal ahead sign, alerts you to possible hazards and road conditions. A **guide sign,** such as an interstate sign, gives directions.

Regulatory Signs

Regulatory signs tell you about laws that you must obey. The most important signs, STOP and YIELD, have unique shapes. All other regulatory signs are either white squares or rectangles with red or black lettering.

Stop Sign

A STOP sign is used on a road that crosses a main highway or a through street. The STOP sign is a red octagon with white letters and border.

Always come to a **full stop** at a STOP sign. Once stopped, you must yield the right of way to pedestrians or other vehicles in or approaching

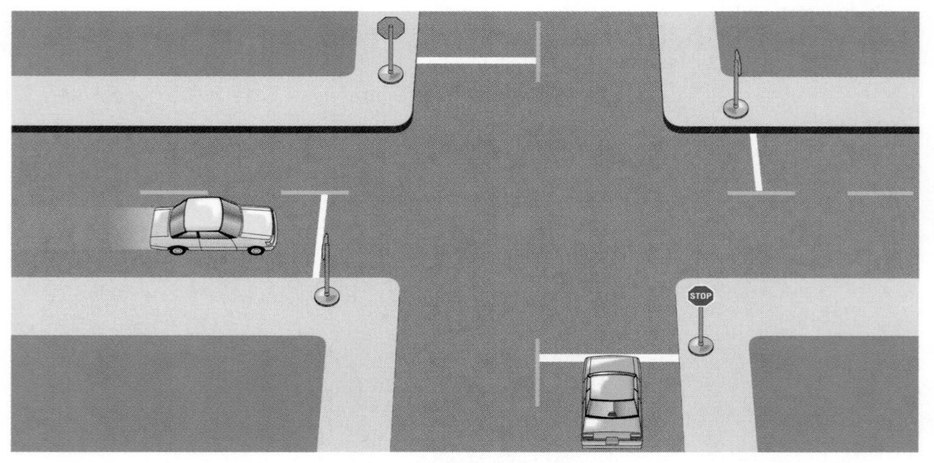

If you were driving the yellow car, the other car should yield the right of way at this 4-way stop. Car colors in all traffic model pictures are as follows:

- Yellow—action car
- White—other cars in motion
- Blue—parked cars

the intersection. To **yield** means to allow others to use the intersection before you do. Using the **right of way** means you accept the privilege of immediate use of the roadway. If another driver on a through street must slow or stop after you leave a STOP sign, then you have not yielded the right of way.

The location of a STOP sign or stop line indicates where to make a legal stop. If there is only a STOP sign, stop before entering the intersection. Stop where you can see approaching traffic, but stop before you reach any crosswalk. The yellow car in the picture on the left shows where to stop when a stop line is present.

If your view is blocked as you approach an intersection and you cannot see cross traffic clearly after stopping, move ahead slowly and prepare to stop again. Make sure the way is clear before driving into the intersection.

At some intersections, STOP signs are posted at all four corners. Each STOP sign might include a small sign that says "4-WAY" or "ALL WAYS." Follow these steps at a 4-way stop:

1. The driver who stopped first should be allowed to go first, as the picture shows.
2. When vehicles stop to the right or left of each other at the same time, the driver on the left should yield to the driver on the right.
3. When stopped across the intersection facing oncoming traffic, the driver going straight should be allowed to proceed. A driver turning left should wait.

Traffic Sign Shapes

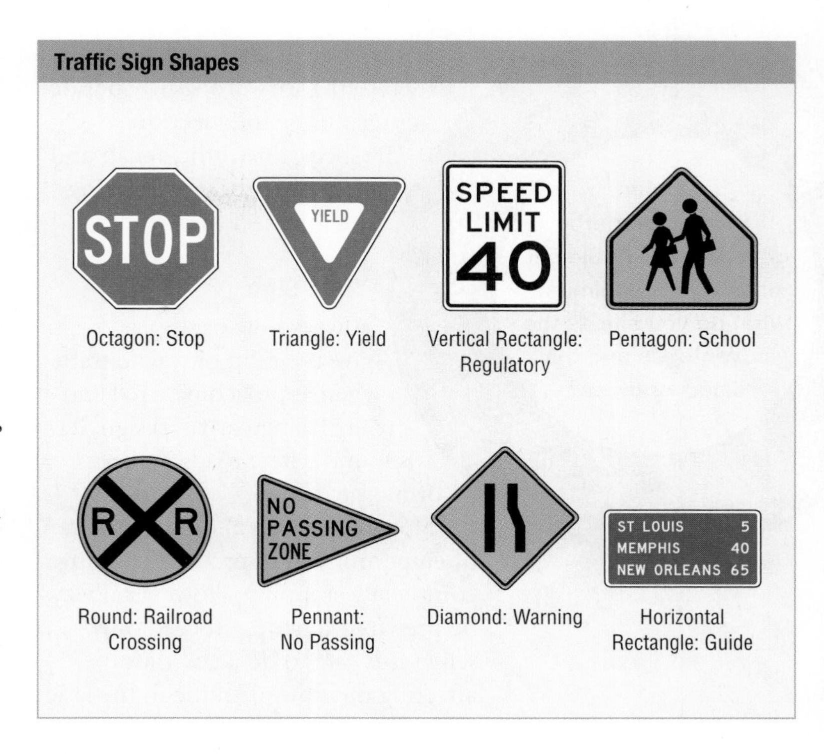

Traffic Sign Colors

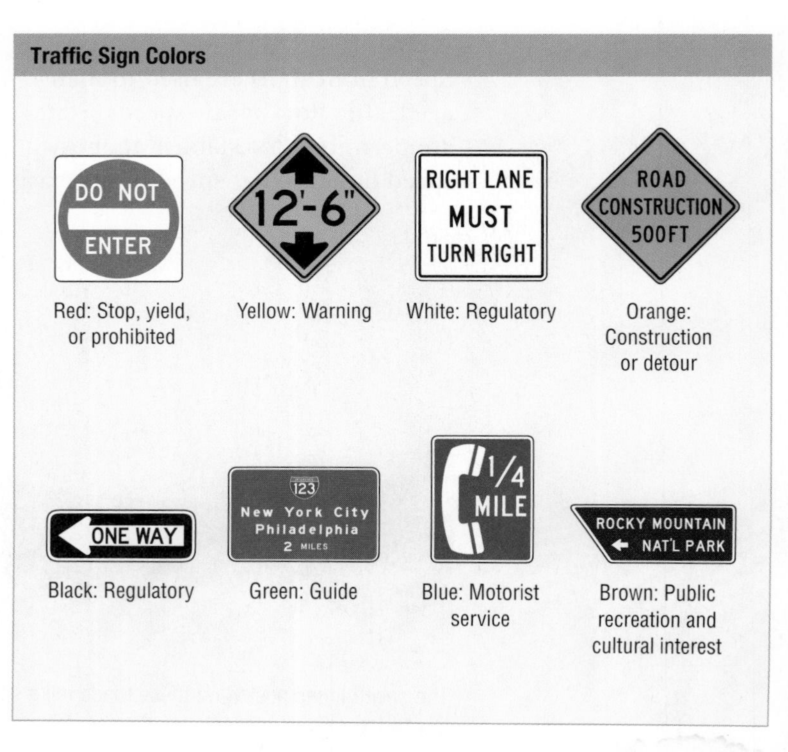

What Do You Think?

Do you think the federal government should set national speed limits? What do you see as the advantages and the disadvantages?

4. Show your intention to proceed by moving forward slowly before entering the intersection.
5. Check for traffic ahead and to the sides before entering the intersection.

Yield Sign

Always slow or stop, and give the right of way to traffic when approaching a red and white triangular YIELD sign. It is found where roadways cross or merge.

Slowing enough ahead of time can often permit you to proceed without completely stopping. However, always be prepared to stop. Proceed only when it is safe to do so, without affecting the flow of traffic in the lane you are entering.

Speed Limit Signs

Speed limit signs are used to manage traffic flow at safe speeds. States are permitted to establish their own speed limits. What speed limits exist in your state? Check the speed limits of other states before traveling there.

Speed limits are set for ideal driving conditions. When traffic, roadway, or weather conditions are not ideal, you must obey the **basic speed law.** This law states that you may not drive faster than is safe and prudent for existing conditions, regardless of posted speed limits.

A **minimum speed limit** is set on some roadways to keep traffic moving safely, such as primary highways and expressways. This speed limit tells you not to drive slower than the posted minimum speed unless conditions are less than ideal. If conditions are bad, follow the basic speed law and drive slower than the minimum speed limit.

Advisory speed limits are set for special conditions such as sharp curves. The signs are often posted below a warning sign. They indicate the maximum suggested speed under

The speed limits posted on these roads tell a safe speed for ideal conditions. When conditions are bad, you must drive slower than posted speeds.

ideal conditions. Speed should be slower when conditions are less than ideal.

In some areas, special speed limits are set for different times of the day. For example, school zones have special speed limits when children are present or during school hours. Night driving speed limits may be lower than daylight limits.

Other Regulatory Signs

Regulatory signs such as those shown above right are used to

- direct traffic to turn or go straight
- direct one-way traffic
- control parking and passing

Signs with red words on white or white words on red usually tell what *not* to do. Black-lettered words usually tell what you can do. Some signs have a black symbol in a red circle and crossed by a red, diagonal slash. The red circle and slash indicate that a certain action is prohibited.

Warning Signs

A warning sign can help you avoid surprise situations. Most warning signs are diamond-shaped. Warning signs have black symbols or lettering on a yellow background.

Diamond-Shaped Warning Signs

Yellow, diamond-shaped signs such as these warn of a danger ahead. Be prepared to slow or stop when you see a warning sign.

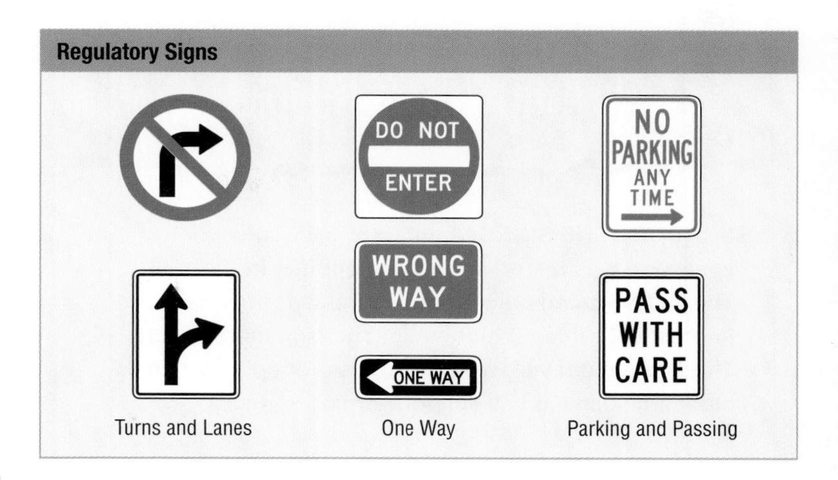

SCHOOL ZONE SIGNS A different colored school zone sign was tested around the country in the 1990s. The yellow-green background is made from a new fluorescent material that makes the sign more visible. The fluorescent yellow-green signs are replacing the standard yellow on all school warning signs.

School Zone

School Crossing

No Passing

School Signs

Two signs are used in school zones. A **school zone** is a portion of a street or highway near a school that is subject to special speed limits. A school zone sign, only showing two children, is posted within a block of a school. A school crossing sign shows children in a crosswalk area. This sign is posted near intersections or crossings used by children. Notice the difference between these two signs.

Be extra alert in a school zone. Children might dart out into the street without looking. They might ride bicycles on the wrong side of the street or take other unexpected actions. Be ready to obey a crossing guard's directions in a school zone.

No-Passing Sign

A yellow, pennant-shaped sign with black letters, as shown below left, may be posted on the left side of the roadway. The sign appears at the start of a no-passing zone and provides advance warning of where a no-passing zone starts. A no-passing sign is used together with a solid yellow line on the roadway. If you intend to pass, you must safely complete your pass before reaching this sign.

Construction Signs

An orange sign, in a diamond or rectangular shape, alerts you to construction zones. Orange, triangular warning signs might be used on a construction vehicle to warn that the vehicle is slow-moving. Be alert in a construction zone, as shown in the picture below. Be ready to slow, stop, or drive around workers and equipment. Follow directions from signs and any worker directing traffic. Many states now increase fines for violations in construction zones.

Be alert in a construction zone. What does the orange sign tell you to do?

The round, yellow sign warns you that a railroad crossing is near. The white crossbuck is at the crossing.

Railroad Signs

A round, yellow sign with a black "X" and two "Rs" warns of a railroad crossing ahead. This sign is posted about 250 feet before a railroad crossing in an urban area. A railroad crossing sign is posted about 750 feet before a railroad crossing in a rural area. A large "X" might be painted on the roadway as an additional warning. The crossing itself is marked with a white crossbuck sign. It may have the number of tracks posted below the sign. Flashing red lights and/or crossing gates might be added to alert you when a train is coming. A driver must treat the crossbuck sign as a yield sign and flashing lights as a stop sign.

Guide Signs

A guide sign provides a variety of information. Guide signs mark routes, intersections, service areas, and other points of interest or information.

Route Signs

Local, state, U.S., and interstate routes are posted with route signs. Notice below that route signs vary according to the type of roadway. State and county route markers will vary from state to state. All the signs below display route numbers.

Interstate route signs are red, white, and blue shields. Notice below that a special numbering system is used for interstate routes.

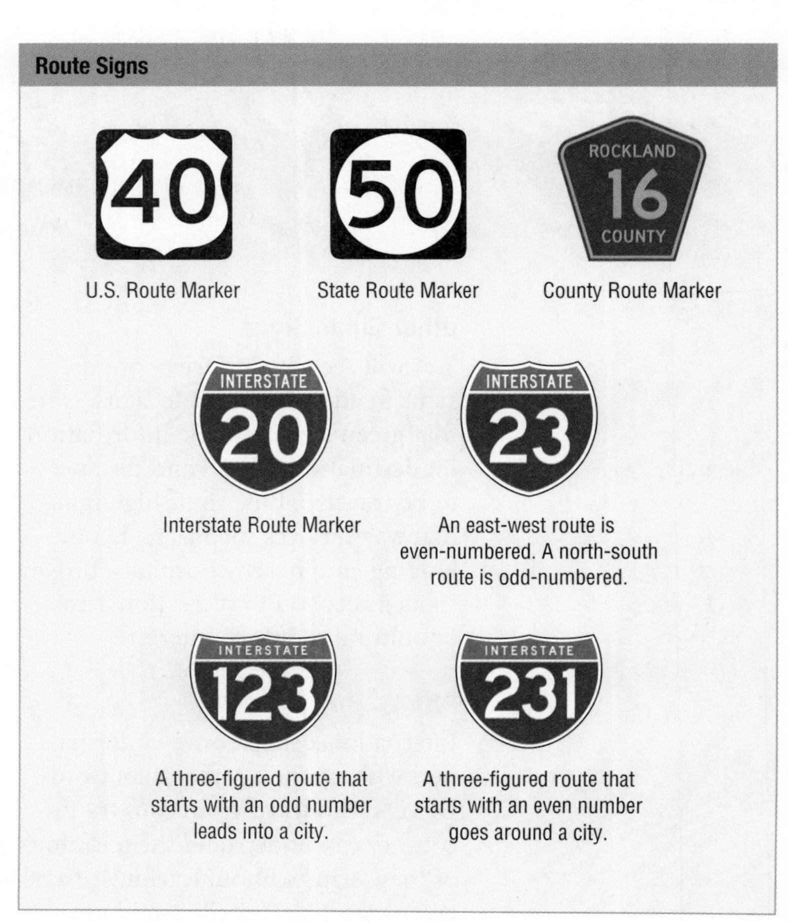

Guide Signs

ST LOUIS 5
MEMPHIS 40
NEW ORLEANS 65

Green signs provide information on mileage to other destinations

Blue signs guide you to services near the highway.

Brown signs indicate points of interest.

International Signs

Stop

Yield

Road Narrows

No Right Turn

Other Guide Signs

You will see a wide variety of guide signs in addition to route signs. Note that green signs provide information on destinations ahead and distances to be traveled. Blue signs highlight highway services such as fuel, food, lodging, and nearby hospitals. Brown signs direct you to recreation areas or cultural points of interest.

International Signs

International signs convey information with symbols rather than words. Drivers who travel from country to country can understand the meaning of these signs without learning several languages. The United States has adopted several **international symbols** for use on highway signs. More and more of these symbols will be used as international travel increases.

Review It

1. What do the eight shapes and colors of traffic signs mean?
2. What actions should you take at STOP, YIELD, and speed-limit signs?
3. What are some situations where warning signs might be used?
4. What information do guide signs and international signs provide?

2.2 Traffic Signals

Traffic lights, arrows, flashing signals, lane signals, and pedestrian signals are used to help traffic flow smoothly. Each of these devices is a **traffic signal.** All traffic signals have specific colors. Red means stop. Yellow means caution: be ready to stop. Green means go: proceed if the way is clear and safe.

Objectives

1. Explain what to do at a green light, a yellow light, and a red light.
2. Describe the action to take when you approach a flashing red signal or a flashing yellow signal.
3. Describe the actions to take with pedestrian signals and traffic control officers' signals.

Traffic Lights

Various combinations of traffic lights can be placed at intersections to control traffic. Remember the following types of lights so you will be familiar with them while driving.

Proceed at a green light only if the intersection is clear.

Green Light The first picture shows a green light. You can proceed only if the intersection is clear. When approaching a green light, check traffic to the left, front, and right before entering the intersection. When approaching a light that has been green for some time, be prepared for the light to turn yellow. The green light will be mounted at the bottom or to the right on the traffic signal.

A yellow light means caution and prepare to stop.

Yellow Light The second picture shows a yellow light. Make every effort to stop safely for a yellow light. Sometimes you might be too close to stop safely when a yellow light appears. You then will have to proceed with caution. The yellow light will appear in the center on the traffic signal.

At a red light, come to a complete stop before the entrance to the intersection.

Red Light The third picture shows a red light. You must come to a full stop at a red light. Stop behind the stop line, crosswalk, or before entering the intersection if no stop lines are used. The red light will be mounted on the top or to the left side on the traffic signal.

Computerized Traffic Lights
Computerized traffic light systems are often used to control the flow of traffic. A computer coordinates traffic lights at several intersections. With this system, traffic can flow for several blocks at or near the speed limit without stopping.

Traffic lights also can be set to change when traffic approaches. A sensor in the roadway detects oncoming or stopped traffic. This system can be used where most of the traffic comes from one direction, such as a left-turn lane. They can also be used to regulate traffic entering a limited access highway.

Right-Turn-on-Red

All states now allow drivers to make a **right-turn-on-red.** This means turning right when the signal is red. However, some cities restrict such

Before you make a right-turn-on-red, you must yield the rig
way to any vehicle in, or approaching, the intersection.

turns. Procedures for turning right on red are discussed in Chapter 7.

Left-Turn-on-Red

Some states permit drivers to make a left turn on a red light when turning from a one-way street into a one-way street. This turn must be made cautiously and only after stopping. A few states permit left-turns on a red light from a left turn lane into a one-way street. Be sure state laws and local ordinances permit such

The flashing red light lets drivers at a distance know that they are approaching a stop.

turns. The intersection and cross-walk must be clear of traffic and pedestrians before you turn either left or right on a red light.

Flashing Signals

A **flashing signal** alerts drivers to dangerous conditions or tells them to stop. These signals are used at intersections and other dangerous locations.

Note the flashing red signal in the bottom picture on the opposite page. Make a full stop when you come to a flashing red signal. A STOP sign and stop line may be used with this signal. After you stop, yield to traffic, and proceed only when the intersection is clear.

When you see a warning sign and a flashing yellow signal, slow down. Be prepared to stop at the traffic light.

Arrows

Traffic must flow in the direction that a green arrow is pointing. Look at the arrows shown here. These arrows are used together with traffic lights. If you are driving in a lane with a green arrow pointing to the left or right, you must turn in that direction. Remember first to yield to other traffic and pedestrians.

Some cities use left-turn arrows to permit drivers to turn left before oncoming traffic proceeds. Other cities use green left-turn arrows only after oncoming traffic has cleared or has been stopped by a red light. You should be cautious if you are unfamiliar with the left-turn signals you encounter. Always be prepared to yield.

GO left only. Be sure that oncoming traffic does not run the red light.

GO right only. Yield to pedestrians and vehicles already in the intersection.

GO straight ahead only after yielding to vehicles and pedestrians within the intersection.

WARNING. The red arrow is about to appear.

STOP. You may not go in this direction.

When the pedestrian signal says DON'T WALK, predict that your green light will soon change.

Lane Signals

Sometimes traffic in some lanes needs to go in one direction for a certain period of time and in the opposite direction at another period of time. The direction of these lanes is reversed on some streets and expressways to control morning and evening rush-hour traffic. In these situations, lights hanging overhead show whether or not a lane can be used at that time. Each light is a **lane signal.** These signals are different from the arrows that regulate turns. You will learn more about lane signals on expressways in Chapter 11.

Pedestrian Signals

A **pedestrian signal** is used at an intersection with heavy traffic. These signals or symbols are mounted near traffic lights as seen in the picture. Pedestrians should only cross at an intersection when they face a WALK signal or symbol. Pedestrians must clear the intersection or wait on a curb when the DON'T WALK signal or symbol flashes or remains lit.

Normally, the WALK signal or symbol and the green traffic light will be on at the same time for pedestrians and drivers going in the same direction. The DON'T WALK signal or symbol usually begins to flash just before the yellow light appears for drivers. If you approach an intersection and see the DON'T WALK signal flashing, predict that your green light will soon change.

The pedestrian DON'T WALK signal will remain on when a green right- or left-turn signal is permitting a driver's path of travel to cross the crosswalk. Pedestrians must wait until their WALK signal or symbol is lit. When turning on a green left-turn signal, drivers should be alert to pedestrians crossing.

Officer's Signal

You must obey signals given by a traffic control officer, even if the officer's signals contradict the traffic signal. A hand held up with the palm toward you means stop. A hand waving you on means go. Signals can be given with lighted wands during times of low visibility.

Review It

1. What should you do when you approach a red light? a yellow light? a green light?
2. What action should you take as you approach a flashing red signal? a flashing yellow signal?
3. How do pedestrian signals and officer's signals help you when driving?

2.3 Roadway Markings

A **roadway marking** gives you a warning or direction. These markings are usually lines, words, or arrows painted yellow or white on the roadway. Sometimes special markings are used on curbs and other surfaces.

Objectives

1. Describe the difference between broken yellow lines and broken white lines.
2. Explain the differences between a shared left-turn lane and a left-turn lane.
3. List six types of special roadway markings.

Yellow Line Markings

A broken yellow line separates two-way traffic. It also means a driver may pass only when no traffic is coming from the opposite direction.

A solid yellow line on the driver's side of the center line indicates that passing is not allowed. Passing is allowed only when the solid yellow line no longer appears on the driver's side of the highway. Turning left across a solid yellow line into a driveway or alley is allowed after yielding to oncoming traffic.

Passing is allowed across a broken yellow line.

No passing is allowed on the side of a road that has a solid yellow line.

Two solid yellow lines that divide traffic prohibit passing that involves crossing the solid lines, as shown in the picture on page 32. Some cities permit you to make left turns across these lines after yielding to oncoming traffic.

Many cities use a **shared left-turn lane** to help drivers make safer mid-block left turns to and from businesses on a busy street. Solid and broken yellow lines are used with left-turn arrows from both directions to identify a shared left-turn lane.

White Line Markings

Broken white lines separate lanes of traffic that are moving in the same

TIP

SAFE DRIVING

Do not use the shared left-turn lane to advance your position in preparation for a left turn at an upcoming intersection. Use the shared left-turn lane only for turning mid-block.

direction. You may cross these broken white lines when changing lanes.

Solid white lane lines keep drivers in their lanes and restrict lane changing. Solid white lines indicate that you should not cross them. These lines identify locations where changing lanes is hazardous. Plan ahead to prevent crossing solid white lane markings.

White arrows are painted in lanes to tell you when and where to turn. If you are in a lane with an arrow and the word ONLY, you *must* continue in the direction of the arrow. You may turn or go straight if there is a curved and straight arrow in your lane.

Solid white lines are used along the side of a roadway to mark the edge of the roadway. These lines help you to see the edge of the roadway at night or under poor visibility driving conditions.

Solid white lines are also used to mark pedestrian crosswalks and stop lines. Some crosswalks have diagonal or perpendicular lines between them or are painted a different color to highlight the area. You must yield the right of way to pedestrians in crosswalks. Stop lines across your lane at intersections show where to stop at a STOP sign or a traffic light.

No passing is allowed if it involves crossing a double yellow line.

Solid white lines separate traffic lanes and mark pedestrian crosswalks and stop lines. Arrows with the word ONLY indicate the direction you must go when driving in these lanes.

Rumble Strips and Raised Roadway Markers

Rumble strips are short sections of corrugated roadway. These strips alert you through the noise your tires make when you drive over them. Rumble strips warn of hazards such as a major or dangerous intersection, a toll plaza, or an unexpected need to stop or reduce speed. Sometimes a rumble strip is used to warn that you are driving too close to the roadway edge, as the picture shows.

On some highways, drivers might have a difficult time seeing the driving lane at night. Raised or lowered roadway markers are used in such situations. These markers act as small reflectors. They are raised in areas where snow seldom occurs. In snow removal areas, these markers will be lower than the surface of the roadway.

Roadway markers are color coded. White markers are used at the edge of a roadway or between lanes, just as white lines are used. Yellow markers may locate the left edge of an expressway. If you are driving and see red roadway markers, pull off the roadway immediately. These red markers warn that you are driving in the wrong direction. Safely get your car going in the proper direction.

Other Roadway Markings

A special white marking on the roadway is used to show you where an exit ramp starts. It is dangerous and illegal to make a last minute decision to cross this area.

The railroad markings using an "X" and two "Rs" on each side of the roadway warn you that a railroad crossing is ahead. Do not pass near railroad crossings.

This type of rumble strip will let you know when you have wandered off the roadway.

Roadway markers shine when struck by headlight beams to help drivers see the driving lane at night.

You may not park alongside this yellow curb marking.

These parking spaces are reserved for handicapped drivers or passengers.

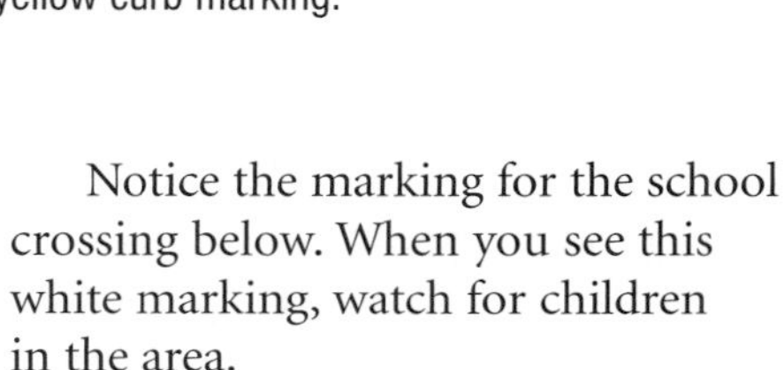

Notice the marking for the school crossing below. When you see this white marking, watch for children in the area.

Curbs alongside a road might be painted to indicate warnings or that parking is not permitted. No-Parking zones often are near fire hydrants, curves, and intersections. The curb marking in the top left picture shows a No-Parking zone. The markings may be red, yellow, or white.

The top right picture shows a parking space reserved for vehicles having handicapped drivers or passengers. Check for signs that say HANDICAPPED PARKING ONLY and signs and pavement markings with the handicapped parking symbol. It is illegal to park in this space without proper permit.

Predict that children could be crossing ahead.

Review It

1. What is the basic difference between broken white lines and broken yellow lines?
2. What are the functions of shared left-turn lanes versus regular left-turn lanes?
3. What are six types of special roadway markings?

Chapter 2
Review

Reviewing Chapter Objectives

1. Traffic Signs

1. What are the meanings of the eight shapes and eight colors used for traffic signs? (20–21)
2. What actions should you take at STOP, YIELD, and speed limit signs? (20–23)
3. What are five situations where warning signs might be used? (23–25)
4. How can guide signs and international signs help you when driving? (26)

2. Traffic Signals

5. What should you do at a green light, a yellow light, and a red light? (27–28)
6. What action should you take when approaching a flashing red signal or a flashing yellow signal? (29)
7. What actions should you take with pedestrian signals and traffic control officers' signals? (30)

3. Roadway Markings

8. What is the difference between broken yellow lines and broken white lines? (31–32)
9. What is the difference between a shared left-turn lane and a left-turn lane? (31)
10. What are six types of special roadway markings? (31–34)

Projects

Individuals

Research Find out about the speed-limit laws in your state. Then find the same information about neighboring states. Notice any similarities or differences in the laws. Write a report comparing the laws.

Observe Traffic Observe for fifteen minutes pedestrians and vehicles at an intersection that has a pedestrian signal. Count the number of pedestrians that cross the street. Notice whether the pedestrians and the vehicles are obeying the signals. Compare your results with those of your classmates.

Groups

Debate Divide your group into two and debate the pros and cons of having the federal government set speed limits. Make a list of all the reasons your group mentions. Compare your list with the other groups in your class.

Practice Make color flashcards for all the signs shown in this chapter. With a partner from your group, test each other on the meanings of the signs.

Chapter 2
Review

Chapter Test

Check Your Knowledge

Multiple Choice Copy the number of each sentence below on a sheet of paper. Choose the letter of the answer that best completes the statement or answers the question.

1. What does a round traffic sign mean?
   (a) yield to other traffic (c) stop
   (b) railroad crossing (d) pedestrian crossing
2. A construction zone sign is
   (a) yellow. (c) green.
   (b) blue. (d) orange.
3. Which of the following is not an example of a traffic signal?
   (a) flashing lights (c) school zone sign
   (b) arrows (d) pedestrian signals
4. Two solid yellow center lines on a two-lane highway indicate
   (a) no passing from either way.
   (b) passing both ways.
   (c) passing only with caution.
   (d) passing on the left only.

Completion Copy the number of each sentence below. After each number, write the word or words that complete the sentence correctly.

5. A _____ signal is used at heavy traffic intersections to tell people who are walking whether they should proceed or wait.
6. International traffic signs use _____ rather than words.
7. A lane on a busy street that helps drivers make safer mid-block left turns is called a _____.
8. A _____ sign controls traffic.

Review Vocabulary

Copy the number of each definition in list A. Match the definition in list A with the term it defines in list B.

List A

9. sign that alerts you to possible hazards and road conditions
10. signal that alerts drivers to dangerous conditions or tells them to stop
11. sign set on roadways like primary highways and expressways to keep traffic moving safely
12. signal, usually overhead, that tells whether a lane can or cannot be used at a specific time
13. speed limits set for special conditions such as sharp curves
14. sign that gives directions

List B

a. flashing signal
b. lane signal
c. warning sign
d. advisory speed limits
e. guide sign
f. minimum speed limit

Think Critically

Write a paragraph to answer each question.

1. What is the difference between a *basic speed law,* a *minimum speed limit,* and an *advisory speed limit?*
2. You are planning to drive in a foreign country that has a different language from yours. What can you do to be sure that you will understand the traffic signs?

Decision Making

1. What is the speed limit in this situation? What speed law might make driving at the posted speed limit illegal?

2. You will be making a left turn at the traffic light ahead. Are you in the correct lane to make that turn? Explain your answer.

3. The orange sign and arrow ahead are used to warn drivers about what condition? If you were driving the vehicle that the scene is viewed from, what mistake would you have already made?

4. You want to pass the slower moving vehicle ahead. Is it safe and legal to pass here? Why or why not?

CHAPTER 3
Basic Vehicle Control

You Are the Driver!

For all drivers and especially for new drivers, safety is your primary responsibility. To be a safe driver, you must know the location and function of your vehicle's control devices. Since vehicles differ in so many ways, it is important that you read and understand your owner's manual.

You also must know the procedures to follow when entering, starting, moving, stopping, and leaving your vehicle. What should you check before entering the vehicle? What is the odometer? What should you do before starting the engine? This chapter describes a vehicle's instruments and control devices and how to use them.

For: Chapter 3 online activities
Visit: PHSchool.com
Web Code: cak-9999

3.1
Instruments, Controls, and Devices

Objectives

1. Identify each gauge and warning light on an instrument panel and explain its function.
2. Explain the purpose of each control used to operate a vehicle.
3. Describe the use of the safety, communication, and comfort devices.

When you are ready to begin your driving experiences, you must know what the warning lights and gauges on the instrument panel tell you. Read the owner's manual to learn the location and operation of the devices for safety, comfort, and communication.

Instrument Panel

The instrument panel is the panel directly in front of you as you sit in the driver's seat. The location of the gauges and warning lights varies from one vehicle to another. No matter where these gauges and lights are located, their purposes are the same. You can make sure the warning lights are working if they light when the ignition switch is turned to On.

The picture on the next page shows one example of the location of the gauges and warning lights in a vehicle, though not all vehicles have the same indicators. The numbers correspond to the gauges and lights explained on this and the next page.

Speedometer (1) This instrument tells you the speed you are traveling in both miles per hour and kilometers per hour. Some vehicles have a digital speedometer.

Tachometer (2) Some vehicles have a tachometer that indicates the engine revolutions per minute. Engine damage may occur if the needle enters the red zone.

Odometer (3) The **odometer** indicates the total number of miles the vehicle has been driven. Some vehicles have an additional trip odometer that can be set back to zero when you want to know the number of miles driven during a certain period of time.

Fuel Gauge (4) The fuel gauge shows the amount of fuel in the tank. If you let the fuel tank get below one-quarter full, you risk running out of fuel.

Try to keep the fuel tank at least half full in cold weather to help prevent fuel-line freeze. This can occur when moisture condenses and freezes inside the tank and fuel line. Ice particles can then block the flow of fuel.

Temperature Light or Gauge (5) This light or gauge warns you when the coolant in the engine is too hot.

Oil Pressure Warning Light or Gauge (6) This warning light or gauge warns you when the oil is not circulating at the proper pressure. However, it does not tell you the amount of oil in the engine.

Alternator Warning Light or Gauge (7) Your vehicle's electrical system is in trouble if this light comes on or the gauge shows "discharge" while the engine is running. The alternator is not generating enough electricity to run the vehicle. When this happens, the engine must use stored electricity from the battery.

The **alternator warning light** or gauge warns that the battery is being drained. The more electricity used, the sooner the battery will be dead. Turn off as many electrical devices as possible, and have the system checked without delay.

Brake System Warning Light (8) This warning light serves two purposes. First, the light reminds you to release the parking brake before moving the vehicle. Second, if the light comes on while you are pressing the foot brake, or while you are driving, it means that part or all of the braking system is not working properly. If this occurs, brake gradually to a stop, have the vehicle towed, and have the problem corrected.

Antilock Braking System Light (9) This light tells you if the **antilock braking system** (ABS) is functioning properly. ABS keeps the wheels from locking if the driver brakes hard. If this light comes on, it indicates a problem with the system.

Safety Belt Light (10) This light reminds you to fasten your safety belt before moving your vehicle. This light comes on when you turn the key. In some vehicles the light stays on for a few seconds after the engine is started.

Air Bag Warning Light (11) This light tells you if the air bags are in proper working condition. When the ignition is turned on, the air-bag light comes on for a few seconds and then goes off. If the air bags are not in proper operating condition, the warning light will stay on.

Turn-Signal Indicators (12) These indicators tell you the direction you have signaled to turn. Each indicator is usually a small green arrow that flashes when you signal for a turn. The arrow stops flashing after you make the turn or when the turn signal is cancelled.

High-Beam Indicator (13) This light glows when the high-beam headlights are on. This indicator usually appears as a small light in some area of the instrument panel.

Vehicle Controls

The characteristics and locations of vehicle controls vary from one model to another. However, each control performs the same function in each vehicle. The numbers in the pictures on the next four pages match the controls explained.

Your car's instrument panel might look different, but all vehicles have similar devices to provide information.

TIP

Be aware of any warning light that comes on while you are driving. The light tells you there is a problem, but it does not tell you what the problem is.

Devices for starting and controlling the movement of a vehicle.

Cruise control should *never* be used when road surfaces are wet or slippery or in heavy traffic. You have much less control if a conflict occurs. Using cruise control in areas of steep grades wastes fuel and puts added stress on the engine.

Steering Wheel (14) The steering wheel controls the direction of the front wheels. Turn right to go right; turn left to go left. Use the same steering procedure when backing the vehicle.

Steering Wheel Adjustment Lever (15) Some vehicles have an adjustable steering wheel. The wheel can be tilted up or down for better driving comfort.

Selector Lever (16) Move the selector lever in an automatic transmission vehicle to choose forward or reverse gear. This control is located on the steering column or on the **console.** The console is the compartment mounted between the front seats in a vehicle.

Gear-Shift Lever (17) In a stickshift vehicle, shift gears by moving the shift lever to the desired position. This lever is located on the console.

Ignition and Starter Switch (18) Start the engine by putting the key into the **ignition switch.** The picture below shows all of the positions of the key in the starter switch.

Cruise Control (19) This is an optional feature you can have on your vehicle. **Cruise control** is a device that lets you maintain your desired speed without keeping your foot on the accelerator. Tap the foot-brake pedal to cancel cruise control.

Parking Brake (20) The parking brake keeps the vehicle in place when it is parked. In many vehicles the parking brake is a pedal located on the far left. Push down on the pedal to set the parking brake. To release the parking brake, push down on the pedal until you hear a click, then lift your foot off the pedal. Some vehicles have a brake-release lever on the left side under the instrument panel. In other vehicles, the parking brake is a lever mounted on the floor or on the

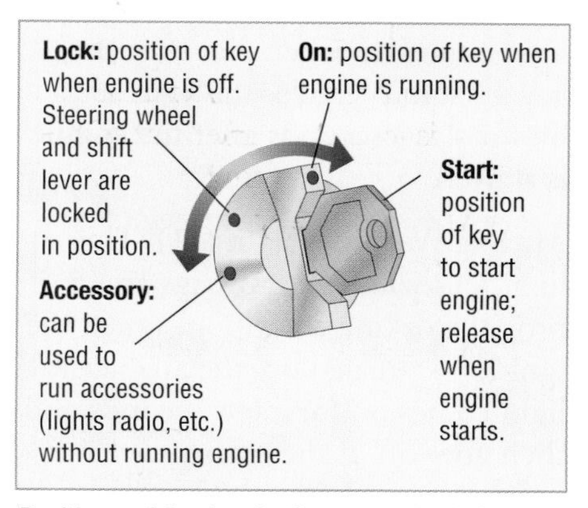

Positions of the key in the starter switch (18)

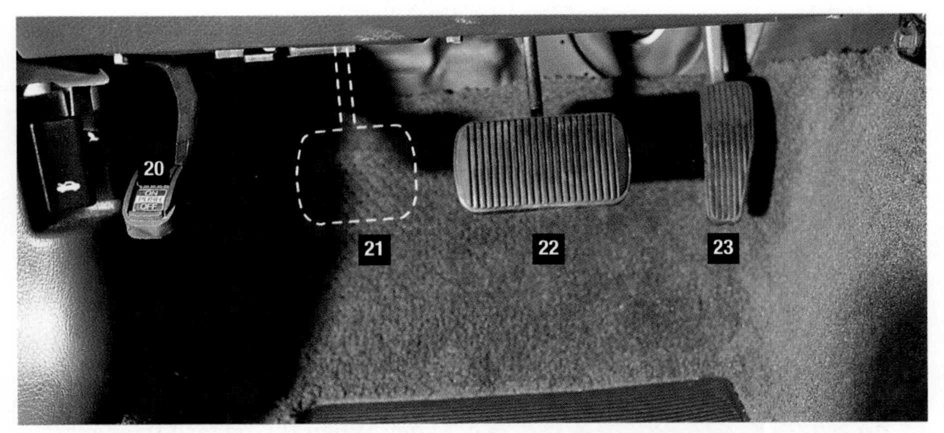

All vehicles have a foot-brake pedal and an accelerator pedal. Some vehicles also have a clutch pedal and/or brake pedal.

console to the right of the driver's seat. Push in the button at the tip of the lever and lower the lever to release this type of brake.

Clutch Pedal (21) In a stickshift vehicle, the **clutch pedal** is located to the left of the foot-brake pedal. Pushing this pedal down lets you shift gears.

Foot-Brake Pedal (22) Pushing down on the foot-brake pedal slows or stops the vehicle. Depressing this pedal also turns on the brake lights in the back of the vehicle.

Accelerator Pedal (23) The accelerator pedal is located to the right of the foot-brake pedal. Pushing the accelerator down increases speed; releasing it slows the vehicle.

Devices for Safety, Communication, and Comfort

Locate and understand the operation of the following devices on any vehicle you drive.

Safety Belts (24) Always wear your safety belt when your vehicle is in motion. Safety belts are your best protection against injury in a collision. Fasten your safety belt to a

Safety devices help protect you and your passengers.

The dark shading indicates "blind spots"—areas that you cannot see with your mirrors.

snug fit before starting your engine. Most states require drivers and passengers to wear safety belts.

Head Restraints (25) Most vehicles have **head restraints,** padded devices on the backs of front seats. Head restraints help reduce whiplash injuries in a collision, especially if your vehicle is struck from the rear.

Inside and Outside Rearview Mirrors (26–27) The inside mirror (26) shows the view through the rear window. The left outside mirror (27) shows a view to the left and rear of your vehicle. The right outside mirror shows a view to the right rear. Even when these mirrors are adjusted properly, there are areas they cannot show the driver. These areas, as shown here, are called **blind-spot areas.** For this reason, *never* rely completely on your rearview mirrors when turning. Always glance over your shoulders to check these areas before changing lanes.

Horn (28) The horn usually is located on the steering wheel. Know how to use the horn on each vehicle you drive.

Hazard Flasher Control (29) This switch usually is located on the steering column or on the instrument panel. When the **hazard flasher** is on, both front and rear turn-signal lights flash at the same time. These lights warn others that your vehicle is a hazard or that you are in trouble.

Turn-Signal Lever (30) This lever is located on the left side of the steering column. Move the lever up to signal a right turn and down to signal a left turn. The turn signal stops flashing when the steering wheel is straightened. You might have to cancel a signal manually if the turn is slight. Hold the signal up or down lightly to signal a lane change. When released, it will cancel.

Windshield Wipers and Washers (31) One switch usually operates both the wipers and the washer to clean the outside of the windshield. This control is often mounted on the turn-signal lever. Use a windshield antifreeze solution in winter in the windshield washer container under the hood.

Light Switch (32) The light switch is usually a knob or switch located on the left of the instrument panel or on the turn-signal lever. In some vehicles it may be a separate lever

What Do You Think?

Do you think that a federal law should be passed requiring all drivers in the country to have their headlights on whenever they are driving? Why or why not?

These are some of the instruments that control safety and comfort.

attached to the steering column. This device controls headlights, taillights, and side-marker lights, as well as the instrument panel, license plate, and dome light. You can change the headlights from low to high beam by using the dimmer switch, usually located on the turn-signal lever.

Hood Release Lever (33) This lever usually is located on the left side under the instrument panel. Pull this lever to release the hood. You will need to operate a second release in the front of the vehicle before the hood will open.

Heater, Air Conditioner, and Defroster Heating and air-conditioning systems warm or cool the inside of the vehicle. The defroster keeps the windshield and windows free of moisture. Some vehicles have a separate switch for a rear-window defroster.

Sun Visor The sun visors are located above the windshield. Pull the visor down or to the side, to help cut glare from bright sun.

Seat Adjustment Lever This lever is usually located at the lower front or left side of the driver's seat. In vehicles with electric seats, the controls are usually on the lower left side of the driver's seat.

Review It

1. What warnings do the temperature gauge, oil pressure gauge, and brake system lights give you?
2. What is the purpose of the ignition and starter switch?
3. Why must you not rely completely on what your rearview mirrors show you?

3.2
Getting Ready to Drive

Objectives

1. List in order the checks you make when preparing to drive.
2. Describe how to enter a vehicle from the street side.
3. Describe the correct positioning of the seat and outside rearview mirrors.

Before you take your place behind the wheel to drive, you should follow certain checks and procedures. People who just get into a vehicle and drive away, with little thought or concern for themselves or others, are demonstrating high-risk driving behaviors.

Inspect your vehicle and the area around it before you get in to drive. An oil stain under the vehicle, for example, indicates there could be a problem.

Be alert for small children playing near your vehicle. Many deaths each year are attributed to driveway back ups. Also look for tools, toys, or any kind of debris that might be near your vehicle. Follow the same steps in the same order each time you get ready to drive to develop safe pre-driving habits.

Outside Checks

1. Walk around your vehicle with keys in hand and look for objects in the path you intend to take. Also look for water or oil marks under the vehicle.
2. Glance at the tires to see they are inflated properly.
3. Notice the direction the front wheels are pointed. If they are not pointed straight ahead, your vehicle will go to the left or right as soon as you begin to drive.
4. Make sure the windshield, windows, headlights, and taillights are clear. If windows are covered with snow or ice, clear them completely. Do not clear off just enough for a "peephole."
5. Check the back window ledge for loose objects. Remove any objects before driving.
6. Look inside the vehicle to be sure you do not have unwanted passengers.

If you have been driving for some time on wet roadways, your headlights may be covered with road dirt. Develop the habit of cleaning the headlights often, and clean them every time you get fuel.

Once you have completed all the outside checks, follow these steps in order to safely enter your vehicle.

Getting into the Vehicle

1. If you enter your vehicle from the street side, have your keys in hand ready to unlock the door. If you use a remote-control device, unlock the vehicle before you walk into the street.
2. Walk around the front of the vehicle toward the back. You then can see oncoming traffic and reduce the risk of being hit. Do not open the door if an oncoming vehicle is near.
3. Get in quickly, close the door, and lock it. Put the key in the ignition.

Inside Checks

1. Lock all doors. Locked doors are less likely to fly open in a collision.
2. Adjust the seat for comfort and best control of foot pedals and steering wheel. Sit with your back firmly against the back of the seat. Sit high enough to see over the steering wheel. Adjust the seat so you are at least 10 inches back from the hub of the wheel to avoid injury in a crash.
3. Your hands should be in a balanced, comfortable position on the steering wheel with your elbows slightly bent. Reach for the accelerator and brake pedal with your right foot to judge a comfortable distance. Your knees should be slightly bent.
4. Adjust the head restraint to the middle of the back of your head.

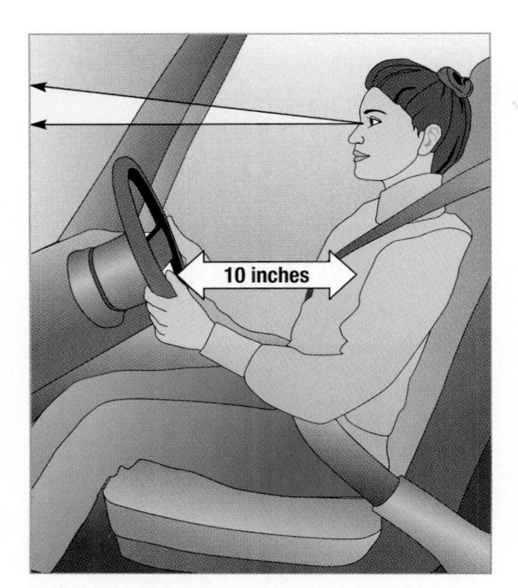

Make adjustments so you are comfortable before driving.

You Are the Driver!
What procedures is the driver following to enter the car safely?

5. Adjust the inside rearview mirror so it shows the area behind you through the rear window.
6. Adjust the left and right outside rearview mirrors so they show a slight amount of the sides of the vehicle.
7. Fasten your safety belt and ask all passengers to fasten theirs.

Review It

1. What outside checks should you make before entering the vehicle?
2. Why should you walk around the front of the vehicle when entering from the street side?
3. What is the correct way to position the driver's seat and mirrors of your vehicle?

3.3

Driving a Vehicle with Automatic Transmission

Objectives

1. Explain the use of each gear.
2. Describe the procedure for starting an automatic transmission vehicle.
3. List the steps for putting an automatic transmission vehicle in motion.
4. Tell the correct procedure to follow when leaving an automatic transmission vehicle from the street side.

Learning the correct steps for starting, moving, and stopping an automatic transmission vehicle is not difficult. You choose the gear you want by moving the gear selector lever. Practice each step in the correct order so that the procedures become a habit.

Selector-Lever Positions

The **shift indicator** shows the gear positions. This indicator may be located on the steering column, on the instrument panel, or on the console to the right of the driver. The first picture shows the shift indicator on the instrument panel and tells you the vehicle is in PARK. The second picture shows the indicator mounted on the console and tells you the vehicle is in PARK.

PARK (P) This gear position locks the transmission. Your vehicle should be in PARK before you start driving. You should also shift to PARK every time you stop driving since the vehicle cannot roll in this gear. Never shift to PARK when the vehicle is moving. In many vehicles you can remove the key from the ignition only when the lever is in PARK.

REVERSE (R) This gear is used for backing. Always come to a complete stop before shifting into REVERSE. Expensive damage to the transmission can result from shifting to REVERSE when the vehicle is moving forward.

When you shift to REVERSE, the **backup lights** come on. These are white lights at the rear and tell others that you are backing.

NEUTRAL (N) This position allows the wheels to roll without engine power. If the engine stalls while you are driving, shift to NEUTRAL (not PARK) to restart the engine. Shift to NEUTRAL if you are stopped in traffic for more than a few minutes.

DRIVE (D) This position is for moving forward. To keep your vehicle from "jumping" forward, keep firm pressure on the brake pedal every time you shift to DRIVE.

Gear indicators can be on the control panel or on the console.

Many vehicles are equipped with overdrive, shown by a "D." At speeds of 40–45 mph the vehicle automatically shifts into overdrive. Driving in this gear saves fuel and can be used for all normal forward driving.

LOW (L1 and L2, or 1 and 2) These positions allow the engine to send more power to the wheels at lower speeds. Both positions are for slow, hard pulling and for going up and down steep hills. LOW 2 is used when driving in snow. Use LOW 1 when going up or down very steep grades and when pulling heavy loads.

Starting the Engine

Use this procedure to start the engine of a vehicle with an automatic transmission. The pictures correspond to the steps listed.

1. Make sure the parking brake is set.
2. Make sure the selector lever is in PARK. If you are starting the vehicle after the engine has stalled, place the selector lever in NEUTRAL.
3. Keep your foot off the accelerator.
4. Turn the ignition switch to On. Continue turning the key to start the engine. Release the key as soon as the engine starts.
5. Check the gauges, warning lights, and fuel supply.

Never try to start the engine when it is already running. Expensive damage to the starter can result. Press lightly on the accelerator so you will know whether or not the engine is running. When in doubt, turn the key to "Off" and repeat the starting procedure.

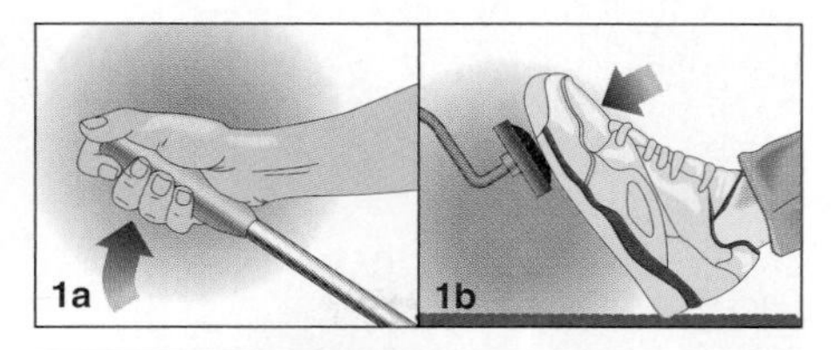

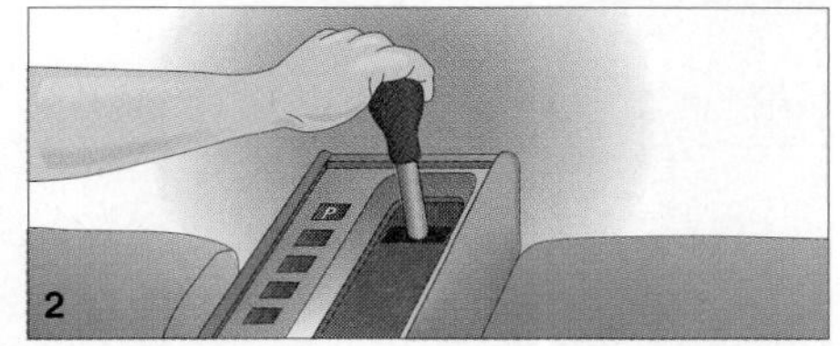

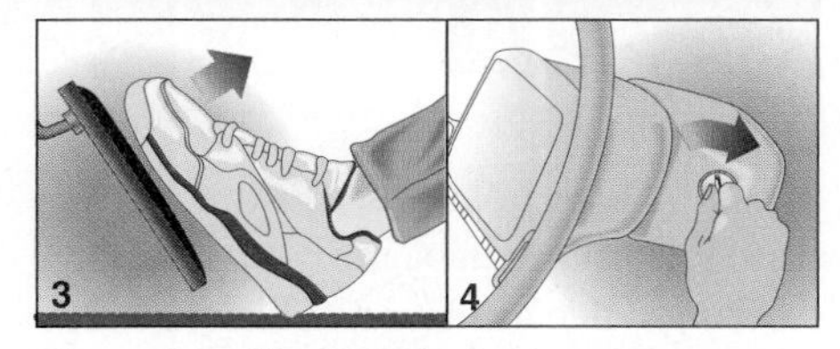

These steps illustrate the basic procedure for starting a vehicle with an automatic transmission.

Hand Positions for Controlled Steering

Steering is not just a matter of pointing the vehicle in the direction you want it to go. Controlled steering involves a comfortable and balanced hand position on the steering wheel.

Using the proper grip on the steering wheel is just as important as using the proper grip in sports like tennis or golf. With your hands in a comfortable position on the rim of the steering wheel, grip the wheel firmly on each side in a balanced position.

Imagine that the steering wheel is the face of a clock. Many drivers place their hands at the 10 o'clock and 2 o'clock, or the 9 o'clock and 3 o'clock, positions. Other drivers place their hands at the 8 o'clock

and 4 o'clock positions. To avoid injury from an airbag in your vehicle's steering wheel during a collision, keep your hands between the 9 and 3 o'clock position and the 8 and 4 o'clock position.

Always keep your knuckles outside the rim of the steering wheel. Some safety specialists recommend that the thumbs also be outside the rim of the steering wheel to reduce injury in a collision.

Steering the Vehicle

Once you have selected your comfortable and balanced hand position, you are ready to develop steering-control techniques. Begin your steering practice by picking a **target** far out in the distance. A target is a stationary object that appears in the distance in the center of your path of travel. The target is really the "aiming point" where you want your vehicle to go. Look far ahead to identify clues and hazards that could cause conflicts. In Chapter 4 you will learn different systems of seeing and identifying all the critical areas around your vehicle.

Keeping your vehicle in a straight line requires slight but critical steer-

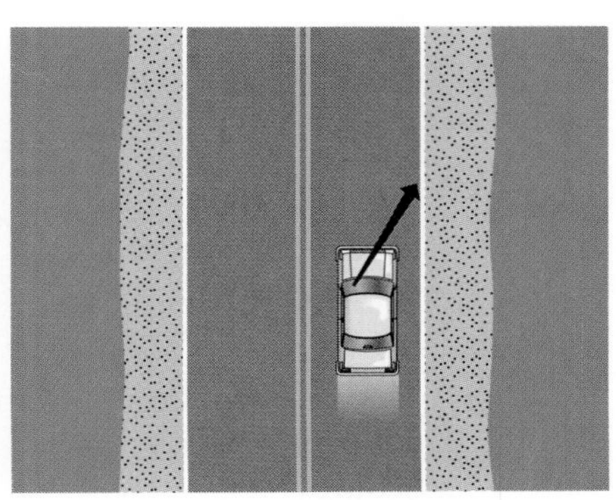

Don't use the road lines as a guide for where to look when you practice steering.

ing corrections. Avoid looking directly in front of your vehicle. Do not use the road lines as guides when you practice steering. Making these mistakes, as the pictures on the bottom of page 50 show, does not allow you to see far in the distance toward the path you want to follow.

Once you learn how to make steering adjustments, you will make them automatically. You then can concentrate on the total driving task.

Most vehicles are now equipped with air bags. Even with an air bag as an added safety device, it is extremely important that you always wear your safety belt when you travel in a vehicle.

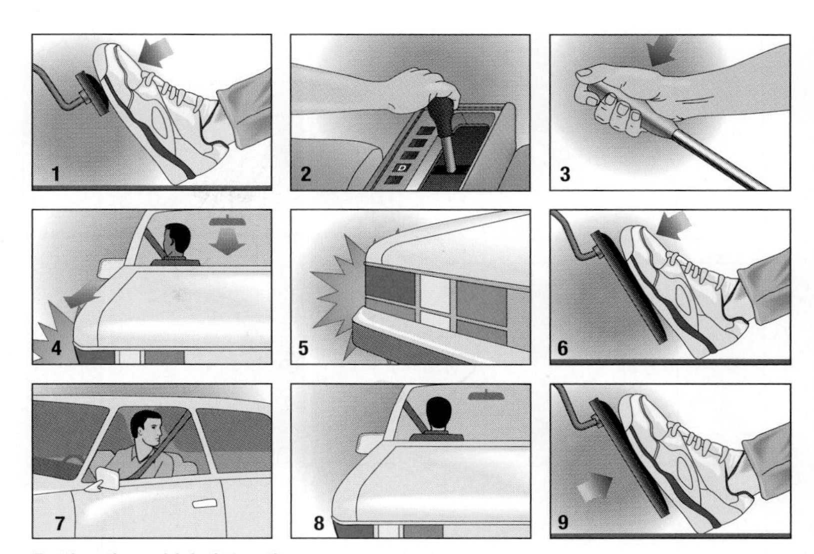

Putting the vehicle in motion

Putting the Vehicle in Motion

After you have started the engine and checked all the gauges, you are ready to put your vehicle in motion. Follow these steps in the same order each time you move your vehicle. The numbered steps correspond to the numbered pictures above.

1. Press firmly on the foot brake.
2. Move the selector lever to DRIVE.
3. Release the parking brake while still pressing the foot-brake pedal.
4. Check for traffic ahead and in rearview mirrors. Look over your left shoulder to see if a vehicle is approaching from the rear.
5. If you are going to move away from the right curb, use the left turn signal to alert other drivers. Check mirrors again.
6. When you know the roadway is clear, release the foot-brake pedal and press gently on the accelerator to increase speed smoothly.
7. Quickly check again over your left shoulder for traffic.
8. Cancel the signal, if necessary.
9. As you reach your desired speed, let up a little on the accelerator. Adjust your speed to traffic.

For best control of the brake pedal and accelerator, rest the heel of your foot on the floor. This position lets you pivot the front part of your foot back and forth between the two pedals as you drive.

In a vehicle with automatic transmission, always come to a full stop before shifting to another gear. This keeps your vehicle from moving before you are ready.

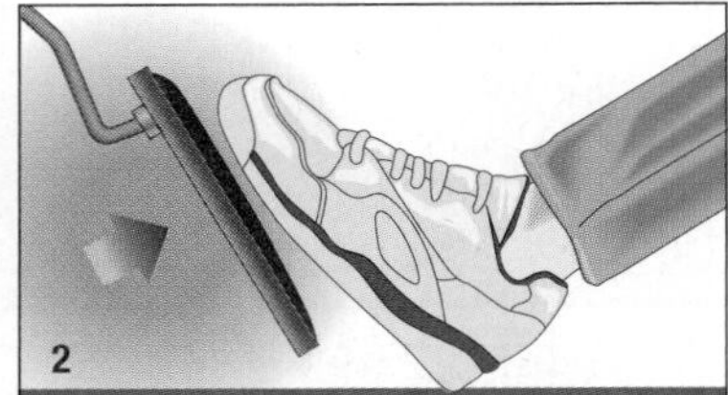

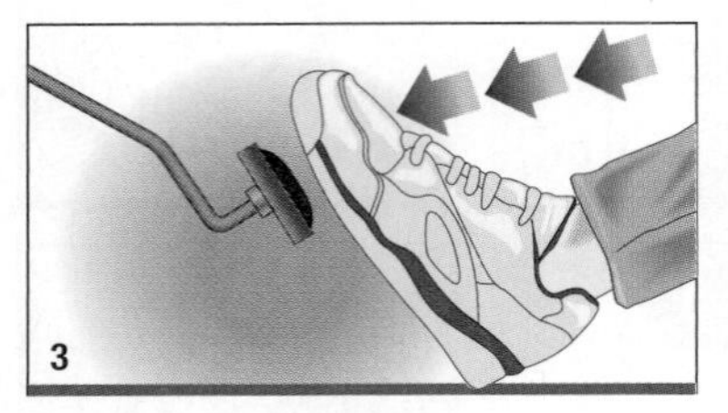

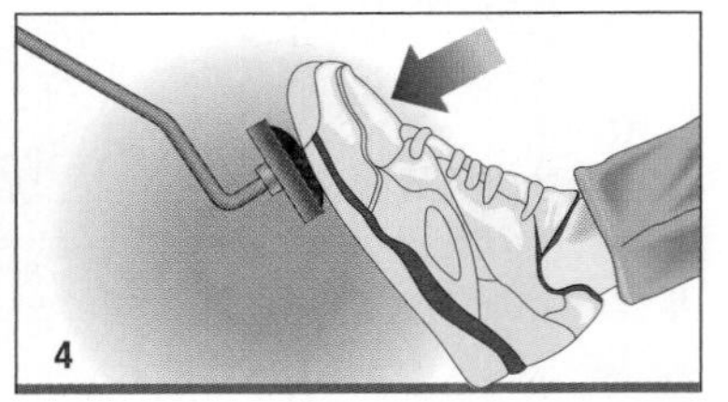

Stopping the vehicle

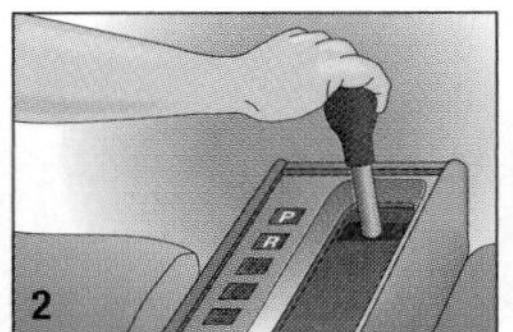

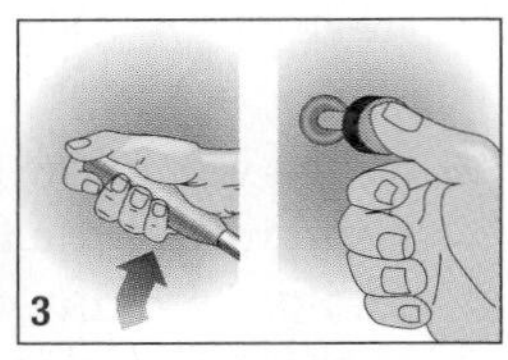

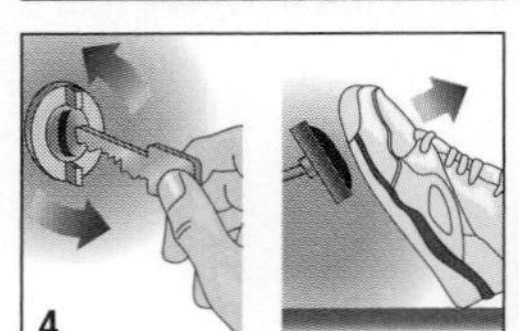

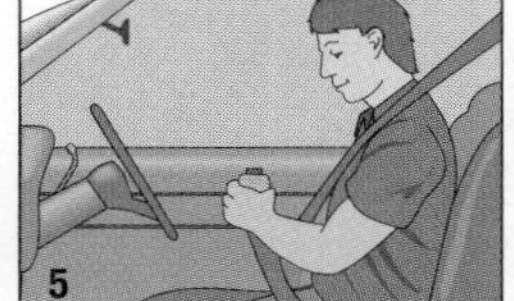

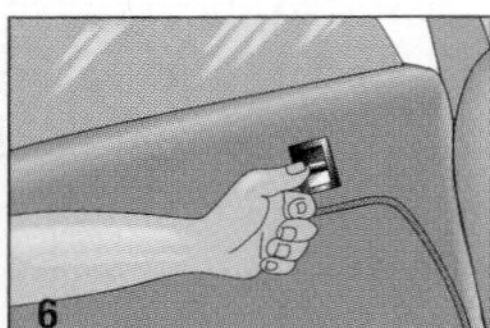

Securing the vehicle

Stopping the Vehicle

The numbered steps correspond to the numbered pictures.

1. Check traffic in both mirrors before slowing down.
2. Let up on the accelerator.
3. Tap the foot brake lightly.
4. Gradually press down on the foot-brake pedal. Ease up on the brake just before stopping. Leave the selector lever in DRIVE if you plan to start moving again immediately. Otherwise, shift to PARK.

Securing the Vehicle

This procedure applies to both automatic and stickshift vehicles.

1. Once you have stopped, continue pressing the foot brake.
2. Shift to PARK in an automatic or to REVERSE in a stickshift vehicle.
3. Set the parking brake. Turn off all accessories. Close all windows.
4. Turn off the ignition switch. Remove the key. Release the foot brake.
5. Unfasten your safety belt.
6. Lock all doors.

Leaving the Vehicle

If you leave the vehicle from the street side, follow these steps.

1. Check inside and outside mirrors.
2. Make sure you have your keys.
3. Glance over your left shoulder before opening the door.
4. When it is safe, open the door and get out quickly.
5. Make sure all doors are locked. Walk around the rear of the vehicle to reduce your risk of being hit.

Review It

1. What is the purpose of each gear in an automatic transmission?
2. How do you start an automatic transmission vehicle?
3. How do you put an automatic transmission vehicle in motion?
4. What procedure do you follow when leaving the vehicle?

3.4 Driving a Vehicle with Manual Transmission

Learning to drive a vehicle with manual (stickshift) transmission is not difficult, especially if you already know how to drive an automatic transmission vehicle. You must learn how to coordinate using the clutch with the accelerator and gearshift lever. The key to mastering stickshift driving is to engage the clutch smoothly and control the **friction point.** The friction point is where you feel the engine take hold and the vehicle starts to move.

Selector-Lever Positions

Most stickshift vehicles have either a four-speed or a five-speed shift pattern as the pictures below show. REVERSE is usually in the upper-left corner, or in the lower-left or right corner.

FOURTH gear is used for highway driving, and FIFTH gear is used for speeds over 45 or 50 mph. These gears save fuel because they allow the engine to run slower at any speed.

Using Stickshift Gears

NEUTRAL (N) This position is the crossbar of the pattern. Use this gear when standing still or when starting the engine.

FIRST (1) Use FIRST gear to start the vehicle moving to a forward speed of 10 to 15 mph. Use FIRST gear also to pull heavy loads and when driving up or down steep hills.

SECOND (2) Use SECOND gear to accelerate to a speed of 15 to 25 mph. Use SECOND gear also for hills or driving on snow or ice.

THIRD (3) Use THIRD gear to accelerate to speeds of 25 to 40 mph.

FOURTH (4) In a four-speed transmission, use FOURTH gear for highway driving. Shift to FOURTH gear at speeds above 35 mph.

FIFTH (5) In a five-speed transmission, use FIFTH gear to drive at speeds over 45 or 50 mph.

REVERSE (R) This gear is used for backing. Never shift into REVERSE while the vehicle is moving forward.

Using the Clutch

Always press the clutch pedal to the floor before starting the engine, before shifting, or before coming to a stop. Shift smoothly from one gear position to the next. The speeds given here for shifting are only guidelines. Read your owner's manual to know the recommended shifting speeds for your vehicle.

Objectives

1. List the procedures for starting a stickshift vehicle.
2. Tell the correct procedure for moving a stickshift vehicle in FIRST gear.
3. Explain the procedure for stopping from higher gears.
4. Define downshifting and explain its purpose.

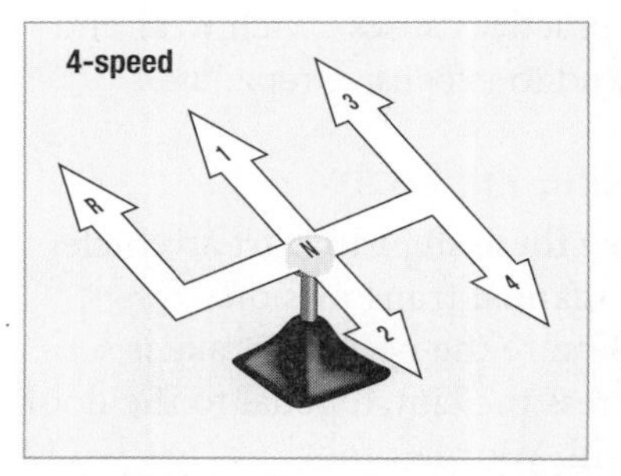

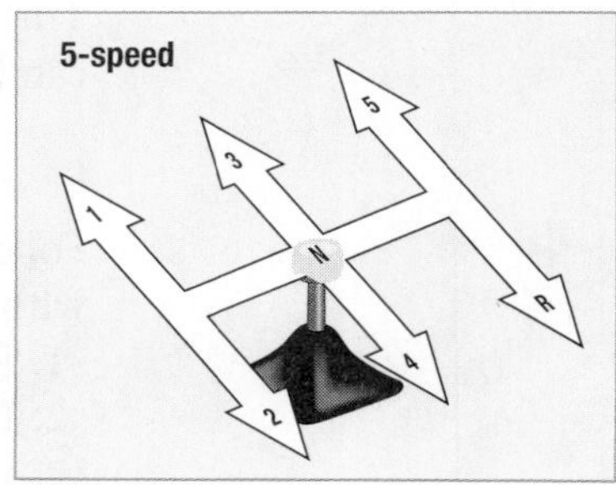

Typical patterns of gear positions for four- and five-speed transmissions. Positions may vary, especially for REVERSE.

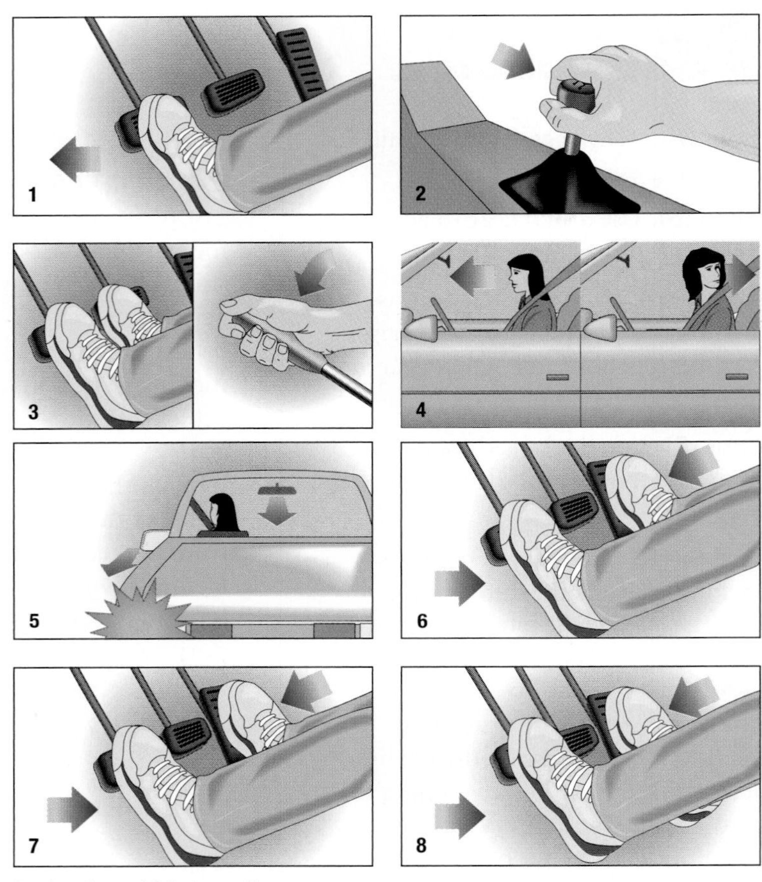
Putting the vehicle in motion

Do not develop the habit of **riding the clutch.** That means resting your foot on the clutch pedal while driving. This practice causes clutch wear and can lead to expensive repairs.

Starting the Engine

Follow these steps to start a vehicle with manual transmission:

1. Be sure the parking brake is set.
2. Press the clutch pedal to the floor with your left foot.
3. Put the gear-shift lever in NEUTRAL.
4. Turn on ignition switch and check warning lights.
5. Turn the key forward until the engine starts, then release it.

Putting the Vehicle in Motion

Once the engine is running, follow these steps to put the vehicle in motion. Each numbered step is pictured.

1. Press the clutch pedal to the floor.
2. Move the gear-shift lever to FIRST.
3. Depress the foot brake and release the parking brake.
4. Check traffic ahead and in rear-view mirrors. If you are moving away from the curb, glance over your left shoulder to see if any vehicle is approaching from the rear.
5. Use the turn signal to alert other drivers.
6. If the roadway is clear, accelerate gently and gradually and release the clutch slowly to the friction point. Releasing the clutch suddenly causes the vehicle to jerk forward or stall the engine.
7. Hold the clutch momentarily at the friction point until the vehicle starts to move.
8. Continue gradual acceleration, and let the clutch up all the way.

Shifting from FIRST to SECOND

At about 10 to 15 mph follow these steps to shift from FIRST to SECOND:

1. Press the clutch down and release the accelerator at the same time.
2. Move the gear-shift lever to SECOND. Pause slightly as you go across NEUTRAL into SECOND. This action helps you shift more smoothly.

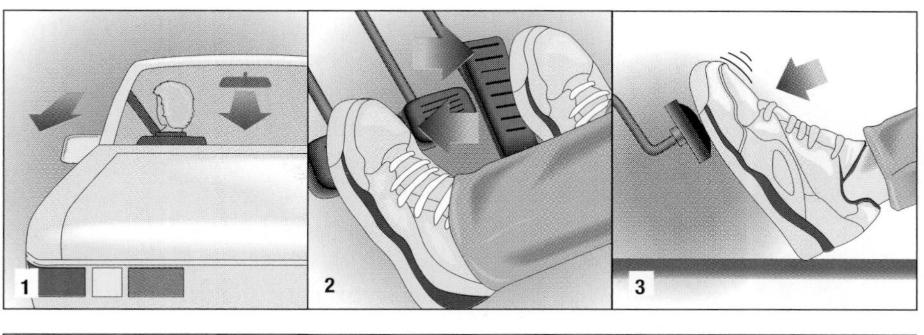

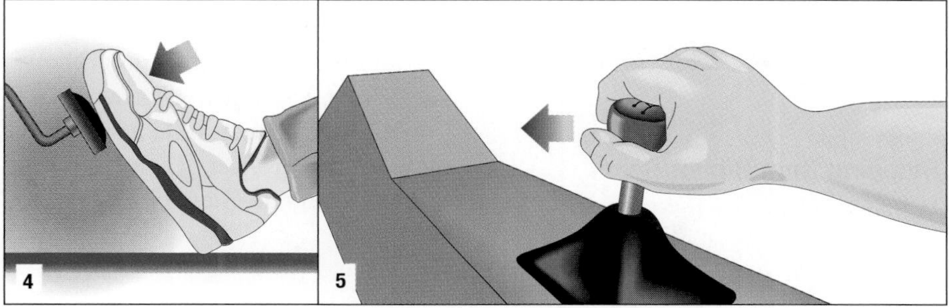

Stopping from FIRST, SECOND, or REVERSE

3. Accelerate gently as you slowly release the clutch. Hesitate briefly at the friction point, then release the clutch all the way.

Stopping from FIRST, SECOND, or REVERSE

The pictures on this page correspond to these steps:

1. Check traffic in mirrors.
2. Press the clutch pedal down while releasing accelerator.
3. Tap the brake pedal lightly to signal for a stop.
4. Press the foot brake gently to a stop.
5. Shift to NEUTRAL when stopped.

Shifting to THIRD, FOURTH, and FIFTH

Once you have accelerated to the higher-speed ranges described for THIRD, FOURTH, and FIFTH gears, follow these step for shifting:

1. Press the clutch down.
2. Release the accelerator.
3. Shift to the desired gear. Do not hurry the shift or you may shift to the wrong gear.
4. Accelerate gradually while releasing the clutch smoothly.

SHIFTING GEARS There is no one correct speed for shifting from one gear to another. Speed for each gear depends on engine power and type of transmission. As you drive different stickshift vehicles, you will develop a feel for proper accelerating and shifting in each one.

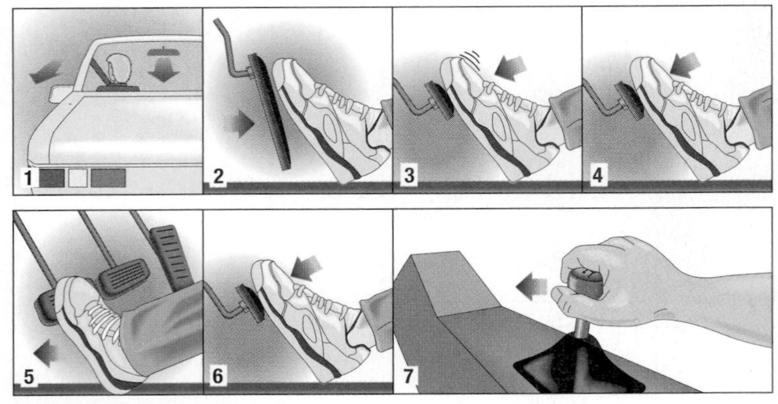

Stopping from higher gears

Stopping from Higher Gears

When stopping from THIRD, FOURTH, or FIFTH, slow down before depressing the clutch. The engine helps slow the vehicle. The pictures on this page correspond to these steps:

1. Check the mirrors for traffic.
2. Let up on the accelerator.
3. Tap the brake to signal a stop.
4. Brake to about 15 to 20 mph.
5. Press the clutch pedal down.
6. Brake to a smooth stop.
7. Shift to NEUTRAL when stopped.

Downshifting

The term **downshifting** means shifting from a higher to a lower gear. The engine has greater pulling power in lower gears than in higher ones. If you have slowed below 30 mph in FOURTH gear, or if you are going uphill, you must downshift to THIRD in order to regain speed. Follow these steps to downshift:

1. Press the clutch pedal down and shift to THIRD. Accelerate gradually while releasing the clutch.
2. Accelerate to over 30 mph. Press the clutch pedal and shift back to FOURTH gear. If you are going uphill, you may have to stay in third gear longer.

You can downshift for added control, as when slowing before a sharp turn. However, be sure to downshift before starting the turn. You need both hands ready to steer.

You can also downshift to gain extra power when climbing long or steep hills. Use a lower gear to go down long or steep hills to prevent wear on the brakes. Let the clutch out smoothly after every downshift.

Review It

1. What is the procedure for starting a stickshift vehicle?
2. What are the steps for moving a stickshift vehicle in FIRST gear?
3. What steps should you follow when stopping from higher gears?
4. What is meant by downshifting and for what reasons might you downshift?

Chapter 3

Review

Reviewing Chapter Objectives

1. Instruments, Controls, and Devices

1. What is the name and function of each gauge on the instrument panel? (40–41)
2. What is the purpose of each control used to operate a vehicle? (42–43)
3. How do you use the safety, communication, and comfort devices on a vehicle? (43–45)

2. Getting Ready to Drive

4. What checks should you make when preparing to drive? (46)
5. How should you enter a vehicle from the street side? (46–47)
6. How do you position the seat and outside rearview mirrors of your vehicle? (47)

3. Driving a Vehicle with Automatic Transmission

7. What is the use of each gear in an automatic transmission vehicle? (48–49)
8. What is the procedure for starting an automatic transmission vehicle? (49)
9. What are the steps for putting an automatic transmission vehicle in motion? (51)
10. What is the correct procedure to follow when leaving an automatic transmission vehicle from the street side? (52)

4. Driving a Vehicle with Manual Transmission

11. How do you start a stickshift vehicle? (53–54)
12. What is the correct procedure for moving a stickshift vehicle in FIRST gear? (54)
13. What is the procedure for stopping a stickshift vehicle from higher gears? (56)
14. What does "downshifting" mean? (56)

Projects

Individuals

Demonstrate Make a poster that illustrates the instrument panel on your family vehicle. Present the illustration to the class, describing the location, function, and operation of each device on the panel.

Investigate Research the antilock braking system (ABS). Who invented this system? How does the system work? When was it first available? What were the first vehicle models to feature the system? Investigate the differences between antilock brakes and brakes that are not antilock. Write a report on your findings.

Groups

Use Technology Each group member should observe the driver of a stickshift vehicle. Record the speed at which the driver shifts out of each gear. Make a group spreadsheet of your findings.

Demonstrate Make a video demonstrating the outside checks you should make before getting into and driving a vehicle. Group members should take turns demonstrating the steps. Present the video to your class.

Chapter 3

Review

Chapter Test

Check Your Knowledge

Multiple Choice Copy the number of each sentence below on a sheet of paper. Choose the letter that best completes the statement or answers the question.

1. Which of the following is *not* found on a vehicle's instrument panel?
(a) speedometer (c) tachometer
(b) horn (d) fuel gauge

2. When entering a vehicle from the street side, you should
(a) be ready to unlock the door.
(b) walk around the front of the vehicle toward the back.
(c) get in quickly, then close and lock the door.
(d) all of the above

3. When starting an automatic transmission vehicle, the selector lever should be in
(a) LOW-L1 or L2, or 1 or 2 (c) PARK-P or NEUTRAL-N
(b) DRIVE-D (d) REVERSE-R

4. The friction point is the point
(a) where the vehicle starts to move.
(b) where you feel the engine turn off.
(c) when you suddenly release the clutch.
(d) none of the above

Completion Copy the number of each sentence below. After each number, write the word or words that complete the sentence correctly.

5. The _____ pedal in a stickshift vehicle enables a driver to shift gears.

6. A vehicle's rearview mirrors cannot show _____ areas.

7. The alternator warning light warns that the _____ is being drained.

Review Vocabulary

Copy the number of each definition in List A. Match the definition in List A with the term it defines in List B.

List A

8. compartment mounted between the front seats in a vehicle

9. device on the instrument panel indicating the total number of miles the vehicle has been driven

10. stationary object appearing in the distance in the center of your intended path of travel

11. shifting from a higher to a lower gear

12. device that shows the different driving gears and the one being used

13. padded devices on the backs of front seats that help reduce whiplash injuries in a collision

List B

a. downshifting
b. odometer
c. head restraints
d. console
e. shift indicator
f. target

Think Critically

Write a paragraph to answer each question.

1. Explain the term downshifting, and give two reasons for using this action.

2. List and explain the procedure you should follow for securing your vehicle once you have stopped.

Chapter 3 Review

Decision Making

Fuel

Alternator

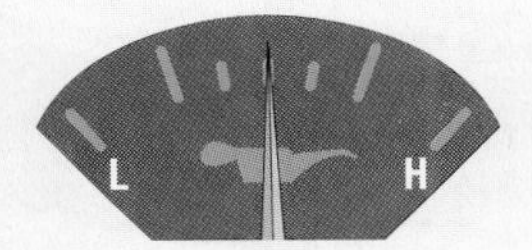

Oil Pressure

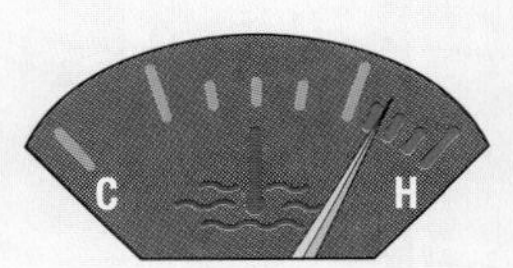

Temperature

1. While you are driving, the gauges on the instrument panel could look like the pictures above. What does each gauge tell you? What problems might you have? What should you do?

2. The driver is going to enter the car and drive. Identify the incorrect procedure the driver is following. Explain why the procedure is unsafe. What error should the driver correct? What safety checks should the driver make?

3. What steps did this driver forget when getting ready to drive? Is this a safe steering position? How might the driver achieve more controlled steering? What safety device is missing?

4. You are preparing to turn this very sharp curve. You are driving a four-speed car in FOURTH gear. What should you do before entering the curve? Describe the procedure you would use.

8·871·18

CHAPTER 4
Managing Risk with the IPDE Process

4.1 The IPDE Process

4.2 Identify and Predict

4.3 Decide and Execute

4.4 Using the IPDE Process

You Are the Driver!

Imagine you are approaching the intersection in this picture. You have a green traffic light. What possible hazards can you identify? Should you predict the light will stay green? What action should you take if your intended path of travel becomes closed? If you decide to change speed or direction, how can you communicate with the drivers behind you?

This chapter presents the IPDE Process with its components, the Smith System and the Zone Control System. The IPDE Process will help you reduce risk by making wise decisions and executing safe driving actions.

For: Chapter 4 online activities
Visit: PHSchool.com
Web Code: cak-9999

4.1

The IPDE Process

Objectives

1. Name three major factors that can contribute to the degree of risk you encounter while driving.
2. Name the four steps of the IPDE Process.
3. List the five rules of the Smith System.
4. Explain the structure of the Zone Control System.

Nearly every driver uses some kind of system or process to drive. Drivers who do not use some kind of organized system will have more close calls and collisions. Drivers who use an organized system will be better equipped to manage risk and thus reduce the possibility of damage or harm.

Risk

All activities throughout a person's life involve some degree of risk. Whether playing a sport, working on the job, or driving a vehicle, some degree of risk with the possibility of suffering harm is always present. The risk you take when driving a vehicle is the ever-present possibility of conflict.

Driving a vehicle in today's environment can cause you to be at a very high degree of risk. Risk factors can be contributed by the driver, by the vehicle, and by the roadway and environment. Some examples of driver-contributed factors are

- adjusting radio
- being angry
- having blurred vision
- combing hair
- drinking while driving
- using a cellular phone

Driver-contributed risk factors also apply to other drivers on the roadway. These other drivers can increase or decrease your level of risk and chance of conflict.

Some risk factors are contributed by the vehicle. However, most vehicle-related risk factors are really contributed by the vehicle owner. Ownership responsibility requires proper maintenance and repair of your vehicle. Some of these risk factors are

- bald tires
- poorly adjusted brakes
- dirty windshield
- broken headlight
- worn wiper blades

Risk factors contributed by the roadway and the environment may include the following:

- bright sun
- construction
- dark shadows
- snow and ice
- sharp curve

As you drive, be aware that all of these risk factors, and many more, play a major role in the level of risk you face.

Because some degree of risk is always present, try to make sure

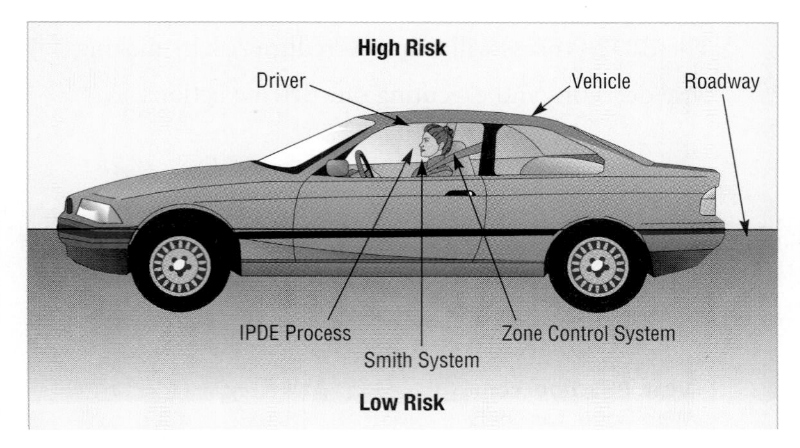

nothing about your own condition or the condition of your vehicle raises your level of risk.

Some drivers deliberately take chances. They put not only themselves but others at a high degree of risk. Deliberately taking a chance with a vehicle, with its great capacity for harm and destruction, should be unthinkable. The potential for suffering harm and loss is too great, and the possible penalties are too serious. Drivers who take unnecessary chances demonstrate risk-taking behaviors. A driver who continues to practice these behaviors can develop high-risk habits with the possibility of becoming an unsafe driver.

Good drivers make every effort to manage risk in order to lower the probability of conflict, and thus enjoy more stress-free driving. As you begin your driving experience, make every effort to develop low-risk driving behaviors. Then, through continual practice, these low-risk behaviors will become your safe driving habits.

The IPDE Process

Good seeing habits and your ability to manage space in the roadway are basic tools for low-risk driving. The IPDE Process, along with the Smith System and Zone Control System, can enable you to enjoy low-risk and low-stress driving.

Safe driving depends upon your ability to see and analyze traffic situations correctly. Good seeing habits are the basic critical factor necessary for staying out of high-risk situations. However, just being able to see well is no guarantee you will identify all critical clues and make correct driving responses in every situation.

The driving task is primarily a thinking task. Your hands and feet do only what your brain tells them to do. Most responsible drivers use a system that deals with all the traffic possibilities they will encounter. These drivers have fewer close calls and collisions than drivers who do not use some kind of system.

The IPDE Process is an organized system of seeing, thinking, and responding. The Smith System and the Zone Control System will help you apply the IPDE Process. The four steps of the IPDE Process are

1. Identify
2. Predict
3. Decide
4. Execute

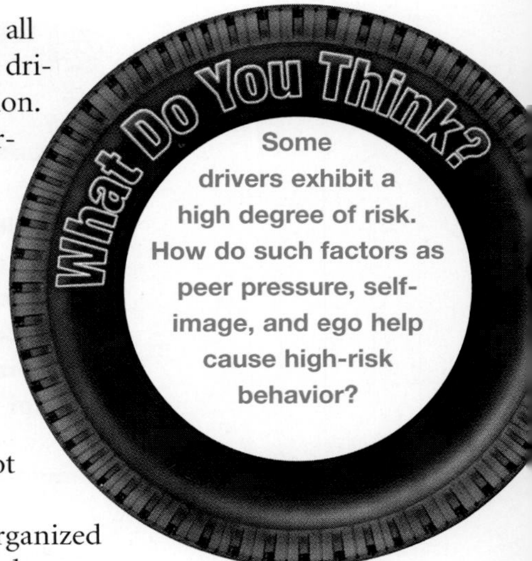

What Do You Think?

Some drivers exhibit a high degree of risk. How do such factors as peer pressure, self-image, and ego help cause high-risk behavior?

IPDE Process

1 Identify

Use visual search pattern to identify
- open and closed zones
- specific clues
- other users
- roadway features and conditions
- traffic controls

2 Predict

Use knowledge, judgment, and experience to predict
- actions of other users
- speed
- direction
- control
- points of conflict

IPDE

3 Decide

Decide to use one or more actions to
- change or maintain speed
- change direction
- communicate

4 Execute

Execute your decisions to
- control speed
- steer
- communicate
- combine actions

THE SMITH SYSTEM® Years ago, Harold L. Smith introduced a system for safe driving. The Smith System stresses eye discipline and the idea of a space cushion. Later, the Ford Motor Company asked Mr. Smith to share his system of driving with drivers throughout the United States. This system is still considered basic for safe driving habits.

You begin the IPDE Process by "reading" traffic situations to gather information for your decisions and actions. To process this information properly, you must identify hazards and predict conflict. You then decide how to avoid the conflict by executing the correct action.

The Smith System® is an organized method to help drivers develop good seeing habits by using five keys for driver safety. The five keys of the Smith System are

1. Aim high in steering.®
2. Get the big picture.®
3. Keep your eyes moving.®
4. Leave yourself an "out."®
5. Make sure they see you.®

The Zone Control System is an organized method for managing six zones of space surrounding your vehicle. Zone Control allows you to see and respond to changes in the traffic environment at a time when best control can be achieved.

The structure of the Zone Control System includes the following steps:

1. See a zone change.
2. Check other zones.
3. Create time and space by getting the best speed control, lane position, and communication.

Using the Smith System and Zone Control System with the IPDE Process can put you well on the road toward low-risk driving behaviors.

Review It

1. What three major factors contribute to your degree of risk while driving?
2. What are the four steps of the IPDE Process?
3. What are the five keys of the Smith System?
4. What is the structure of the Zone Control System?

4.2
Identify and Predict

The Identify and Predict steps of the IPDE Process are critical in every driving environment. These two steps begin your thinking process for every situation you encounter. With practice and experience, these steps will seem to occur in your thinking process as happening almost at the same time. As you search in and around your path to identify possible problems, you will be making judgments and predictions about what conflicts may occur.

Identify

The first step of the IPDE Process is **identify.** This step involves much more than just seeing. When you identify, you give meaning to what you see. You must know when to look, where to look, how to look, and what to look for.

Any aspect of the Highway Transportation System (HTS) can become a hazardous situation. This includes the roadway, your own vehicle, other vehicles or pedestrians, and traffic controls. Clues you identify may cause you to change direction or speed, signal others, or perform any combination of maneuvers. The sooner you identify a possible hazard, the more time you will have to react safely.

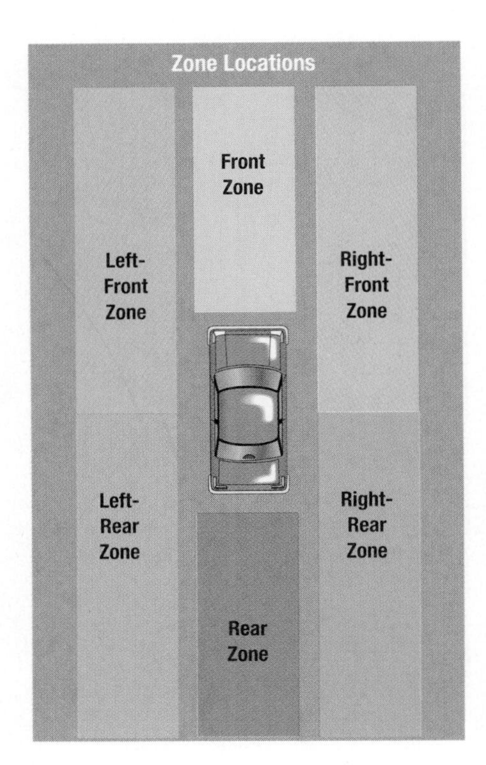

Zones and Searching Ranges

The Zone Control System helps you make quick and accurate use of the IPDE Process by setting a standard of what to identify and what to do when you find it. A **zone** is one of six areas of space around a vehicle that is the width of a lane and extends as far as the driver can see. The picture shows the six zones around your vehicle. Straight ahead is the front zone, to the left is the left-front zone, and to the right is the right-front zone. Behind you is the rear zone, the left-rear zone, and the right-rear zone.

An **open zone** is space where you can drive without a restriction to your **line of sight** or to your intended **path of travel.** Your line of sight is the distance you can see

Objectives

1. Describe the location of each of the six zones of the Zone Control System.
2. Explain what is meant by an open zone and a closed zone.
3. Describe an orderly visual search pattern.
4. Explain how knowledge and experience help you make accurate predictions.

What is your open zone in this situation?

ahead in the direction you are looking. Your intended path of travel is the space your vehicle will occupy. Your path of travel is directed toward the **target area.** The target area is the section of the roadway where the target is located in the center of your intended path, and the area to its right and left.

A **closed zone** is a space not open to you because of a restriction in your line of sight or intended path of travel. A red traffic light is an example of a closed front zone. A parked vehicle to your right represents a closed right-front zone. A closed rear zone might be a vehicle that is following you too closely. The sooner you identify a closed zone, the more time you have to respond. With more time, the better chance you have to achieve control of the situation by lowering the degree of risk.

The driver in the picture on the left has identified the car that is about to enter his or her intended path of travel. The driver will need to treat the front zone as closed, and therefore slow down to open the front zone.

In order to keep alert to the conditions of your zones, there are three searching ranges that need to be evaluated. A searching range is a certain distance ahead of the vehicle where the intended path of travel is systematically evaluated. The picture below shows the three searching ranges. The first searching range is the **target area range,** which is the space from your vehicle to the target area. You search this range to detect early any conditions that might affect your intended path of travel.

Next you will search the **12–15 second range,** which is the space you

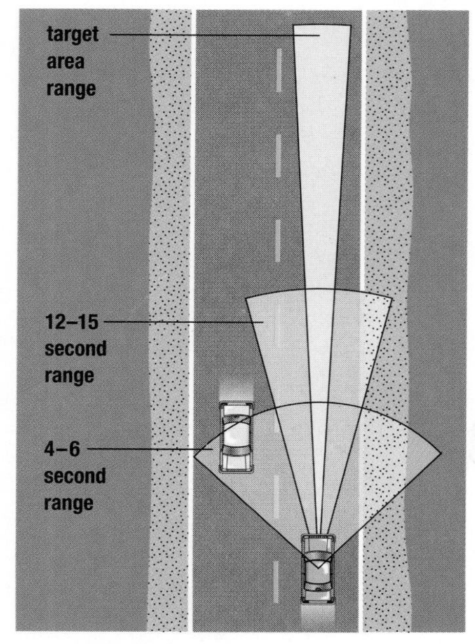

Three searching ranges

will travel in during the next 12–15 seconds. This range is where you need to identify changes in your line of sight or path of travel to make decisions about controlling your intended path. Try to identify the possibility of closed zones by searching to the left and right for anything that might come into your zones.

The **4–6 second range** is the space you will travel in during the next 4–6 seconds. This range is where you need to get the final update of how you are controlling your intended path of travel.

AVOID STARING Many beginning drivers develop the habit of staring. They fixate for several seconds on the same clue or event. They do not look far into target-area ranges, and often drive with swerves and jerky movements. Do not let yourself become a "stare" driver.

Orderly Visual Search Pattern

You can use any of several patterns to help develop your own identifying process. An **orderly visual search pattern** is a process of searching critical areas in a regular sequence. To use an orderly visual search pattern, look for clues in and around your intended path of travel in a systematic manner. Below is an example of an orderly visual search pattern for straight-ahead driving.

1. Look ahead to your target area range.
2. Evaluate your left-front, front, and right-front zones in the 12–15 second range. Search driveways and intersections for possible changes in your line of sight and path of travel.
3. Glance in rearview mirror to check your rear zones.
4. Evaluate your 4–6 second range before entering that space.
5. Look ahead again to evaluate another 12–15 second range.
6. Check your 4–6 second range.
7. Glance in rearview mirror.
8. Check speedometer and gauges.

You will repeat this pattern continually as you move forward. Each look or glance should last only an instant as you evaluate your zones and the areas to the left and right. Be careful not to stare as you search. Practice using your orderly visual search pattern as a passenger—in addition to when you are driving—so it will become a safe driving habit. You will then be able to adjust your search pattern for any maneuver or driving environment.

Where and How to Look

Different driving environments and traffic situations present a variety of visual search problems. As you gain driving experience, you will learn what kinds of clues and situations are most important to identify in order to keep an open zone in your path of travel.

The area you can see around you, while looking straight ahead, is called your **field of vision**. Many of us can see an area of about 90 degrees to each side, for a total picture of 180

Even though your peripheral vision is not sharp and clear, it is very important to you while you are driving. When you see some kind of movement or a vehicle or pedestrian in your peripheral vision, you can turn your eyes in that direction to see if there is a potential problem.

degrees. The area you can see clearly and sharply is seen with your **central vision.** This is a narrow cone of only up to 10 degrees. The area you can see to the left and right of central vision is your side vision, or **peripheral vision.** As the distance from central vision increases toward the outer edge of peripheral vision, the less clearly you can identify clues and events.

Three of the Smith System keys can help you learn where and how to look as you develop your visual search pattern.

Aim High in Steering® To "aim high" means that you look ahead 12–15 seconds into your target area as you drive. Do not just look at the close area in front of or at the sides of your vehicle. Be a high-aim driver. Looking far ahead with your line of sight will help you identify clues and analyze situations before your zone becomes closed. There are many restrictions to your line of sight that can cause a closed zone. Some such restrictions are curves, hills, large vehicles, weather conditions, buildings, trees, or even a dirty windshield.

Keep Your Eyes Moving® Looking near and far, side to side, and in the mirrors will help you see a zone change before it becomes critical. Keeping your eyes moving does not mean just moving them constantly. You must fixate on an object or an event for an instant in order to identify it. Do not fixate for longer than an instant or you will find yourself staring. Keeping your eyes moving will prevent you from staring at any one object or clue.

Develop the art of **scanning,** glancing continually and quickly with very brief fixations through your orderly visual search pattern. You are looking and seeing as you scan, but not staring at any one event or clue. Staring blocks out side vision, causes lack of attention, and

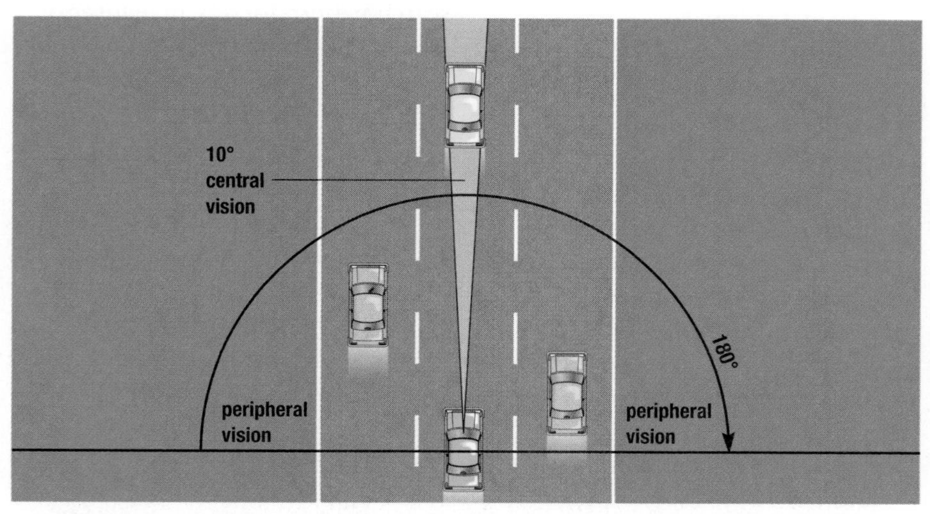

You see most clearly in the area of central vision, but peripheral vision is equally important.

tends to create high-risk driving habits. Keeping your eyes moving helps you stay more alert with your attention at a higher level. You are then more likely to keep up with all the changes in your field of vision.

Get the Big Picture® Getting the big picture is the mental process of putting together the critical clues you have selected. It is the result of aiming high and keeping your eyes moving.

What to Look For

Knowing where and how to look does little good if you do not know what to look for in your target area. Develop the technique of selective seeing in your identifying process. Selective seeing means that you identify and select only those clues and events that restrict your line of sight or can change your intended path of travel.

Look for Open Zones Use your visual search pattern to look for specific driving-related clues that might cause an open zone to close. When searching parked cars on a street, you might identify an important clue, such as front wheels turned toward the street, as the picture shows. You might also identify vapor coming from an exhaust pipe or a driver sitting in a car. These clues indicate that a car might enter your path of travel and cause your front zone to close.

The kinds of clues you search for will change as you drive in different environments. When driving in the city, search for intersections, parked cars, pedestrians, and traffic. On open highways, search areas much farther ahead. Look for crossroads, slow-moving vehicles, and animals. Any of these can suddenly cause an open zone to close, resulting in the need to change your intended path of travel. When you drive on expressways, speeds are higher and scanning all zones becomes even more critical. Regardless of the driving environment, you should always look for other roadway users, roadway features, changing conditions,

Front wheels turned toward the street are a clue that the car might pull out and close your zone.

You Are the Driver!
What procedure would you follow to avoid a possible conflict if your front zone becomes closed?

and traffic controls that may affect your intended path of travel.

Look for Other Users Look for other users who might affect your intended path of travel. Watch for movement of other users, especially in areas that have shadows or shade. Watch for pedestrians and bicyclists. A large truck is easy to identify. However, it creates a restriction in your line of sight and may prevent you from seeing another user. Develop the habit of **ground viewing** as part of your visual search pattern. Ground viewing is making quick glances to the roadway in front of your vehicle. When other vehicles are approaching, use ground viewing to see where they are headed by checking the direction of their front wheels.

Always be on the lookout for problem drivers. Problem drivers usually give clues by their driving behavior. Some fast drivers might be problem drivers. They may try to pass without enough room or in a no-passing zone. They frequently change lanes, trying to get ahead of the normal traffic flow, and can cause a sudden change in your open zone condition.

Look for Roadway Features and Conditions The roadway itself is another important area to watch. Identify intersections, hills, and curves early. Be aware ahead of time that the width of your lane might be reduced for road construction or other obstacles. An intersection is a high-risk area where the management of your path of travel needs constant attention. Stopped traffic or entering traffic can cause line-of-sight restrictions or even a closed

Drivers need to look for many different roadway users and roadway conditions that will affect their path of travel.

zone. A hill is a line-of-sight restriction which could hide a closed zone as you go over the hill. Here are some reasons for changes in roadway features and conditions:

- **Change from multilane to single lane** Multilane roadways often narrow into single-lane roadways. Identify signs warning you of this change early enough to avoid a closed zone in your intended path. When signs indicate roadway repairs ahead, you can expect your front zone will close. Check your left-front, right-front, and rear zones before moving into the through lane. Drivers who wait until the last instant and then try to squeeze into the through lane are demonstrating high-risk behavior with no concern for other drivers.
- **Change in width of lane** Standing water, patches of snow, potholes, or objects in the roadway can cause an open zone to close. Identify the conditions early and then check your rear zone to find out if there will be a problem in case a stop is needed. Check your left-rear zone and left-front zone, as the driver in the picture above is doing, to see if you have space to go around the problem safely.
- **Roadway surface** Identify the roadway surface and condition each time you begin to drive. There will be times when the weather will change while you are driving. Roadway surfaces may be dry when you start out and then become wet and slippery with rain, snow, or ice as you are driving. Be prepared to adjust your driving for changing weather conditions that might affect the roadway surface. A gravel surface can cause sliding or skidding just like a wet or slippery surface.
- **Roadside hazards** Your identification process should keep you scanning for bicyclists, pedestrians, parked vehicles, and animals. Watch for shopping center entrances and exits, roadside stands, and restaurants. Other drivers can appear from almost any location and cause your open zone to close. Continual scanning of your target areas will help you identify these other drivers in time to avoid sudden actions or conflict.

Check your rear zones and left-front zone when an object is in the roadway.

Look for Traffic Controls Learn to look in different places for traffic controls. At major intersections, controls can be overhead, in the center, or on a corner. Identify traffic controls as early as possible so you are ready to make correct responses.

Predict

Once you have identified a hazard, **predict** how this hazard might affect your intended path of travel. When you predict, you interpret the information you have identified. You predict where possible points of conflict can occur. You try to foresee what might happen, how changes in zones may occur, and how you would check other zones for alternate paths. Your predictions will be based upon those conditions that may reduce your line of sight or could change your intended path of travel.

If you had to face just one hazard at a time, you could more easily predict the possible outcome. However, most of the time you will be faced with more than one possible hazard or conflict, so predicting can become more complex.

How to Predict

Predicting involves what is happening in your zones, what could happen, and if it does happen, how the change could affect you. To predict, you must evaluate the situation and make a judgment about the possible consequences. The more complex a situation is, the more difficult it is to identify and predict. As you gain driving experience, you will become more selective about which hazards or possible conflicts are critical.

Imagine you are driving the car on the right in the picture below. Your left-front zone is blocked by the bicyclists and oncoming car. You should predict that one or both of the bicyclists might swerve or fall. If so, predict that the oncoming car might enter your front zone, causing it to close.

Using Zone Control, you would check your rear zone in case you need to stop. Check your right-front zone in case you need to move in that direction. You should also check the right-rear zone before moving to the right. Scanning your target areas can help you predict hazards that may affect your path of travel. Your ability to predict and make sound judgments will improve as you gain knowledge and experience.

Knowledge One basic part of your driving knowledge comes from the study of traffic laws and driver-education material. Whenever you drive, you also gain knowledge by gathering more information and learning from others.

Think of storing driving knowledge as adding to your safe-driving memory bank. The more you drive, the more you add to your memory bank of knowledge. This knowledge

What might you predict if this was your oncoming traffic?

will help you identify and predict more quickly and accurately and increase your chances of becoming a low-risk driver.

Judgment Making a judgment about a traffic situation involves measuring, comparing, and evaluating. As you drive, you judge speed, time, space, distance, traction, and visibility. You make judgments about your own driving performance as well as the actions and performance of other roadway users. Make every effort to develop the ability to make sound judgments that lead to accurate predictions.

Experience In addition to knowledge, experience helps you improve your ability to predict accurately. Exposure to a wide variety of driving experiences provides a solid base for making sound judgments later.

What to Predict

Nearly all predictions you make as a driver will be related to predicting changes in zones and looking for an "out" or an alternative path of travel. Two major elements in the traffic scene you must make predictions about are

- the actions of other roadway users
- your control of your vehicle and consequences of your actions

Predicting Actions of Others Do not assume other roadway users will always take the correct action. Instead watch for clues to what they might do to alter zone conditions. The most important types of predictions to make concerning the actions of others are

- **Path** Where might the other driver go? What zone might be closed? Will I have an open zone for an "out"? The Smith System rule of leaving yourself an "out" is critical when predicting possible closed zones.
- **Action** What action will other users take? Is more than one action possible? Where will I be then?
- **Space** Will I have an open zone?
- **Point of Conflict** If I have no open zone for escape, where might our paths cross and a conflict occur?

Imagine that you are driving toward the intersection in the picture below. The oncoming driver is signaling for a right turn. Assume the worst and predict that the driver

What Do You Think?

Both knowledge and experience are important. Which adds more to your safe-driving memory bank—knowledge or experience?

What might the oncoming driver do? What might the pedestrians do?

You Are the Driver!
What effect does the oncoming car have on your IPDE Process?

will turn left into your front zone. Also predict that the pedestrians will step off the curb and close your right front zone. By making these predictions you will be able to slow, swerve, or stop in order to avoid a conflict.

Predicting Control of Your Vehicle and Possible Consequences Speed is probably the most important factor in maintaining control of your vehicle. Always be prepared to adjust your speed for different zone conditions and situations. Different traffic, roadway, and weather conditions can change the amount of time and space needed for safe reactions.

The basic requirement for vehicle control is **traction.** Traction is the actual gripping power between the tires and the roadway surface. The more traction there is, the greater the gripping power.

In the picture above, the driver knows the roadway is wet and presumes it is slippery. Visibility is restricted by the weather. The driver predicts that stopping for the STOP sign will take longer than if the roadway were dry. Based on this prediction, the driver checks the rear zone and then slows and brakes earlier.

In many situations you may have a choice of actions to predict. Try to judge and compare the possible consequences before deciding on the best action.

Review It

1. What is the location of each of the six zones of the Zone Control System?
2. What is an open zone and a closed zone?
3. Give an example of an orderly visual search pattern.
4. What effects do knowledge and experience have on your ability to make accurate predictions?

4.3

Decide and Execute

Once you have identified a situation and predicted a possible conflict, you then **decide** upon an action. Deciding, like predicting, is also a mental task. There is probably no task more important, though, than making wise decisions and then executing actions to avoid conflict. Drivers must continually identify and predict until they have enough information to make correct decisions.

Once you make a decision, the **execute** step of the IPDE Process will follow. To execute a decision means that you carry out an action that you have decided upon. In order to do this, you will use your vehicle's controls and safety devices.

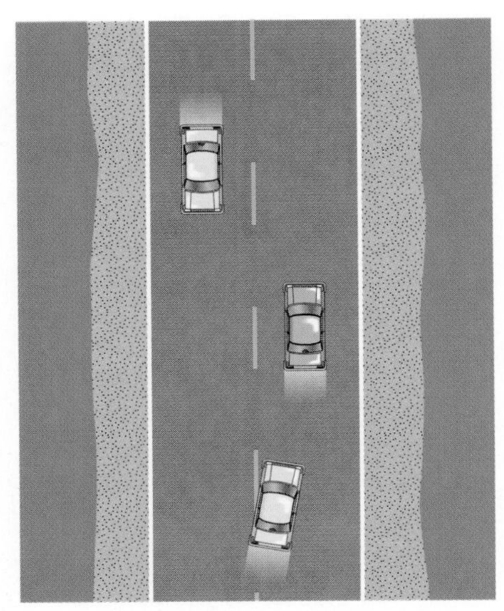

The driver of the yellow car decided to accelerate to provide space for the passing driver to return to the right lane.

Decide

As you follow a selected path, your decision might be to maintain speed, change speed, change direction, or communicate your plan to others. Or you might decide to use a combination of these actions. Be prepared to rethink your decisions as zones close and greater hazards are presented. Practice and experience, as well as your judgment and stored knowledge, are the tools you can use to avoid conflict and develop low-risk driving behaviors.

Decide to Change Speed Any decision you make will be influenced by the speed of your own vehicle as well as the speed of other vehicles. Many drivers think that slowing down is the only way to avoid a conflict. In many situations, however, you will decide to maintain your speed. Your other choices of actions, rather than maintaining your speed, are to decelerate, brake, or accelerate. Base your decision about speed control on your evaluation of the situation as well as the possible consequences of your actions.

The driver of the yellow car on the two-lane road in the picture decided to accelerate. This decision provided space for the passing driver to return to the right lane. Had the driver of the yellow car decided to brake, there could have been a major collision in that driver's left-front zone.

Decide to Change Direction In order to change your position in the

Objectives

1. Name the three decisions you must make when applying the IPDE Process.
2. Describe the three different lane positions available to you within your lane.
3. Explain what is meant when you minimize or separate a hazard or compromise space.
4. List the three most important actions you can take to avoid conflict.

roadway, you will steer to the right or left. A greater change of direction might even be a lane change.

The Smith System® key to leave yourself an "out" allows you to change direction when necessary. You then can use an escape path into an open zone to avoid conflict. This area of space all around your vehicle is called a **space cushion.**

Three different lane positions are available to you within your lane. You could change to one of these positions in order to avoid a closing zone. Notice the three lane positions in the diagram below.

- **Lane position 1:** The car is centered within the travel lane. This should be your selected and safest position under normal driving conditions. In this position you have the most space around your vehicle.
- **Lane position 2:** The car is three to six inches away from the left line of your lane. You might decide to use this position when there is a closed right-front zone with an open left-front zone. Just a slight adjustment to the left is necessary.
- **Lane position 3:** The car is three to six inches away from the right line of your lane. Use this position when there is a closed left-front zone with an open right-front zone.

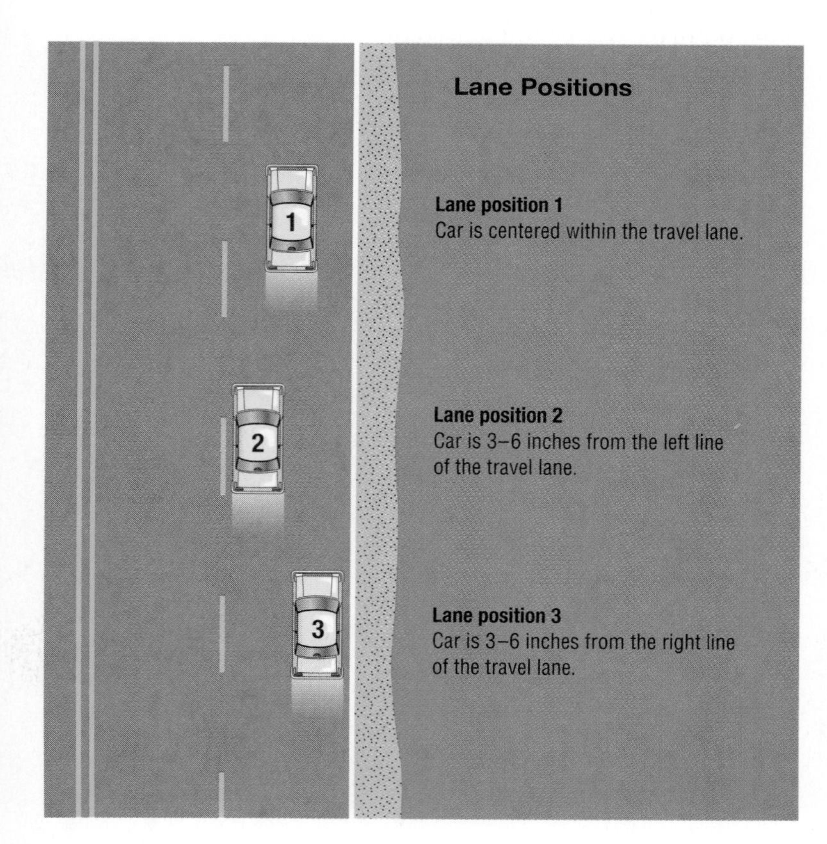

There may be times when the situation requires a greater change in direction than the three lane positions. You may decide that the best position, in some situations, is to straddle a lane line. In these situations, return to lane position 1 as soon as it is safe to do so.

In order to make consistently low-risk decisions, try to detect a changing zone condition at least 15 seconds ahead in your searching area. This gives you ample time to decide on the best action.

Decide to Communicate Communicating is the process of sending and receiving messages to and from other users of the roadway. The decision to communicate with others helps reduce the possibility of conflict. The Smith System® key, "Make sure they see you®," tells others where you are and what you plan to do. You can decide to communicate with others by using lights, horn, vehicle position, eye contact, and body movement.

A change in direction or speed can be executed with less risk if you have communicated your intentions to other users. Try to avoid changes in speed or direction without communicating first. Surprises of sudden actions can result in high-risk situations.

You can decide to communicate with others in a variety of ways:

- headlights, taillights, and brake lights
- turn signal lights
- parking lights and hazard flashers
- back-up lights
- horn
- car position
- eye contact and body movement

After deciding the best method of communicating, you will execute that action to inform others of your decision. The driver in the picture below is using body movement by waving the driver on the left through the intersection first.

Traffic Flow

The IPDE Process, the Smith System, and the Zone Control System will help you make decisions that will enable you to avoid hazards and conflicts in your intended path. The safest position in traffic is the place where the fewest vehicles surround you. Your objective is to keep your vehicle surrounded by space. Continually analyze your left, front, and right zones and make decisions to adjust your speed or direction if one of your zones begins to close. By deciding to adjust your speed or direction, you will avoid unnecessary stops and thus reduce your risk of conflict.

Use body motions to communicate.

Use the following techniques to manage time, space, and distance in order to maintain your safe path of travel.

Minimize a Hazard You always want to **minimize a hazard,** or reduce the possibility of conflict by deciding to put more distance between yourself and the hazard. As the yellow car in the picture on the right approaches the parked cars on the right, the driver predicts a car door might open. Since there is no oncoming traffic, the driver decides to steer away from the parked cars into lane position 2. After passing the parked cars, the driver will return to lane position 1. The driver has minimized the hazard by using more space.

Minimize the hazard of the parked cars by moving to lane position 2.

Separate Hazards There will be times when you face more than one hazard at a time. When this occurs do not try to handle both or all hazards at once. Instead, decide to adjust your speed so you deal with only one hazard at a time. By following this strategy, you will **separate the hazards.**

The driver of the car in the picture on the left sees the oncoming motor home in the left-front zone and the pedestrians in the right-front zone. The best decision is for the driver to adjust speed by slowing down. The motor home can then pass the pedestrians first. The driver would then meet the motor home with ample space before passing the pedestrians. In this situation, the driver separated the hazards and handled only one at a time.

The driver must separate two hazards—the pedestrians on the right and the approaching vehicle on the left.

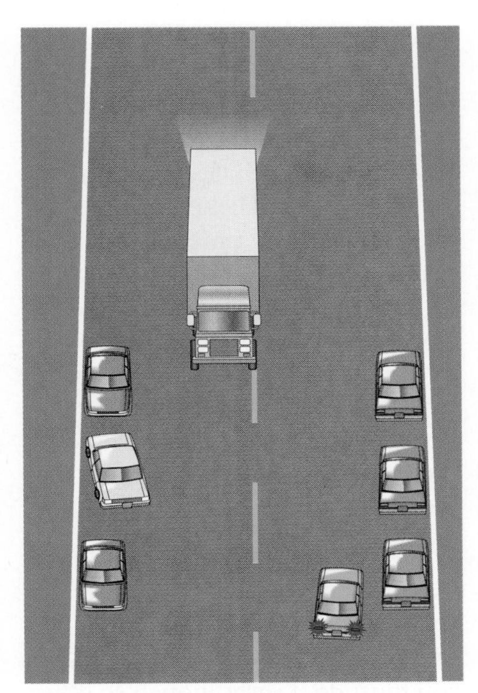

The driver of the yellow car is compromising space to give more space to the greater hazard—the truck.

Compromise Space Sometimes hazards cannot be minimized or separated. When this occurs, you must decide to **compromise space** by giving as much space as possible to the greater hazard.

The truck in the picture on this page might enter the front zone of the yellow car to avoid the parked car leaving the parking space. Although the cars on the right present a hazard, the driver of the yellow car should decide to steer right as far as possible. This decision gives more space to the greater hazard, the approaching truck. In every situation, the action you decide on should be the one involving the least amount of risk.

Execute

Carrying out your decision in order to avoid conflict is the execute step in the IPDE Process. This step involves the physical skills used in driving. In most cases, you will execute routine actions and maneuvers. Some actions will be using your vehicle's controls such as heater, defroster, wipers, gearshift lever, and others. More important actions, however, involve timing and placement of your vehicle to avoid conflict. The important actions you will execute are

- control speed
- steer
- communicate

Control Speed Your decisions to control speed can result in a variety of actions. At times the action you take will be to maintain the speed you are going. Other times your action may be to decelerate. This action can be used successfully as you approach a red light. If you merely release the accelerator far enough before the intersection, you often will arrive at the intersection when the light is green. In this situation, you also may use gentle pressure on the brake if more slowing is needed. Check your rear zone before decelerating.

When greater deceleration is needed, you will execute the action of more firm braking. The amount of braking needed will vary with the situation, the speed of your vehicle, the condition of the roadway, and the condition of your brakes.

Always check your rear zone before decelerating or braking in any

The IPDE Process is a constant interaction of the I, P, and D functions. Don't become a high-risk driver who only *executes*.

What Do You Think?

Some vehicles now come with daytime running lights. Should daytime running lights be mandatory equipment on all vehicles?

manner. Avoid locking the brakes in an emergency stop. Locked brakes make steering impossible because wheels must be turning to provide traction for steering. Some newer vehicles have an antilock braking system. Such a system helps prevent loss of steering control. An antilock braking system, through the use of computers, helps brake your vehicle in an emergency. All you need to do is to apply the brakes hard, continually. No pumping action is needed.

As the driver of the car in the picture below enters the intersection, the white car from the right makes a right turn and enters the driver's path. The driver avoids locking the brakes so as not to lose steering control. Locking the brakes could have caused the car to slide and result in a conflict.

Steer When you decide to steer away from a possible conflict, execute just the amount of steering needed. Oversteering can cause you to lose control of your vehicle, especially at higher speeds. Higher speeds also require more space for your maneuver.

Understeering can also present a problem. Try to steer just enough to avoid a conflict without making jerky or sudden movements. Drivers who keep space cushions around their vehicles usually have an escape path to steer into, thus reducing risk.

Communicate In many instances your only action will be to communicate. When you do communicate, you must do it early enough so other users know your intentions. Communicate by using the following:

- **Headlights, taillights, and brake lights** Use headlights during

You Are the Driver!
What procedures would you follow to avoid conflict? Assume that your vehicle has an antilock braking system.

periods of reduced visibility. Using headlights during daylight hours, as the driver in this picture is doing, is a safety practice that makes your vehicle more visible to other drivers. Some new vehicles are equipped with daytime running lights—headlights that come on automatically whenever the vehicle is operated. The advantage of these lights is to improve the visibility of the vehicle. Research shows that the use of daytime headlights reduces daytime crashes of all types.

- **Turn-signal lights** Turn them on three to five seconds before making any change in direction.
- **Parking lights and hazard flashers** When you are parked along the roadway but not in an emergency situation, have your parking lights turned on. If your vehicle is disabled, turn on your hazard flashers. Be prepared to change your path of travel when you see the blinking or flashing lights of a stopped delivery truck. The driver in the picture below has identified the blocked zone in time to safely pass the truck.
- **Back-up lights** White back-up lights let others know you are backing up. Look for back-up lights on vehicles in parking lots.
- **Horn** A light tap is usually enough for a warning. In an emergency, a loud blast may be necessary.

Your vehicle can be seen more easily if your headlights are on, even in daytime.

Be prepared to change your path to go around stopped vehicles.

What actions would you take to avoid a conflict?

- **Vehicle position** The position of your vehicle in the roadway communicates a message. It indicates to others your intended path of travel. Other drivers may or may not see a light signal, but the position of the vehicle in the lane sends a message.
- **Eye contact and body movement** Try to develop eye contact with other roadway users. You can communicate many messages this way. Body movements such as a wave of the hand may tell a driver to proceed. Other hand movements may ask drivers to wait while you proceed.

Combine Actions

You often will need to execute a combination of actions. Sometimes you might need to accelerate and steer at the same time. In other situations, you might need to brake, communicate, and steer at the same time.

If you were driving alongside the parked car in the picture above, you would need to combine several actions. You would first check your rear zone and your left-front zone to see if they are open. Then communicate by signaling as you brake and steer around the open car door. The precision and timing with which you execute these actions will determine whether or not a conflict will occur.

Review It

1. What are the three basic decisions you make in the Decide part of the IPDE Process?
2. What three different lane positions are available to you within your lane?
3. What are the three techniques you can use to maintain a safe path of travel?
4. What three actions can you execute to avoid conflict?

4.4

Using the IPDE Process

Using the IPDE Process, along with the Smith System and the Zone Control System, helps you plan and execute maneuvers to reduce hazards. It is up to every driver to manage space, time, and speed in order to further increase safety within the HTS.

You must continually practice using the IPDE Process so that it will become habit. Once you have developed the habit, you will

- see more
- make accurate predictions and correct decisions
- execute maneuvers more successfully

IPDE Takes Practice

Practice is necessary for the development and improvement of any skill. As you ride with other drivers, practice the I-P-D steps of the IPDE Process. You can then judge if the actions taken by others were based on correct decisions.

Commentary Driving

Commentary driving is a system of "thinking out loud" as you practice the IPDE Process. When using commentary driving, you verbalize what you identify, predict, and decide.

Imagine you are the driver in the picture on the right practicing commentary driving. Using the IPDE Process, what would you say? Now turn the page to see the picture at the bottom. Did you identify and predict correctly? What action did you decide to execute? Practicing commentary driving will help make the IPDE Process a basic part of your safe driving behavior.

Putting IPDE Into Action

Use the four steps of the IPDE Process in order. Once you have learned the techniques for identifying, add the predicting step. You identify the hazards or events, then predict how they might affect your intended path of travel. You then perform the third step, deciding. Finally, you execute your maneuvers based on your decisions.

Selective Use of IPDE

There will be times when you do not carry out the total IPDE Process. Conditions may change in one or more zones so the process need not be completed. You can use the IPDE Process selectively by beginning a new cycle before completing the previous one.

Objectives

1. Explain what is meant by commentary driving.
2. Describe what is meant by selective use of the IPDE Process.
3. Explain why the IPDE Process takes time.

What warning clues are in this picture? What would you predict? What would you do?

You Are the Driver!
How would you use the IPDE Process if you were the driver in this situation?

As you become a more experienced driver, you will learn the more important clues and trouble spots in different areas of the HTS. You will then be able to adjust your selective application of the IPDE Process for those specific areas.

IPDE Takes Time

Remember that the IPDE Process takes time. You must have time to identify clues and changing zones. You must have time to predict the actions of others and the possibility of closed zones. The more complex the traffic situation and the more risk factors present, the longer it takes to carry out the IPDE Process.

At times your own feelings and physical condition can cause you to take more time to complete the IPDE Process. Do not allow complacency or laziness to creep into your driving habits. By making a conscious effort to continually apply the IPDE Process, you can achieve the reward of low-risk, low-stress driving enjoyment.

Warning clues were the ball in the street and the children in the yard. Did you predict and react correctly?

Review It

1. What is commentary driving?
2. Explain what is meant by selective use of the IPDE Process.
3. What factors can cause the IPDE Process to take more time?

Chapter 4
Review

Review Chapter Objectives

1. The IPDE Process

1. What are the three major factors that can contribute to the degree of risk you encounter while driving? (62)
2. What are the four steps in the IPDE Process? (63)
3. What are the five rules of the Smith System? (64)
4. How is the Zone Control System structured? (64)

2. Identify and Predict

5. What is the location of each of the six zones of the Zone Control System? (65)
6. What do "open zone" and "closed zone" mean? (65–66)
7. How do you use the identifying process known as an orderly visual search pattern? (67)
8. How can knowledge and experience help you make accurate predictions? (72–73)

3. Decide and Execute

9. What three decisions must be made when applying the IPDE Process? (75)
10. What are the three different positions available to you within your lane? (76)
11. How do you minimize a hazard, separate a hazard, and compromise space? (78–79)
12. What are the three most important actions you can take to avoid conflict? (79)

4. Using the IPDE Process

13. What does "commentary driving" mean? (83)
14. When is it appropriate to use the IPDE Process selectively? (83)
15. Why does the IPDE Process take time? (84)

Projects

Individuals

Investigate Visit your library to find more information about Harold Smith, founder of the Smith System. Write a short report about your findings.

Observe Traffic As a passenger in a vehicle during heavy traffic, observe the driver's use of the IPDE Process. In your opinion, were the driver's actions based on correct decisions? Discuss your observations with the class.

Use Technology Use the Internet to access the State Highway Patrol home page for your state to find information about traffic fatalities. List the risk factors that contributed to the fatalities and present your findings to the class.

Observe Traffic Ask students to make observations of the roadways they travel on as passengers to record locations where they are able to find actual examples of line-of-sight restrictions. Also, ask them to try to record five line-of-sight restrictions that were not listed during class. Have them bring their papers back to class for further discussion.

Groups

Observe Traffic Observe for 15 minutes the drivers of the cars that drive past your school. Note risk factors you see. Compile a list of any driver-contributed risk behaviors that you see. Discuss the impact of these behaviors with your class.

Investigate Each person in the group should use a different Internet search engine to find more information about the IPDE Process. Discuss your findings with your group and class.

Chapter 4
Review

Chapter Test

Check Your Knowledge

Multiple Choice Copy the number of each sentence below on a sheet of paper. Choose the letter of the answer that best completes the statement or answers the question.

1. Which of the following risk factors is contributed by the roadway and environment?
   (a) blurred vision (c) bald tires
   (b) bright sun (d) broken headlight
2. Six areas of space around a vehicle that are the width of a lane and extend as far as the driver can see are called
   (a) ranges. (c) zones.
   (b) fields. (d) paths.
3. Peripheral vision refers to the area you can see
   (a) while looking straight ahead. (c) clearly and sharply.
   (b) to the left and right of central vision. (d) behind you.
4. Which of the following terms describes glancing continually and quickly through your orderly visual search pattern?
   (a) ground viewing (c) steering
   (b) selective seeing (d) scanning

Completion Copy the number of each sentence below. After each number, write the word or words that complete the sentence correctly.

5. An open zone is space where you can drive without a restriction to your ______ or to your intended path of travel.
6. Making quick glances to the roadway in front of your vehicle is called ______.
7. Almost every ______ you make as a driver will be related to anticipating zone changes and looking for alternative paths of travel.

Review Vocabulary

Copy the number of each definition in list A. Match the definition in list A with the term it defines in list B.

List A

8. area as far ahead as you can see a target in the center of your intended path, and to its right and left
9. space where you can drive without restriction to your line of sight or intended path of travel
10. cone-shaped area of up to 10 degrees in which you can see clearly while looking straight ahead
11. one of six areas of space around a vehicle that is the width of a lane and extends as far as the driver can see
12. all the area a person can see while looking straight ahead
13. side vision area to the left and right of central vision
14. process of adjusting the speed of a vehicle to handle one hazard at a time when two or more hazards threaten a driver

List B

a. open zone
b. peripheral vision
c. separate the hazards
d. zone
e. target area range
f. central vision
g. field of vision

Think Critically

Write a paragraph to answer each question.

1. Explain what it means to develop the art of scanning. Why is scanning important?
2. What is the relationship between the IPDE Process, the Zone Control System, and the Smith System?

Decision Making

1. You are the driver of the car leaving the football game. Your team has just won. You are driving to a restaurant in town. How might your friends in the car contribute to your level of risk as you drive? What procedures will you follow to maintain a low level of risk?

2. How would knowledge and experience help the driver approaching the STOP sign execute a safe stop?

3. What do you predict will occur in your front zone? What steps will you take to reduce risk? Which lane position will you use?

4. You are the driver meeting the oncoming traffic. What do you predict an oncoming vehicle might do? If a vehicle does enter your lane, how will you complete the IPDE Process?

Unit 2

Controlling Your Vehicle

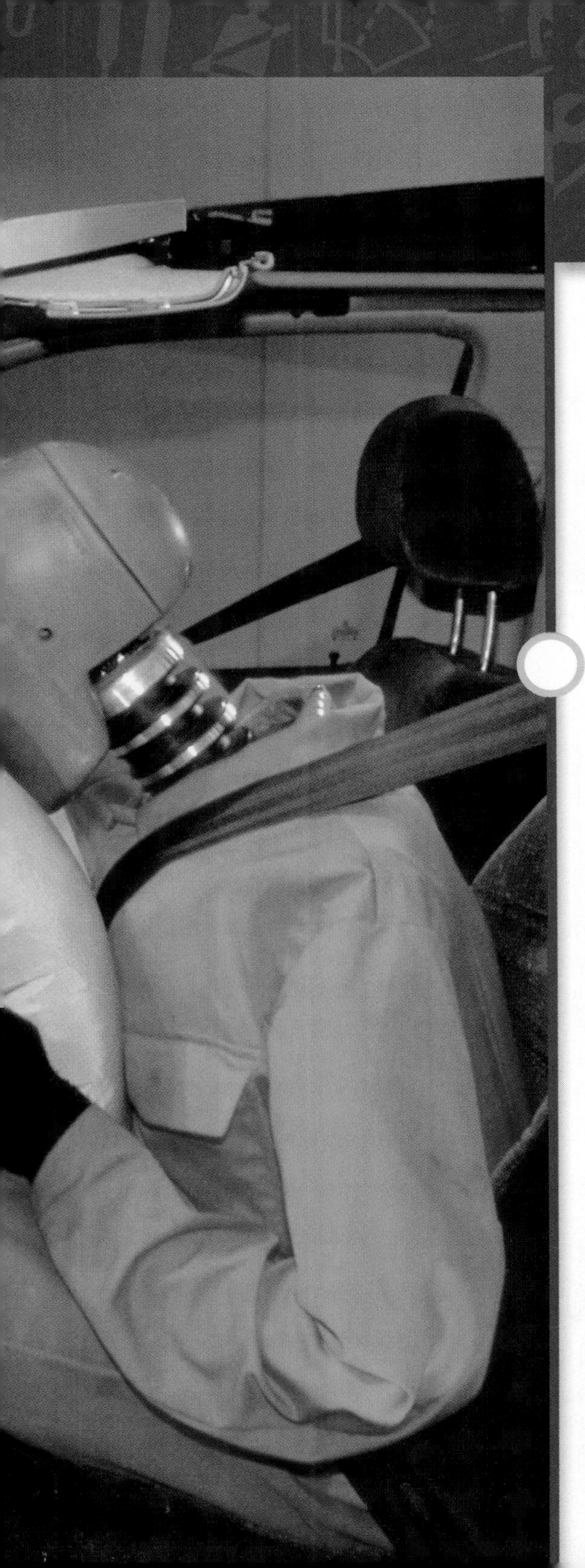

CHAPTER 5
Natural Laws and Car Control

You Are the Driver!

At the very instant that this picture was taken, tremendous forces were being applied. If you had been the driver and were using your safety belt, the air bag would have helped to prevent serious injury. How will natural laws affect your car control? What are the best hand and seating positions for you and your passengers if air bags inflate?

To be a safe driver, you need to know about natural laws. This chapter will introduce you to these laws and explain why you must respect them.

For: Chapter 5 online activities
Visit: PHSchool.com
Web Code: cak-9999

5.1 Gravity and Energy of Motion

Objectives

1. Explain how gravity affects your car.
2. Describe the factors that affect energy of motion.

Gravity and energy of motion are natural laws that will affect the way your vehicle performs. When you operate a light vehicle like a bicycle at low speeds, you can easily maintain control. Control can be tricky, however, when you drive a car or a light truck that weighs almost two tons. In emergency situations, natural laws can create forces that can work for or against you.

Gravity

Gravity is the force that pulls all things to Earth. The lack of gravity in outer space lets astronauts float. However, if you hit a ball, drop a rock, or drive your vehicle over a pothole, gravity pulls each to Earth.

Driving Up and Down Hills

You can feel the pull of gravity as you drive up and down hills. When you drive uphill, you will lose speed unless you use extra power. To hold the same speed, you must increase the vehicle's power to overcome the pulling force of gravity. On a steep hill in a standard stickshift vehicle, you will have to use a lower gear to increase power and maintain speed.

Gravity will increase your speed on a downhill road unless you control it. It will take you longer to stop, so you will need to think further ahead. Start braking early and shift to a lower gear on a long downhill stretch of road. This will let the engine—instead of the brakes—slow your vehicle.

How will an uphill or downhill situation affect your intended path of travel? In an uphill situation, your actual braking distance will be shortened a little. On a downhill road, your actual braking distance will be longer. The steeper the incline, the longer your stopping distance will be.

Center of Gravity

The point around which an object's weight is evenly distributed is called its **center of gravity.** For example, high-wire circus performers use this law by holding long poles to help them maintain balance. As the ends of the pole curve down, the performer's center of gravity is lowered.

A vehicle's stability decreases as its center of gravity rises.

This lower center of gravity helps the performers to maintain balance and walk the thin wire without falling.

An automotive engineer tries to make a vehicle's center of gravity low so that it can perform better. Look at the vehicle in the pictures on the left. See how raising the vehicle's center of gravity could make it unstable on a steep hill or sharp turn. How would this vehicle perform in a sudden stop or swerve situation?

Energy of Motion

When an object moves, it acquires energy. This force is called **energy of motion,** or kinetic energy. The faster your vehicle moves, the more energy of motion it has. Energy of motion is also affected by the weight of the moving object.

The pictures on this page show how a truck's energy of motion increases dramatically as weight and speed increase:

- The truck's energy of motion doubles when its weight is doubled by a load. When the truck weighs twice as much, it needs about twice the distance to stop.
- The truck's energy of motion will change in proportion to the *square* of its change in speed. When the truck's speed doubles, it needs about *four times* the distance to stop. If you triple your speed, you will need *nine times* the distance to stop.

Once you really understand this natural law, you can adjust to traffic situations ahead of time. You will see how important it is to slow before an emergency situation develops. Every time you cut your speed in half, you cut your energy of motion by four times.

As a driver, you will feel the laws of gravity and energy of motion affecting your vehicle. Remember these laws when you need to judge how long it will take you to stop your vehicle.

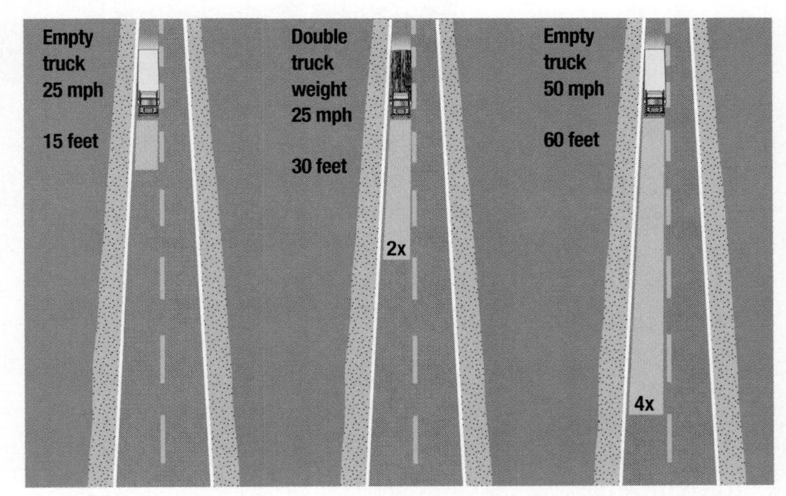

A vehicle's energy of motion increases dramatically with increases in weight and speed.

Review It

1. How does the force of gravity affect your car going downhill?
2. What factors affect energy of motion?

5.2
Friction and Traction

Objectives

1. Explain how traction controls your car.
2. List three things that can reduce traction.
3. Describe how you can check traction while driving.
4. List factors that affect your car in a curve.

Many people believe their steering wheel, brake pedal, and accelerator control their vehicle. Actually, your four tires, and their footprints that touch the road, are the first and one of the most important parts to the control system. Look at the picture below and spot the four footprints created by the car's tires. Each footprint is about as big as a page of this book.

Friction is the force that keeps each tire from sliding on the road. You can feel this same force by rubbing your hands together.

The friction created by the tire on the road is called **traction.** Traction makes it possible for your vehicle to grip the road so you can change speed and direction. Press the accelerator, and the drive wheels rotate. The traction of the tires mounted on these wheels makes your vehicle go forward.

Push the brake pedal, and braking friction will slow the four wheels on your vehicle. As the tires on these wheels slow, traction between the tires and the road will slow your vehicle. This same system will enable your vehicle to turn left or right when the front wheels turn.

Tires

Tires make a difference in the way your vehicle performs. The simple mistake of driving with low pressure in your tires can mean the difference between avoiding a collision or hitting something.

Tread and Traction

The grooved surface of a tire that grips the road is called the **tread.** When the road is wet, the tread allows water to flow through the grooves and away from the tire. This action allows the tire tread to cut through the water and grip the road. Thus, the tire will not float on the water and lose traction. This gripping action on wet roads is critically important in preventing skids and hydroplaning (see page 252).

A tire's gripping ability will increase as the amount of tread

The four footprints of your tires on the road are the only contact between your car and the road.

touching the road increases. Tire size will also affect the amount of tread and traction on the road. Use care when putting larger tires on a vehicle. Check the owner's manual for your vehicle for the maximum recommended size of tire to use.

A worn, bald tire is dangerous. A bald tire will not grip a wet or icy road. Because it has no tread, the tire may puncture. If this happens, the tire could suffer a **blowout** when all the air escapes at once. Check page 96 to see how to check your vehicle's tire tread depth.

Inflation and Traction

Each tire is designed to work best between a range of high- and low-inflation air pressures. Check your owner's manual for the best pressure to use. The pictures on this page show how too much or too little pressure can change the amount of tread, or footprint, on the road. The dark gray areas show the best traction areas. The more dark gray area, the better. When your tire pressure is right, you will get your best control. You also will get your best gas mileage and tire wear because tires roll easier at the right pressure.

Underinflation When you drive on an underinflated tire (see the middle picture on this page), only the outside edges of the tire provide traction. That means the outside edges will wear out first. When this happens, the life of the tire is shortened. More importantly, in an emergency, the underinflated tire will not perform properly. Finally, an underinflated tire is likely to heat up and fail more quickly than a properly inflated tire.

Overinflation Overinflating a tire should also be avoided. If the tire has too much pressure, only the center of the tire will grip the road properly (see bottom picture on this page). Over time, the overinflated tire will wear out its center tread more quickly than a normal tire.

Outside air temperatures can change the pressure in your tires, too. If the air gets colder, tire pressures will drop. Hot temperatures will increase pressures. Check tire pressures on a regular basis to make sure they have the right amount of air. To assure an accurate reading, check tire pressures when your tires are cold, before you start driving.

Split Traction

Even under ideal conditions, the amount of traction your tires can produce is limited. The way you use the amount of traction you have is up to you.

In a straight-line braking situation, all traction is used to slow down your vehicle. However, when you are braking and turning, you divide your traction limit. You may use some of your traction to turn and some to slow. Or, you may use some traction to turn and some to speed up. In turning-braking situations, you will have to ease up on your brake pedal to avoid skidding. And remember, always try to drive at a speed where you can hold some traction in reserve.

Many vehicles today are four-wheel, or all-wheel drive. That means they can apply power to all four of

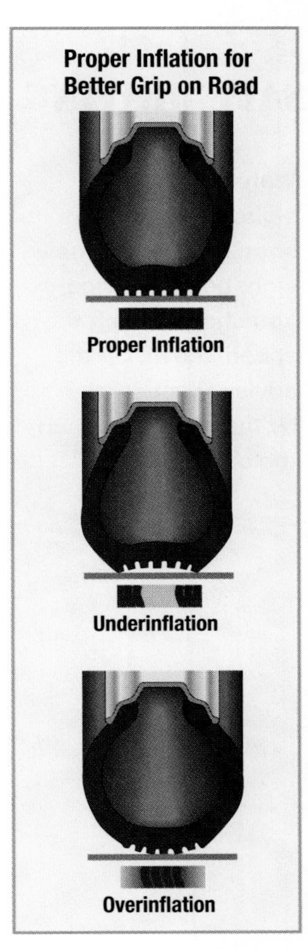

The boxes show the areas of best traction—properly inflated tires grip evenly; underinflated tires grip only by the outer edges; overinflated tires grip only in the center.

Watch for warning signs for curves. As soon as you see the sign, begin slowing. You should reach the speed shown on the advisory speed sign by the time you reach the curve.

their wheels for added pulling power. But again, the basic laws of nature apply. Both two-wheel-drive and four-wheel-drive vehicles can use almost all of their four wheels of traction for stopping or turning. In a split-traction situation, however, you must divide the amount of available traction between stopping or starting and steering.

Reduced Traction

You need two things to maintain ideal levels of traction. First, your vehicle must be in good condition. Second, the road must be smooth, paved, level, and clean.

Vehicle Condition

When your vehicle is new, it is easy to control. But as it ages, you need to work hard to make sure it is maintained in top condition so it will perform correctly. If you allow tires, shock absorbers, or steering system parts to wear, traction and control will be reduced.

Good shock absorbers are very important for maintaining traction. Worn shock absorbers will cause your tires to bounce off a rough road and limit your control. Worn shock absorbers must be replaced to regain control.

Worn or improperly inflated tires also will limit your control. In an emergency situation, you will need all the control your tires can provide. Check tire pressure and tread frequently. You can check tire tread with a gauge or a penny. Make sure there is at least one-sixteenth of an inch, as the driver in the picture is doing.

Road Surface

When you drive on a straight, dry, flat road, traction and control are great. But, if you drive the same vehicle on the same road on a rainy or snowy day, control will be reduced dramatically. When you see the road is about to change, reduce your speed before you reach the reduced-traction area.

Icy weather can be especially dangerous for driving. When ice is covered with water, traction control will be reduced to almost nothing. Be alert that water will freeze in shaded areas and on bridges *before* it does on regular roads.

Checking Traction When road conditions are bad, slow down your vehicle. You can use these steps to check how much traction you have:

1. Check your rear zone to make sure no traffic is near.
2. Brake *gently* to see how your vehicle responds.
3. If your vehicle does not slow or if your antilock brakes start to work, reduce speed even further.

If you can see all of Lincoln's head on the penny, switch the tire.

Curves

Energy of motion and traction will work on your vehicle as you drive around a curve. The energy of motion in your vehicle will try to make it go straight in a curve. The higher your vehicle's speed, the more it will tend to go straight.

Tire traction is the second force working for you in a curve. But if your speed is too high, you might not have enough traction to make the curve.

Vehicle Control in Curves

Your vehicle's speed, the sharpness of the curve, the bank of the curve, and your vehicle's load will affect the control you have in a curve.

Speed You have no control over how sharp a curve is, but you can adjust your speed. To reduce your chance of skidding, lower your speed before entering a curve. Remember, your energy of motion will change in proportion to the square of your increase or decrease in speed. If you cut your speed in half, the force pushing you off the road will be cut four times.

Sharpness of Curves The sharper a curve, the more traction your vehicle needs to grip the road. Use lower speeds for sharp curves.

Banked Curves A curve that is higher on the outside than it is on the inside is called a **banked curve.** This type of curve helps to overcome your vehicle's tendency to move to the outside of the curve. This can be very helpful on a road that has a crowned, or higher, center.

This driver slowed ahead of time for this curve.

What should the driver do to adjust for the extra load?

Load Your vehicle's load affects your control in a curve. How will adding the load to the vehicle in the right picture affect control? To maintain control, the driver must slow when heavily loaded.

Vehicle Capabilities

Vehicles of different sizes and power handle differently. Small vehicles like a motorcycle are light and can accelerate quickly. Large trucks and recreational vehicles, on the other hand, take lots of power just to accelerate to highway speeds. Large vehicles can take a long distance to stop. You need to remember these differences when you use the IPDE Process.

Review It

1. How can traction control your vehicle?
2. What are three things that can reduce your traction?
3. What three steps can you take to check traction while driving?
4. Name three factors that can affect your vehicle in a curve.

5.3 Stopping Distance

Objectives

1. Define total stopping distance.
2. Explain how to use the four-second rule.
3. Name four factors that affect braking distance.

When you are driving and have to stop, three things must happen. You must perceive the hazard in your path of travel, react, and brake your car to a stop.

Total Stopping Distance

The distance your car travels while you make a stop is called your **total stopping distance.** The picture on this page shows how this distance is measured from the point you first see a hazard to the point where your vehicle stops.

Perception Time and Distance

The length of time you take to identify, predict, and decide to slow for a hazard is called your **perception time.** Perception time will vary greatly depending on visibility, the hazard, and your abilities at the time. The distance your vehicle travels during this time is your **perception distance.**

You cannot consistently estimate your perception distance because your ability to perceive will change. Sometimes it will take longer to perceive a complex driving situation than it will take to brake to a stop. To help compensate for your long perception time, aim high and look 12 seconds or more down the road.

Reaction Time and Distance

Once you recognize a hazard, the length of time you take to execute your action is your **reaction time.** An average driver's reaction time is

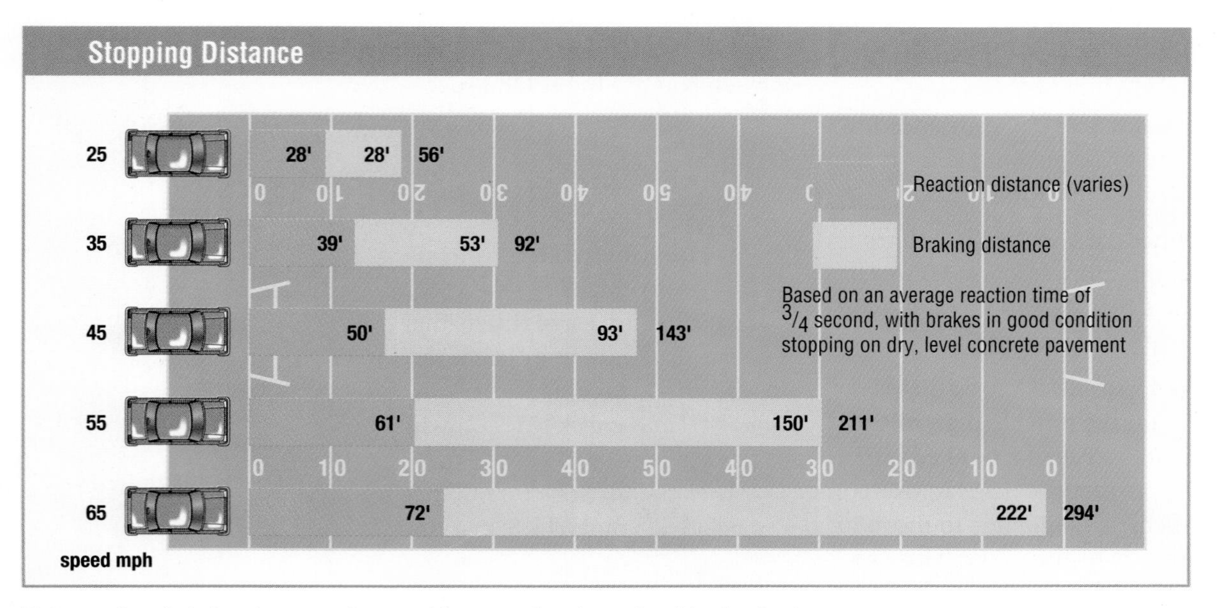

Distances traveled at various speeds once driver perceives hazard and begins to stop

three-fourths of a second. The distance your vehicle travels while you react is called your **reaction distance.**

Braking Distance

The distance your vehicle travels from the time you apply the brake until you stop is called **braking distance.** A vehicle's energy of motion—and your braking distance—are proportional to the square of the increase in speed. If you accelerate from 20 mph to 40 mph, your braking distance will be about four times longer. If you know you are going to be driving into a high-risk situation, why is it so important to drive at a lower speed?

Estimating Stopping Distance

The chart on this page shows your reaction distance and braking distance from different speeds.

Use the four-second rule, which enables you to project your approximate stopping distance under ideal conditions at any speed.

1. Pick a fixed checkpoint (a mark or shadow on the road) ahead where you think you could stop.
2. Count off four seconds: "one-thousand-one, one-thousand-two, one-thousand-three, one-thousand-four."
3. Check your vehicle's position. If you have just reached your fixed checkpoint, you can assume the distance you estimated in Step 1 was the approximate distance it would have taken you to stop.

Practice estimating your stopping distance from various speeds. Keep in mind it will take you almost 300 feet, or the length of a football field as shown in the chart, to stop if you are traveling at 65 mph.

Factors That Affect Braking Distance

These seven factors can affect your total braking distance:

- **Speed** The higher your speed, the longer your braking distance.
- **Vehicle Condition** A vehicle with worn tires, shock absorbers, or brakes needs a longer distance to stop.
- **Roadway Surface** Rain, snow, ice, dirt, wet leaves, and gravel reduce road traction and increase stopping distance.
- **Driver Ability** If you are distracted or impaired, you will take longer to stop your vehicle.
- **Antilock Braking System (ABS)** If your car has an antilock braking system, you can better control your stopping distance while turning.
- **Hills** Your braking distance increases when driving downhill.
- **Loads** Heavy loads increase your braking distance.

Total stopping distance

Review It

1. What three parts add up to your total stopping distance?
2. How can you estimate your stopping distance?
3. What factors can affect your braking distance?

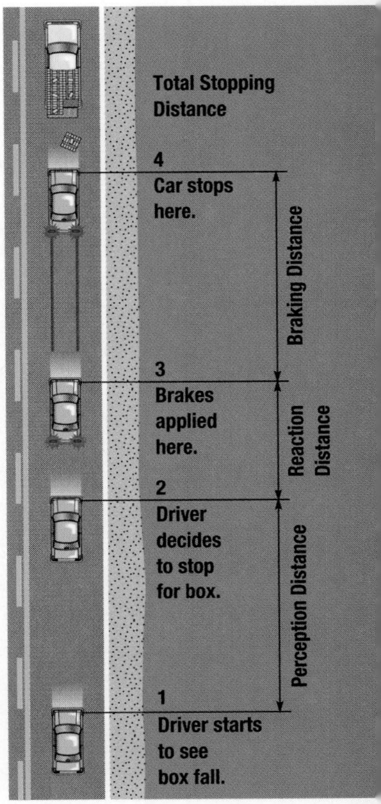

5.4 Controlling Force of Impact

Objectives

1. List three factors that will change your vehicle's force of impact in a collision.
2. Explain the correct way to adjust safety belts.
3. Describe how a driver and passengers should position themselves to benefit from air bags.
4. Explain how to best position and use child safety seats.

If you have ever seen a severe traffic collision, then you know that collisions happen with blinding speed—usually in less time than it takes to blink your eye—and that these collisions can be violent. The following pages will show you how to protect yourself and your passengers if you are involved in a severe collision.

Force of Impact

In a violent collision, vehicle occupants need all the protection they can get. If they are not protected, they will be thrown against the vehicle's interior in a second collision or ejected from the vehicle.

The force with which a moving object hits another object is called **force of impact.** Three factors determine how hard something will hit another object—speed, weight, and distance between impact and stopping.

Speed Speed is the most important factor in determining how hard a vehicle will hit another object. The force of impact is in proportion to the square of the increase or decrease in the vehicle's speed. Any reduction in speed will greatly reduce the damage inflicted. Always try to reduce speed in an emergency.

Weight The heavier a vehicle, the more damage it will cause in a collision. A vehicle weighing twice as much as another vehicle will hit a solid object twice as hard.

Distance Between Impact and Stopping The distance a vehicle covers between the instant it hits an object and the moment it comes to a stop can vary greatly. Imagine hitting barrels filled with sand sitting in front of a light post rather than hitting the post itself. The barrels will slow you as you hit them rather than stopping you like the post would. This is why traffic engineers put cushioning materials in front of solid roadside objects.

Safety Belts

Three collisions occur when a vehicle hits a solid object. First, the vehicle hits the object and stops. Second, the occupants either hit the inside of the vehicle or their **restraint devices.** Third, occupants may suffer internal collisions as their organs impact inside their bodies.

A restraint device is any part of a vehicle that holds an occupant in a crash. A **passive restraint device,** such as an air bag, is a part that works automatically. A device you have to engage, like a safety belt, is called an **active restraint device.**

How to Wear Safety Belts

What can you do ahead of time to reduce the possibility of serious injury? Using safety belts is your number one defense. Safety belts will hold you in place during an emergency and prevent you from being thrown from your vehicle. Any time you are in a vehicle, you need to follow these steps for wearing your safety belt:

1. Adjust your seat to a comfortable upright position. Make sure your safety belt is not twisted.
2. Snap the metal fitting on the end of the safety belt into the buckle. Then adjust the lap part of your safety belt so that it is low and snug across your hips. The bottom edge of the safety belt should just touch your thighs. By making this adjustment, any crash forces will be applied to your pelvic bones.
3. Finally, adjust the shoulder part of your safety belt across your chest. Your shoulder belt should be snug.

These adjustments will work for all normal-height individuals, including expectant mothers. For children, see the section on child safety seats later in this chapter. Like the driver shown in the picture, you are responsible for everyone in your vehicle.

Everyone needs to take responsibility for a safe trip.

Air Bags

An air bag is a balloon-type device that automatically inflates to protect you. Look at the first page of this chapter to see an inflated air bag. If collisions happen in the blink of an eye, air bags work even more quickly. They deploy at speeds over 200 mph. The following description of a collision between two air-bag-equipped cars will give you some idea of their effectiveness.

> The investigation revealed exactly what happened. Driver A had seen

INVENTOR OF SAFETY BELTS Nils Bohlin is the engineer who invented the modern three-point lap and shoulder safety belt while working for the Volvo Automobile Company in Sweden. These belts appear in most vehicles around the world.

According to Mr. Bohlin's design, the belts should fit snugly across the chest. Belts that are too loose will not restrain the chest properly in a crash.

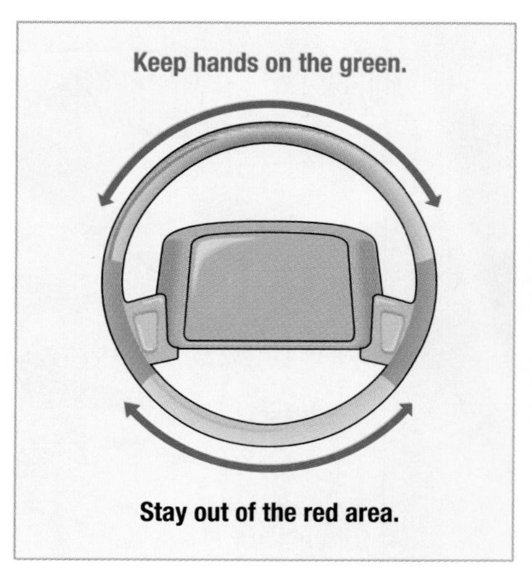

A balanced steering position between the 9 and 3 o'clock or the 8 and 4 o'clock position is best to avoid injury from an air bag.

You must have 10 inches or more between your chest and the air bag in the steering wheel.

a car heading toward him on his side of the road and had virtually stood on his brakes. Then he was aware that his face was being buried in a balloon-like pillow. Driver B remembers her bag suddenly billowing in front of her nose. "It was a jolt, but not a hard jolt. Like when you were a kid and jumped on a mattress...."

The Insurance Institute for Highway Safety team established that the crash was the equivalent of each of them hitting a stationary object at 68 mph. As the cars slammed together, each driver's head was thrown forward with 1700 pounds of force....

By the time the hood of each car began to crumple, both bags were fully inflated and positioned directly in line with the head and torso of each driver. As their heads slammed forward, the folds of the air bag softened the impact, like a big balloon. At maximum inflation, the bags began to vent nitrogen gas to ensure the gentlest impact possible.

Thanks to air bags, both drivers recovered from this collision.

To receive full benefit from air bags, you need to know the following:

- Air bags are designed to work with safety belts. That is why air bags are called a supplemental restraint system. Most air bags protect in frontal collisions only. Safety belts provide front, side, and rollover protection. Some vehicles also have overhead and side-door air bags for extra protection.
- To avoid an air-bag injury, keep your hands on the steering wheel between the 9 and 3 o'clock and the 8 and 4 o'clock position. This balanced steering position will give you your best ready position for steering. Look at the picture above left to see this range. If your hands are too high or too low in an air bag collision, you could suffer a serious hand, arm, head, or eye injury.

- Sit away from an air bag after you are belted. As the driver, your chest should be at least 10 inches away from the steering wheel hub, as shown in the right-hand picture on the opposite page. Use approved pedal extensions if needed to attain this distance. As a front-seat passenger, move your seat as far back as possible.
- If you have a tilt steering wheel, tilt it so your air bag will deploy toward your chest.
- Children in child seats and young people up to the age of twelve must sit in the back seat as shown in the picture. When children, and even short adults, ride in the front seat of an air-bag-equipped vehicle, they can be injured if the air bags deploy.

Always use child seats in the back seat.

Air Bag Improvements

The air bag has proved to be an effective life-saving device. Engineers are now designing features to make air bags even more effective. The following list highlights some of the features that are being developed:

- **Advanced air bags** Because some people have suffered serious injuries as the bag deploys, some vehicles are now equipped with air bag systems with advanced features. Sensors can measure weight and seat position of passengers and severity of the crash. Then, the air bag deploys in two stages with appropriate speed and intensity.
- **Air bag switches** To give vehicle owners a choice about using an air bag, some owners may ask permission to have a switch installed to turn off the front passenger air bag. This is an enormous compromise. If you are considering this option, check your insurance policy to make sure it will be in full force if you switch off an air bag. Also check your safety belts to see if they are designed to stretch. If you install the switch, you will need to replace those safety belts with belts that do not stretch.

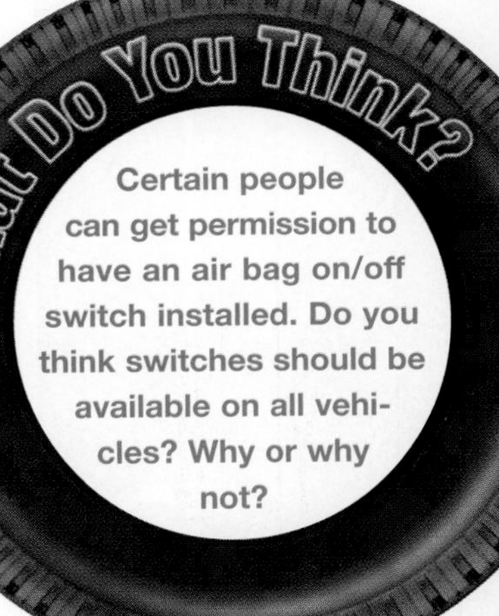

Other Protection Devices

To reduce risk in collisions, automobile engineers have designed

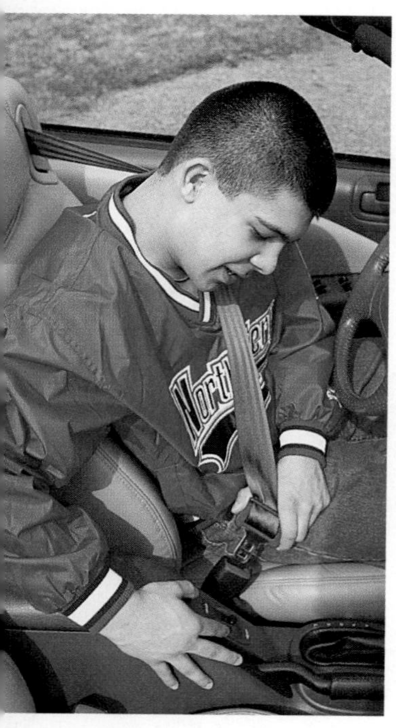

Make sure your lap belt is used with your shoulder belt.

Adjust your head restraint to reach the middle of the back of the head.

additional devices in new vehicles to protect you. These are a few of them:

- **Automatic safety belts** Some vehicles have automatic safety belts for occupant protection. To use these belts, you must make sure your lap belt is buckled low and across your hips. Then when your door is shut, your shoulder belt is drawn into place as shown in the picture.
- **Front and rear crush areas** Vehicles are now designed to have their front or rear end crush on impact. When this happens, the dramatic force of impact is lessened for occupants in the vehicle.
- **Energy-absorbing bumpers** Most vehicles are now equipped with bumpers that are designed to absorb low levels of impact under 5 mph without damage. This will provide protection in many minor collisions.
- **Side door beams** Many vehicles now have steel beams built into the side doors. These beams provide valuable protection in collisions where you are hit on an angle.
- **Reinforced windshield** To avoid flying glass in a collision, vehicles now have laminated windshields. This means the windshield is really two pieces of glass with a thin layer of plastic in the middle.
- **Energy-absorbing steering wheel and column** This type of steering wheel and column is designed to compress when hit.
- **Padded dash** This design feature can reduce injury in all crashes.
- **Child seats** The use of special seats for infants and small children is required in every state. These seats must be used in the back seat of your vehicle, as shown in the picture on page 103. If used in the front seat of a vehicle with air bags, an air bag could seriously injure a child in the event of a crash. Always follow your child seat manufacturer's instructions.
- **Head restraints** Padded head rests on the top of seats are designed to protect you against whiplash injuries. To make sure you get the full benefit of this protection, adjust your head rest as shown in the picture.

Review It

1. What three factors can affect force of impact?
2. What three steps should you take when putting on safety belts properly?
3. What are the two key steps you should take to protect yourself as the driver of a car with air bags?
4. Where should all child seats be secured in a car?

Review

Reviewing Chapter Objectives

1. Gravity and Energy of Motion

1. How does gravity affect your vehicle? (92)
2. What are the factors affecting energy of motion? (93)

2. Friction and Traction

3. How does traction control your vehicle? (94)
4. What three things can reduce traction? (95–96)
5. How can you check traction while driving? (96)
6. What are the factors that affect your vehicle in a curve? (97)

3. Stopping Distance

7. What is total stopping distance? (98)
8. How do you use the four-second rule? (98–99)
9. What are four factors that affect braking distance? (99)

4. Controlling Force of Impact

10. What are three factors that will change your vehicle's force of impact in a collision? (100)
11. What is the correct way to adjust safety belts? (101)
12. How should a driver and passengers position themselves to benefit from air bags? (102)
13. How do you best position and use child safety seats? (103–104)

Projects

Individuals

Investigate With the owners' permission, examine the tires of at least 10 vehicles. Check for signs of worn tread or bald spots. Write a short report about your findings. In the report, describe the condition of each vehicle's tires. Also give the percentage of vehicles that you checked that have worn tread or bald tires.

Use Technology Using a tire-pressure gauge, determine the tire pressure of the vehicles you checked in the Investigate project above. Make a computer spreadsheet for your findings. Your spreadsheet should also include your observations about the conditions of the tire treads.

Groups

Research Observe at least 50 vehicles at a busy intersection. One-third of the group should record the number of drivers wearing safety belts; one-third should record the number of passengers wearing safety belts; one-third should record the number of child seats, and whether the child seat was in the front or back seat of the vehicle. Discuss your results with the class.

Investigate Gather advertisements for tires from newspapers or magazines. Make a group list organized by sizes of tires you see in the ads. Also include prices and special features (such as special treads or other safety-related features). Compare your group lists in class.

Chapter 5
Review

Chapter Test

Check Your Knowledge

Multiple Choice Copy the number of each sentence below on a sheet of paper. Choose the letter of the answer that best completes the statement or answers the question.

1. When an object moves, it acquires
   (a) friction. (c) energy of motion.
   (b) traction. (d) speed.
2. The length of time you take to execute an action is called your _____ time.
   (a) total stopping (c) braking
   (b) perception (d) reaction
3. Which of the following is an example of a supplemental restraint system?
   (a) air bag (c) lap and shoulder belt
   (b) safety belt (d) antilock brakes
4. In a _____ situation, you must divide the amount of available traction between stopping or starting and steering.
   (a) reduced traction (c) sharp curve
   (b) split traction (d) banked curve

Completion Copy the number of each sentence below. After each number, write the word or words that complete the sentence correctly.

5. The force that pulls all things to earth is called _____.
6. A vehicle's energy of motion will change in proportion to the _____ of its change in speed.
7. The gripping ability of a tire will _____ as the amount of tread touching the road increases.
8. The _____ your speed, the longer your braking distance.

Review Vocabulary

Copy the number of each definition in List A. Match the definition in List A with the term it defines in List B.

List A

9. grooved surface of a tire that grips the road
10. point around which an object's weight is evenly distributed
11. restraint device that you have to engage
12. distance your vehicle travels while you make a stop
13. force that keeps each tire from sliding on the road

List B

a. active device
b. friction
c. tread
d. total stopping distance
e. center of gravity

Think Critically

Write a paragraph to answer each question.

1. Explain the relationship between traction and the amount of air in a vehicle's tires. Use the terms "underinflation" and "overinflation" in your answer.
2. Discuss how speed, sharpness of curve, and your car's load affect how you control your vehicle in a curve. Why are banked curves often beneficial?

Chapter 5
Review

Decision Making

1. What two things has this driver done to adjust to the air bag?

2. You are driving the yellow car and have locked your standard brakes to avoid a head-on collision. Your wheels are sliding. You want to head for the shoulder to avoid trouble. What should you do?

3. You are approaching this curve at 40 mph. To maintain control, when should you adjust your speed?

4. The driver ahead is braking to maintain control. What two factors might increase the stopping distance in this situation?

Spring
DOWNTOWN EVANSTON
TOYOTA CAMRY
Z 34 421
WRR 968
B 610 096

CHAPTER 6
Performing Basic Vehicle Maneuvers

You Are the Driver!

Suppose you are the driver approaching this intersection. What clues tell you that you are traveling on a one-way street? What hazards do the angle-parked vehicles on the left present to you and to their drivers? What conflicts might you anticipate in your right-front zone?

This chapter explains the basic maneuvers of steering, changing lanes, turning, and parking. You will also learn how to turn your vehicle around and how to start and park on hills. Finally, you will learn when and where to perform these maneuvers safely.

For: Chapter 6 online activities
Visit: PHSchool.com
Web Code: cak-9999

6.1 Steering, Signaling, and Changing Lanes

Objectives

1. Explain how to steer straight forward and backward.
2. Describe the correct use of hand signals and explain when they might be used.
3. List the proper steps for changing lanes.

Steering control is critical to safe, successful driving. Developing steering control involves acquiring visual habits, such as looking far ahead into your intended path of travel, using space correctly, controlling speed, and continually adjusting the steering wheel.

Steering Straight Forward

Use a comfortable, balanced hand position, as explained in Chapter 3, as you begin steering control practice. Aim far ahead into your intended path with your visual search. Avoid looking down at your hands or feet.

The steering adjustments you need to make to drive in a straight line are small but critical. Some new drivers tend to turn the steering wheel too much, or **oversteer.** When you oversteer, your vehicle will weave from side to side.

Other new drivers might tend to **understeer.** These drivers do not turn the steering wheel enough to keep the vehicle in the planned path. If you understeer, you continue too far in one direction before you can correct and steer toward your target. Correct understeering by turning the steering wheel only slightly and more often.

Practice will help you think of your vehicle as an extension of yourself. You soon will be able to accurately judge the space your vehicle uses while it is moving and the space you need to make various maneuvers.

Steering Straight Backward

Backing your vehicle may feel strange at first. Steering when moving backward involves knowing where to look and how to control direction and speed. Before backing, make sure your rear zones are clear, and follow these steps:

1. Hold the brake pedal down and shift to REVERSE.
2. Turn your body to the right, and put your right arm over the back of the passenger seat. Look back through the rear window.
3. Put your left hand at the top

The driver is in the correct position for backing straight.

of the steering wheel at the 12 o'clock position.

4. Release pressure on the brake just enough to allow the vehicle to creep backward slowly.
5. While looking back through the rear window, move the top of the steering wheel toward the direction you want the back of the vehicle to go.
6. Keep your foot over the brake pedal while your vehicle is moving backward. Glance quickly to the front and sides to check traffic. Continue to look back through the rear window as you brake to a stop.

Backing a Stickshift Vehicle

You can back slowly in a stickshift vehicle by carefully controlling your use of the clutch pedal at the friction point. Follow these steps for backing in a stickshift vehicle:

1. Push the brake and clutch pedals down.
2. Shift to REVERSE.
3. Release the brake, and let the clutch come out slowly to the friction point.

Holding the clutch at the friction point allows you to back the vehicle at a slow, controlled speed. Releasing the clutch suddenly may cause the vehicle to jerk back quickly.

Most stickshift vehicles can move slowly in REVERSE with the clutch at the friction point and with no acceleration. Keep your right foot over the brake pedal, ready for a stop. When stopping, push the clutch pedal down and brake to a smooth stop. Continue to look back until the vehicle is completely stopped.

Signaling

Develop the habit of signaling every time you plan to turn, change lanes, slow, or stop. Signal well in advance before you begin any maneuver. Doing so gives other drivers time to react.

Even though all vehicles have turn-signal devices, there will be times when you use hand signals for further protection. Hand signals are often easier to see in bright sunlight. If your turn-signal device does not work, use hand signals. Many times a combination of turn lights and hand signals will be more effective.

Notice the hand and arm positions in the pictures. The first picture shows the left arm and hand pointing up for a right turn. The second shows the left arm and hand extended straight out for a left turn. The third picture shows the left arm extended downward, indicating slow or stop.

When using hand signals, use your right hand to maintain steering control. Make all hand and arm signals well in advance of entering a turn. Return your left hand to the steering wheel before you begin to execute the turn.

Right turn

Left turn

Slow or stop

Changing Lanes

Drivers must be able to execute the lane-change maneuver smoothly and safely before they learn to pass other vehicles. Changing lanes is a maneuver you will use often on a roadway with two or more lanes of traffic moving in your direction. You also may need to change lanes before making right or left turns.

At times, changing lanes gives you a better position or view when

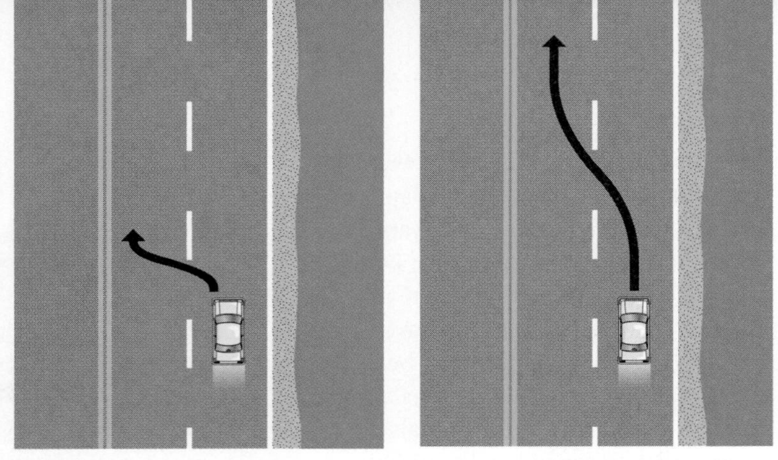

Oversteering can cause you to take an incorrect path for changing lanes. The picture on the right shows the correct path of travel for a smooth lane change.

driving in traffic. For example, you might change lanes when following a large truck on a multilane highway. By moving to a different lane, you increase your sight distance and get a broader view of the traffic scene.

Steering control is a critical factor as you learn the lane-changing maneuver. Oversteering can cause your vehicle to turn too sharply as you start to enter the adjoining lane. The first picture shows this oversteering error. At higher speeds you could lose steering control.

Change lanes as smoothly as possible. The second picture shows the safe path of travel of a vehicle executing a smooth lane change.

Always follow the same procedure for making a lane change, regardless of your reason for making the lane change. Before changing lanes, check all zones for possible hazards. Make sure you can see far ahead in the lane of your intended path of travel and that there are no obstructions in either lane.

Follow these steps when making a lane change to the left:

1. Check traffic in the front and left-front zones. Check rear zones through the rearview mirrors.
2. Signal and make a blind-spot check over your left shoulder to see if any vehicle is about to pass you.
3. Increase your speed slightly as you steer smoothly into the next lane if it is clear.
4. Cancel your signal and adjust your speed.

Follow the same procedure when making a lane change to the right, with one exception. After checking traffic ahead and through both mirrors, check the blind-spot area over your right shoulder. Take only a glance to make the check. Be careful not to pull the steering wheel to the right as you turn to glance over your right shoulder. Keep steering straight as you check your blind spot. If the lane is clear, complete the lane change to the right the same way you would make a lane change to the left.

Review It

1. Describe the procedures for steering straight forward and backward.
2. What are the three hand and arm signals for turns and stopping? When might these signals be used?
3. List the steps to follow when changing lanes.

6.2 Making Turns and Turning the Vehicle Around

Making turns properly depends on steering control, speed control, and good visual habits. Look far ahead as you approach the turn. Identify where your vehicle will go, any hazards in your path, and how much to turn.

Hand-Over-Hand Steering

You use **hand-over-hand steering** by pulling the steering wheel down with one hand while your other hand crosses over to pull the wheel farther down. Follow these steps for a left turn:

1. Begin the turn from a balanced hand position.
2. Start pulling down to the left with your left hand. Your right hand pushes the wheel toward the left about a quarter turn.
3. Release your left hand from the wheel and cross it over your right hand to grasp the wheel near the top. Continue pulling down.

You can complete the turn by continuing to pull down with the left hand as you release the right hand.

Some steering wheels will straighten after a turn if you relax your grip. However, be ready to unwind the wheel hand-over-hand, especially at lower speeds, with front-wheel drive vehicles, and when backing.

Push-Pull Steering

Some drivers prefer **push-pull steering** for some maneuvers. You push the steering wheel up with one hand and pull it down with the other hand. This method allows you to keep both hands on the wheel at all times.

To use this method, one hand grasps the steering wheel near the 4 or 8 o'clock position. That hand then pushes the wheel up to near the 12 o'clock position. At the same time, the other hand slides up to the 11 or 1 o'clock position and pulls down. As the pulling hand comes down, the pushing hand returns to the original position to continue the process. With this method, you never cross your arms while driving.

Making Left and Right Turns

Make left and right turns only after checking all traffic. Take

Hand-over-hand steering

Push-pull steering

Objectives

1. Describe hand-over-hand steering.
2. List the steps for making right and left turns.
3. Describe how to back left and right.
4. Describe five turnabouts and tell which is the safest to use.

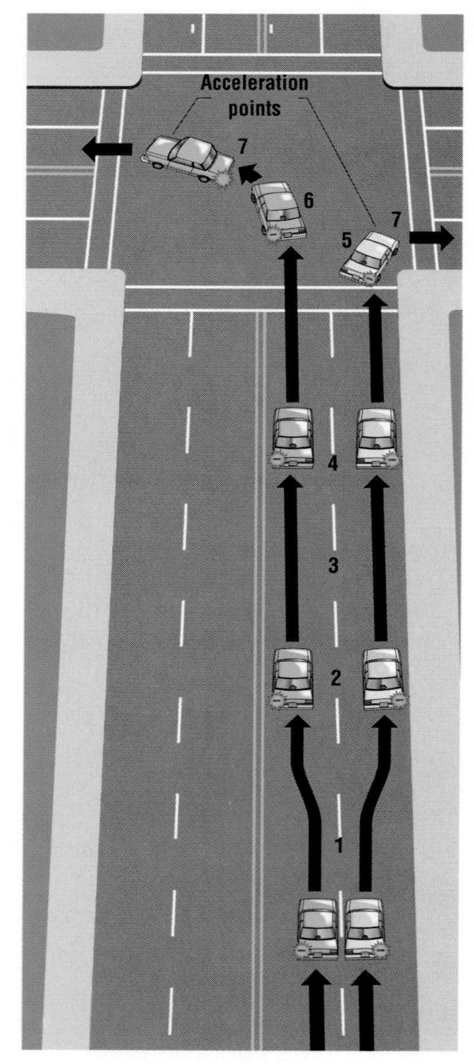

Steps for making left turns (yellow car) and right turns (white car)

these precautions when executing turns:

- Look for pedestrians and oncoming vehicles. Check rear zones for vehicles about to pass you.
- Plan turns well in advance. Be in the correct lane about a block before your turn.
- Obey all traffic signs, signals, and roadway markings. Remember that you must yield to oncoming traffic when preparing to turn left.

When turning in a stickshift vehicle, you might need to downshift before entering a sharp turn. Downshift and release the clutch before the turn so you have both hands free for turning.

Procedures for Turning The numbers in the picture on the left match the following steps for turns:

1. Position your vehicle in the correct lane for the turn. For a right turn, be in lane position 3 if there are no parked vehicles. For a left turn, be in the lane nearest the center line in lane position 2. (On a one-way street, be in the far left lane.) Signal about half a block before the turn.
2. Brake early to reduce speed.
3. Use your visual search pattern to check the front zones for vehicles, pedestrians, and bicyclists.
4. Slow to about 10 mph just before the crosswalk.
5. For a right turn, check to the left again before turning. Then look in the direction of the turn. Begin turning the wheel when your vehicle's front bumper is even with the curbline.
6. For a left turn, check traffic to the left, then right, then left again. Turn the steering wheel just before the front of your vehicle reaches the center of the intersection. Continue looking left into the lane you will enter.
7. As you begin your turn, make a quick blind-spot check through

A shared left-turn lane

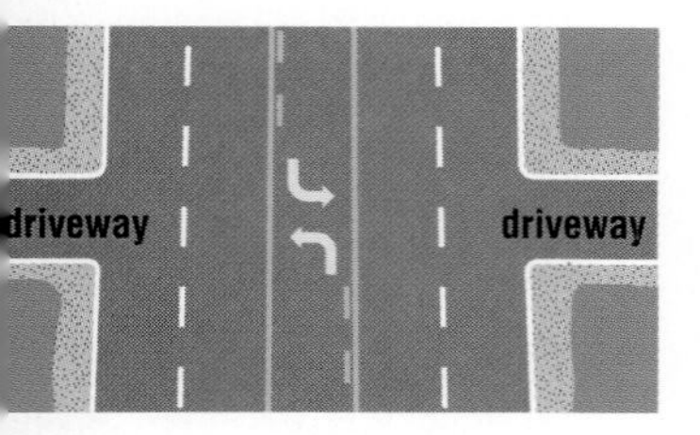

the right side window. Check front and rear zones. If the intersection is clear, turn into the nearest lane of traffic going in your direction.

Accelerate about halfway through the turn as you return the wheel to the straight-ahead position.

Shared Left-Turn Lane

Some left turns into business areas can be made in midblock from a center lane. This is called a **shared left-turn lane.**

This type of left turn can be hazardous. Before making a turn from a shared left-turn lane, search your front zones. Follow the proper procedure to enter the center lane. Look ahead for oncoming traffic and be prepared to yield to any vehicle whose path you will cross.

Backing Left and Right

When backing to the left, your visual search will be primarily over your left shoulder through the left side windows. When backing right, you will look over your right shoulder and through the right side windows. Use hand-over-hand steering and follow these steps to make sharp turns when backing.

1. Before backing, check for traffic, pedestrians, parked vehicles, and any stationary objects in front, around, and behind you. Turn your head toward the direction you will be backing.
2. Keep both hands on the wheel, ready for hand-over-hand steering. Pull the wheel to the left to back left. Pull the wheel to the right to back right. The back of your vehicle will go in the direction you turn the wheel. Look back toward the direction you want the vehicle to go.
3. Back slowly as you enter the turn. Make quick glances to the front and sides to be sure no one is near. Begin to unwind the steering wheel to finish the turn in a straight position.

When backing left, allow a wide space on the right side. The front wheels will move far to the right of the rear wheels. The front of your vehicle will swing wide to the right. When backing right, allow a wide space on the left side.

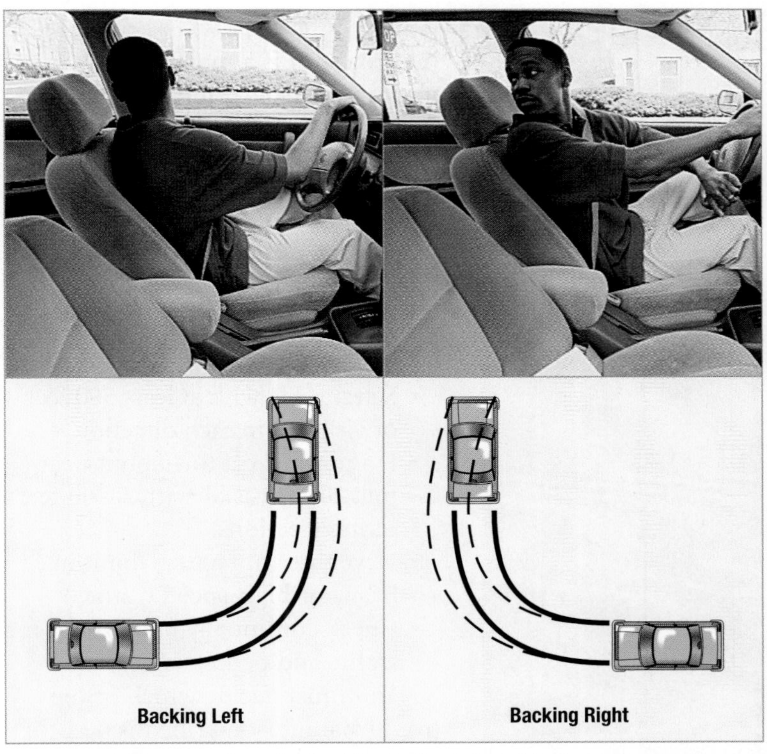

The correct driver positions for backing to the left and to the right, and the space and path of travel the car takes during backing

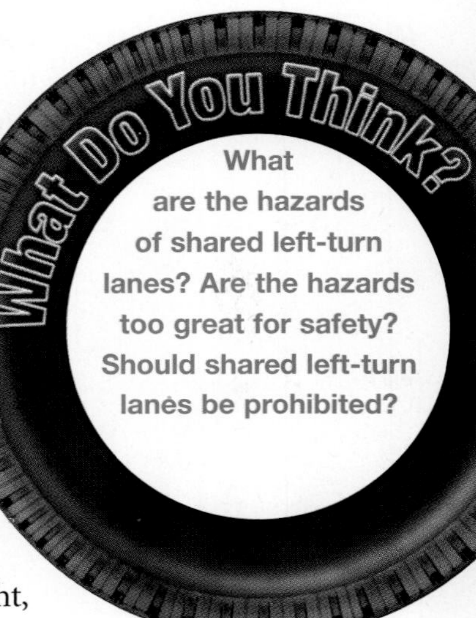

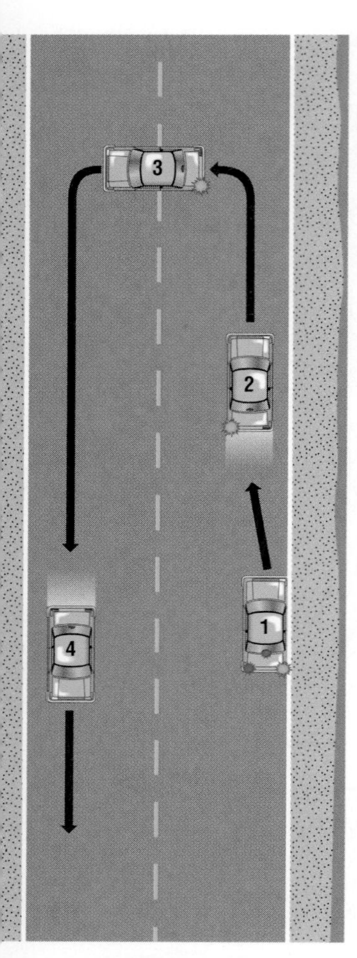

Midblock U-turn

Turning the Vehicle Around

A **turnabout** is a maneuver for turning your vehicle around to go in the opposite direction. Because turnabouts often require drivers to cross or back into traffic, they should be considered a high-risk maneuver.

Take these precautions when you plan to make a turnabout:

- Be sure local laws permit the turnabout.
- Select a site with at least 500 feet of visibility in each direction.
- Do not make a turnabout near hills or curves or within 200 feet of intersections.
- Never attempt a turnabout in heavy or high-speed traffic.
- Check continually in all zones for traffic and pedestrians.

You must decide which of the five turnabouts described is best for each situation. The steps for each turnabout match the numbered car locations shown in the pictures.

Midblock U-turn Make sure local and state laws permit this type of turnabout. You need a wide space to make a U-turn. A U-turn is risky because you must cross several lanes of traffic to execute it.

1. Check traffic ahead and to the rear, and then signal right. Pull to the far right and stop at location 1.
2. Signal left and move toward location 2.
3. Check your front and left-rear zones. Check your left blind spot. Turn sharply left while moving slowly toward location 3. Do not stop if you have enough space to complete the turn.
4. Move slowly toward location 4. Check all zones. Straighten the wheels while you accelerate gently into the proper lane.

Back into Driveway on Right Side
Choose this turnabout if a clear driveway is on the right and there is no close traffic in your rear zones. This turnabout has the advantage of letting you reenter traffic going forward.

1. Check traffic to the rear. Begin to slow as you proceed beyond the driveway.
2. Stop about three feet from the curb and with your rear bumper just beyond the driveway. Check traffic, and back slowly to the right to location 3. Use hand-over-hand steering. Stop when your vehicle is completely off the street.
3. Signal a left turn. Check traffic.

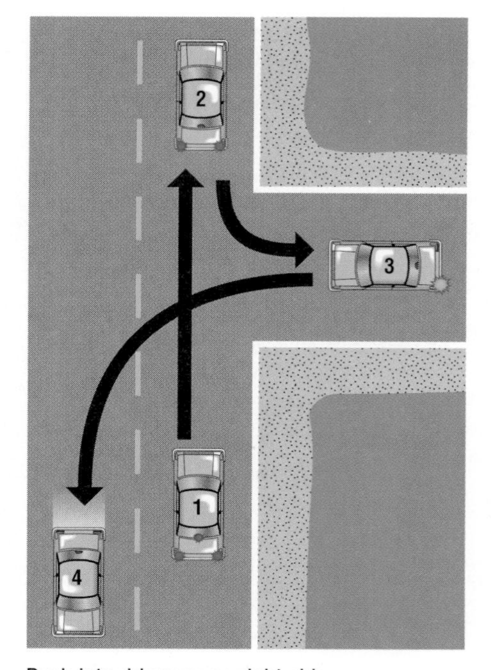

Back into driveway on right side

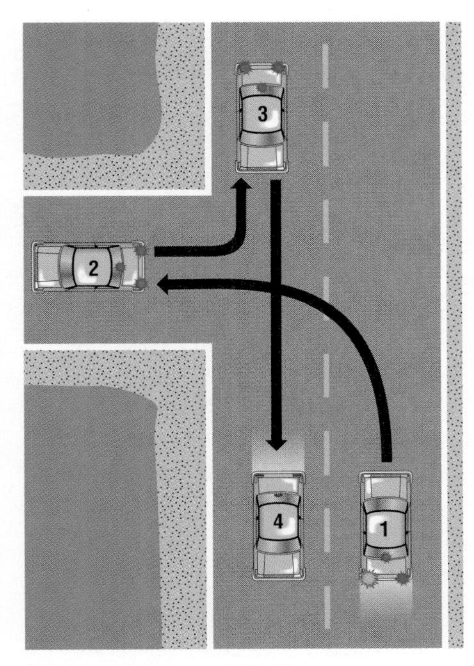

Pull into driveway on left side

4. When your path is clear, drive forward to location 4.

Pull into Driveway on Left Side
You might choose this turnabout if oncoming traffic is light and a driveway on the left is available. The disadvantage is that you must back into traffic before moving forward.

1. Check traffic in front and rear zones. Signal a left turn and use the left-turn procedure to move to location 2. Stay as close to the right side as possible. Stop with your wheels straight when your vehicle is completely off the street.
2. Check traffic again, especially from the right. Back slowly to the right to location 3. Look to the right rear and side while backing. Stop with the wheels straight.
3. Accelerate gently, scanning all zones, as you drive forward toward location 4.

Pull into Driveway on Right Side
This type of turnabout is a high-risk maneuver. To complete it, you must back across two lanes of traffic and into oncoming traffic before moving forward. Avoid this turnabout whenever possible.

1. Check traffic in front and rear zones. Signal a right turn and use the right-turn procedure to move to location 2. Stop when your vehicle is off the street.
2. Check traffic again from both directions. Back slowly across the street, turning left toward location 3. Look to the left, rear, and side when backing. Glance to the front, then continue looking back while

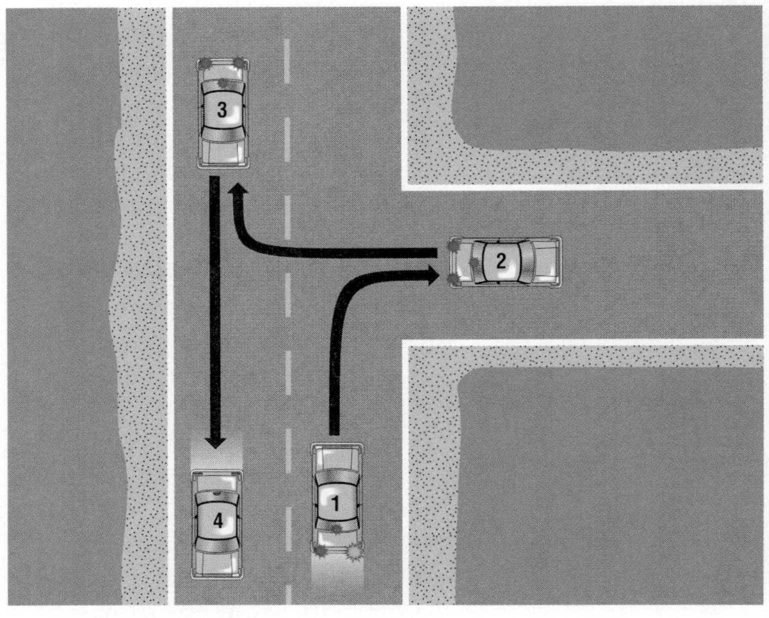

Pull into driveway on right side

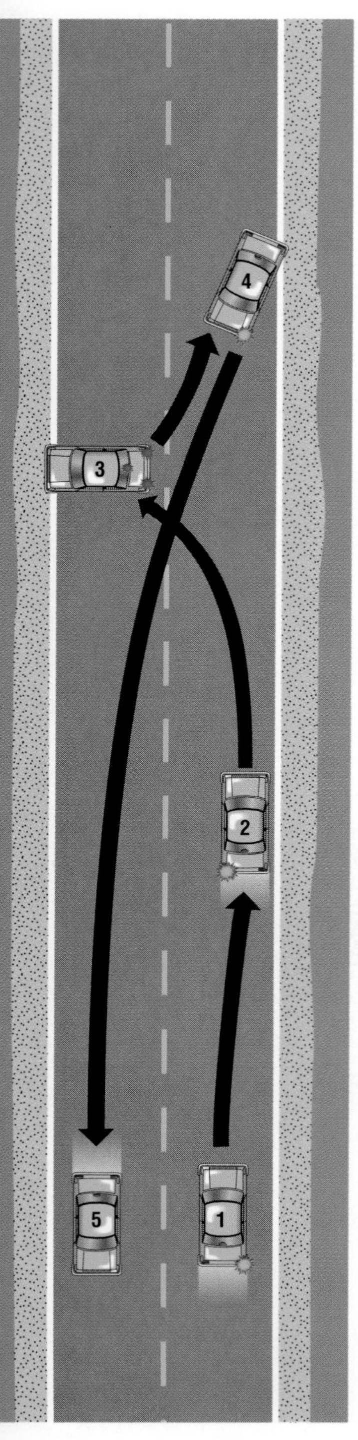

Three-point turnabout

stopping with the wheels straight in location 3.

3. Accelerate gently, and drive forward to location 4.

Three-Point Turnabout This turnabout is hazardous to perform. You not only cross traffic lanes, but your vehicle is stopped across a traffic lane. Executing this maneuver may put you in a high-risk situation.

1. From location 1 check front and rear zones. Signal right and stop close to the curb as shown in location 2. Check traffic ahead, to the rear, and over your left shoulder. Signal a left turn.
2. Search front and rear zones as you turn sharply left. Move to location 3 with wheels straight. Stop before hitting the curb.
3. Check all traffic again. Turn the wheels sharply right while backing slowly to location 4. Back only as far as necessary to complete the maneuver and before hitting the curb. Stop with wheels straight.
4. Check traffic again and signal left. Move slowly forward while steering left toward location 5.

Deciding Which Turnabout to Use

Consider these factors when deciding which turnabout to use:

- legality of the turnabout
- amount of traffic
- types of driveways available
- need to enter traffic lanes forward or backward
- ample space to enter traffic
- number of traffic lanes to cross

Backing into a driveway or alley on the right side is usually the safest type of turnabout to use because you can enter traffic forward.

Sometimes you might need to make a turnabout in light traffic. If there are driveways on both the left and right sides, choose the left driveway to turn into. This turnabout lets you back into your own lane rather than across both lanes. Select a gap in traffic that gives you ample time to complete the maneuver.

A three-point turnabout should rarely be used. Use this turnabout only when you are on a dead-end street or on a rural roadway with no driveways.

Review It

1. What is the procedure for hand-over-hand steering?
2. What are the steps for turning left and right?
3. What procedures do you follow to back to the left and to the right?
4. What is the safest type of turnabout to use? Why is that type the safest?

6.3
Parking

Some drivers find parking a vehicle a difficult maneuver to execute, because the size of the parking space often is limited. Parking your vehicle requires speed control, steering control, and accurate judgment.

Parking is easier and safer if you consider these factors:

- Try to find a parking space with ample room for entering and exiting easily. The size of your vehicle is the main factor in determining the space you choose.
- Avoid spaces at the end of parking lanes and near a large vehicle that might block your view. In end spaces your vehicle has a greater chance of being struck by other moving vehicles.
- Avoid spaces with a poorly parked vehicle on either side.
- Use reference points when executing parking maneuvers.

To use a standard reference point, the driver's line of sight sees the center of the hood at Arrow A and the curb at Arrow B. This tells the driver that the right tires are close to the curb.

Reference Points

Many drivers use reference points to serve as guides in determining the position of the vehicle in the roadway. A **reference point** is some part of the outside or inside of the vehicle, as viewed from the driver's seat, that relates to some part of the roadway. Reference points can be developed for the front, side, or rear to help you know where your vehicle is located in the roadway. A **standard reference point** is the point on the vehicle that is typical for most drivers. This could be a sideview mirror, a hood ornament, or the center of the hood. The photograph shows how the center of the hood is used for a standard reference point.

Once you learn standard reference points, you can develop your own **personal reference points.** A personal reference point is an adaptation of a standard reference point for one's own vehicle. You will learn to use different parts of your own vehicle such as wiper blades, door handles, or rearview mirrors as guides.

As you begin to practice parking maneuvers, you will learn which parts of your vehicle to use as personal reference points. You will be able to line up these points with parts of other vehicles to help execute the maneuvers.

Objectives

1. Discuss reference points and how to use them as guides when parking your vehicle.
2. Describe the procedures for angle, perpendicular, and parallel parking.
3. Describe how to park uphill and downhill with and without a curb.
4. Explain how to start from an uphill parking space without rolling backwards.

Angle parking

The following parking procedures refer to entering a parking space to your right. When parking to your left, adjust your actions and visual checks for the left side. The steps for each procedure match the numbered car locations in the pictures.

Angle Parking

Use **angle parking** to park your vehicle diagonally to the curb. Angle parking is often used in parking lots and shopping centers.

1. Check for traffic and pedestrians. Position your vehicle at least six feet from the row of parked vehicles. Signal a right turn, check traffic to the rear, and begin braking.
2. Flash your brake lights to warn drivers behind. Check your right blind spot and continue braking.
3. Creep forward until you can see the center of the space without your line of sight cutting across the parking line. This is your reference point to begin turning. Turn the wheels sharply to the right. Slowly enter the stall.
4. Straighten the wheels when you are centered in the space. Determine your forward reference point to place the front of the bumper even with the curb or parking line.

Perpendicular Parking

Use **perpendicular parking** to park your vehicle at a right angle to the curb.

1. Position your vehicle at least eight feet from the row of parked vehicles, or as far to the left of the lane as possible. Flash your brake lights and signal a right turn. Check your right blind spot, and begin to brake.
2. Check traffic to the rear, and continue braking.
3. Determine your personal reference point to know when the front bumper of your vehicle passes the left rear taillight of the vehicle to the right of the empty parking space. Turn the wheel sharply right. Slowly enter the stall. Check your right-rear fender for clearance.
4. Straighten the wheels when you are centered in the space. Use a forward reference point, like the driver's side-view mirror, to stop before the wheels strike the curb.

Some drivers prefer backing into a perpendicular parking space. These drivers consider this a safer maneuver because they do not back out into traffic when leaving the space.

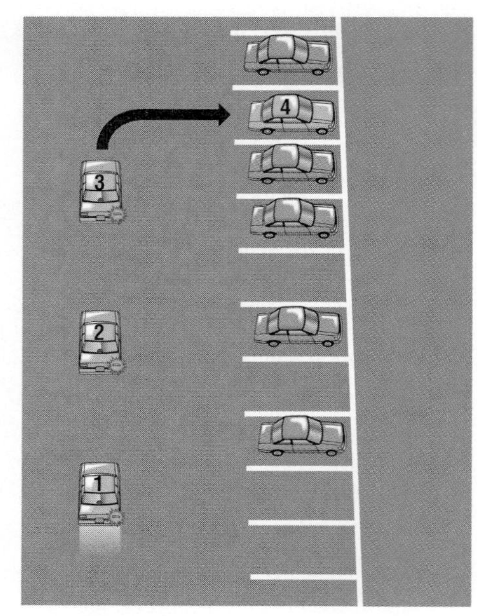

Perpendicular parking

Leaving an Angle or Perpendicular Space

Your view often will be blocked as you begin to back into moving traffic. Back slowly. Look to the rear and to the sides as you search for other roadway users and pedestrians.

1. Creep straight back while you control speed with your foot brake. (Hold the clutch at the friction point in a stickshift vehicle.)
2. When your front bumper is even with the rear bumper of the vehicle on your left, begin to turn right.
3. Back into the nearest lane and stop with the wheels straight. Shift to a forward gear and proceed as you scan your front and rear zones.

Parallel Parking

Use **parallel parking** to park your vehicle parallel to the curb. Select a space that is five to six feet longer than your vehicle. During the maneuver, the front of your vehicle will swing far to the left. Check over your left shoulder to be sure this needed space is clear.

1. Flash brake lights, and signal a right turn. Stop two to three feet away from the front vehicle with the two rear bumpers even. Shift to REVERSE. Check traffic. Look back over your right shoulder. Back slowly as you turn right. Aim toward the right-rear corner of the space. Control speed with your foot brake (clutch at friction point in a stickshift vehicle).
2. When the back of your seat is even with the rear bumper of the front vehicle, straighten the wheels. Determine your personal reference point for this position. Slowly back straight. Look over your shoulder, through the rear window.
3. When your front bumper is even with the front vehicle's back bumper, turn your wheels sharply left. Back slowly. Look out the rear window.
4. When your vehicle is parallel to the curb, straighten wheels and stop before you touch the vehicle behind. Develop reference points

Steps for parallel parking

PARKING REGULATIONS Parking regulations in most states specify the maximum distance a vehicle may legally be parked from the curb. This distance is usually 6–18 inches. Know the regulations in your state or city.

to know your distance from the curb and from the vehicle behind you. Slowly pull forward to center your vehicle in the space.

Leaving a Parallel Parking Space

You are responsible for avoiding a collision when leaving a parallel parking space. Yield to all traffic.

1. Back straight slowly until your rear bumper almost touches the vehicle behind. Turn wheels sharply left as you stop.
2. Signal a left turn. Check your left blind spot. Move forward slowly.
3. Check the right-front corner of your vehicle for clearance.
4. Turn your wheels slowly to the right when you are halfway out of the parking space. Scan front zones and accelerate gently as you center your vehicle in the traffic lane.

Parking on Hills

When parallel parking on a hill, you must be sure your vehicle will not roll down into traffic. Always turn the front wheels and set the parking brake to prevent the vehicle from rolling downhill. Procedures for uphill and downhill parking apply to parking on the right side of the street or roadway. Adjust your actions and visual checks when parking on the left side.

Uphill Parking with a Curb

1. Using personal reference points, position your vehicle close to the curb. Just before stopping, turn the steering wheel sharply left as shown in the first picture on the opposite page.
2. Shift to NEUTRAL. Let the vehicle creep back slowly until the back of the right-front tire gently touches the curb.
3. Shift to PARK (FIRST in a stick-shift), and set the parking brake.
4. When leaving the parking space, signal, check traffic, and accelerate gently into the lane of traffic.

Uphill Parking with No Curb

1. Pull as far off the roadway as possible. Just before you stop, turn the steering wheel sharply right, as in the second picture.
2. Shift to PARK (FIRST in a stick-shift), and set the parking brake.
3. When leaving the parking space, let the vehicle creep backward while straightening the wheels. Signal and check traffic. Shift to DRIVE (FIRST in a stickshift), and accelerate gently into traffic.

Downhill Parking with a Curb

1. Position your vehicle close to the curb and stop.
2. Let the vehicle creep forward slowly while turning the steering

wheel sharply right, as in the third picture. Let the right-front tire rest gently against the curb.

3. Shift to PARK (REVERSE in a stickshift), and set the parking brake.
4. When leaving the parking space, check traffic and back a short distance while straightening the wheels. Signal and check traffic again. Shift to DRIVE (FIRST in a stickshift), and accelerate into traffic.

When parking uphill against a curb, turn the front wheels to the left.

Downhill Parking with No Curb

Follow the same procedure as downhill parking with a curb. Turn wheels sharply right as you creep as near to the shoulder as possible. Note this position in the second picture. Use the same steps for parking downhill with a curb to complete the maneuver and to leave the parking space.

When you leave any hilly parking space, make sure you have a big enough gap to enter traffic safely. Traffic coming down the hill may be approaching faster than you think it is.

When parking uphill or downhill where there is no curb, turn your wheels to the right.

Starting on a Hill

At times, you might have to stop while going up a hill. You must then be able to start moving forward again *without rolling back.* Starting on an uphill grade without rolling back involves timing and coordination.

Using Automatic Transmission

One method for starting on a hill without rolling back involves using

When parking downhill against a curb, turn the front wheels to the right.

the parking brake. Follow these steps when using this method:

1. While holding the foot brake down, set the parking brake firmly.
2. Move your foot to the accelerator, and accelerate until you feel the engine start to pull.
3. Release the parking brake as you continue to accelerate.

A second method for starting on a hill involves using only the foot brake.

1. Hold the foot brake down with your *left* foot.
2. While still holding the foot brake with your *left* foot, accelerate gradually until the engine starts to pull.
3. Release the foot brake gently as you increase acceleration to move forward.

Using a Stickshift One method for starting on a hill in a stickshift vehicle involves the use of the parking brake. Follow these steps in a stickshift vehicle:

1. Be sure the parking brake is set. Shift to FIRST.
2. Use one hand to hold the steering wheel. Hold the parking brake release with the other hand.
3. Accelerate to a fast idle. Let the clutch out to the friction point.
4. Release the parking brake slowly when you feel the engine begin to pull.
5. Increase pressure on the accelerator, and let the clutch all the way up as your vehicle begins to move forward. Completely release the parking brake.

You might be able to coordinate the clutch and accelerator to move forward without using the parking brake. Follow these steps:

1. Shift to FIRST while stopped.
2. Keep the foot brake down while releasing the clutch slowly, just to the friction point.
3. Move your right foot quickly from the foot brake to the accelerator. Accelerate gently.
4. Release the clutch smoothly, and accelerate gradually.

Starting on a hill in a stickshift can be difficult. Practice first on gentle slopes away from traffic before you need to start moving on a steep hill. Use the method with which you feel most secure and comfortable.

Review It

1. What are standard reference points? How can you adapt them to become personal reference points?
2. What are the steps for angle parking? perpendicular parking? parallel parking?
3. Which way should your front wheels be turned when parking uphill with a curb? uphill with no curb? downhill with a curb? downhill with no curb?
4. How do you use the parking brake to start on a hill without rolling backwards?

Chapter 6
Review

Reviewing Chapter Objectives

1. Steering, Signaling, and Changing Lanes

1. How do you steer straight forward and backward? (110)
2. How do you use hand signals correctly and when should you use them? (111)
3. What are the proper steps for changing lanes? (112)

2. Making Turns and Turning the Vehicle Around

4. What is hand-over-hand steering? (113)
5. What are the steps for making right and left turns? (114)
6. How do you back left and right? (115)
7. How do you execute the five turnabout maneuvers, and which is the safest to use? (116–118)

3. Parking

8. What are reference points and how do you use them as guides when parking your vehicle? (119)
9. What are the procedures for angle, perpendicular, and parallel parking? (120–122)
10. How do you park uphill and downhill with and without a curb? (122–123)
11. How do you start from an uphill parking space without rolling backwards? (123–124)

Projects

Individuals

Investigate Research your state's laws on turnabouts. Which of the turnabouts described in the text are legal in your state, and which are illegal?

Observe Traffic Locate a busy street in your area on which vehicles must parallel park. Observe vehicles parallel parking for at least a half hour. Record how many attempts to parallel park each vehicle makes. What are the most common errors the drivers make in attempting to parallel park?

Practice Establish personal reference points in your family vehicle that you can use when you park. Compare your personal reference points with those of your classmates. Are the reference points you have in common "standard reference points"? Why or why not?

Groups

Debate Divide the group into two smaller groups to debate the pros and cons of shared left-turn lanes. Make a list of the pros and cons your group discusses. Share the list with your class.

Demonstrate Take turns demonstrating the hand and arm signals you use when turning and stopping. Present your group demonstration to the class.

Chapter 6
Review

Chapter Test

Check Your Knowledge

Multiple Choice Copy the number of each sentence below on a sheet of paper. Choose the letter of the answer that best completes the statement or answers the question.

1. To steer straight forward, look
(a) at your hand position on the steering wheel.
(b) at the center line or lane lines.
(c) left and right to judge available space.
(d) far ahead toward the center of your path.

2. To make the correct hand signal for a left turn, your left arm and hand should be
(a) extended straight. (c) pointing down.
(b) pointing up. (d) waving left.

3. The first step to take before you begin a lane-change maneuver is to
(a) check the blind spot over your left shoulder.
(b) check that roadway ahead has no obstructions.
(c) hand signal a stop.
(b) steer slightly into the next lane.

4. Backing a stickshift vehicle requires skillful use of the
(a) brake pedal. (c) gearshift lever.
(b) turn signals. (d) clutch pedal.

Completion Copy the number of each sentence below on a sheet of paper. After the number, write the word or words that complete the sentence correctly.

5. Before backing, make sure your _____ zones are clear.

6. _____ signals are easier to see in bright sunlight.

7. When changing lanes, _____ can cause your vehicle to turn too sharply.

8. Perform a _____ only when there are no driveways to use for another type of turnabout.

Review Vocabulary

Copy the number of each definition in list A. Match the definition in list A with the term it defines in list B.

List A

9. a part of the outside or inside of the vehicle, as viewed from the driver's seat, that relates to some part of the roadway
10. not turning the steering wheel enough
11. parking vehicle diagonally to curb
12. maneuver for turning your vehicle around to go in the opposite direction
13. parking vehicle at right angle to curb
14. pushing the steering wheel up with one hand and down with the other
15. turning the steering wheel too much

List B

a. turnabout
b. push-pull steering
c. reference point
d. perpendicular parking
e. oversteering
f. understeering
g. angle parking

Think Critically

Write a paragraph to answer each question.

1. You are driving down a two-way, two-lane street in a residential area at night during a storm. You notice that a large tree has fallen down across the roadway ahead of you. What type of turnabout should you make and why?

2. When parking on a hill, what can you do to make sure that your vehicle will not roll down into traffic?

Decision Making

1. You are the driver in this picture and need to make a turnabout. What type of turnabout would you choose? Why would you choose this type?

2. If you were planning to park in the row of angle-parked vehicles, which parking space would you choose to use? Why is this space the safest?

3. What procedure must the driver of the blue car follow when leaving the parallel parking space? If there is a collision, who is at fault? Why?

4. Which direction should the front wheels be turned for the vehicles parked uphill? For the vehicles parked downhill? Why is this important?

CHAPTER 7
Negotiating Intersections

7.1 Searching Intersections

7.2 Controlled Intersections

7.3 Uncontrolled Intersections

7.4 Determining Right of Way and Judging Gaps

You Are the Driver!

Imagine you are driving the brown pickup truck waiting for the light to change. You plan to go straight. Are you stopped in the proper location? Where should you search? Your decisions require intensive searching of all zones for accurate assessment of your intended path of travel.

In this chapter, you will learn how to identify and search controlled and uncontrolled intersections for a conflict-free path of travel. You also will learn how to interact safely with other roadway users at intersections.

For: Chapter 7 online activities
Visit: PHSchool.com
Web Code: cak-9999

7.1
Searching Intersections

Objectives

1. Explain how to search an intersection after it has been identified.
2. Tell when you are at the point of no return.
3. Describe what you should do when you have a closed front zone at an intersection.

The chances of a collision are greater at intersections than at any other point on a roadway. Intersections are dangerous because many drivers' paths cross there, and many unexpected stops occur there. More than one-third of all collisions and one-fourth of all fatal collisions take place at intersections.

One reason for the large number of collisions at intersections is the driver's failure to identify a safe path of travel through the intersection. In order to identify a safe path of travel you first need to locate the intersection.

Look for these clues to identify an intersection ahead:

- street signs and street lights
- roadway markings
- crossing traffic
- parked vehicles on cross streets
- turning traffic
- rows of fences and mailboxes
- traffic stopping
- power lines

What clues identify this intersection?

Intersections can be found in various designs. Most are simply two roadways crossing or a railroad crossing a roadway in a + or an X pattern. Others may form a Y when one roadway divides into two or when two join to form one. Some meet to form a T. A few are formed when several roadways meet at a circle—commonly called a **traffic circle.** A driver needs to know how to identify and be able to safely negotiate each design.

Approaching an Intersection

After identifying an intersection, you will need to determine if you have an open zone for your intended path of travel into and through the intersection. You will need to search the left-front, front, and right-front zones to be certain that they are open. You also need to look for line-of-sight restrictions that will prevent you from seeing if your intended path of travel is going to be safe. You should search for changes in those zones that could make them closed for your travel as shown in the top picture on the next page.

Remember, line-of-sight restrictions can be caused by the environment or by other highway users. When your line of sight is restricted, your zone checks should become more frequent. You should still primarily be checking your front zone to make sure it is still open for your intended path of travel.

Your search will change when you have identified a closed zone caused

Search for changes in your zones to keep your intended path of travel safe.

by a line-of-sight restriction. That is also true when you make a left turn, make a right turn, or continue through an intersection.

Once you are within 4–6 seconds of the intersection, your searching pattern should widen to include more information from the right and left of your path of travel. If your front zone is clear, you can keep moving. If it is not clear, you will need to prepare to stop or change your path of travel.

When you identify a line-of-sight restriction, you should perform a search of that area. Search for such things as a car stopped on the left, a parked vehicle on the right, or a double-parked delivery truck. Turn your head 45 degrees to the right or left in an attempt to see beyond the line-of-sight restriction as shown in the picture on the right. When searching, you need to briefly pause at each zone to detect objects in that location. Do not move your eyes in a constant scan. If you do not pause at each zone, you could miss objects as large as a car.

Continue Moving Ahead

You may continue ahead if the traffic light is green, or if the intersection has no signals or signs, and the front, right-front, and left-front zones are open. At an intersection a driver needs to locate open front zones to move ahead safely. Many times it takes numerous checks of a zone because of a line-of-sight restriction.

If your path of travel is clear, continue searching the left-front, front, and right-front zones for a path-of-travel change or a line-of-sight restriction.

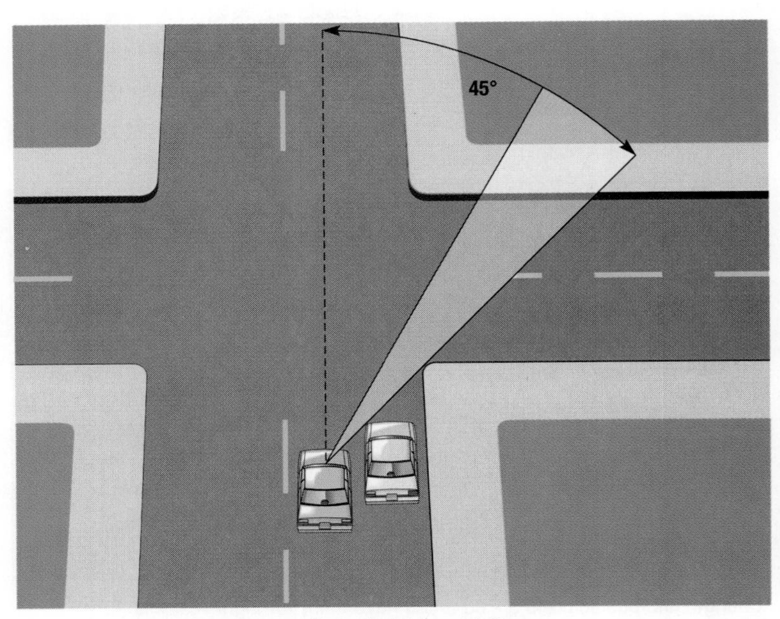

Move your head to see beyond line-of-sight restrictions.

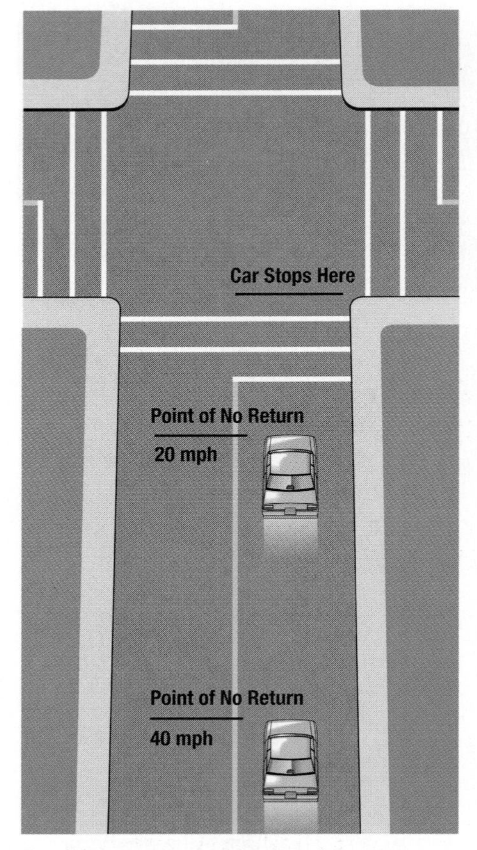

Every intersection has a point of no return.

Once you have passed the point-of-no-return, you should continue through the intersection. The **point-of-no-return** is the point beyond which you can no longer stop safely without entering the intersection. Under normal conditions, that point is two seconds from the intersection as shown in the picture on the left.

If you do have a line-of-sight restriction, you may want to change your lane position and reduce your speed. This will give you more time to see what is hidden. If the restriction is on the right and you have an open left-front zone, move to the left side of your lane into lane position 2 and reduce your speed. If the restriction is on the left and you have an open right-front zone, move to lane position 3 and reduce speed. When your left-front and right-front zones are closed, stay in lane position 1 and further reduce speed. By improving your position and reducing your speed, you will have more time to see as well as be seen by others.

When your path of travel is closed and there is a line-of-sight restriction, a lane change may be needed. *Remember, you are not allowed to make lane changes within an intersection.* Therefore, you should select the best path of travel before entering an intersection. You must check your new path of travel before you change your lane position or change lanes.

Change lane position and speed if you have a line-of-sight restriction.

Deciding to Stop

You may have to stop at an intersection when you identify or predict a closed zone or a line-of-sight restric-

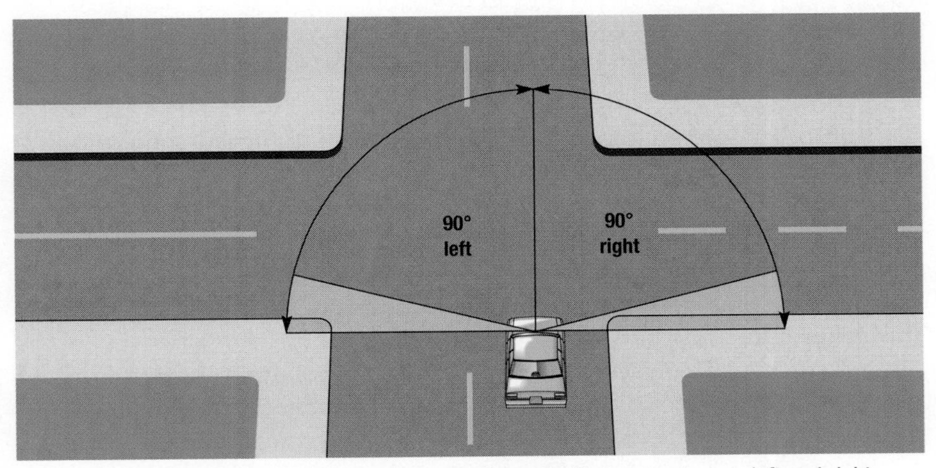

After you have stopped, check your front zone and search 90 degrees to your left and right.

tion ahead. By reducing your speed you can more easily check the zone having a line-of-sight restriction.

A closed front zone is identified by the presence of a yellow or red traffic light, a YIELD sign, or something moving into your intended path of travel. All of these situations would give you less than 10 seconds of an available path of travel and make it a closed zone.

If you have identified a closed zone at an intersection, you will need to prepare to reduce speed or stop. As soon as you identify a closed zone, check your rear zone. If it is open, begin to brake. If the rear zone is closed, tap your brake pedal a few times so that your brake lights communicate to the driver to the rear that you are stopping.

Moving After a Stop

After you have stopped and your front zone is clear, search at 90-degree angles to the right and left before you begin moving. Pause briefly at each target area to get a clear view of possible conflicts.

When turning, your last check should be in the direction of your intended path of travel. You need to know if your intended path of travel is open before you enter an intersection.

If you are stopped behind another vehicle, wait one second after it begins to move before you move. This gives you room to respond to any sudden stop made by the vehicle ahead.

Review It

1. Which zones should you search when approaching an intersection?
2. Where is your point of no return?
3. What should you do when you identify a closed front zone at the next intersection?

7.2 Controlled Intersections

Objectives

1. Explain how to approach a controlled intersection.
2. Tell how to move from a STOP sign when your view is blocked.
3. Describe how to make right turns and left turns at controlled intersections.

A **controlled intersection** is one at which traffic signals or signs determine the right of way. Obey all signs and traffic signals when you approach a controlled intersection. Yield the right of way to through traffic.

Controlled Intersections with Signs

Two kinds of signs control intersections: STOP and YIELD. You must come to a **full stop** for a STOP sign, crosswalk, or stop line. At a YIELD sign, slow and yield the right of way to vehicles on the through street.

Blocked View at Stop Sign

Sometimes parked vehicles or other objects cause a line-of-sight restriction. Follow these steps to cross intersections safely and merge with traffic after stopping.

Crossing Traffic Follow this procedure when you need to cross traffic through an intersection:

1. Look around and search at a 45-degree angle at location 1 in the picture on the top right. Continue to search left, front, and right as you creep forward. Check your rear zone.
2. Check your path of travel for pedestrians and prepare to make the legal stop before you move beyond location 2. Look for vehicles making turns into your path.
3. Stop with your front bumper even with the curb. Search 90 degrees to the left and right of your target area. When there are parked vehicles, your ideal searching location is when your front bumper is even with the left side of the parked cars, as in location 3.
4. When you have an open front zone and a clear gap of at least seven seconds from the left and right, proceed by accelerating to the proper speed. Once through the intersection, check your rear zone.

Joining Traffic—Right Turn Take these steps when turning right to join traffic:

1. At location 1 in the picture in the middle on the right, search your front zones for pedestrians and vehicles turning onto your street. Check your rear zone, and stop.
2. Stop at location 2 where your front bumper is even with the curb. Search 90-degrees to the left and right. Evaluate the target path and your left-front, front, and right-front zones. When clear of any line-of-sight restrictions and with a gap of at least seven seconds, begin your turn. Turn your head toward your target, begin to accelerate, and turn the steering wheel. When you have a line-of-sight restriction to your left that prevents you from clearly seeing at a 90-degree angle, creep forward slightly to improve your view to

the left. Turn your head toward your target path as you accelerate and turn.

3. At location 3, turn so that you end up no farther than three to four feet away from the curb. Accelerate to adjust to traffic and check the rear zone.

Joining Traffic—Left Turn Follow these steps when turning left:

1. Before moving beyond location 1 in the picture on the bottom right, your vehicle should be in lane position 2. Search front zones for pedestrians and vehicles turning onto your street. Check your rear zone and stop.
2. Stop when your front bumper is even with the curb. Evaluate your left-front, front, and right-front zones. When you are clear of any line-of-sight restrictions and have a gap of at least seven seconds, begin your turn. Move forward slightly to where your body is even with the curbline. Check your front zones; turn your head toward your target area; accelerate; and turn the steering wheel.
3. At location 3, turn so that you end up in lane position 2. Accelerate to adjust to traffic and check the rear zone.

Controlled Intersections with Signals

Traffic signals usually have three lights to each cycle—red, yellow, and green. Signals also can have a fourth or fifth light, such as a yellow arrow and a green arrow. Imagine you are

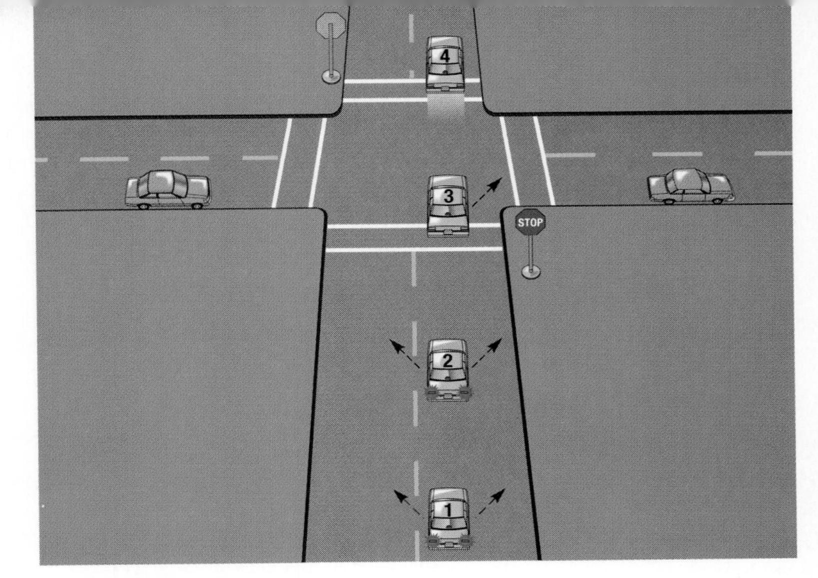

Crossing traffic

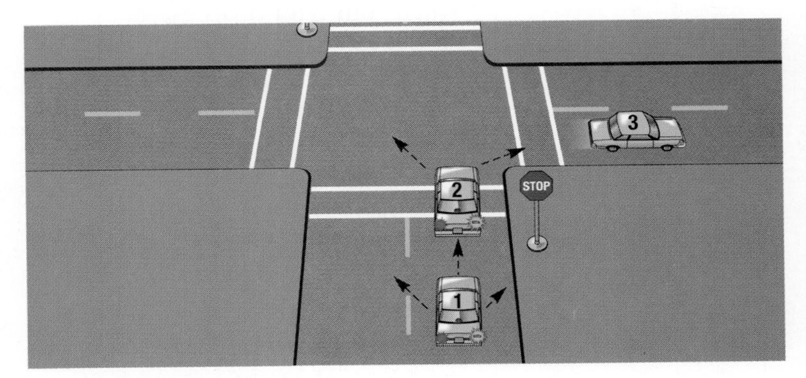

Joining Traffic—Right Turn

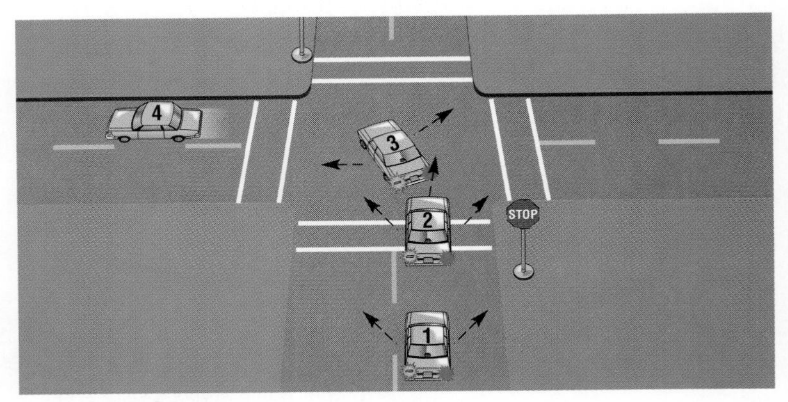

Joining Traffic—Left Turn

The green arrow permits you to make a protected left turn.

stopped at the red light in the picture above. Think of what is about to take place. Proceed with caution when your light turns green.

As you drive toward a signal-controlled intersection, consider if the signal is about to change. Treat each intersection as a separate problem. Searching 12–15 seconds ahead, evaluate the next intersection to see what color that light is. Look for any traffic moving on the cross street. Before you reach the point where you must brake to stop at an intersection, quickly check your front zones. If you predict the light is going to be red, or if cross traffic has closed your front zone, check your rear zone, reduce speed, and be prepared to stop.

Signals

Use the IPDE Process to handle traffic signals properly. Identify the color of a signal as soon as you see it. Predict that the color might change as you approach the intersection.

Stale Green Light A **stale green light** is a light that has been green for a long time. If a light remains green after you first identify it, be prepared to slow. Predict that it will turn yellow soon.

Fresh Green Light A **fresh green light** is a light that has just turned green. A fresh green light does not guarantee that you will have a safe path of travel. *Be sure that no driver on the cross street is running the red light.* Check for an open zone before you proceed.

Yellow Light When you approach an intersection as the light turns yellow, you must decide whether to stop or proceed. If the light turns yellow before you reach the point of no return, check in the rear zone.

You Are the Driver!
What will you do when your signal turns green?

If it is safe to stop, do so. Otherwise, go through the intersection.

Be very careful before making a left turn on a yellow light. Wait for all oncoming traffic to stop before you start your turn.

Red Light When the light is red, you must stop. Check your rear zone as you begin to slow.

If you have a vehicle ahead of you, stop at a point where you can see its rear wheels touching the roadway. If you have no vehicles behind you, continue checking your rear zone often.

Unprotected Left Turns

An **unprotected left turn** is made at a signal-controlled intersection that does not have a special left-turn light. When you turn left, you must yield to oncoming traffic.

Protected Left Turns

You can make a **protected left turn** when a special left-turn light, green arrow, or delayed green light lets you turn left while oncoming traffic is stopped. Left turns might be prohibited when the protected left-turn signal ends by a sign or a red arrow. If the turn is allowed, respond to it as you would to an unprotected left turn.

Left-Turn Light A left-turn light provides a protected left turn. Some left-turn lights are located over the turn lane without using signs.

Green Arrow A green arrow can appear with the normal red, yellow, and green signals. In many places the green arrow simply turns off to indicate the protected turn has ended. Others are followed with a yellow arrow as a warning. Watch for oncoming drivers who might proceed, thinking your green arrow is their green light.

Delayed Green Light A **delayed green light** indicates that one side of an intersection has a green light while the light for the oncoming traffic remains red. This light allows traffic from one side to turn or go straight before the light for oncoming traffic turns green. Obey your signal only. Do not assume that you can proceed when oncoming traffic proceeds.

Turns on Red

All states and the District of Columbia now permit turns on red. A few local governments may not. Watch for signs posted that prohibit turning on red.

Right on Red Before turning right on a red light, come to a full stop as you would at a STOP sign. Move to a position where you can see clearly. Search the front zones for openings. You must yield the right of way to any vehicle or pedestrian in, or approach-

TIP

SAFE DRIVING

When a light turns yellow as you approach an intersection, prepare to stop. Do not speed up to try to get through the intersection.

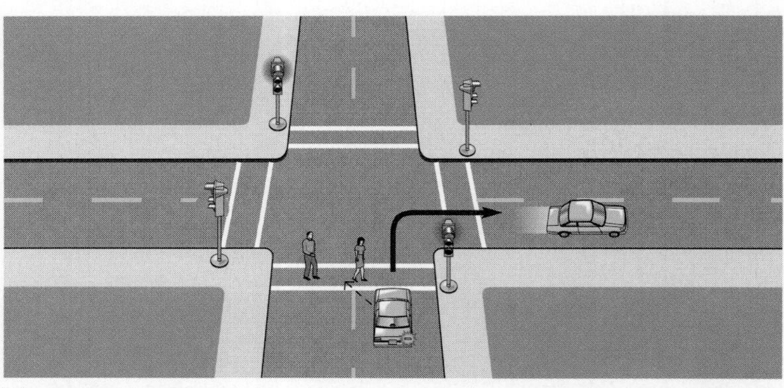

Where should you search for vehicles and pedestrians when turning right on red?

TRAFFIC SIGNALS In the early 1920s, Garret Morgan noticed that the traffic signals at a busy intersection did not help traffic move smoothly enough through the streets of Cleveland, Ohio. The signals did not have a caution position to alert drivers that they would soon have to stop. Morgan made a three-position signal. He then sold his idea to a large electric company that developed the red-yellow-green traffic lights still prevalent today.

ing, the intersection. Complete your turn into the nearest right lane.

Left on Red Most states also permit a left turn on red if the turn is from a one-way street onto another one-way street. A few states also permit turning left on red from a left-turn lane on a two-way street onto a one-way street. Follow the same procedure as in a right turn on red, but look for traffic in your front and right-front zones. Then turn into the nearest left lane.

Controlled Railroad Crossings

A **controlled railroad crossing** usually has red lights along with crossing gates. Make a complete stop when the lights are flashing and/or the gates are down. Remain stopped until the lights stop flashing and the gates have raised. It is illegal, unsafe, and costly to drive around the gates. When the crossing is clear, proceed cautiously.

Stop when the gate is down.

Review It

1. How should you approach a controlled intersection?
2. When your view is blocked at a STOP sign, what should you do?
3. How would you make a right turn or a left turn at a controlled intersection?

7.3
Uncontrolled Intersections

Objectives

1. Tell how to identify an uncontrolled intersection.
2. Explain the procedures to follow at an uncontrolled intersection.
3. Describe the proper procedures for crossing uncontrolled railroad tracks.

An **uncontrolled intersection** has no signs or signals to regulate traffic. These intersections usually are found in areas of light traffic, such as residential areas. Although these streets usually are quiet, they can be dangerous because drivers might not be expecting cross traffic or pedestrians.

Sometimes a driver fails to identify an intersection as uncontrolled. The driver assumes the other driver will stop or, on a quiet street, assumes that no one is there. If you do not see a traffic sign or signal, assume that the intersection is uncontrolled. Predict that other traffic will not stop. Reduce speed, search aggressively, and always be prepared to stop.

Approaching Uncontrolled Intersections

Once an intersection has been identified, check your rear zone for following traffic. Then, you will need to determine if you have an open path of travel into and through the intersection. You will need to search the left-front, front, and right-front zones to be certain that they are open for your use. You need to continue to look for line-of-sight restrictions that could prevent you from seeing if your path of travel is going to be safe.

Be certain that you can clearly see open space in your left-front, front, and right-front zones before entering the intersection. You must search for zone changes that could make them closed.

Your search pattern will change when you have identified a closed zone caused by a line-of-sight restriction. If you identify a closed zone in your path of travel, check your rear zone again. Remove your foot from the accelerator and cover or apply the brake.

If a vehicle is coming from the left or right, the driver on the left must yield to the driver on the right. However, predict the worst in each case. *Never assume that the other driver will yield.* The only safe action is to slow and be prepared to stop.

You Are the Driver!
Where are the signs and signals at this intersection?

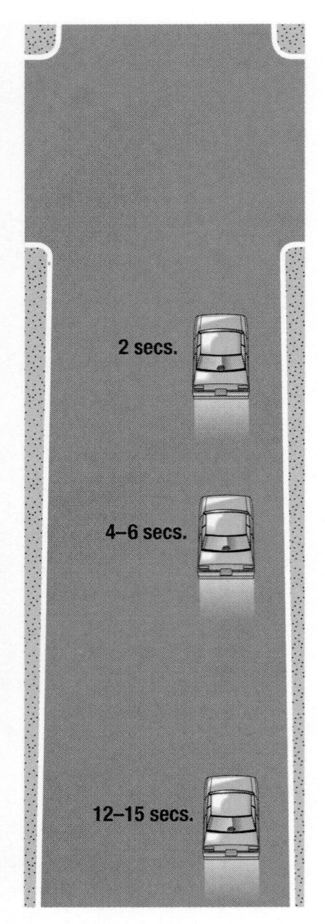

You should perform a series of steps at each of these three locations near uncontrolled intersections.

Treat an uncontrolled intersection as you would a YIELD sign and always be prepared to stop.

At a traffic circle you must yield to vehicles already in the circle. Vehicles in the traffic circle will be coming from your left. When you are in the circle, be alert for vehicles entering in your right-front zone.

Always let pedestrians go first—no matter where the pedestrian is crossing. As a driver, you must yield to pedestrians even if they are breaking a traffic law.

Procedures at Uncontrolled Intersections

When you search your target area and identify an uncontrolled intersection, there are three critical locations at which you must use the IPDE Process. Each location corresponds to a time period measured in seconds. When you approach an uncontrolled intersection, you must perform a series of steps at each of these locations.

IPDE Process at 12–15 Seconds from Intersection

1. Check roadway conditions as you approach the intersection. Check for closed zones to the left front, front, and right front.
2. Identify whether or not the intersection is controlled.
3. Identify other roadway users in or near the intersection.
4. Search the view to each side. Look for line-of-sight restrictions. Check 45 degrees to each side. When you identify closed zones, solve the problems before you enter those spaces.
5. Locate your point of no return. You cannot stop after passing that point.
6. Check the rearview mirror for following traffic, and slow your vehicle. The more line-of-sight restrictions, the more time you need to use the IPDE Process.

IPDE Process at 4–6 Seconds from Intersection

1. Recheck your immediate path of travel.
2. Search left front and right front again for an open zone.
3. If a vehicle is coming from the left or right, prepare to stop.
4. Recheck traffic to the rear.

IPDE Process at 2 Seconds from Intersection

1. Pause your search briefly as you continue evaluating zones for potential conflicts. This is your last chance to stop safely—your point of no return.
2. Brake to a stop if your front zone in the intersection closes.
3. Search again to the left and right.
4. Proceed through the intersection when your path of travel is clear.

Uncontrolled Railroad Crossings

Trains warn others of their approach, but it is primarily up to the vehicle driver to avoid a collision. Stopping distances of trains will vary. You can be sure that a train's stopping distance will always be longer than that of a car.

An **uncontrolled railroad crossing** does not have flashing red lights or crossing gates. However, nearly all are marked with a sign as you approach them. In towns and cities, a round, yellow railroad-crossing sign is posted about 250 feet from the actual crossing. In rural areas this warning sign is about 750 feet from the crossing. A **crossbuck,** a large white X-shaped sign, is located beside the crossing. Many times a large white X is painted on the roadway near the crossing.

Treat uncontrolled crossings the same as an intersection with a YIELD sign. Slow and be prepared to stop.

Slow and be prepared to stop at uncontrolled railroad crossings.

Crossing Railroad Tracks

Take these actions when you approach an uncontrolled railroad crossing:

1. Slow down. Check tracks to both sides and traffic to the rear as you approach the crossing sign.
2. Turn off the radio, air conditioner, or heater fan to listen for train sounds. Open the window if the area is noisy.
3. Reduce speed to handle a possible rough-road crossing or if there is a line-of-sight restriction. Note the number of track sets.
4. If a train is approaching, stop at a safe distance before the tracks.
5. Wait for the train to clear. Then carefully check the crossing. Be sure another train is not approaching on another set of tracks.
6. If it is safe to cross, increase your speed up to at least 20 mph. Then your vehicle can roll across the tracks should its engine stall.
7. If you have a stickshift vehicle, shift to a lower gear before crossing to prevent stalling on the tracks. Never shift while crossing tracks.
8. Drive onto the tracks only after you have enough space and speed to clear the tracks. Make sure any vehicles ahead clear the tracks before you start to cross. Never stop on railroad tracks while waiting for traffic ahead to move.
9. When you follow buses or trucks hauling flammable contents, be prepared to stop. Many states require such vehicles to stop before crossing railroad tracks.

Review It

1. How can you identify an uncontrolled intersection?
2. What should you do at an uncontrolled intersection?
3. What are the procedures to use when going through an uncontrolled railroad crossing?

7.4 Determining Right of Way and Judging Gaps

Objectives

1. Define right of way.
2. Describe situations in which you, the driver, must yield the right of way.
3. Identify how long it takes to cross and join traffic.

A safe driver knows that conflicts often occur at intersections and is prepared to handle these conflicts. To be a safe driver, you need to know when to yield the right of way.

What Is Right of Way?

The term **right of way** describes the privilege of having immediate use of a certain part of a roadway. You have the right of way only when other drivers give it to you. It is not something you can take.

You will often have to **yield,** by letting others go first, to be safe. Letting others go first is called "yielding the right of way." Sometimes you must yield to prevent a collision. At other times, yielding is an act of courtesy. Most of the time, laws determine who should yield the right of way.

Situations When You Must Yield

Remember these points in yield situations:

- Your action should not cause those to whom you should yield the right of way to slow, stop, or change their intended path of travel.
- Traffic signs and signals only show who should yield the right of way. They do not stop traffic for you.
- Others can give you the right of way. Do not assume others will always yield to you.
- Many times it is better to yield the right of way even when the law requires the other driver to yield.
- Failure to yield the right of way is one of the most frequent violations in fatal collisions.

You must yield the right of way in many situations. Knowing right-of-way laws will help you make safe decisions. These drawings show the most common situations regarding yielding the right of way. In each situation the yellow car is required to yield.

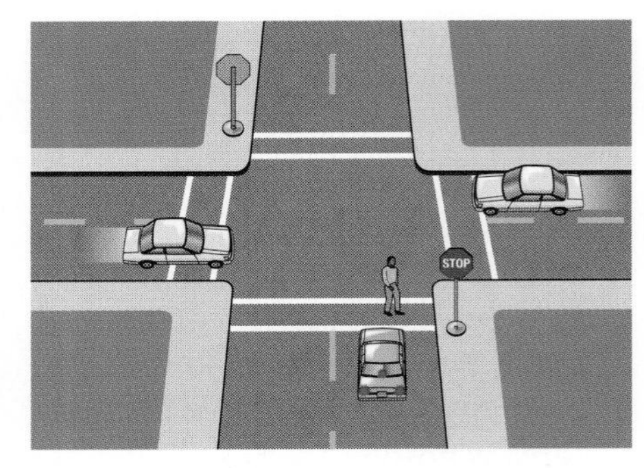

Yield at STOP signs to
- pedestrians in or near the crosswalk
- all traffic on the through street

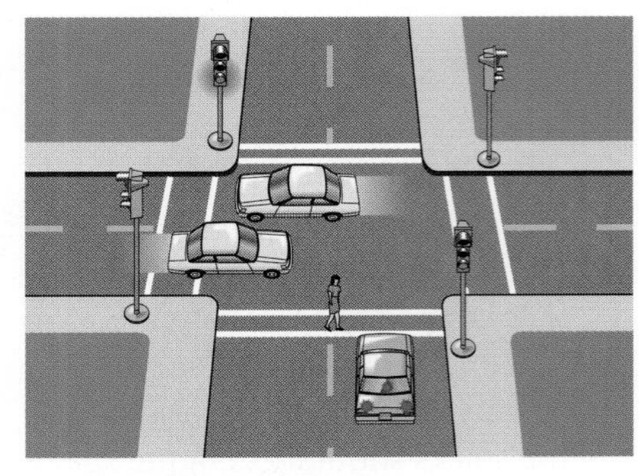

Yield at fresh green lights to
- pedestrians still in the crosswalk
- vehicles still in the intersection

Yield coming from an alley, driveway, or private roadway to
- pedestrians before reaching the sidewalk
- all vehicles on the street (Make two stops.)

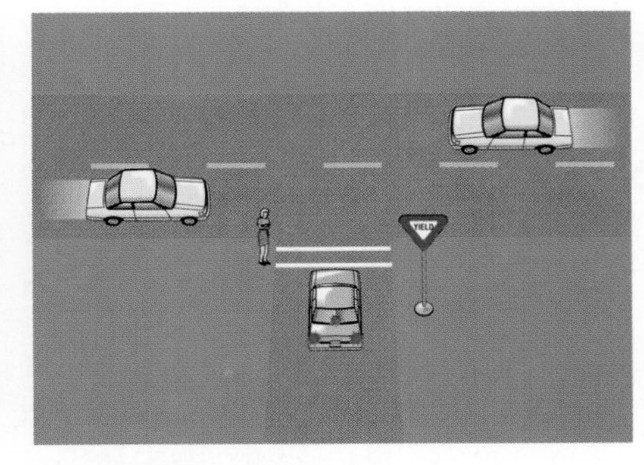

Yield at all YIELD signs to
- all pedestrians in or near crosswalks
- all vehicles on the cross street

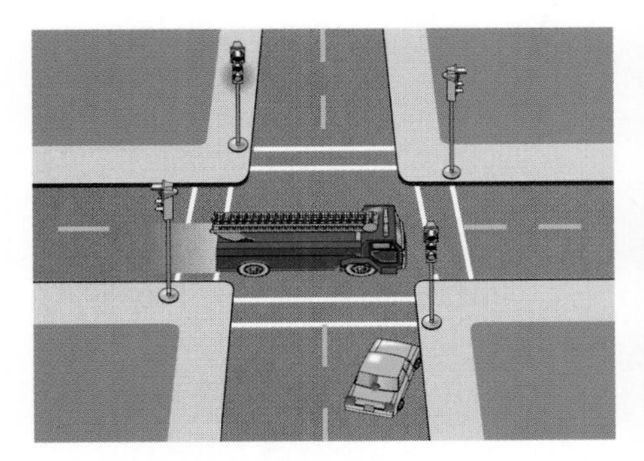

Yield to emergency vehicles
- sounding a siren or using a flashing light (Stop clear of the intersection close to curb. Wait for emergency vehicle to pass.)

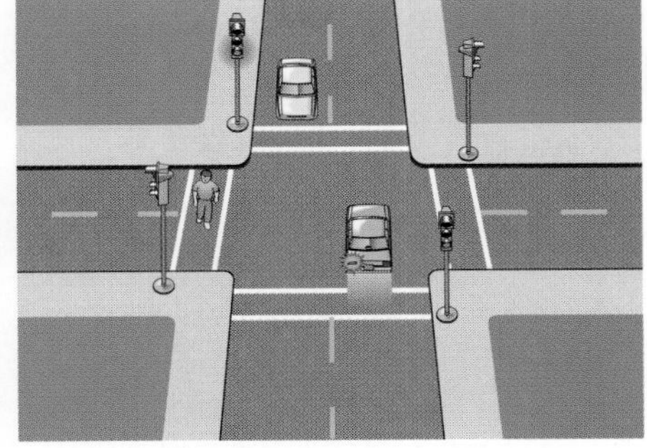

Yield when turning left at any intersection to
- all pedestrians in your turn path
- all oncoming vehicles that are at all close

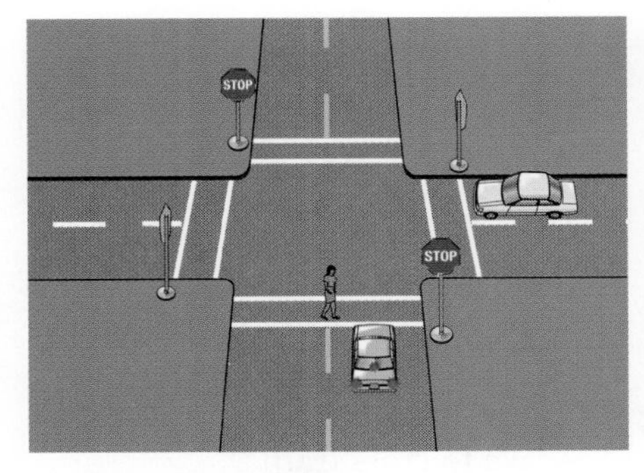

Yield at four-way stops to
- all pedestrians in or near crosswalks
- vehicles that arrive first
- a vehicle from the right if you arrive at the same time

Yield at uncontrolled intersections to
- pedestrians in or near the crosswalk
- any vehicle that has entered the intersection
- a vehicle from the right if you both arrive at the same time

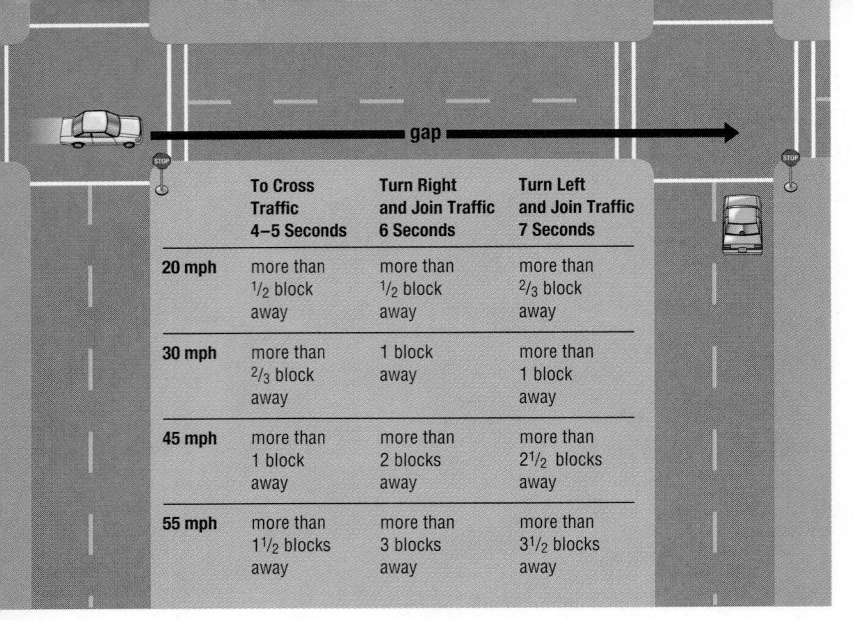

	To Cross Traffic 4–5 Seconds	Turn Right and Join Traffic 6 Seconds	Turn Left and Join Traffic 7 Seconds
20 mph	more than 1/2 block away	more than 1/2 block away	more than 2/3 block away
30 mph	more than 2/3 block away	1 block away	more than 1 block away
45 mph	more than 1 block away	more than 2 blocks away	more than 2 1/2 blocks away
55 mph	more than 1 1/2 blocks away	more than 3 blocks away	more than 3 1/2 blocks away

Gap selection for crossing or joining traffic

Judging the Size of a Gap

You must be able to judge the gaps between vehicles and how long it takes to pass through or enter intersecting traffic lanes.

A **gap** is the distance between vehicles. When you enter a through street after stopping, you must judge the size of the gaps in traffic.

You need different size gaps depending on the maneuver you plan to make and the speed of traffic. From the picture above you see that crossing a two-lane street takes about four to five seconds. Turning right and accelerating to 30 mph takes about six seconds. Turning left and accelerating to 30 mph takes about seven seconds. The same process to judge following distance is adapted to judge gap sizes.

Crossing and Joining Traffic

You must know how long it takes to turn right, to turn left, and to cross traffic at an intersection. Turning right or left into lanes of other vehicles is called *joining traffic.* Look at the picture to visualize situations that follow.

Crossing an intersection takes four to five seconds from a stop. If traffic on the through street is traveling 30 mph, you need a gap of about two-thirds of a block in each direction.

You need a larger gap to join traffic when turning right than when crossing. You need about six seconds to reach the speed of through-street traffic without interfering with the flow of traffic.

A left turn is more dangerous than a right turn. You cross the paths of traffic from the left before entering traffic from the right. The gap to the left should be greater than when you make a right turn. At 55 mph, you need a gap of more than three and one-half blocks.

Review It

1. What is meant by "yielding the right of way"?
2. Give six examples of when you should yield the right of way.
3. How many seconds does it take to cross traffic?

Chapter 7
Review

Reviewing Chapter Objectives

1. Searching Intersections

1. How should you search an intersection once you have identified it? (130–131)
2. How can you tell when you are at the point of no return? (132)
3. What should you do when you have a closed front zone at an intersection? (132–133)

2. Controlled Intersections

4. How should you approach a controlled intersection? (134)
5. How should you move from a STOP sign when your view is blocked? (134)
6. How would you make a right turn or a left turn at a controlled intersection? (136–138)

3. Uncontrolled Intersections

7. How would you identify an uncontrolled intersection? (139)
8. What procedures should you follow at an uncontrolled intersection? (140)
9. What procedures should you follow at an uncontrolled railroad crossing? (141)

4. Determining Right of Way and Judging Gaps

10. What does the term "right of way" mean? (142)
11. In what situations must a driver yield the right of way? (142–143)
12. How would you judge a gap in traffic? (144)
13. How would you cross and join traffic properly? (144)

Projects

Individuals

Observe Traffic Keep a record for a week of all the railroad tracks you cross as a passenger in a car. Note whether (1) the crossing was controlled or uncontrolled, (2) a train was approaching or proceeding down the track, and (3) the driver took the appropriate actions when approaching the tracks. Discuss your findings with the class.

Investigate Clip two articles reporting intersection collisions from your local newspaper. Analyze each report to determine which vehicle should have yielded the right of way. Write a summary of your findings and compare your opinions with classmates who analyzed the same collisions.

Groups

Observe Traffic As a group, observe traffic at an intersection controlled by a STOP sign. Use a stopwatch to measure the gaps between vehicles proceeding through the intersection. Record your measurements, organizing them in a spreadsheet format. Measure gaps for vehicles (1) crossing traffic, (2) joining traffic—right turn, and (3) joining traffic—left turn.

Use Technology Make a video of cars progressing through an intersection controlled by traffic signals. In the narration, group members should identify the types of traffic signals and analyze the drivers' responses to the signals.

Chapter 7

Review

Chapter Test

Check Your Knowledge

Multiple Copy the number of each sentence below on a sheet of paper. Choose the letter that best completes the statement or answers the question.

1. As you approach a yellow or red traffic light, your front zone
(a) widens. (c) opens up.
(b) closes. (d) narrows.

2. What is the term for a light that has just turned from red?
(a) yellow light (c) fresh green light
(b) stale green light (d) stale red light

3. With which of the following does one side of an intersection have a green light?
(a) fresh green light (c) controlled green light
(b) stale green light (d) delayed green light

4. Which of the following terms means to allow others to go first?
(a) stop (c) yield
(b) proceed (d) cycle

5. Which of the following signs identifies an uncontrolled railroad crossing?
(a) STOP sign (c) crossbuck
(b) YIELD sign (d) red flashing lights

Completion Copy the number of each sentence below on a sheet of paper. After each number, write the word or words that completes the sentence correctly.

6. Your chances of collision are greater at a/an _____ than at any other point on a roadway.

7. When turning after a stop, your last check should be in the direction of your _____.

8. As a driver, you must always _____ to pedestrians.

Review Vocabulary

Copy the number of each definition in List A. Match the definition in List A with the term it defines in List B.

List A

9. intersection at which traffic signals or signs determine the right of way
10. complete stop as required at a stop sign or red light
11. privilege of having immediate use of a certain part of a roadway
12. distance between vehicles
13. intersection that has no signs or signals to regulate traffic
14. light that has been green for a long time

List B

a. right of way
b. full stop
c. stale green light
d. controlled intersection
e. uncontrolled intersection
f. gap

Think Critically

Write a paragraph to answer each question.

1. Imagine you are driving a car that is approaching an intersection controlled by a STOP sign. You wish to make a left turn. Describe in detail the steps you would take before, during, and after your turn.

2. What is the difference between a protected left turn and an unprotected left turn? Why do you suppose some left turns are protected at signal-controlled intersections, while others are not?

Decision Making

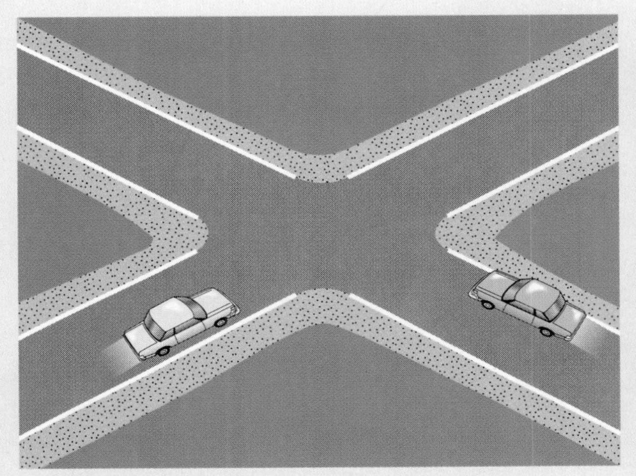

1. You are driving the yellow car and are approaching an uncontrolled intersection. You and the other car are the same distance from the intersection. What do you predict about the other car? What should you do?

2. You have just stopped at a red light. You wish to turn left. Is a left turn at this intersection legal on a red light? Where should you search before turning?

3. You are driving the red car. The light turns yellow just after the car in front of you crosses the railroad tracks. Where should you stop? What could happen in this situation?

4. You are driving this car that is stopped at the STOP sign. At what speed would you assume the cars on the through roadway would be traveling? How far away would the cars have to be for you to make a safe left turn?

CLASSES OFFERED
Days, Evenings, Weekends
Short-Term and Online
www.lacitycollege.edu
LACC
LOS ANGELES CITY COLLEGE
An Urban Oasis
of Learning
rmont

CHAPTER 8
Sharing the Roadway

8.1 Sharing the Roadway with Motorcyclists

8.2 Motorcyclist Actions Can Affect You

8.3 Bicycles, Mopeds, and Motor Scooters

8.4 Pedestrians and Special Vehicles

8.5 Sharing the Road with Trucks

You Are the Driver!

As a driver, you will be sharing the roadway with a variety of other vehicles and pedestrians. These other users present their own special problems in every driving environment. Many vehicles are small in size and, like pedestrians, have very little protection if a conflict with a larger vehicle occurs.

What problems might the motorcyclist have in this traffic scene? What should the car driver predict? This chapter explores problems presented by other roadway users and explains your responsibility for protecting other less-protected users.

For: Chapter 8 online activities
Visit: PHSchool.com
Web Code: cak-9999

8.1 Sharing the Roadway with Motorcyclists

Objectives

1. Tell why you have the responsibility for protecting motorcyclists.
2. Explain how to use the IPDE Process to protect motorcyclists.
3. Describe situations where you should look for motorcyclists.

Even though many drivers will never ride a motorcycle, they will be safer drivers if they understand problems involved in the cyclist's driving task. Motorcyclists have the same privileges within the HTS as drivers of other vehicles. They also share an equal responsibility for following safe driving practices.

Even though motorcycle registrations make up a very small percentage of all vehicle registrations, about 2,000 cyclist fatalities occur each year. Injuries and deaths from motorcycle crashes result primarily from the exposed position of the rider. Unlike the driver of a larger vehicle, a motorcyclist has little or no protection when conflicts occur.

As a driver of a larger vehicle, you must accept the major share of responsibility for protecting motorcyclists as they interact within the HTS. Show cyclists the same courtesy you show other drivers.

Using the IPDE Process

Most low-risk drivers tend to be alert for other cars and larger vehicles that might cause conflict. Because motorcycles are smaller and are driven in several different lane positions, they often are not identified in time to prevent conflict. Make a special effort to use the IPDE Process.

The Identify step is crucial for drivers because motorcycles are more difficult to see. Search all the zones so you will not be surprised by the sudden appearance of a motorcycle.

Predict actions of motorcyclists that might enter your path. Base your decisions on the problems that confront the motorcyclist, and execute your actions. Use every technique possible before a closed zone or conflict occurs. The driver in the yellow car in the picture is looking through the approaching car's windows to see the motorcyclist or other roadway users.

Where to Look for Motorcyclists

Look for motorcyclists in the following situations.

Vehicle Turning Left in Front of Motorcyclist When you plan to turn left across one or more lanes of traffic, be sure your planned path of travel is clear. Even though the cyclist in the top picture on the opposite page is signaling for a left turn, the car driver

Scan through the windows of other vehicles to see motorcyclists or other roadway users.

Both the car driver and the motorcyclist want to make left turns. The driver of the car should let the motorcyclist start the turn first.

should predict that the cyclist will continue straight. The car driver should complete the left turn only after scanning front and side zones and after the cyclist has entered his left-turn path.

When you make left turns at night, be especially watchful for oncoming vehicle headlights. The single headlight of a motorcycle can be confused with a larger vehicle that has only one working headlight.

Vehicle Turning Right at Intersection or Driveway Drivers of larger vehicles who do not check their rear zones frequently might not be aware of traffic to the rear. Therefore, they may turn right directly in front of a motorcyclist, as the picture below shows.

Motorcyclist Turning Left When you are approaching an intersection and there is oncoming traffic, expect

You Are the Driver!
How could you have avoided a possible conflict with this motorcyclist?

smaller vehicles to appear in your path. An approaching motorcyclist who is about to turn left could be blocked from your view. Search your front zones and be aware of any limited sight distance to your left. Be prepared to act to avoid conflict.

Motorcyclist in Driver's Blind Spot Because of its relatively small size, a motorcycle is often difficult to see in the blind-spot areas behind your vehicle. The roof-support columns on the back and sides of vehicles add to the problem. Always check the blind spots in your left- and right-rear zones by glancing over your shoulder before turning or changing lanes.

Tailgating Motorcyclist The only way to know if you are being tailgated by a motorcyclist is to check your rear zone often. When you see a tailgating cyclist, try to avoid sudden braking. If the driver of the yellow car in the picture brakes suddenly to let the car on the shoulder in, the tailgating motorcyclist could lose control. The motorcyclist does not have enough following distance to stop in time. Check your rearview mirrors often and increase your following distance if a cyclist is following you.

Motorcyclist Passing Vehicle on Right or Left Check your rearview mirrors and blind spots frequently as part of your visual search pattern. Anticipate that motorcyclists will pass you. The failure of many drivers to check their rearview mirrors and blind-spot areas can easily lead to conflict with motorcyclists.

Be especially aware of being passed on either the right or left at an intersection where there may be more space. Even though motorcyclists should not pass at intersections, always watch for them so you can avoid conflict. When you are being overtaken by a motorcyclist, maintain both your lane position and your speed.

Motorcyclist Meeting an Oncoming Vehicle You are more likely to see an oncoming motorcyclist in the daytime if the motorcycle's headlight is on. Many states require that the motorcycle's headlight be on at all times. All motorcycles manufactured today have the headlight come on when the ignition is turned on. Whenever you see an oncoming motorcyclist, stay on your side of the roadway until the motorcyclist has passed. Remember also that having your headlights on at all times makes you more visible to the cyclist.

Watch for tailgating motorcyclists if you must slow or stop suddenly.

TIP — SAFE DRIVING

Motorcyclists should never assume that all other drivers see them. They should make every effort to be as visible as possible in the traffic scene.

Passing a Motorcyclist

Never tailgate a cyclist before passing. The appearance of a very close vehicle in the cyclist's rearview mirror could cause an unexpected action and result in conflict. When you plan to overtake and pass a motorcyclist, stay well back until you start to pass.

When the way is clear, execute your passing maneuver. Use the entire left lane for passing, as the car driver in the picture is doing. When you can see the cyclist in your rearview mirror, signal, check your right blind-spot area, and return to the right lane.

Protecting Motorcyclists

Unlike a driver protected inside a larger vehicle, a motorcyclist is fully exposed to dangers that could cause injury or death. For this reason, you must accept an extra share of responsibility for avoiding conflicts with cyclists. With a larger vehicle under your control, you have the power to cause far more harm than a cyclist. Handle this power with respect.

Develop an attitude of helping others who are less protected. Make it your responsibility to demonstrate habits and behavior that show you care for the safety of your fellow roadway users.

Motorcyclists Can Lack Experience and Skill Be alert when approaching a cyclist. Predict judgment and control errors due to inexperience and lack of skill. Some motorcyclists ride rented or borrowed cycles and might not have enough practice to develop sound judgment and good control. Others, who own their own motorcycles, might not have received proper riding instruction.

Handling Traits of Motorcycles
Help protect motorcyclists by being aware of the handling traits of motorcycles and how they operate.

Use the entire lane when passing a motorcyclist.

Motorcyclists lean when making turns. Watch a motorcyclist's shoulders to anticipate turns.

Notice in the picture that the motorcyclist leans to the side when making a turn. Control of a motorcycle is difficult in a turn or sharp curve. The cyclist can have even more difficulty handling the cycle in a strong wind, or if the roadway is rough or slippery.

Increase Your Following Distance

A motorcyclist's balance and stability depend on two small areas of tires that grip the roadway. Water, sand, oil, wet leaves, potholes, or loose gravel reduce traction and can make motorcycle control even more uncertain.

Watch for a motorcyclist's balance and stability problems. Predict that the cyclist might swerve or even fall. Give cyclists extra space by increasing your following distance.

Make the Motorcyclist Aware of You

When following a motorcyclist, do not assume the cyclist is aware of your presence. Traffic and wind noises make it more difficult for the cyclist to hear. Protective helmets worn by cyclists might also muffle some traffic sounds.

The small size of the mirrors on the handlebars and the vibration of the motorcycle can restrict the motorcyclist's view to the rear. Keep extra space in your front zone when you think a cyclist is unaware of your presence.

Review It

1. Why must drivers of other vehicles accept responsibility for protecting motorcyclists?
2. How can you use the IPDE Process to help protect motorcyclists while driving?
3. Where are five places you should look for motorcyclists while driving?

8.2 Motorcyclist Actions Can Affect You

Objectives

1. Explain the difference in acceleration and braking abilities between motorcycles and other vehicles.
2. Describe the protective equipment motorcyclists should wear.
3. Explain motorcyclists' special riding problems.

Although you share the responsibility for protecting motorcyclists, they have the primary responsibility for avoiding conflict. How motorcyclists ride, how they use protective equipment, and how they handle special problems affect all other roadway users.

How Motorcyclists Ride

Because motorcyclists share the roadways with others and present special problems, they should develop safe riding skills. All states offer motorcycle safety courses taught by instructors certified by the Motorcycle Safety Foundation. Proper training and widespread helmet use have helped reduce motorcycle fatalities. The student riders in the picture are practicing balance and turns in a motorcycle-riding course taught by a certified instructor.

With proper instruction and training—and an attitude of responsibility and caring—motorcyclists can become cooperative, low-risk users of the HTS.

Braking and Accelerating

A vehicle driver needs only to step on the foot brake to stop a vehicle. However, a motorcyclist must operate separate brakes for front and rear wheels. A lever on the right handlebar operates the front brake. This brake supplies most of the braking power for stopping. A foot pedal controls the rear brake. A cyclist must coordinate both foot and hand brakes carefully for maximum braking. If either brake is applied too hard it can lock and cause loss of control.

A motorcyclist must coordinate the hand throttle, hand clutch, and foot-gearshift lever to accelerate

Taking a certified training course can help motorcyclists reduce their risks.

What Do You Think?

Many states have passed laws requiring motorcyclists to wear helmets. Should wearing helmets be required by law in all states?

smoothly. Balance problems can occur if these actions are not coordinated.

Loss of Balance

Unlike four-wheel vehicles, a motorcycle might have difficulty remaining upright while in motion. Be alert and anticipate that the cyclist can lose control, especially if the roadway is wet or covered with oil drippings.

Following Distance

Motorcyclists should increase their following distance to reduce risk of collisions. Increased following distance also helps prevent cyclists from being hit by pebbles or dirt thrown back by the vehicle ahead. As a driver, check your rearview mirror often. Be aware of following motorcyclists, and avoid making sudden stops.

Identify the protective gear that this motorcyclist is wearing.

Use of Protective Equipment

Because other vehicles can severely injure motorcyclists in a collision, motorcyclists must make every effort to protect themselves. Cyclists can reduce or prevent injuries by using **protective equipment,** as has the rider in the picture.

A motorcyclist's protective equipment includes the following items:

- helmet—the headgear worn to reduce or prevent head injuries
- eye-protection—goggles or a face shield
- heavy shoes or boots
- full-length pants and jacket made of durable material
- full-fingered gloves

Helmets are required by law in most states and are important in saving lives. In a collision, a cyclist who does not wear a helmet is far more likely to suffer fatal neck and head injuries than a rider who does wear a helmet.

Special Riding Problems

Weather and roadway conditions present greater problems to cyclists than they do to drivers of other vehicles. Allow extra time and space for motorcyclists in all adverse weather conditions. When following motorcyclists who are crossing railroad tracks or carrying passengers, leave extra space.

Adverse Weather Conditions A motorcyclist cannot cope with adverse weather conditions as well as a driver in a four-wheel vehicle can. For example, a puddle might hide a pothole that jolts your vehicle.

That same hidden pothole can throw a motorcycle out of control.

Like drivers of other vehicles, the worst time for motorcyclists is immediately after it starts to rain. As rain mixes with dirt and oil on the roadway, traction is greatly reduced. Because balance is important for motorcycle control, reduced traction is far more critical to motorcyclists.

You can turn on your windshield wipers when it rains. When dirt from the roadway splashes up on the windshield, you can use windshield washers. A cyclist has neither device. Therefore, the motorcyclist's vision is greatly reduced and can be distorted under these conditions.

Motorcyclists should use extra caution when riding on or crossing painted lines on a wet roadway. Painted lines can become slippery when wet. Motorcyclists gain extra traction on wet roads by riding in another vehicle's wheel track, as the picture shows.

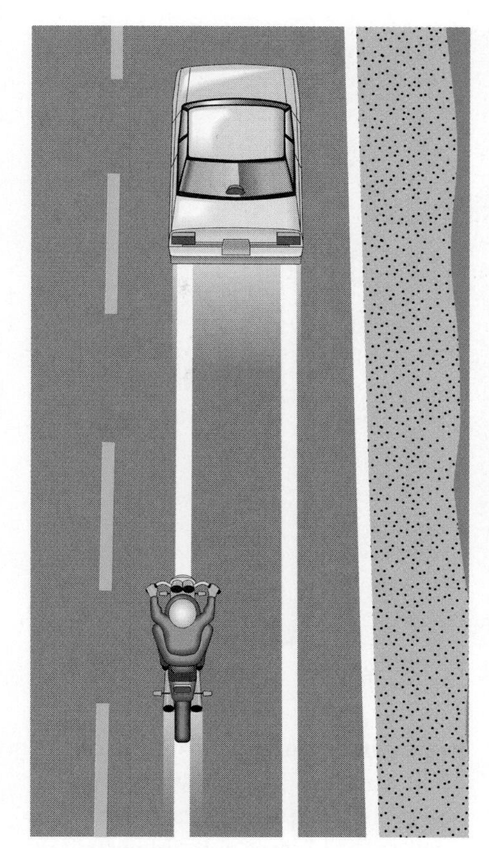

Motorcyclists can gain traction on wet roads by riding in another vehicle's wheel track.

Motorcyclist Crossing Railroad Tracks Railroad tracks are a special problem for motorcyclists. Motorcycle tires can get caught in the grooves of the crossing, causing the motorcyclist to lose balance. A cyclist should cross railroad tracks as close to a right angle as possible, as long as this does not cause the cyclist to enter another lane.

Motorcyclists Carrying Passengers A motorcycle carrying two people requires extra caution from other vehicle drivers. Be alert for a difference in acceleration, braking, and turning when a motorcyclist is carrying a passenger. A passenger can create balance and control problems for the cyclist by leaning the wrong way in curves and turns.

How Motorcyclists Can Help Other Vehicle Drivers

Motorcyclists should use all their skills and techniques to reduce their risks of conflicts. However, nothing the cyclist does should diminish the caution other drivers must practice near motorcyclists. Remember, you must always be ready to yield to cyclists.

By riding offset, motorcyclists are more easily seen.

Riding in Groups Motorcyclists often travel in groups. When you see one cyclist, be prepared to see others. Cyclists should not ride side by side in traffic. They should be in an offset position, as the picture shows. By riding offset, each cyclist is more easily seen by others and has more space to swerve safely, if necessary.

Like you, motorcyclists should prepare for turns by moving into the correct lane well before the turn. If they are riding in groups, they should be in single file as they approach, enter, and complete the turn.

Being Visible in Traffic Motorcyclists should position themselves in traffic so other roadway users can easily see them. Riding in lane position 2 usually makes a motorcyclist more visible. A rider in the correct position is visible to the driver ahead as well as to oncoming drivers.

Riding in lane position 2 also forces other drivers to use the other full lane to pass. This position adds a degree of safety to the passing maneuver. It also reduces the chance that the cyclist will be forced off the roadway.

Motorcyclists should not ride between lanes of moving vehicles. This practice is dangerous for everyone. In many states it is illegal.

Riding at Night It is far more difficult for drivers of other vehicles to judge the speed and position of a motorcycle at night. Because a motorcycle's taillight is relatively small, drivers behind may have difficulty seeing it.

Motorcyclists should take added precautions when riding at night. They can make themselves more visible by putting reflective tape on helmets and clothing and by having reflectors on the motorcycle.

Review It

1. How do a motorcycle's braking and acceleration differ from those of other vehicles?
2. What protective equipment should a motorcyclist use?
3. What special riding problems can affect a motorcyclist's control?

8.3

Bicycles, Mopeds, and Motor Scooters

Bicycles and low-powered, two-wheel vehicles continue to be popular for transportation, recreation, and business. Bicycles use no gasoline, create no pollution, and provide exercise for the rider. Because of their small sizes, mopeds and motor scooters create very little pollution and provide an economic means of transportation.

Users of smaller two-wheel vehicles have the same privileges and responsibilities as other drivers. Riders of these vehicles should use the IPDE Process and develop a visual search pattern to help themselves be more aware of possible conflicts with other roadway users. However, drivers of larger vehicles, with their greater protection, must accept the major responsibility for avoiding conflict.

Just as you have a major responsibility for protecting motorcyclists, you should be even more cautious and aware of these smaller vehicles because they are so unprotected.

Bicyclists' Responsibilities

Bicyclists must share the responsibility for avoiding conflicts with other roadway users.

Be a responsible bicyclist by following these safe-riding practices:

- Wear a helmet for protection.
- Know and follow the laws regarding roadway riding, lane position, and sidewalk riding.
- Obey all signs, signals, and laws.
- Wear light-colored clothing and have lights and reflectors on bicycles when riding at night.
- Do not wear earphones while bicycling. Wearing earphones while bicycling or driving a motor vehicle is illegal in many states.
- Keep bicycles in safe operating condition.

When riding at night use a headlight that is visible for at least 500 feet. Reflective tape on the frame and fenders of your bicycle, as well as on your helmet, adds safety for night riding.

Protecting Bicyclists

As a driver of a larger vehicle, give bicyclists extra space whenever possible. Some bicyclists might not be able to control their bicycles well. When following a bicyclist, be aware of the possible path the bicyclist might take. Vehicle doors opening, railroad tracks, storm drains, potholes, puddles, and other roadway hazards may cause a bicyclist to swerve into your path.

Use the IPDE Process constantly as you encounter bicyclists. Scan wide enough to include the sides of the roadways as well as sidewalks. Try to build into your visual search pattern a special awareness of bicyclists and where they might be. Allow more time and space for bicyclists to change their intended path of travel.

Preventing Conflicts with Bicyclists
Passing bicyclists on a two-lane

Objectives

1. Tell how you can help protect bicyclists from conflict.
2. List the guidelines that moped and motor scooter drivers should follow when riding.

BICYCLING ON WET ROADS Wet or slippery roadways can be especially dangerous for bicyclists. Hand-operated brakes on a bicycle do not operate effectively when the bicycle wheels are wet. Bicyclists should allow a greater stopping distance under these conditions.

roadway presents a problem for both drivers and riders. Consider the position of the cyclist in traffic when you plan to pass.

Start your passing maneuver well behind the bicyclist. You should have at least one-half lane between your vehicle and the bicyclist, as the picture shows. Be even farther away if the traffic lanes are narrow.

Use these techniques to further prevent conflicts with bicyclists:

To pass a bicyclist safely, move to lane position 2.

- Check rear zones and signal early when you plan to slow or stop.
- Help others identify a bicyclist by adjusting your position. At night, use low-beam headlights or a flick of high-beam headlights so that others can see the cyclist.
- Reduce speed and increase space when you are unsure of a bicyclist's control.
- Look for bicyclists before opening the street-side door of your vehicle.

Large tricycles have become popular in many communities, especially in retirement areas. Even though these tricycles are larger than most bicycles and are more readily visible, they can present a hazard. Be alert for and protective of riders of these large tricycles when they are a part of your traffic environment.

Mopeds and Motor Scooters

A **moped** is a two-wheeled vehicle that can be driven with either a motor or pedal. Its name comes from *mo*tor-driven bicycle and *ped*al-driven bicycle. Like a bicycle, a moped can be pedaled and can be stopped with a hand brake. Like a motorcycle, a moped is powered by an engine and controlled by a hand throttle.

A **motor scooter** is also a low-powered two-wheeled vehicle. It is more powerful than a moped. A motor scooter is similar to a motorcycle, though most motor scooters require no shifting.

Moped and Motor Scooter Restrictions Most states require moped and motor scooter operators to have an operator's license. Mopeds and motor scooters are restricted from certain high-speed roadways. Both the speed and the acceleration of mopeds are limited. Because they do not accelerate to traffic speed as quickly as a motorcycle or other vehicles, they may be unable to keep up with the traffic flow.

Responsibilities of Moped and Motor Scooter Drivers Even though these vehicles are smaller than motorcycles, their drivers also can benefit from taking a rider-training course.

In addition to observing laws and local requirements, moped and motor scooter drivers should follow these guidelines:

- Wear protective clothing. At night, wear clothing that has reflective tape on it, as the picture shows.
- Have the headlight on at all times.
- Position the vehicle in the lane so it can be seen by others.
- Keep a space cushion between themselves and other vehicles.
- Use extra care when riding on wet or slippery surfaces.

Reflective tape makes the motor scooter rider more visible to other drivers at night.

- Concentrate on the driving task and use the IPDE Process.

Drivers of other larger vehicles should predict possible sudden actions from drivers of mopeds and motor scooters. Be especially alert when driving near a moped or motor scooter.

Review It

1. In what ways can you help protect bicyclists?
2. What guidelines should drivers of mopeds and motor scooters follow?

8.4
Pedestrians and Special Vehicles

Objectives

1. Explain why you should use extra caution and care to protect pedestrians.
2. List areas where you can expect to see pedestrians.
3. Explain procedures to follow to clear the way for emergency vehicles.

Of all highway users, pedestrians are the most vulnerable. Motorists have a strong moral and legal obligation to protect pedestrians in every situation.

Pedestrians

Many pedestrians who do not drive are not fully aware of traffic laws and signals. Children and older people are most at risk. Children are less visible to drivers and often lack the judgment to know when it is safe to cross streets. Older people may not hear or see well and may be unaware of possible conflicts.

Other adult pedestrians may just get careless. They are drivers of vehicles and fully understand traffic laws. However, when they are in a hurry or are trying to escape bad weather, they may take chances and forget the risks involved.

Communicate with pedestrians so they will know you are there. A tap on the horn or a wave of your hand can give the message that you are there. Use the IPDE Process continually and always be ready to yield to pedestrians.

Learn where you can expect to see pedestrians and be extra alert when approaching the following areas.

Alleys and Driveways Approaching a sidewalk from an alley can be risky if a pedestrian or a bicyclist suddenly appears. The driver in the picture should expect movement from either side when approaching the sidewalk.

Make two stops when driving from an alley. First, stop before the sidewalk and look both ways for pedestrians and bicyclists. Tap your horn as a warning. Second, be pre-

Be especially alert for pedestrians as you drive out of an alley or driveway because buildings can obstruct your view. Be prepared to stop.

pared to stop again as you look for traffic just before you enter the street.

Business Districts Many collisions involving pedestrians occur at intersections and crosswalks in business districts where there is often a high volume of traffic. Many pedestrians assume that drivers will yield the right-of-way to anyone in the crosswalk. Drivers, however, are often looking at traffic signals and other vehicles and may not see the pedestrian in time to avoid a conflict.

Rain and snow often cause pedestrians to be more concerned about protection from weather than protection from traffic. Be extra alert under these conditions. It is often difficult to identify pedestrians at night and during adverse weather conditions.

Residential Areas Many residential streets are used by children as play areas, as the picture shows.

Regardless of the legal aspect of children playing in the street, it is the driver's responsibility and obligation to make the utmost effort to prevent conflict. Search for pedestrians coming from between parked vehicles on residential streets.

Jogging Areas Although joggers are safer using a sidewalk or a jogging path, expect to see them on streets and in traffic lanes. Joggers should yield to moving traffic—but do not expect this to happen. Always be ready to slow, steer around, or stop for joggers.

Watch for children playing on the street.

The Driver as a Pedestrian

As soon as you step out of your vehicle, you are a pedestrian. You no longer have the protective shield of your vehicle. Because you understand traffic rules and laws, you should be a responsible pedestrian.

Exercise special care at night. Wear something white or carry a light, particularly in rural areas. Try to be where drivers expect to see you. Do not walk into traffic lanes from between parked vehicles.

Regardless of the behaviors practiced by some pedestrians, you should always demonstrate an

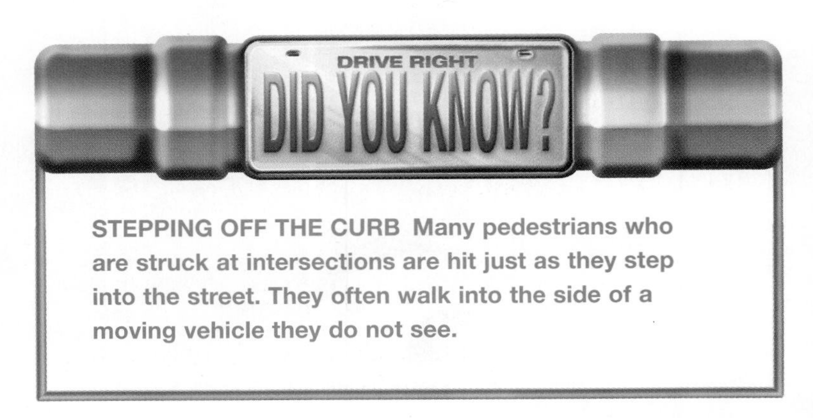

STEPPING OFF THE CURB Many pedestrians who are struck at intersections are hit just as they step into the street. They often walk into the side of a moving vehicle they do not see.

attitude of responsibility in your driving. Remember how destructive a large vehicle can be to these less-protected users. Exercise special care whenever pedestrians are around.

Parking Lots

Parking lots present a high-risk area for drivers, riders, and pedestrians. Like many residential streets, parking lots sometimes are used as recreational areas. Even though drivers are traveling at low speeds, a bicyclist or a skateboarder can cause conflict. Many property damage collisions and injuries occur in parking lots, even at very slow speeds. As a pedestrian in parking lots, you should look for brake lights and backup lights on parked vehicles.

Follow these guidelines to lower your risk when driving in parking lots:

- Obey parking-lot speed limits.
- Follow the routes for traffic flow. Do not drive diagonally across parking-lot lines.
- Be alert for pedestrians, bicyclists, roller-bladers, and skateboarders.
- Avoid tight parking spaces. Try to avoid parking in end spaces.
- Drive far enough into the space so the front or rear of your vehicle will not extend into the path of moving traffic.
- Position your vehicle properly in the parking space.
- Secure the vehicle properly.
- Continually scan in all directions when backing out of a parking space. If vision is blocked by a large vehicle, tap the horn before you back out.
- Watch for others who may back out toward you and may not see your vehicle. The drivers in the picture nearly collided because they were not aware that the other driver was backing out.

Special-Purpose Vehicles

Besides sharing the roadway with cyclists and pedestrians, you must also share it with an increasing number of special-purpose vehicles. Some special-purpose vehicles can be expected at different times of the

Be alert for parking spaces designated for "Handicapped Parking Only." Do not park in these spaces.

Be alert when leaving a parking space.

Allow extra space to increase your sight distance, and use caution when passing.

year. For example, snow plows can be expected in winter months in cold climates. In rural areas large, slow-moving farm machinery should be expected. When mobile homes are being transported, they often are preceded and followed by vehicles that carry a "Wide Load" sign. Use extra caution when meeting or passing such vehicles.

A **recreational vehicle** is a type of vehicle used mainly for pleasure and travel. Some of the more common types of recreational vehicles are vans, motor homes, campers, travel trailers, pickup trucks, and sports utility vehicles. Because of their size, some of these vehicles can decrease your sight distance or completely block your view. Allow these larger vehicles extra space in traffic and increase your following distance.

Buses

Local buses and school buses are the two most common types of buses you will encounter. Laws governing school buses are more strict than those governing local buses. School buses usually stop for students right in the lane of traffic. Most states require traffic going in both directions on a two-way street to stop when a school bus stops to load or unload passengers. A school bus has flashing red lights and, in some states, a STOP sign that swings out from the side of the bus. Some buses have flashing yellow lights before the flashing red lights begin. Do not proceed until all the lights stop flashing, the STOP sign is withdrawn, and the bus begins to move.

Most states do not require traffic from either direction to stop for local buses. When stopping to discharge or pick up passengers, local buses usually pull in toward the curb out of the lane of traffic. However, just because a stop is not required for local buses, it is your responsibility to keep alert for pedestrians near the bus who might cause a conflict.

Yield to emergency vehicles at all times.

Use the following guidelines to protect pedestrians near buses:

- Expect to see school buses more frequently in mornings and afternoons during school opening and closing times.
- Identify school buses by their yellow color, and then be prepared for stops. Expect some local buses to be used as school buses. Although you are not required to stop for local buses, exercise caution when you approach them.
- Expect pedestrians hurrying to catch a bus to be unaware of your presence. Communicate with horn and eye contact.
- Search areas around stopped or parked vehicles that might hide pedestrians.
- Give buses extra space. When passing a stopped bus, be sure no pedestrian who is blocked from view will enter your path.
- Reduce speed and cover the brake, if needed, to give yourself more time to respond.

Emergency Vehicles

Always yield to emergency vehicles with sirens and flashing lights—regardless of the direction the vehicle is traveling. When you see the lights or hear the siren, pull over to the right as far as possible. Stop if there is space and it is safe to do so. The drivers in the picture have pulled off the roadway and stopped.

If you are in heavy traffic, move in the direction other drivers are moving. Leave as much space for the emergency vehicle as possible.

Some drivers become careless about their response to emergency vehicles. They fail to pull over or stop. Not only are they putting themselves and the emergency vehicle at risk, but they may be harming others who are waiting for the emergency vehicle.

Review It

1. Why should you use extra caution for pedestrians?
2. In what areas should you expect to see pedestrians?
3. What steps should you follow to clear the way for an emergency vehicle?

8.5

Sharing the Road with Trucks

Trucks help transport nearly everything we eat, wear, and use in our daily lives. They are an essential part of our national economy.

Types of Trucks

The three main classifications of trucks are light, medium, and heavy. Most trucks are light or medium and are the types you commonly see as service trucks, pickup trucks, and delivery trucks. Heavy trucks include dump trucks and tractor trailers.

Tractor Trailers

A truck that has a powerful tractor that pulls a separate trailer is called a **tractor trailer.** The tractor is the front part that includes the engine and the cab. The most common size tractor trailer is the **tractor-semitrailer.** This is a tractor that pulls one trailer and is commonly called an "eighteen wheeler." Next in size is the double trailer, two trailers pulled by a tractor. The largest trucks, triple trailers, consist of three trailers pulled by a tractor.

Even though most truck drivers practice a high degree of safe-driving behavior, be aware that there are times when drivers suffer from fatigue or loss of sleep. Drivers often face the problem of tight scheduling and drive over long periods of time.

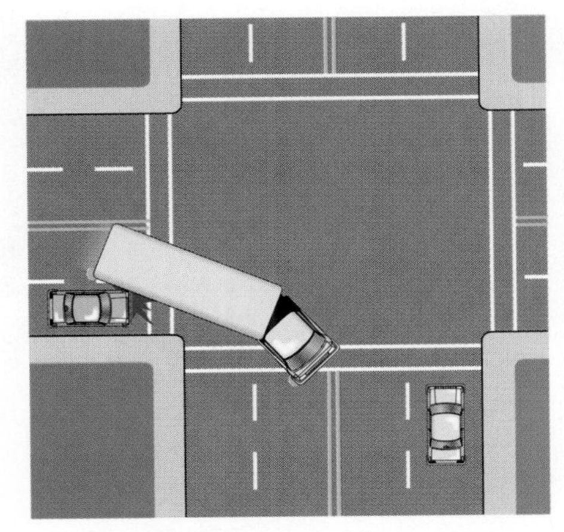

To avoid conflict, keep out of the open space to the right of a tractor-semitrailer making a right turn.

Large Trucks Making Right Turns

Many drivers following a tractor-semitrailer assume that if the truck moves to the left it is preparing to make a left turn. However, drivers of large trucks usually swing out to the left as the first step in making a *right* turn. If you begin to pass on the right at that time, you could be caught in the "right-turn squeeze," as the picture shows. Always check a truck's turn signals before you start to pass.

Following Large Trucks

Drivers of large trucks sit high above the road and have an excellent view of the roadway ahead. However, their view to the sides and rear is often restricted by the size of their rig.

Large trucks often create visibility problems for other drivers. When you follow a large truck, the truck causes a line-of-sight restriction.

There are large blind spots in front, to the sides, and to the rear

Objectives

1. Define "no-zones" around large trucks.
2. Explain precautions to take when following large trucks.
3. List guidelines to follow when passing large trucks.

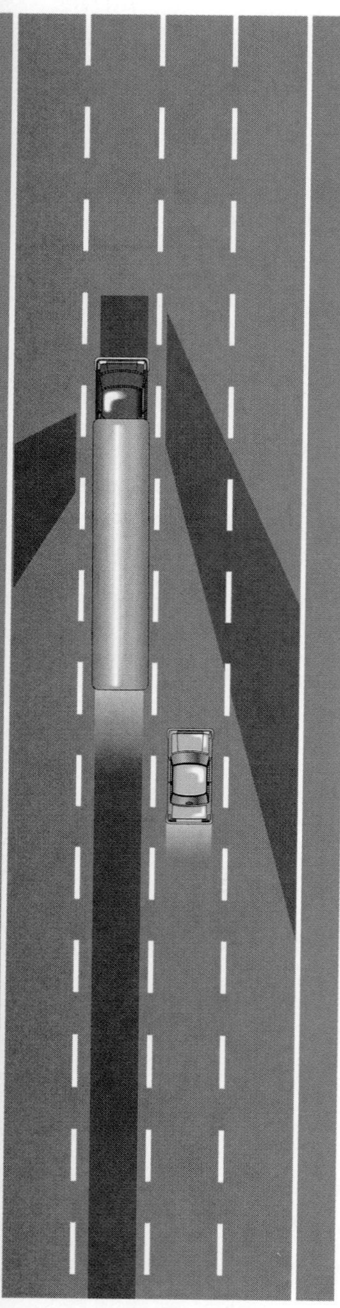

Stay out of the No-Zones where truck drivers cannot see you.

of every large truck. These blind-spot areas, called **no-zones,** are where truck drivers cannot see other vehicles and where most collisions occur. The picture at left shows these no-zones.

When drivers travel in a truck's no-zones, they put themselves at a high degree of risk because they cannot be seen by the truck driver. When you are following a large truck, increase your following distance to allow clear sight distance ahead. Stay far enough back so you can see the sideview mirrors of the truck. If you can't see one of the driver's sideview mirrors, then the driver can't see you.

Passing Large Trucks

Whenever possible, plan to pass a large truck when the driver shifts gears to gain speed. Passing is more easily done when you leave a STOP sign or a traffic light. Do not begin to pass until you are both clear of the intersection.

Use the following guidelines when passing large trucks:

- Check front and rear zones, signal a lane change, and change lanes smoothly.
- Stay in lane position 2 during the passing maneuver, and complete your pass as quickly as possible.
- After you can see both headlights in your rearview mirror, signal, check over your right shoulder, and return to the right lane. CAUTION: *In many trucks, the front no-zone can extend over 20 feet. Be sure you are well beyond that distance before you return to the right lane.*
- Do not slow during or after completing the pass. Maintain your highway speed.

Passing a large truck during rain or snow increases your level of risk. Both traction and visibility are reduced. When passing under such conditions, flash your headlights so the truck driver will know you are passing.

Meeting Large Trucks

You do not have much room when meeting large trucks on narrow two-lane highways. When you meet a large truck, move to lane position 3. Look well ahead and drive in a straight line. Try to choose a meeting point where the shoulder offers an escape path. Hold the steering wheel firmly because you might encounter a wind gust as you meet the larger vehicle.

Review It

1. Where are the no-zones?
2. What precautions should you take when following a large truck?
3. How should you pass large trucks?

Chapter 8

Review

Reviewing Chapter Objectives

1. Sharing the Roadway with Motorcyclists

1. Why do drivers have responsibility for protecting motorcyclists? (150)
2. How would you use the IPDE Process to protect motorcyclists while driving? (150)
3. In what situations should you look for motorcyclists while driving? (150–152)

2. Motorcyclist Actions Can Affect You

4. What is the difference in acceleration and braking abilities between motorcycles and other vehicles? (155)
5. What protective equipment should motorcyclists wear? (156)
6. What are motorcyclists' riding problems? (156–157)

3. Bicycles, Mopeds, and Motor Scooters

7. How can you help protect bicyclists? (160)
8. What guidelines should moped and motor scooter drivers follow when riding? (161)

4. Pedestrians and Special Vehicles

9. Why should you use extra caution and care to protect pedestrians? (162)
10. In what areas will you see pedestrians? (162–163)
11. What procedures should you follow to clear the way for emergency vehicles? (166)

5. Sharing the Road with Trucks

12. What are the "no-zones" around large trucks? (167–168)
13. What precautions should you take when following large trucks? (167–168)
14. What guidelines should you follow when passing large trucks? (168)

Projects

Individuals

Investigate Research driving rules or laws in your state as they pertain to motorcyclists. Make a list of rules or laws that motorcyclists must follow that are not required of other drivers.

Interview Interview someone you know who drives a truck for a living. Ask the person how driving a truck is different from driving a car. Write a report based on your conversation. (If you don't know anyone who drives a truck, interview a person who drives a motorcycle. Ask how driving a motorcycle is different from driving a car.)

Observe Traffic Observe the traffic for fifteen minutes at a busy intersection in your area. Make a record of the different types of vehicles you see (including cars, trucks, bicycles, motorcycles, etc.) Compare your results with those of your classmates.

Groups

Debate Break your group into two and discuss the pros and cons of having two-wheeled vehicles (such as motorcycles, mopeds, and motor scooters) share the roadways with other vehicles.

Use Technology Make a group video about bicycle safety. Share the video with your class.

Chapter 8

Review

Chapter Test

Check Your Knowledge

Multiple Choice Copy the number of each sentence below on a sheet of paper. Choose the letter of the answer that best completes the statement or answers the question.

1. Why do car drivers have responsibility for avoiding collisions with motorcyclists?
(a) Cars need less stopping distance.
(b) Motorcycles maneuver more easily.
(c) Car drivers have more protection.
(d) Motorcyclists have less experience.

2. Which of the following is NOT a safe practice for bicyclists?
(a) wearing a helmet
(b) obeying signs, signals, and traffic laws
(c) having reflectors on bicycles
(d) listening to music with headphones while bicycling

3. When meeting a truck on a two-lane road,
(a) flash your headlights.
(b) pull off the road and stop.
(c) move to lane position 3 and drive straight ahead.
(d) move to lane position 1 and slow down.

Completion Copy the number of each sentence below. After each number, write the word or words that complete the sentence correctly.

4. To reduce risk of collision, motorcyclists should increase their _____ .

5. Users of mopeds have limited speed and _____.

6. Many collisions involving pedestrians occur at crosswalks and intersections in _____.

Review Vocabulary

Copy the number of each definition in list A. Match the definition in list A with the term it defines in list B.

List A

7. two-wheeled vehicle that can be driven either with a motor or pedal

8. large blind-spot areas where truck drivers cannot see other vehicles

9. items a motorcyclist wears to protect head, eyes, and body

10. truck that has a powerful tractor that pulls a separate trailer

11. large vehicle used for pleasure and travel

12. type of tractor trailer commonly called an "eighteen wheeler"

List B

a. no-zones
b. tractor trailer
c. moped
d. recreational vehicle
e. protective equipment
f. tractor-semitrailer

Think Critically

Write a paragraph to answer each question.

1. Why is it important for drivers of four-wheel vehicles to use the IPDE Process when encountering two-wheel vehicles?

2. Discuss the different ways in which rain and snow affect pedestrians and motorcyclists.

Decision Making

1. What is the car driver's responsibility in avoiding a collision? How could the car driver have avoided this possible conflict?

2. What is wrong with the motorcyclists' position in the traffic lane? Why is this position hazardous? What is the correct position for the cyclists in the traffic lane?

3. What should the car driver do to clear the way for the emergency vehicle?

4. If you were the driver of the car following this truck, what error would you be making? What procedure should you follow when driving behind a large truck?

NISSAN
SUZUKI
1KHC607

Unit 3

Driving in Different Environments and Situations

California
SAN FRANCISCO CITY TOURS

CHAPTER 9
Driving in Urban Traffic

You Are the Driver!

Welcome to San Francisco, one of the great international cities of the world. When you drive in this and other cities, you will encounter a wide range of vehicles and numerous pedestrians. In addition, you will have to manage your vehicle in new, unfamiliar, and crowded situations. How will the driver of the red car in this picture have to adjust to zone and line-of-sight changes in this situation?

This chapter will show you how to use the IPDE Process in urban areas. You also will learn how to handle special driving situations so that you can become a low-risk driver in any city.

For: Chapter 9 online activities
Visit: PHSchool.com
Web Code: cak-9999

9.1 Adjusting to Urban Traffic

Objectives

1. Name two factors that can make driving difficult in city traffic.
2. Describe how to use the IPDE Process for city driving.

Once you are comfortable making basic maneuvers and using the IPDE Process, you will be ready to start driving in city traffic. City driving will test your best abilities.

Traffic Complexity

When you drive on a little-used rural road in good weather at a moderate speed, you probably will encounter few critical hazards. However, driving in heavy, fast-moving, city traffic is different and more challenging.

Two main factors make city driving difficult:

- Traffic is more dense in urban areas than it is in rural areas. There are more cars, buses, trucks, and pedestrians per mile.
- City traffic hazards are closer to you than they are in rural areas. Those hazards can quickly block your path.

In rural driving situations, the number of hazards per mile is low; you usually have an adequate "space cushion." You have time to adjust to the traffic scene. However, in city driving you may have to respond to several close hazards and possible conflicts at the same time.

Number of Hazards Mile for mile, city roads have the highest number and variety of hazards. Compare the two pictures of the same location on this page. Which situation is harder to handle. Why?

Time, Distance, and Speed As you drive, remember it takes time to use the IPDE Process. You will have to contend with many situations with closed zones and line-of-sight restrictions. If you cannot increase the distance between your vehicle and a hazard, you must change your lane position, slow, or stop to give yourself time to solve the conflict.

Using the IPDE Process

Heavy urban traffic will test your driving skills. Focus your attention on driving to avoid conflicts and distractions. You might see other

The number of urban hazards can vary dramatically.

You need to slow when your left- and right-front zones are closed.

drivers using cellular phones. You also will see aggressive drivers who needlessly increase the risk in a situation by challenging other drivers. Some extremely angry or thoughtless drivers will actually charge at others as though they are in a rage. In "road rage" situations, be cool and drop back. Give the angry, distracted, or absent-minded driver distance. You can control these situations by avoiding them.

Study the picture above and think about how you would apply the IPDE Process. As you drive, focus on the IPDE Process in these ways:

- **Identify** Be vigorous in using your visual skills. "Aim high" and look well ahead to your target area. Check your searching ranges to make sure your front zone is open and you have time to spot things like a line-of-sight restriction.
- **Predict** Predict possible points of conflict quickly and gain valuable time to respond.
- **Decide** Always be ready to communicate or adjust your vehicle position by changing speed and/or using distance effectively.
- **Execute** Be ready to use your vehicle's controls to make smooth low-risk maneuvers in traffic.

Review It

1. What two factors can make city driving difficult?
2. How can you best use the IPDE Process in city driving?

Studies have shown that using a cellular phone while driving can increase the risk of collision. Drivers should not split their attention between driving and other attention-intensive activities.

9.2 Following and Meeting Traffic

Objectives

1. Describe how to use the 3-second following-distance rule.
2. Describe how you can safely manage a tailgater.
3. List the steps to take to avoid conflicts with oncoming traffic.

You need to maintain an ample space cushion between your vehicle and possible hazards in all driving environments. Managing the space cushion, or distance, between your vehicle and the vehicle ahead is the first step.

Following Others

An adequate following distance has these advantages:

- You can see further ahead to get the "big picture."
- Others can see you better.
- You have more time to use the IPDE Process.
- You are in a better position to avoid the car ahead if it stops suddenly.

3-Second Following Distance

A 3-second following distance provides a safe space cushion from the vehicle ahead in most normal driving situations. Use these steps to measure your 3-second following distance.

1. Pick a fixed checkpoint on the road ahead. Road marks or shadows make good fixed checkpoints.
2. When the vehicle ahead of you passes your checkpoint, count: "one-thousand-one, one-thousand-two, one-thousand-three," for your 3-second count.
3. Now, check to see that your vehicle is still short of your fixed checkpoint. If not, slow and add more distance.

Check your following distance frequently. Imagine you are driving the car in the picture below. Do you have a 3-second following distance?

This 3-second technique works well at all speeds for measuring a normal following distance. As your speed increases, so does the distance your vehicle travels during your 3-second count. Thus, when you count off 3 seconds, your following distance will increase at higher speeds.

This 3-second distance is not the total stopping distance you need to avoid hitting a stationary object. A 3-second following distance only protects you from colliding with the vehicle you are following.

Increase your following distance to more than 3 seconds under adverse conditions, or if you need more time to complete the IPDE Process. Maintain extra distance in these situations:

To determine a 3-second following distance, start counting as the rear of the car ahead passes your fixed checkpoint (bridge shadow).

- You are just learning to drive. Your ability to use the IPDE Process is not yet fully developed.
- A tailgating driver has closed your rear zone.
- You are approaching a line-of-sight restriction.
- Traction is low.
- You are carrying a heavy load or pulling a trailer.
- The driver ahead seems unsure.
- You are following a motorcycle.

Looking Beyond the Vehicle Ahead

The 3-second rule is only one technique to use when following other vehicles. Also look over, through, and around the vehicle you are following. You can even see the reflection of brake lights on wet pavement by looking under the vehicle ahead. Be alert for brake lights, including high-mount brake lights, as shown in the picture on this page. Always try to anticipate what the driver ahead is likely to do in response to a changing zone condition.

Areas for Sudden Stops

Be alert in areas where sudden stops can occur. Three high-risk areas where closed zones and sudden stops can happen are

- intersections where drivers may have to stop for traffic or pedestrians
- lanes next to parked vehicles
- business driveways with high-volume traffic

When to Look Away

Imagine driving in an unfamiliar area while also looking for an address. If you are looking away from the road and the driver ahead stops suddenly, you may collide. Take these steps to prevent making this mistake:

- Make sure the zone ahead is stable and open. If you are following another vehicle, increase your following

distance to more than three seconds.
- Lower your speed even further when you have line-of-sight restrictions.
- Keep your eyes moving; take split-second glances rather than one long look.
- If you have a passenger, ask that person to look for an address.

Being Followed

You are in a high-risk closed rear zone situation when someone **tailgates,** or follows too closely. You can take several steps to lower the risk in this type of situation.

Tailgaters Are Hazards

A tailgater is a hazard because if you have to stop fast, the tailgating driver can hit you from the rear. Tailgating drivers often think they can save time or make other drivers go faster. Neither is true.

Managing Tailgaters If you are being tailgated, take these actions to avoid being hit from the rear:

- Increase your following distance to at least four seconds. Imagine you are driving the yellow car in the picture above. You have identified the tailgating driver and determined your rear zone is closed. By using a following distance of at least four seconds, you have increased your space cushion from the vehicle ahead. If you must slow or stop, you can do it more slowly and give the tailgater more time to respond.
- Move slightly to the right. Look at both pictures on this page. How have the drivers being tailgated helped the tailgating driver to see better?
- Signal early for turns, stops, and lane changes. Flash your brake lights ahead of time to warn a tailgater that you plan to slow or stop. Slow sooner to make a gradual stop.

The yellow car driver has added tailgater protection by using a following distance longer than three seconds.

The driver ahead has moved slightly to the right to allow the tailgater to see traffic farther ahead.

- In extreme situations, change lanes, or pull out of traffic to avoid the tailgater. To reduce stress and risk, your best defense is to avoid tailgaters.

You Are the Driver!
If you were driving a car approaching this intersection, what would you predict the driver of the blue car might do?

Responding to Oncoming Traffic

If a driver closes your front zone by crossing the center line, you must react instantly. Knowing how to predict and respond to this type of situation ahead of time may give you enough time to avoid a collision.

Reasons for Crossing the Center Line

A driver might cross into your path of travel for these reasons:

- **Driver impairment** A driver might be drowsy, distracted, confused, intoxicated, or ill.
- **Poor judgment** A driver might misjudge speed, distance, or position.
- **Poor visibility** Direct sunlight, blinding headlights, or bad weather can reduce a driver's ability to see.
- **Reduced space** A snowbank, narrow bridge, or an object in or near the road might force a driver across the center line.
- **Sudden moves by others** Children, bicycles, pedestrians, animals, or a vehicle door opening can force a driver to make a last-second move.
- **Vehicle failure** A driver might lose control of a vehicle due to mechanical failure.
- **Turning buses and trucks** Long vehicles need extra room just to make normal turns. Vehicles pulling trailers can create the same situation.
- **Double-Parked Vehicles** Drivers or delivery drivers may park carelessly and close your front zone.

Avoiding Conflicts

If a vehicle comes at you, take these actions to avoid a collision:

- Slow until the other driver can return to the normal lane. You can also slow so that you meet the other driver at a point where there is room to pass.
- Turn on or flash your headlights and blow your horn.
- If your right-front zone is open, move to the right to give the oncoming driver more room. Swerve sharply to an open space on the right if needed.

Review It

1. How many seconds should you use for a normal following distance?
2. What can you do to manage a tailgater safely?
3. How can you avoid a conflict with an oncoming vehicle in your lane?

9.3 Managing Space in Urban Traffic

Objectives

1. Describe how far ahead you should look in city traffic.
2. Tell how to cover the brake.
3. Explain how to select the proper lane for driving.

When driving in urban traffic, you must respond to a wide variety of situations. Unfamiliar streets, line-of-sight restrictions, small zones created by narrow lanes, and high-density traffic all make your driving task difficult. To manage these situations, you will need to use your best skills combined with a positive, heads-up, alert attitude.

Looking Ahead While Staying Back

How far ahead should you look to make sure you are aiming high enough while driving in the city? In addition to looking around your vehicle, look a block or more ahead. By looking far ahead to your target area to protect your path of travel, you will be able to spot zone problems in time to adjust your speed and/or position as needed.

Imagine you are the driver following the truck in these pictures. Maintain a safe following distance of three seconds or more to have a good view of the road ahead. By doing so, you can identify and predict possible points of conflict. You also will be able to better manage the distance between your vehicle and the truck ahead.

Approaching Traffic Signals

Look at your target area to detect traffic signals. By doing so, you will have more time to respond.

If the light is red, slow and be ready to stop. If the signals on your street are synchronized to work together, you should be able to drive at or near the speed limit for several blocks as lights turn green.

If the light is green when you first see it, predict it will change

The truck creates a line-of-sight restriction ahead because you are tailgating.

View of road ahead with 3 or more seconds of following distance.

The flashing DON'T WALK signal is a warning that your green signal is about to turn yellow.

soon. A traffic light that has been green and will soon turn yellow is called a stale green light. Watch for a DON'T WALK pedestrian signal that has started to flash like the one in the top picture on this page. This signal warns you that the light is about to turn yellow. If the signal is flashing, you must decide if you have time to drive through the intersection safely before the light turns yellow. Your decision will depend on your distance to the intersection and your speed.

Never speed up to get through a green light before it changes. At any speed, you will reach a point-of-no-return, or a point where you must start braking if you are going to stop before the intersection. If you were the driver in the bottom picture, could you stop before the light turns red? How might a tailgater force you into a collision?

Covering the Brake

You can maintain a normal speed if you are driving into a stable, hazard-free traffic situation. But, if you are driving into a scene like the one shown on the top of page 184, you might have to stop quickly. To get

In this changing zone situation, you need to check your speed, distance, and other traffic when deciding whether to stop.

Be ready for doors to open at the last second.

ready to stop, you need to **cover the brake.** Take your foot off the accelerator, and hold it over the brake pedal. You can use this technique whenever you sense a possible conflict. This could cut your reaction time and help you avoid a collision.

When you cover your brake, make sure not to rest your foot on the brake pedal, or **ride the brake.** When you do so, your brakes heat up and wear faster. In addition, your brake lights stay on, confusing drivers behind you. Only flash your brake lights to warn drivers behind you when you know you are going to slow or stop.

Take these actions to identify and respond to the risk of parked vehicles:

- Cover your brake and move left in your lane to lane position 2.
- Look for drivers through the windows of parked vehicles.
- Be alert for the parked vehicles' brake lights, exhaust, or wheels turned out.
- Lightly tap your horn if needed.
- Be ready to stop or swerve. Swerve only if your left-front zone is open.

While driving past parked vehicles, watch for doors that might

Adjust your speed early as you enter a town after driving on a highway.

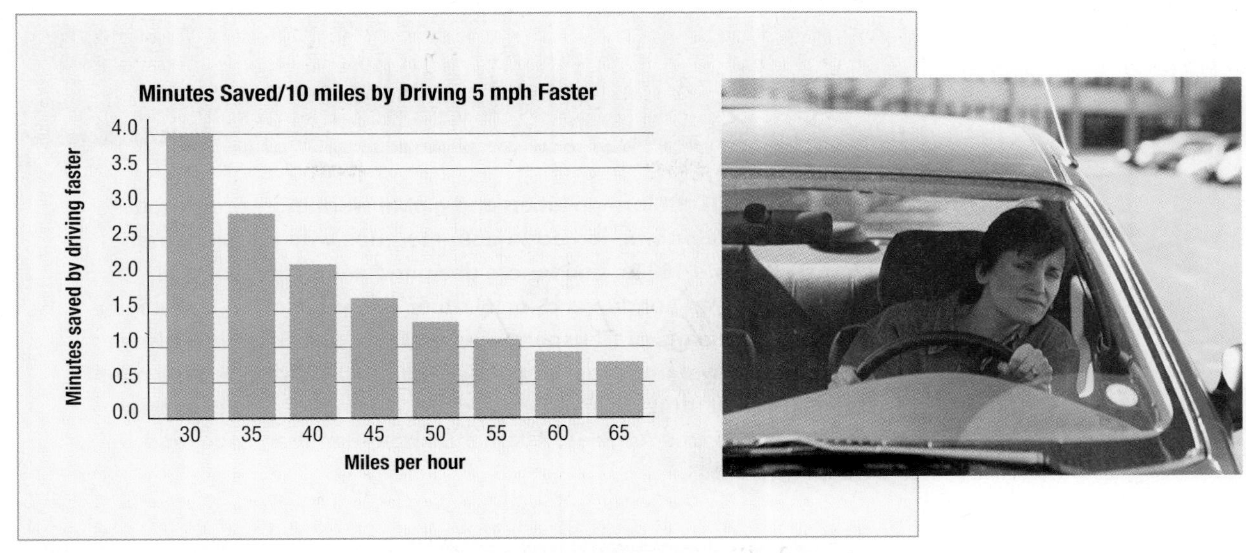

Look at the graph to see how much time you save by driving 5 mph faster for 10 miles. Is driving faster worth it?

open unexpectedly, as shown in the top picture on left page. Try to drive at least one car door's width away from parked vehicles. Otherwise, reduce speed.

Adjusting Speed

Imagine that you have been driving for an hour on a highway. You are just entering the town shown in the bottom picture on left page. The speed limit is 25 mph. However, traffic conditions should tell you to adjust your speed, and drive even slower.

Blending into traffic is one of the most common city driving skills you will need. Use these techniques to select your best driving speed:

- Drive with the traffic flow.
- Stay within the speed limit.
- Adjust speed and position ahead of time for other drivers who might block your way.

Look at the graph and driver pictured on this page. If you are as hurried as this driver, remember this: You only save a few seconds by driving even 5 mph faster. And, the time savings are less and less at higher speeds.

Selecting the Best Lane

When driving in multilane traffic, you will use different lanes at different times. Select the lane or zone with the fewest number of hazards.

The left lane is usually for faster traffic. But at times, traffic can be held up by drivers waiting to turn left. These left-turning drivers can be a problem when only two lanes are going in your direction.

If your street has multiple lanes going your way, choose the lane where the traffic flow is smoothest. Imagine driving the yellow car in the picture on the next page. Why is the center lane the best for drivers going straight?

DRIVE RIGHT DID YOU KNOW?

MASS TRANSIT Before pollution and global warming were serious concerns, London was forced to come to grips with crippling traffic jams. In the late 1800s, Londoners designed and built a subway system. Today in London and many other European cities, subways are the best means of transportation. In the United States, subways and light-rail systems are expanding. Thousands of people who might drive or ride at street level now travel by these rail systems in New York, Chicago, Los Angeles, Atlanta, Boston, San Francisco, and Washington, D.C.

Lane Positioning Use these techniques to position your vehicle in multilane city traffic:

- Increase your following distance to more than three seconds in heavy traffic.
- Adjust your speed and lane position as needed to stay out of other drivers' blind-spot areas.
- Move to another lane if your front zone closes.

Through traffic should use the center lane to avoid slowdowns or stops.

Changing Lanes

Once you start driving in a lane, try to stay in that lane. If you must change lanes, follow these steps:

1. Use your mirrors to check traffic in your rear zones.
2. Signal your lane change early.
3. Quickly check your blind-spot area.
4. Change lanes without slowing.
5. Cancel your signal.

Repeat this procedure if you need to change more than one lane.

Overtaking and Passing

At times, you might decide to **overtake,** or pass, a vehicle ahead. To overtake another vehicle, use the lane-changing procedure and drive

Carpooling saves time and fuel. It also reduces traffic and parking problems.

past the slower moving vehicle. Signal briefly and return to your lane when both headlights of the vehicle you have passed appear in your inside rearview mirror. You will learn more about the procedures for passing in Chapter 10.

Passing in a city can be dangerous. You must be alert for pedestrians, cross traffic, signals, and an endless number of line-of-sight restrictions.

If you must overtake another moving vehicle on a two-lane two-way street, make sure you can do so safely and legally. It is illegal to pass at intersections or over double-yellow center lines.

Special Traffic Lanes

To help move rush-hour travel, many cities now have special lanes for bus and/or carpool drivers. Drivers who travel alone must use the regular, more crowded, slower lanes. By using these special lanes, people, as shown in the picture above, ride together to save time and fuel, and to reduce pollution and parking problems.

Review It

1. How far ahead should you look in city traffic?
2. How do you cover your brake?
3. How do you select the best lane on a multilane street?

9.4 Special Urban Situations

Objectives

1. Describe the procedure for turning left or right from a one-way street.
2. Explain how to warn a driver who is driving the wrong way on a street.

You will encounter a wide range of situations in city driving. By using the IPDE Process, you will be ready to adjust to each situation ahead of time.

Driving on Two-Way Streets

Most city roadways are two-way streets with one lane going in each direction. Other streets have two or more lanes going in the same direction.

Many city intersections do not have traffic controls. You cannot be sure what other drivers will do as you approach an uncontrolled or blind intersection.

Some intersections have special left-turn lanes. If you turn left at an uncontrolled intersection, you must yield to oncoming traffic.

Driving on One-Way Streets

One-way streets can move a greater volume of traffic with fewer conflicts than two-way streets. Generally, one-way streets are less congested than two-way streets, so fewer conflicts occur.

Identifying One-Way Streets

When you come to an unfamiliar street, first determine if it is a one-way street. These clues can help you identify a one-way street:

- ONE WAY signs are posted on most one-way streets.
- All moving traffic and parked vehicles point in the same direction.
- Broken white lines are used to separate lanes.
- Most traffic signs will be facing the same direction. If you are driving on a street and the signs are facing the other way, you probably are going the wrong way on a one-way street.

Entering One-Way Streets

Imagine you are driving the yellow car in the top picture on the opposite page. To enter the one-way street, turn from the right lane to the nearest right lane.

To make a left turn onto a one-way street, position your vehicle in the nearest left lane. Make a sharp

You Are the Driver!
Imagine you are approaching this intersection. What clues identify this as a one-way street?

left turn into the nearest lane going left. Signs are used to alert you when your street is about to become a one-way street.

Lane Choice on One-Way Streets

If you plan to drive on a one-way street for a distance, try to avoid a lane that is next to parked vehicles. A parked vehicle could pull out and close your front zone. Each parked vehicle creates a line-of-sight restriction. If a center lane is available, use it to reduce possible conflicts.

When you plan to turn, position your vehicle ahead of time. Move into the right or left lane at least one block before your turn.

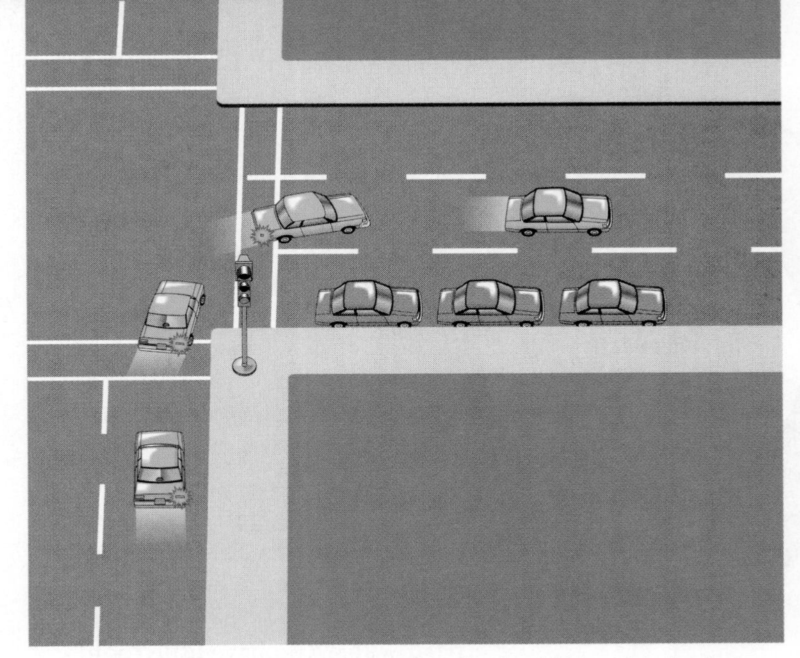

To turn right onto a one-way street, turn from the far right lane into the first available right lane.

Leaving One-Way Streets

Imagine you are driving the yellow car in the picture on the right. To turn left from your one-way street, position your vehicle in the far left lane ahead of time. To turn right, position your vehicle in the far right lane ahead of time. Complete your turn by entering the nearest lane going your way.

On some one-way streets, the outside lane may be for turns only. On other one-way streets, you can turn into a multilane street from more than one lane. Road markings or overhead signs will direct you.

You will need to adjust when a one-way street turns into a two-way street. Your left lane might end. Signs or lights will warn you when a one-way street is about to change to a two-way street.

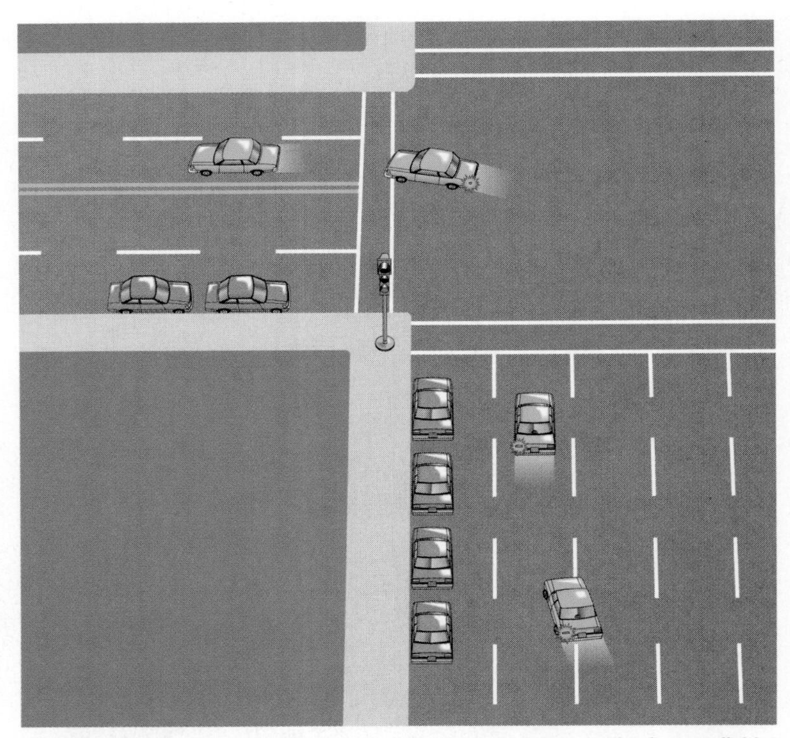

To turn left from a one-way street, turn from the far left lane to the first available lane going left.

What Do You Think?

High-speed city traffic and residential neighborhoods don't mix—especially when small children are involved. How can traffic be controlled in these settings?

Signaling Wrong-Way Drivers

If you encounter a vehicle headed the wrong way on a one-way street, slow, steer right, and sound your horn. If you have time, flash your headlights to warn the other driver.

Unexpected Situations on Crowded Streets

Imagine you are driving in the situation pictured below on the left. A vehicle suddenly emerges from an alley and is about to enter your path of travel. The street is so narrow that you have little room to maneuver.

Slow and cover your brake to maintain a safe path of travel. If necessary, let traffic clear before you move ahead.

When driving on city streets, you should maintain a continuous orderly visual search pattern. Even though drivers may have a green light, they are required to stop for a pedestrian as this driver in the right picture has done.

You might not be able to see a pedestrian in front of a vehicle that is stopped at a green light.

Angle or parallel parking is allowed on most streets. If you must drive close to parked vehicles, be alert for possible conflicts. At the first hint of movement from a vehicle or pedestrian, slow, stop, or move to another lane.

If you cannot move left, be prepared to stop.

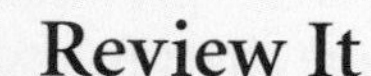

Review It

1. What lanes should you use when making a right or left turn from a one-way street?
2. What can you do if another driver approaches you from the wrong direction on a one-way street?

Chapter 9

Review

Reviewing Chapter Objectives

1. Adjusting to Urban Traffic

1. What are the two main factors that make driving difficult in the city? (176)
2. How do you use the IPDE Process for city driving? (177)

2. Following and Meeting Traffic

3. How do you use the 3-second following-distance rule? (178)
4. How can you safely manage a tailgater? (180)
5. What steps should you take to avoid conflicts with oncoming traffic? (181)

3. Managing Space in Urban Traffic

6. How far ahead should you look when driving in city traffic? (182)
7. What should you avoid doing when covering the brake? (184)
8. How do you select the proper lane for driving on a multilane street? (186)

4. Special Urban Situations

9. What is the procedure for turning left or right from a one-way street? (188–189)
10. How can you warn a driver who is driving the wrong way on a one-way street? (189–190)

Projects

Individuals

Investigate Research local newspapers to find articles about accidents that have been caused by drivers running red lights. Are some intersections mentioned more often than others? Compare your results with those of your classmates.

Observe Traffic As a passenger in a vehicle, look for signs of "road rage" in drivers of other vehicles. Also look for signs of distracted or absent-minded drivers. Make a list of the actions you observe. Discuss your findings with your class.

Groups

Investigate Research alternate transportation systems found in large cities. Each group member should research a different city and make a list of all the transportation systems available in that city. Note similarities and differences among the transportation systems listed. Prepare a group report that contains each group member's findings.

Use Technology Use the Internet to find street maps of large cities in the United States. Each group member should research a different city and observe whether there are more one-way streets or two-way streets in that city. Compare your findings with those of others in your group.

Chapter 9

Review

Chapter Test

Check Your Knowledge

Multiple Choice Copy the number of each sentence below on a sheet of paper. Choose the letter that best completes the statement or answers the question.

1. While driving in urban situations,
(a) keep your vehicle close to others.
(b) cover the brake pedal.
(c) be ready to reduce speed and change vehicle position.
(d) maintain the posted speed.

2. The 3-second following distance technique
(a) should be decreased in adverse conditions.
(b) is safe for most conditions.
(c) is the same as total stopping distance.
(d) is not safe at speeds over 40 mph.

3. You can avoid being hit by a tailgater if you
(a) increase your following distance to four seconds or more.
(b) move to the left side of your lane.
(c) look in the rearview mirror and warn the tailgater.
(d) keep steady pressure on the brake.

4. It is illegal to pass another vehicle
(a) over a broken lane marker.
(b) at an intersection.
(c) on a multilane street.
(d) on a one-way street.

Completion Copy the number of each sentence below. After each number, write the word or words that complete the sentence correctly.

5. To give yourself adequate time to react to a hazard, you should _____ your speed.

6. Urban streets and roads have the highest number of _____ per mile.

Review Vocabulary

Copy the number of each definition in List A. Match the definition in List A with the item it defines in List B.

List A

7. take your foot off the accelerator and hold it over the brake pedal to be ready to brake quickly
8. rest your foot on the brake
9. pass the car ahead
10. follow another vehicle too closely

List B

a. overtake
b. ride the brake
c. tailgate
d. cover the brake

Think Critically

Write a paragraph to answer each question.

1. Driving in urban traffic can be a challenge. What characteristics of urban traffic make driving more difficult than in other environments?

2. You are driving in the right-hand lane of a one-way street. You discover that you need to make a left-hand turn at the next light. What should you do?

3. What are some advantages of driving on one-way streets?

Review

1. How long should it take this car to pass by the speed limit sign?

2. You are following this truck. How can you improve your line-of-sight view ahead?

3. What clue do you have to indicate this is not a stale green light?

4. What can you do to alert this oncoming driver and avoid trouble?

CHAPTER 10
Driving in Rural Areas

10.1 Characteristics of Rural Traffic

10.2 Using Basic Skills in Rural Areas

10.3 Passing and Being Passed on Rural Roads

10.4 Rural Situations You Might Encounter

10.5 Special Driving Environments

You Are the Driver!

About 82 percent of all miles of roadways in the United States are rural roads. Rural roads can be two-lane or multilane. What problems might occur along this rural road? How does it differ from a city street? Will this vehicle most likely be traveling faster or slower than the posted speed limit? What action should you take as you approach this vehicle?

Even if you live in an urban area, you will likely drive in rural areas. This chapter discusses characteristics and problems you might encounter in rural and other environments. It explains how you can apply the IPDE Process to deal with various hazards.

Go Online
PHSchool.com
For: Chapter 10 online activities
Visit: PHSchool.com
Web Code: cak-9999

10.1

Characteristics of Rural Traffic

Objectives

1. Describe rural roadways.
2. Describe factors to consider when selecting a safe speed.
3. Identify traffic controls and how they help inform, warn, and regulate drivers on rural roads.

Wide open spaces and less traffic are common in rural areas. After driving for long periods of time, you might mistakenly assume that conflicts will not occur. However, collisions in rural areas account for nearly twice as many highway deaths as collisions in urban areas.

Roadways

Rural roads are constructed of many different types of materials. Some are paved and others not. Shoulders can be wide or narrow, paved or gravel. Road surfaces may be smooth or in very poor condition.

At night, the lack of adequate lighting causes difficulty in seeing. Be alert to potential changes that could arise. Conditions in rural areas can change suddenly with little warning.

Speed

Determining a safe speed is critical for safe rural driving. Speed affects

- your line of sight
- your stopping distance
- your vehicle control
- the amount of damage and injury in the event of a collision

Many rural roads have a speed limit of 55 mph. Some states allow speeds greater than 55 mph. Where conditions require, lower speeds are posted.

There is a difference between safe speeds and posted speeds. Posted speeds are the maximum speeds allowed under ideal conditions. When conditions are not ideal, safe speeds should be used. These are slower speeds. Factors that affect safe speed selection include other highway users, inclement weather, hills, curves, intersections and very nar-

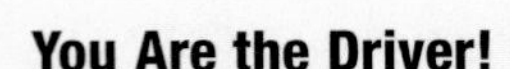

You Are the Driver!
How many traffic hazards can you identify in this picture?

Be prepared to stop as you near the crest of the hill.

row roads or lanes. *Always use your common sense and never drive faster than conditions permit.*

Traffic Controls

Traffic controls—signs, signals, and markings—direct, regulate, inform, and warn drivers. Traffic controls provide advance information and warning of

- hazards that you cannot yet identify
- major intersections ahead
- unusual or hazardous conditions (curves, animal crossings)
- traffic channeled into reduced space

Many warning signs use graphics to warn of a hazardous condition ahead. Note the sign shown above. The hill blocks your line of sight and view of the hazard.

Traffic controls can be complex, especially at intersections where rural highways cross. Identify them early and know their meanings so you can avoid conflicts.

Roadside Hazards

Consider the existing conditions in selecting a safe speed. Rural roads, especially older, narrow, and less traveled ones, present hazards.

Shoulders may be uneven with the edge of the roadway, soft, or narrow. Danger may be only a few feet away. Bridges, guardrails, bushes or trees may be near the road's edge. Sign posts may only be a few feet away from the actual roadway. A steep slope might run from the shoulder down to a drainage ditch.

Entrances to businesses, homes, or fields are always points of possible conflict. Be alert for these areas. Drivers ahead of you could decide at the last moment to turn right or left.

Trees, shrubs, or piles of plowed or drifted snow create line-of-sight restrictions. Drivers trying to enter the roadway may not be able to adequately see traffic. They may turn out into, or across, your path of travel.

What Do You Think?

Federal law no longer mandates a maximum speed limit. Do you think there should be a maximum national speed limit? Why or why not?

Review It

1. What roadway conditions are common to rural driving?
2. What factors need to be considered in selecting a safe speed?
3. What advance information do traffic controls provide?

10.2
Using Basic Skills in Rural Areas

Objectives

1. Explain how the IPDE Process should be used in rural driving.
2. Know the steps to safely handle a curve.
3. List rural situations that require increased following distance.
4. Explain how to enter a multilane rural highway.

A seemingly quiet rural traffic scene can change quickly with little or no warning. Risk is present whenever and wherever you drive, but you can manage the level of risk by applying the IPDE Process.

Applying the IPDE Process

Rural driving typically involves driving at higher speeds. The faster you drive, the greater your chance of having a severe collision. You have less time to identify and respond to a situation or hazard. You may be forced to make an emergency response. Sudden responses at higher speeds increase the risk of losing control of your vehicle.

While traveling on rural roads, there are many ways your zones can become closed. To best apply the IPDE Process, you must manage your speed control. The slower your speed, the more time you have to solve problems. One or two additional seconds can make a great difference in your ability to successfully apply the IPDE Process and manage space. Apply the IPDE Process whenever you drive.

Maintaining vehicle control at higher speeds is more difficult than at lower speeds. It takes longer to stop. Excessive braking or steering can result in a skid and loss of vehicle control.

Drive at a speed where you know you will be able to brake and steer your vehicle without losing control. Assess road conditions and the amount of traction available. Adjust your speed to conditions. Always

Where on this road might conflicts occur?

What do the signs indicate about the curve ahead?

drive at a speed that allows you to stop or swerve to avoid a collision.

Visual Search Pattern

Remember the orderly visual search pattern described in Chapter 4? Apply those same techniques in rural areas. In your 12–15 second search range look for clues of hazards that have the potential of closing your front zone. Higher rural speeds extend the actual distance covered by your 12–15 second search area compared to lower speeds.

Strive to maintain a 12–15 second visual lead. This is the distance your vehicle will travel in the next 12 to 15 seconds. The higher the speed, the greater that distance will be. Maintaining a 12–15 second visual lead will help you to identify hazards early. It also gives you time to predict and execute an appropriate response.

Driving on Two-Lane Roads

Knowing about some common, but important, characteristics of rural roads will help you handle them safely. Some of these characteristics include curves, warning and advisory signs, hills, and intersections.

Curves Rural roads typically have many curves. Collisions occur at curves because speed on the approach is too great. Before approaching a curve, you likely will notice a yellow warning sign that warns of a potential hazard (a curve) ahead. Warning signs are usually placed anywhere from 250 to 700 feet before the actual hazard. A warning sign for a curve has a curved black arrow on it. The sharper the curve of the arrow, the sharper the roadway curve ahead.

Curve warning signs often have **advisory speed signs** posted below

Driving and using a cellular phone or reading a map can be dangerous. Get out of traffic, stop, and then make the call or read the map.

What type of restriction do the shrubs create? Are there any other hazards?

them on the sign post. These indicate suggested travel speeds when conditions are ideal. Follow the recommended speeds, and when conditions are not ideal, use a slower speed. Natural forces work to push you to the outside of the curve when you travel at higher speeds.

When you approach a curve, follow these steps:

1. See the curve in your target area.
2. Check your rear zone.
3. Check your left-front zone for oncoming traffic.
4. Check your right-front zone to determine if it is open or closed to your line of sight and path of travel.
5. Stay in lane position 1.
6. If the curve is sharp, lightly apply your brakes before you turn the steering wheel.
7. As you get closer to the curve, look in the direction the road curves. See if your path of travel is going to be open.
8. Once you are beyond the midpoint of the curve, begin to accelerate gently if conditions permit.
9. Evaluate your new target area and search for zone changes.

Hills Unless they have very steep slopes, hills are usually not marked. Hills restrict your line of sight. Slow as you approach the crest of the hill. Take lane position 1 as you crest the hill. Look for oncoming traffic and an escape path to the right.

Intersections In Chapter 7 you learned about how to handle intersections. Follow the same procedures for rural intersections.

Rural intersections can vary a great deal. Some intersections may have traffic lights; others may just have STOP signs. Early identification of traffic controls will help you predict potential conflicts.

A typical rural intersection is one where a side road crosses a main road. The side road will usually have the STOP sign. Tall crops, trees, or shrubs create line-of-sight restrictions that can block the vision of drivers at the edge of, or across from, an intersection.

Treat driveways like intersections. Look well in advance for clues of driveways, such as:

- loose gravel projecting into the main road
- electrical, phone, and other utility lines crossing the road
- reflectors marking a driveway
- mailboxes, typically located at the edge of, or across from, a driveway

Following Traffic

Establishing and maintaining at least a 3-second following distance is very important in rural areas. At high speeds, a hazard can quickly develop into a conflict. A 3-second following distance provides you space and time to prevent conflicts under normal conditions.

In special situations, you should increase your following distance to four seconds or more. A longer following distance gives you more control when you are

- being tailgated
- driving on a steep downhill slope
- following a motorcycle
- following a snowplow
- pulling a loaded trailer
- following a large vehicle (truck, motorhome, or bus)
- driving on wet or icy roads

Keeping at least three seconds gives you an open front zone. This helps to give you control over the actions of other drivers. When other drivers do dangerous things, it is less likely to affect you if you are following at a distance of three seconds or more.

Driving on Multilane Roads

Many rural roads have four or more lanes of traffic. Posted speed limits usually are higher on two-lane rural roads. Unlike interstate highways, multilane roads may have intersections rather than exit and entrance ramps. Some intersections may have a two-lane road crossing a large four-lane road; others may involve two major multilane roads that cross.

Multilane Roadways with Center Lines Some multilane roadways may only have a yellow line (dashed or solid) separating high-speed traffic moving in opposite directions. Drivers should never cross a solid yellow line or double yellow lines except to make a left turn or clear an obstacle blocking their lane. Whenever you cross a yellow line, you are responsible to do so safely.

You Are the Driver!
You are driving behind this car. Is your following distance adequate?

Divided Roadways Divided roads always have lanes of traffic moving in opposite directions separated in some way. The division may be simply a guardrail or a **median.** A median is an area of ground separating traffic that moves in opposite directions. A median can be a few inches to several feet wide, as seen here.

If you need to cross a multilane highway, cross each half of the multilane road as though it were a one-way street. If a large enough crossover area exists, move into it after you cross the first lanes of traffic. Stop, look for a large enough gap. You will be turning into the fastest lane of traffic, so you may need to look for a gap of six seconds or greater.

Lane Choice Whenever possible, drive in the right lane on a multilane highway, unless signs indicate otherwise. The left lane is usually for passing or preparing to turn left.

Turning at an Intersection When leaving a multilane roadway, turn right from the right lane. When making a left turn, turn from the lane nearest the center line or median strip.

Some intersections may have special turn lanes for right and left turns. To turn, check your rearview mirrors for any possible conflicts in your rear zone. Signal your intention to turn at least five seconds before the actual turn because speeds are much higher on rural multilane roads.

Signaling well in advance gives traffic behind a chance to adjust speed and position to avoid any conflicts. If turning left, keep your wheels straight until you start your turn. If you are hit from behind, you will not be pushed into oncoming traffic.

If you see a vehicle approaching at a high speed from behind, forget your turn, accelerate quickly, and proceed straight ahead across the intersection to avoid being hit from behind. To do this safely, you must be aware of the conditions in the intersection.

Entering a Multilane Road Follow these procedures if you are on a side

A median strip safely separates high-speed traffic that moves in opposite directions.

To make a left turn from a side road onto a multilane highway, a median strip provides a safe place to wait for a gap.

road and wish to enter a multilane roadway:

- To turn right, check to the left and right of where your target area is located. Make sure the left, front and right zones will be open. Enter the nearest right lane as you turn. Steer toward your target and accelerate quickly to the prevailing speed. Change lanes only after you clear the intersection and reach the prevailing speed.
- Left turns require larger gaps than right turns. First, cross the lanes on your side of the roadway. Choose a time when no traffic is approaching in the lane just across from the center line. Then turn into the nearest lane. Accelerate more quickly to the prevailing speed than you would for a right turn.

Entering the roadway from a driveway presents problems similar to entering from a side road. Oncoming drivers may not see you due to a line-of-sight restriction. Though drivers on multilane roadways may have advance warning signs of intersections ahead, there rarely are such signs for driveways.

Review It

1. How should you apply the IPDE Process when driving on rural roads?
2. What steps should you take to safely handle a curve?
3. List five situations that require more than a 3-second following distance.
4. What is the procedure for entering a multilane rural highway?

10.3

Passing and Being Passed on Rural Roads

Objectives

1. List the checks to make before passing another vehicle.
2. List the steps for passing on a two-lane rural road.
3. List situations where passing should never be attempted.

Passing on a two-lane road carries a higher level of risk than passing on a multilane road. When you pass on a two-lane rural road, you will be in the same lane as oncoming traffic for a short period of time. Use parts of the IPDE Process to help lower your risk when passing.

Passing

Passing another vehicle is really a three-stage procedure. You decide to pass, prepare to pass, and execute the maneuver.

Deciding to Pass

Before you pass a vehicle, assess your situation. Ask yourself these questions:

- Is it worth it to pass?
- Is it legal to pass?
- Is it safe to pass?

Consider passing only if you can answer "yes" to all of these questions. The major responsibility for passing safely belongs to the driver who is passing.

Preparing to Pass

Take these actions when preparing to pass:

- When you find your front zone closing to less than three seconds, identify the reasons. Is the vehicle ahead going slower than the posted speed limit? Is it likely to be making a turn? If so, hold back and eliminate passing. If conditions indicate you should pass, continue the steps in preparing to pass.
- Check roadway markings and signs ahead. Make certain that passing is legal.
- Look ahead to your target area. Is your line of sight adequate? You may have to move to lane position 2 to get the best view ahead. Is it safe to pass?
- Check the roadway conditions. If traction is limited, you probably should not pass. If you must pass under poor conditions, you will need to accelerate gently and gradually while passing.
- Check the roadway shoulders and sides ahead that might cause the vehicle you are passing to swerve to the left.
- Check your rearview mirrors for any potential conflicts to your rear zone. If a vehicle is rapidly closing in behind you, delay your pass.
- Glance quickly over your left shoulder. Make sure there are no vehicles in your blind spot.
- Check the oncoming traffic lane again. Make sure no vehicles are approaching and there is enough space for you to pass safely. Any approaching vehicles must be at least 20–30 seconds away. You will need 10–15 seconds to complete the pass. *If in doubt, do not pass.*
- Check ahead for driveways and side roads. Make sure no traffic will be entering the roadway.

Although some states allow passing drivers to exceed the speed limit, it is safer to pass within the posted speed limit.

After you have determined that your left-front zone (the path to be taken) is clear, you are ready to pass. If you identify a problem, slow down and establish at least a 3-second following distance. Repeat the steps to prepare to pass again. In time these steps will become part of your normal driving behavior.

Executing a Pass on Two-Lane Roads

Follow these steps when passing on a two-lane road:

1. Get in your ready position by keeping at least 3 seconds of following distance.
2. When it is safe to pass, signal for a left-lane change and glance over your left shoulder to check your blindspot.
3. Change lanes smoothly.
4. Accelerate at least 10 mph faster than the vehicle you are passing. *All passing should be done within the speed limit.*
5. Make your final evaluations. If you notice a problem that is within 20–30 seconds ahead, you can still change your mind—provided you have not gone beyond the vehicle you are trying to pass. If it is clear, continue to accelerate to the proper speed.
6. Maintain your speed. Remain in the left lane until you can see two headlights of the vehicle you are passing in your inside rearview mirror.
7. Signal for a right-lane change.
8. Return smoothly to the right lane. Do not slow down.

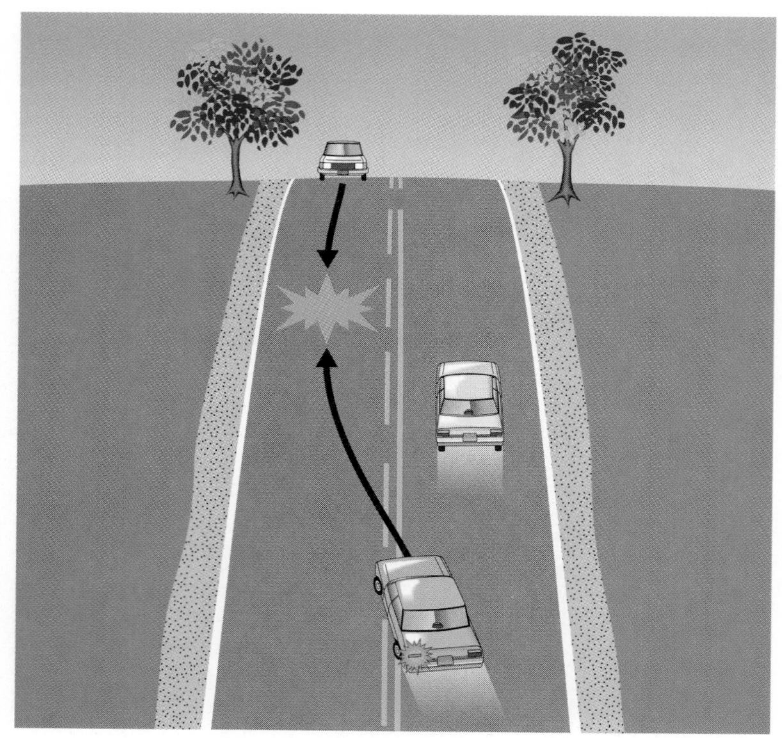

The solid yellow line means that drivers in the right lane must not pass. They would be unable to see vehicles coming over the hill.

Passing at or near an intersection is dangerous. A driver turning from the crossroad might enter your lane.

9. Cancel the signal. Adjust your speed and vehicle's lane position.

If you are passing a large truck, you will need more time and space. It is a good idea to make sure that you have at least 30 seconds of clear space when passing a large truck.

No-Passing Situations

No-passing situations are marked by solid yellow lines, as shown in the pictures. Signs can also mark no passing zones. Rectangular white signs on the right side of the road will indicate DO NOT PASS; yellow pennant-shaped signs are on the left side of the road and indicate NO PASSING ZONE. Passing is illegal and unsafe when

- your line of sight is restricted
- space is narrow, and your front zones are closed
- cross-traffic is present, even if no warning signs or lines are present

How do these conditions apply to the following situations?

No Passing on Roads Going Uphill Passing is not allowed within 700 to 1,000 feet before the top of a hill. Notice that the driver of the yellow car in the top picture has too great a restricted line of sight to pass safely.

No Passing at Intersections Passing is illegal within 100 feet of an intersection. Slow down when approaching an intersection.

Other No-Passing Situations There are other situations where passing is prohibited or should not be attempted. Examples include:

- Within 100 feet before a railroad crossing.

- On a two-lane bridge or underpass.
- On curves, where your line of sight is so restricted you can not see around the curve.
- When the vehicle ahead is traveling at or near the speed limit. Remember, *most passing should not require a driver to exceed the posted speed limit.*
- When your line of sight is limited by fog, snow, or rain.
- When several vehicles are ahead of you, pass only one vehicle at a time.
- When you cannot complete a pass before the start of a no passing zone
- Any time oncoming traffic is too close.
- When you will be stopping or turning soon.

Do not pass on bridges and near underpasses, since they might not have shoulders to provide escape areas.

Passing on Multilane Roads

You need to be cautious on a multilane highway with only a center line to separate traffic. Check all lanes going in your direction before you pass on a multilane roadway. Make sure that no one will move into your front zones taking away your path of travel. The vehicle you intend to pass should be going several miles per hour slower than you.

Generally, all passing should be done in the left lane. Passing on the right is often illegal. Sometimes, it becomes necessary to use the right lane to pass a vehicle. Remember the procedures for passing and follow them every time you pass.

Passing is illegal in both lanes around this curve.

Glance regularly into your mirror to see if a car is about to pass you.

Being Passed

If you are the passing driver, you have the majority of the responsibility for passing safely. However, you also have responsibilities when being passed.

You must be aware that another vehicle is passing, even when the driver of the vehicle fails to properly warn you. Check your mirrors often to identify vehicles approaching from the rear.

When another vehicle passes, it may help to move to lane position 3. By doing so, you provide an extra space cushion and provide the passing driver with a better view ahead.

If the passing driver is having a difficult time trying to pass, slow down to help that driver. *Intentionally speeding up while being passed is illegal.* Only speed up when the driver has decided not to pass and drops back. This will quickly open a space behind you.

Review It

1. What are the checks you should make when preparing to pass?
2. What are the steps for passing on a two-lane rural road?
3. In what situations should you never pass?

10.4 Rural Situations You Might Encounter

In rural areas you may encounter vehicles, animals, and situations that you do not encounter on city streets. Apply the same driving techniques in rural areas as you would in urban areas. For example, in a rural area you would respond to a tractor pulling a plow the same way you would a large truck or bus in the city. Applying the IPDE Process whenever you drive will maximize your ability to more easily recognize conflicts and solve problems.

Slow-Moving Vehicles

A **slow-moving vehicle** is one that is unable to travel at highway speed. Most tractors and other large farm machinery can only travel at lower speeds. They are not designed, nor intended, as means for personal transportation.

Identify slow-moving vehicles as early as possible. The sooner you do, the more time you have to respond. Apply the IPDE Process. Most slow-moving vehicles have an orange and red triangular sign like the one in the picture.

When driving at a higher speed, you will rapidly close in on a slow-moving vehicle. If you find yourself closing to less than three seconds, be aware that you may have a problem. Slow down and prepare to pass when it is safe to do so. Stay far enough behind and in a lane position that gives you the ability to check for oncoming traffic.

Animals

Animals can be a problem on rural roads. They can easily become frightened and dart out into your path. Each year millions of dollars in property damage occur when animals and motor vehicles collide.

Hitting a large animal can result in damage to your vehicle, and serious injury or death to you, your passengers, and the animal. In areas where large wild animals are common, reduce your speed and search

Objectives

1. Explain how to pass a slow-moving vehicle.
2. Explain the steps to take to deal with animals on or along the roadway.
3. Explain how you can allow hazards to separate when meeting traffic.

The vehicle has closed your front zone. Is it safe to pass in this situation?

You Are the Driver!
How should you handle this situation?

a much wider area than usual. If you see one animal, anticipate the presence of more.

You may see warning signs where large animals are common. If you see an animal warning sign, let it serve as a clue, and do the following:

- Evaluate your left- and right-front zones for line-of-sight restrictions from which animals could enter.
- Check your rear zone to determine if you will be able to slow or stop quickly.
- Check your left-front zone to see if it will be open for an escape path.

If you happen to observe one or more animals crossing the road, stop well in advance. Be patient and wait until it is clear to proceed. Do not get out and attempt to hurry any stragglers across the road. You are much safer in your vehicle.

When a smaller animal suddenly appears in your front zone, you may be tempted to brake hard or swerve. Follow the same procedures as above. Be careful not to risk a more serious collision by trying to avoid the animal.

Meeting Oncoming Traffic

Meeting traffic on two-way roads can be dangerous. Very little space separates you from oncoming traffic. With traffic moving at higher speeds, a head-on collision can cause serious damage, injury, or death.

If you identify an oncoming vehicle, check your right-front zone for an alternate path of travel and for line-of-sight restrictions. Try to adjust your timing to have the oncoming vehicle approach you when you have the least problem in your right-front zone.

Use these guidelines for selecting a place to meet oncoming traffic.

- Separate the hazards in or next to your path of travel. Adjust your speed to deal with only one hazard at a time. In most situations slowing down is your best action. Imagine the hazard is a narrow bridge as in the picture. You judge that you might meet the approaching vehicle just about the time you approach the hazard. By slowing down and letting the approaching vehicle clear the hazard first, you separate the hazards.

- Meet where the most space is available. When you must meet oncoming traffic, try to select a location where you have an open right-front zone to move into if you need to swerve to avoid conflict.
- If you are meeting a line of vehicles, slow down and move into lane position 3 to provide a little more space between you and the approaching vehicles.

Oncoming drivers may cross into your lane on rural roads for several reasons. Examples include:

- a blowout, hitting or swerving to avoid a pothole or other debris on the road
- an unexpected loss of traction due to ice, snow, rain, or mud
- a distraction
- an impairment due to alcohol, other drugs, or medications
- an impairment due to illness or fatigue
- a vehicle failure

ANIMAL COLLISIONS More than 4 percent of all collisions reported in the United States involve animals, and that percentage is rising. Most of these collisions occur with deer—about 500,000 a year. Collisions with animals are more likely to occur at dawn or dusk. Most of these collisions occur in October and November during the deer mating season.

Meeting Slow-Moving Vehicles

When you see a slow-moving vehicle or stopped vehicle in your left-front zone, check to the rear of the vehicle for a passing vehicle. The passing

Adjust your speed and position to allow the hazards to separate.

Not all railroad crossings have lights and gates.

driver may not see you. If you are applying the IPDE Process, you will check your right-front zone and move into lane position 3, or onto the road shoulder if necessary. Always know where you have an open zone into which you can move. If you do not have an open zone, brake enough to create space for yourself or the passing driver.

Meeting at Night

Be alert when driving at night. You need to be aware of vehicles in the distance. Keep your windshield clean.

At night, headlights shining over the crest of a hill can warn you of an approaching vehicle. If you have your high beams on, switch them to low beam anytime you are within 500 feet of an approaching vehicle. Do not look directly into the headlights of the approaching vehicle; you could be temporarily blinded, especially if their headlights are on high beam. Glance instead to the right edge of the road. There is often a white line to help you maintain position in your lane.

Railroad Crossings

Many railroad crossings do not have complete controls (flashing lights and gates). In rural areas, trains travel at high speeds. Be alert for railroad-crossing warning signs. Slow and check left and right before crossing. Never cross a railroad crossing until you know it is absolutely safe to do so. Remember, when a vehicle and a train collide, the *train always wins.*

Review It

1. Identify the steps in safely passing a slow-moving vehicle.
2. List the steps to take to deal with animals on or along the roadway.
3. Explain two examples of how you can allow hazards to separate when meeting traffic.

10.5
Special Driving Environments

Driving through mountains and deserts can challenge your patience, energy, and skills. Make certain your vehicle is in good working condition. Adhere to the speed limits and warning signs. Particularly be aware of your vehicle's gauges while driving.

Mountain Driving

Mountain driving presents more problems and special situations than driving in flatter areas. The effects of gravity are constantly at work. Gravity will make your vehicle go faster when going downhill, and slow your vehicle when going uphill.

Mountain roads often zigzag across a mountain with a series of sharp turns called **switchbacks.** A switchback bends sharply in the opposite direction. In the picture, the sign warns that a switchback is ahead.

Driving Up a Mountain

Accelerate steadily when driving uphill to maintain speed because gravity is pulling your vehicle downhill. If the slope is steep, you might need to downshift to a lower gear. An automatic transmission vehicle will downshift by itself. On extremely steep inclines, when extra power is needed, you may need to manually shift an automatic transmission vehicle into a lower gear (LOW 1 or LOW 2).

When you can't see around a curve, reduce your speed, move into lane position 1, and tap your horn. Evaluate your path of travel through the curve. An oncoming vehicle could cross into your lane because it has built up too much downhill speed before the curve. Driving too fast is a leading cause of collisions in the mountains.

Objectives

1. Describe special safety precautions for mountain driving.
2. Describe special safety precautions for desert driving.

At the switchback this road reverses direction.

Loaded trucks, recreational vehicles (RVs), and vehicles pulling trailers move more slowly up mountain roads. Follow these vehicles at their speeds and maintain at least a 4-second following distance. Some mountain roads have locations called **pull-out areas** where an additional right lane is provided for slower-moving vehicles. When slower-moving vehicles move into such areas, it allows faster-moving vehicles an opportunity to safely pass and proceed.

Driving Down a Mountain

When driving down a mountain road, downshift *before* you start traveling downhill. Never coast downhill because the vehicle will speed up and you might lose control.

Some mountain roads have areas along the side of the road for cars to safely pull over and stop.

Adjust your speed with an occasional use of the brakes. Do not ride your brakes, because doing so can overheat them and make them fade. If you are braking often, shift to a lower gear; your transmission can help slow you down and can reduce the need to brake as much. Finally, keep your speed low enough to maintain control and stay in your lane.

Large vehicles can experience serious brake problems going downhill, especially on long steep downgrades. Some mountain roadways have **runaway vehicle ramps,** as the picture on the next page shows. Runaway ramps provide a place for vehicles, especially large trucks, to safely get out of traffic and stop when their brakes are no longer effective.

Weather in the Mountains

Fog, snow, and ice can make mountain driving even more difficult. Some mountain roads become blocked with excessive snow. Weather conditions can suddenly change in the mountains. If weather conditions are poor, call the highway department or state police hotline. Tune your radio to frequencies that update travelers on weather and road conditions. These frequencies are often identified on blue driver-service signs along the side of the road.

Effects of Altitude on Drivers

High altitudes can affect the driver, causing shortness of breath, faster heartbeat, and headache. Lower amounts of oxygen at higher altitudes can reduce concentration and

You Are the Driver! How would this ramp help a runaway vehicle?

cause drowsiness. Effects can be worse for tired drivers. Do not drive if you feel these effects or are tired.

Effects of Altitude on Vehicles

The thin mountain air can affect your vehicle's engine. Climbing power is reduced. Acceleration can become sluggish. The temperature of the water in your radiator may increase significantly and could cause overheating. If your air conditioner is on, turn it off.

Check your gauges and warning lights often. If the temperature light comes on, safely pull over and stop to let the engine cool. Turning on your heater may help remove some of the heat built up in the engine.

Engines can get extremely hot when driving in mountains. When you shut off your engine, vapor lock occurs. The engine will not start because the fuel cannot be pumped in a gaseous state. Allow the engine to cool. Then try restarting it.

If you do a lot of mountain driving, have your vehicle serviced regularly for maximum performance.

Desert Driving

Deserts are often hotter and larger that most drivers realize. Desert driving is hard on the driver, the car, and the roadway. Always prepare yourself and your vehicle in advance.

Effects of Heat on Drivers

Intense daytime heat can cause great stress on you when driving long distances. The sameness of the scenery can lull you into a false sense of security. The glare from the intense sun can reduce your vision.

To help reduce the effects of hot desert driving, you should

- wear good quality sunglasses to help reduce the effects of sun glare
- plan more frequent stops and change drivers often
- carry an ample supply of water

Effects of Heat on Vehicles

Extensive desert driving requires more frequent vehicle service. Battery fluids should be checked daily if the battery is not self-contained. Radiator fluids should be checked at every fuel stop.

CAUTION: *Never remove a radiator cap from a hot radiator.* The steam and hot fluid could burn you. Check the fluid level in your radiator recovery tank. If you must check the level in the radiator, wait until your engine cools.

Check tire pressure regularly. Tire pressure will increase as you drive. Do not reduce the tire pres-

Visibility can be very limited in a sand storm.

sure below the lowest recommended pressure. A tire with low air pressure will run hotter, which could result in tire failure.

The Desert Roadway

Well-designed highways with gentle curves invite higher speeds. Be careful of the sandy roadside shoulders, because your wheels could sink quickly into the sand if it is not firm and compacted. If you need to pull over, make sure the location you select is firm and out of traffic.

Sandstorms and Dust Storms

Windy conditions in deserts often create visibility problems. Avoid driving in sandstorms or dust storms. If you encounter such a storm, slow immediately and find a safe place to pull over. Turn off your headlights and turn on your hazard flashers. Wait in your vehicle until the storm passes.

If you must drive, go slowly. Use your low-beam headlights to help see and be seen. As soon as possible after the storm, have your oil, and oil and air filters changed. Dirt particles from the storm that remain in your fuel injection system and engine oil can cause excessive engine wear and damage.

Flash Floods

A flash flood is a sudden unexpected rush of water from heavy rain. A flash flood can develop quickly and unexpectedly. This condition is especially dangerous in the desert because the ground washes away easily. If you encounter a flash flood, seek higher ground immediately and wait for the water to recede. Stay away from creeks or natural drainage areas.

Do not drive over water-covered roads or streams in the desert. The water may be deeper and running more swiftly than you think.

Review It

1. What safety precautions should you take for driving in mountains?
2. What safety precautions should you take for desert driving?

Chapter 10
Review

Reviewing Chapter Objectives

1. Characteristics of Rural Traffic

1. What are rural roadways like? (196)
2. What factors should you consider when selecting a safe speed? (196)
3. How do traffic controls inform, warn, and regulate drivers on rural roads? (196–197)

2. Using Basic Skills in Rural Areas

4. How should you use the IPDE Process in rural driving? (198)
5. What steps should you take to safely handle a curve? (200)
6. What are some rural situations that require increased following distance? (201)
7. How do you enter a multilane rural highway? (203)

3. Passing and Being Passed on Rural Roads

8. What checks do you make before passing another vehicle? (204)
9. What steps should you take when passing on a two-lane rural road? (205–206)
10. In what situations should you never attempt passing? (206–207)

4. Rural Situations You Might Encounter

11. How do you pass a slow-moving vehicle? (209)
12. What steps should you take to deal with animals on or along the roadway? (209–210)
13. How can you allow hazards to separate when meeting traffic? (210)

5. Special Driving Environments

14. What special safety precautions should you take for mountain driving? (213–214)
15. What special safety precautions should you take for desert driving? (215–216)

Projects

Individuals

Investigate Research to find out which states have a 55 mph speed limit and which do not. Also examine the number of traffic fatalities that occur each year in each state. Is there a correlation between speed limit and number of fatalities?

Use Technology Use the Internet to find out current conditions on mountain roads (either in your state or another state). Discuss with the class what precautions you would take if you were driving in those conditions.

Groups

Debate Divide your group into two and debate the issue of mandatory speed limits. One side should argue for keeping a 55 mph speed limit; the other side should argue for allowing speeds greater than 55 mph.

Demonstrate Make a group poster that illustrates the hazards or other situations you might encounter while driving on a rural road. Present the poster to your class. Group members should take turns explaining what each illustration means and what to do if the hazard or situation is encountered while driving.

Chapter 10

Review

Chapter Test

Check Your Knowledge

Multiple Choice Copy the number of each sentence below on a sheet of paper. Choose the letter that best completes the sentence or answers the question.

1. Posted speed signs indicate
   (a) the safest speeds possible in any conditions.
   (b) minimum speeds under ideal conditions.
   (c) maximum speeds under ideal conditions.
   (d) suggested speeds that legally may be exceeded.
2. Which of the following provides advance information and warning about approaching driving situations?
   (a) roadways (b) road shoulder conditions
   (c) posted speeds (d) traffic controls
3. What effect does increased speed have on the time available to complete the IPDE Process?
   (a) increases time available
   (b) decreases time available
   (c) varies with number of hazards present
   (d) no effect
4. Solid yellow lines indicate
   (a) no passing situations.
   (b) conditions are favorable for passing.
   (c) you must pass with caution.
   (d) hazards in the roadway.

Completion Copy the number of each sentence below. After each number, write the word or words that complete the sentence correctly.

5. _____ roadways have separated lanes of traffic moving in opposite directions.
6. The force that makes your vehicle go slower when driving uphill is called _____.
7. A _____ is a sudden unexpected rush of water from heavy rain.

Review Vocabulary

Copy the number of each definition in List A. Match the definition in List A with the term it defines in List B.

List A

8. place on mountain roads for vehicles to safely get out of traffic when their brakes are not effective
9. sign posts on a curve with suggested speeds for ideal conditions
10. additional right lane on mountain roads for slower moving vehicles
11. area of ground separating traffic moving in opposite directions
12. vehicle unable to travel at highway speed
13. turns that bend sharply in the opposite direction

List B

a. pull-out area
b. slow-moving vehicle
c. advisory speed signs
d. switchbacks
e. runaway vehicle ramp
f. median

Think Critically

Write a paragraph to answer each question.

1. Why do you think that rural collisions account for a majority of highway deaths?
2. What types of animals might you expect to see in areas with animal-warning signs? What should you do if you pass an animal-warning sign while you are driving?

Chapter 10

Review

1. What hazards do you see? Which zones are open? How would you respond to avoid the hazards?

2. You are driving the yellow car, and a car is attempting to pass you. What should you do to help the passing driver?

3. You are approaching a curve. What do you identify and predict? What actions should you take to safely handle the situation ahead?

4. You are driving the yellow car. What possible conflicts do you identify? What should you do?

CHAPTER 11
Driving on Expressways

You Are the Driver!

Imagine you are driving the sport utility vehicle on the entrance ramp to this expressway. The traffic on the expressway is heavy and is moving fast. The driver of the vehicle behind you may be in a hurry and is following you too closely. How can you communicate with that driver? What action should you take as you enter the acceleration lane?

In this chapter you will learn the necessary skills for entering, driving on, and exiting expressways. You will also learn strategies for low-risk expressway driving.

For: Chapter 11 online activities
Visit: PHSchool.com
Web Code: cak-9999

11.1 Characteristics of Expressway Driving

Objectives

1. List five reasons why expressways have lower collision rates than other highways.
2. Describe four different types of expressway interchanges.
3. List strategies for low-risk driving on expressways.

An expressway is a limited-access or **controlled-access highway.** Vehicles can enter and leave expressways only at interchanges. Expressways include interstate highways, freeways, turnpikes, toll roads, parkways, and some beltways. Most of these terms are used interchangeably and designate any type of controlled-access highway.

Advantages of Expressways

Expressways are designed for low-risk higher-speed travel. Despite the high speeds and heavy traffic, you are safer on expressways than on other highways.

Expressways have fewer collisions for five main reasons:

- Cross traffic is eliminated.
- Expressways have a median or barrier between opposing lanes of traffic.
- Pedestrians, nonmotorized vehicles, and slow-moving vehicles are not permitted on most expressways.
- Wide shoulders and extra-wide underpasses provide good escape paths.
- Expressway signs are designed to help drivers anticipate conditions well ahead.

Expressway Interchanges

These pictures show the most common types of expressway interchanges. Interchanges are places where drivers can cross over or under as well as enter or leave the expressway.

Cloverleaf Interchange

A cloverleaf interchange has a series of entrance and exit ramps that resemble the outline of a four-leaf clover. This type of interchange enables drivers to proceed in either direction on either highway.

Diamond Interchange

A diamond interchange is used when a road that has little traffic crosses a busy expressway. A complete cloverleaf is not needed because left turns by exiting traffic can be made easily on the less-busy road.

Trumpet Interchange

A trumpet interchange is used where a side road forms a T intersection with an expressway.

Cloverleaf interchange

All-Directional Interchange

An all-directional interchange is used in complicated intersections with high-volume traffic. From this interchange, traffic is channeled in many different directions.

Safe Driving Strategies

Although expressways have advantages compared to other types of roadways, collisions on expressways are often more serious. Higher speeds often place greater demands on both drivers and vehicles.

When driving on expressways, you should travel at about the same speed as other vehicles. Driving faster than other traffic may cause you to be constantly passing other vehicles. If you drive too slowly, you can block the smooth flow of traffic and become a hazard. Conform to posted minimum and maximum speed limits. Have your headlights on at all times so you are more visible to other drivers.

Use the following strategies to help you become a safe expressway driver.

Prepare Yourself and Your Vehicle

Preparation for driving on any expressway should include a travel plan, regardless of the length of the trip. For short trips, know the name, route, or number for both the entrance and exit you will use.

For long-distance trips, plan stops for food, fuel, and rest. Make every effort to stay alert, use the IPDE Process constantly, and be aware of traffic conditions in all your zones at all times.

Mechanical failure can occur even on a short trip. Keep your vehicle in

Diamond interchange

Trumpet interchange

All-directional interchange

Until you gain experience, avoid driving in heavy rush-hour traffic.

Traveling at the same speed as other traffic on the expressway does not mean that you should keep up with drivers who are exceeding the speed limit or driving too fast for conditions.

top condition to guard against mechanical failure when driving on expressways.

Build Experience Gradually When you first drive alone on an expressway, choose a time when traffic is light. Avoid driving in the heavy rush-hour traffic like this photograph shows. Practice entering and exiting several times before driving in heavier traffic. When you are driving in very light traffic, practice lane changes even when there are no vehicles to pass. Once you develop self-confidence, you will be better prepared to drive in heavier traffic.

Concentrate on the Driving Task Traffic conflicts can develop more rapidly at higher speeds, especially on multilane expressways. Give full attention to the driving task and do not allow yourself to become complacent. Never lose sight of the fact that high-speed expressway driving can present a high degree of risk.

Cooperate with Other Drivers You must cooperate with others when driving on expressways. Resist the urge to challenge other drivers for any reason. Road rage, an extreme act of aggression, can be a serious factor leading to a major conflict in high-speed expressway traffic. React cautiously if someone cuts you off or moves into your front zone too soon.

Review It

1. What are five reasons why fewer collisions occur on expressways than on other types of roadways?
2. What are four different types of expressway interchanges?
3. Explain what strategies you can use to become a low-risk driver on expressways.

11.2

Entering an Expressway

Before you enter an expressway, make sure you are using the correct entrance ramp. Guide signs mark most entrances and give the route number, direction, and name of a major city located in that direction. Many drivers have mistakenly tried to enter an expressway by using an exit ramp. To help prevent this error, most states post signs saying WRONG WAY or DO NOT ENTER.

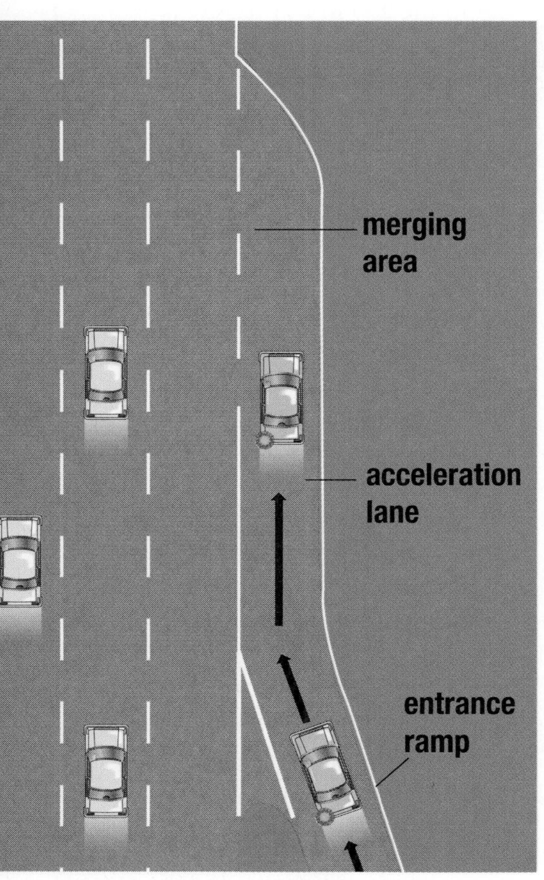

The parts of an expressway entrance

If you start to enter at an entrance you do not want, go ahead and get on the expressway. You can then safely exit at the first opportunity.

Expressway Entrances

Most expressway entrances have three parts:

- The **entrance ramp** gives you time to evaluate zone conditions and determine the best speed as you prepare to enter the expressway.
- The **acceleration lane** is usually long enough for you to search for a gap in which to merge and accelerate to the speed of traffic on the expressway. However, accelerating to expressway speeds in the acceleration lane is determined by the volume of traffic both on the expressway and in the acceleration lane.
- The **merging area** is the third part of an expressway entrance where vehicles blend into the expressway traffic. Evaluate how much time and space you have in your open front zones for merging into the flow of traffic. Try to merge at about the same speed as the vehicles in the nearest lane.

Steps for Entering

Follow these steps to enter an expressway smoothly and safely:

1. Make sure the entrance is the one you want. Look for a red and white WRONG WAY or DO NOT ENTER sign.

Objectives

1. Explain how to enter an expressway properly.
2. Describe four possible entrance problems.
3. Explain why entering an expressway from the left is more hazardous than entering from the right.

Make sure the entrance is the one you want. Check front and rear zones. Find a gap.

When in the acceleration lane, decide where to enter the gap.

Merge smoothly into traffic.

2. Once on the entrance ramp, check your front and rear zones. Signal and take quick glances through your left outside rearview mirror and over your left shoulder to find a gap in traffic where you can safely merge. Look for an entrance ramp signal light and be prepared to stop if it is red.
3. Once you are in the acceleration lane, gradually increase your speed. Continue to quickly glance over your left shoulder and through your outside rearview mirror. Decide when it is a safe time and place to merge into the gap in traffic.
4. Before entering the merging area, decide which vehicle to follow in the flow of the expressway traffic. As you enter the merging area, adjust your speed to match the traffic flow. Position your vehicle at a safe interval behind the vehicle you plan to follow. Merge smoothly.
5. Once on the expressway, cancel your signal and adjust to the speed of traffic. Keep a space cushion around your vehicle.

Possible Entrance Problems

Entrance driver errors cause many conflicts and collisions on expressways. Many drivers feel insecure when they have to merge into fast-moving traffic. Short entrance ramps, short acceleration lanes, and high dividing walls also can cause entrance problems.

Using the IPDE Process at all expressway entrances is critical.

- Make your visual checks and zone evaluations quickly. Identify possible problems on each part of the expressway entrance.
- Predict actions of other drivers.
- Decide on your entrance gap and speed.
- Execute your merge into traffic smoothly and safely.

Entrance Ramp Problems If you make an error and enter the wrong entrance ramp, continue onto the expressway. Drive to the next exit. *Never back up on an entrance ramp or on an expressway.*

If other vehicles are on the entrance ramp, adjust your speed to avoid conflict. Some ramps, particularly ramps with sharp curves, have yellow advisory signs posting a speed limit. Stay within the speed limit.

Begin looking immediately for a gap in traffic if the entrance ramp is short or there is no acceleration lane. If you have a closed front zone, reduce your speed to give the vehicle in front more time to find a gap. Check your rear zone and avoid a sudden slow or stop.

Some entrance ramps have high walls that divide expressway traffic and entering traffic. These walls restrict your line of sight to expressway traffic. On some ramps, you will be very close to the merge area before you can see the expressway traffic. Reduce your speed until you have a clear line of sight.

Entrance Ramp Signal Lights Some entrance ramps have signal lights to help space traffic entering the expressway. The lights are usually red and green. The timing of the signal lights is determined electronically by the volume of traffic at any given time. You must wait for the green light before entering the expressway, as the picture shows.

When the signal light on an entrance ramp is red, wait for the green light before proceeding onto the expressway.

Acceleration Lane Problems During rush hours, the large number of vehicles entering and on the expressway can make it almost impossible to accelerate to expressway speeds. Under these conditions, try to match the speed of traffic around you.

Some entrances have very short acceleration lanes. In such cases, you usually do not have the space to accelerate to the speed of expressway traffic. You need a longer gap to enter traffic and accelerate to the traffic speed.

Make every effort to enter an expressway without stopping. A driver behind you might be looking for a gap and not realize that you are stopped. If you must stop, take these precautions:

1. Flash your brake lights to warn drivers behind you.

Entering an expressway from the left can be more difficult than entering from the right.

If you have to stop before merging onto an expressway, you will need to accelerate more from a stopped position. Consider this as you determine the speed needed for your entry.

2. Pull onto the shoulder at the end of the acceleration lane or merge area.
3. You are now in an emergency situation. Wait for a large, safe gap. Signal and accelerate quickly as you join the traffic flow.

Merging Area Problems Adjusting your speed is critical to timing a smooth entrance into traffic. A closed front zone may cause you to reduce your speed and even to select a new gap. Once you are on the expressway, accelerate as you establish your safe following distance.

Entrance Ramp on Left Some expressway entrance ramps are located on the left of the expressway, as the picture shows. The acceleration lane merges into the far-left lane of expressway traffic. Since this lane is usually used for high-speed traffic, the potential for conflict is greater than when you enter from the right.

Checking fast-moving traffic over your right shoulder can be more difficult than checking to your left. Some vehicle roof supports and head restraints can obstruct your view of the oncoming expressway traffic. You might have difficulty seeing a motorcyclist or a very small car. Signal early as you look for a gap. When you see a gap, accelerate and merge into the traffic lane.

Review It

1. What are the proper steps for entering an expressway?
2. What problems could make entering an expressway difficult?
3. Why is the chance for conflict greater when entering an expressway from the left than from the right?

11.3 Strategies for Driving on Expressways

Once you are on the expressway, stay alert as you adjust to the constantly changing traffic scene. Use your IPDE Process continually. Use the process to predict any conflict and decide accurately how to respond.

Applying the IPDE Process

Expressway driving can make using the IPDE Process more difficult than when driving on two-lane roads. Higher speeds, multiple lanes, and a heavier volume of traffic can make the Identify and Predict steps more difficult.

Identify Expressways are designed to give drivers a long sight distance. However, higher speeds and multiple lanes reduce the amount of visual information you can gather. You need to identify the volume of traffic around you, as well as signs, signals, and roadway markings. You also need to identify closed front zones early. Never allow yourself to become trapped between two large vehicles, as the driver in the picture has done.

Be aware of drivers who do not seem to have their full attention on the driving task. These may be drivers talking on cellular phones or reading a map. Increase your space cushion when you are around these distracted drivers.

Predict A predictable traffic flow is a safety feature of expressways. However, you must search ahead to your target area to watch for sudden slowing traffic or drivers changing lanes. Anticipate closed zones and points of conflict before they occur. Predict that a parked vehicle on the shoulder might suddenly pull onto the expressway or even back up. At a distance, a vehicle backing up may still look like it is moving forward.

Decide Speeds seem to magnify a driver's indecision. Yet faster driving speeds demand that you make quicker decisions. Last-second decisions and driving adjustments can change your safe path of travel into a closed zone or point of conflict. Interchanges can be high-collision areas since so many driver decisions are made there. Open zones can very quickly become closed zones.

Execute Execute your decisions smoothly. Avoid sudden moves.

Objectives

1. Explain how to use the IPDE Process to achieve a safe path of travel.
2. Describe when following distances should be increased for expressway driving.
3. Tell what actions to take when you are being tailgated.
4. Describe three actions that should be automatic when you are changing lanes on an expressway.

The driver of this vehicle has become trapped with closed left-front and front zones and a line-of-sight restriction.

What Do You Think?

Some states do not have a maximum speed limit. Should all states be required to post maximum speed limits on expressways?

Signal early for every maneuver and maintain a safe following distance.

Lane Choice

On the expressway, decide the best lane in which to drive. Generally, it is safer to drive in the right lane and pass on the left. Reserve the center and left lanes for drivers who are passing and for faster traffic.

When traffic is heavy in the right lane, especially at entrance ramps during rush-hour traffic, use the center or left lane to avoid conflicts in the far right lane. Drivers entering, as well as drivers on the expressway, share responsibility for protecting each other from conflict.

Large trucks and vehicles towing trailers are required to travel in the right lane on many expressways. Although you may sometimes share the right lane with them, let the traffic dictate the lane you will use. Avoid driving between two large vehicles. Do not straddle lane lines because this prevents the other drivers from maintaining their proper lane positions.

Signs, Signals, and Roadway Markings

Part of your decision of lane choice is based on information from expressway signs, signals, and roadway markings. You are better able to maintain a safe path of travel and avoid making sudden last-second decisions if you

- know your destination
- read signs and roadway markings
- always think ahead

On some expressways, several overhead signs are posted at the same place. Scan the signs quickly to get the information you need to continue in a safe path. In many states, an overhead sign with a yellow panel indicates the exit lane, as shown in the picture. All traffic in this lane must exit.

Some overhead signs tell you if lanes are open or closed to traffic. A green arrow means that the lane is open for traffic. A yellow X over your

You Are the Driver!
What should you do if you suddenly realize this is the exit that you want to take?

Some signs show special speed limits for different times of day and types of vehicles.

lane warns you that the lane will be closed ahead. In this case you must prepare to move into another lane. A red X farther ahead indicates that the lane already is closed.

Many expressways into and out of cities often have express lanes. In most cases, these lanes have very few entrances and exits. If you are not sure where your exit is, do not enter the express lanes. Otherwise, you may be forced to drive beyond your intended exit.

Speed Limits

Most states post maximum speed limits on expressways. Some states have no maximum speed limit, and others post lower speed limits for trucks and larger vehicles.

When you drive in areas with no posted speed limit, follow the basic speed law. Drive at the speed that is safe and prudent for the weather and roadway conditions.

Minimum Speed Limit Driving too slowly could be very dangerous in fast-moving traffic and could cause rear-end collisions. A minimum speed limit is posted on many expressways to keep traffic from moving too slowly. This speed limit is the lowest legal speed you can drive under ideal conditions. During adverse conditions such as rain, fog, snow, or slippery roadways, driving under the minimum speed limit is both legal and wise. Use the far right lane when you are driving at or under the minimum speed limit.

Common Speed If you drive at the **common speed,** the speed used by most drivers, you can better blend with expressway traffic. Sometimes the common speed is above the maximum speed limit. Resist the temptation to increase your speed to keep up with the faster vehicles. Drivers who exceed the common speed are likely to weave in and out of traffic to pass other vehicles. This practice is dangerous not only to the driver exceeding the speed limit, but also to other drivers on the expressway.

Wolf Packs A responsible driver tries to avoid bunches of vehicles known as **wolf packs.** Reduce your chances of being involved in a conflict by being a "loner" on the expressway. This may be difficult to do in today's high-volume expressway traffic. However, when you travel in the middle of a pack, all zones may be closed. Adjust your speed to avoid wolf packs. The picture shows two wolf packs. The driver of the yellow car in the center lane has wisely chosen to be a "loner" by driving between the packs.

Adjust your speed to avoid being in a wolf pack.

Following

The high speeds of expressway traffic demand that you maintain at least

Which of these drivers is following too closely?

a 3-second following distance. A shorter following distance reduces your sight distance and leaves little time and space to react to a closed front zone.

Applying the 3-second following distance rule on the expressway is a safe plan under ideal conditions. The blue car in the left lane of the picture has a good space cushion and a safe following distance. However, the black vehicle behind the blue car is following too closely and does not have enough space in the front zone. Keeping an ample space cushion around your vehicle gives you both time and space for an "out."

Continually scan the traffic scene around you to be aware of any situation that may affect your safe path of travel. If a driver cuts into your space ahead, keep cool. Do not react in a manner that could cause another driver to exhibit road rage. Slow and reestablish a safe following distance.

Increase your following distance to at least 4 seconds when conditions are less than ideal. Increasing your following distance is especially important when you are

- following a large vehicle that is blocking your vision
- following a motorcyclist
- driving in bad weather or roadway conditions
- driving in heavy traffic
- being tailgated
- driving a heavy vehicle or pulling a trailer
- operating a motorcycle
- entering or exiting an expressway

Blind Spots Remember that you have blind spots in both your left-rear and right-rear zones. Check these zones often and be alert for other drivers who may pass you. When you are behind a vehicle in the next lane, keep far enough back so you are not in that driver's blind spot. Reduce your speed or accelerate and pass in order to stay out of another driver's blind spot.

Being Followed

Vehicles following you too closely, or tailgating, can put you in a dangerous situation. Many drivers tend to think that they have no control over the space in their rear zones. Encourage tailgaters to pass you by reducing your speed gradually. However, do not reduce your speed if heavy traffic prevents tailgaters from passing. If a driver continues to tailgate, change lanes when it is safe to do so. Frequently check your rear zones to stay aware of any tailgaters.

Lane Changing

Avoid changing lanes too often. Unnecessary weaving from one lane to another can lead to a collision. Take these steps to change lanes on the expressway:

1. Change lanes one lane at a time. Signal *every* lane change, whether or not other vehicles are present.
2. Check traffic in the outside and inside rearview mirrors. Check the blind-spot area in the direction you want to move.
3. If your path is clear, accelerate gently and move to the next lane.
4. Cancel your signal after you have changed lanes.

Once you have made a lane change, establish your position in that lane before moving to another. Drive at the speed of traffic in that lane if it is within the speed limit.

Changing lanes on an expressway is more complicated when three or more lanes of traffic are moving in the same direction. Many times a potential conflict is created when two drivers head for the same space at the same time, as the top picture shows. A quick glance over the shoulder lets you check the lane to see if it is open.

Sometimes you will change lanes so traffic entering the expressway can merge safely. Remember that some expressways have entrance ramps on the left as well as on the right. If you are driving in the left lane and see a driver entering from the left, predict a closed front zone. Signal right, check your right zones, and change lanes as the yellow car in the picture is doing.

Lanes are often closed for construction and road repair. When a lane is closed, drive only in the lanes open for traffic. It is both illegal and hazardous to use the shoulder or

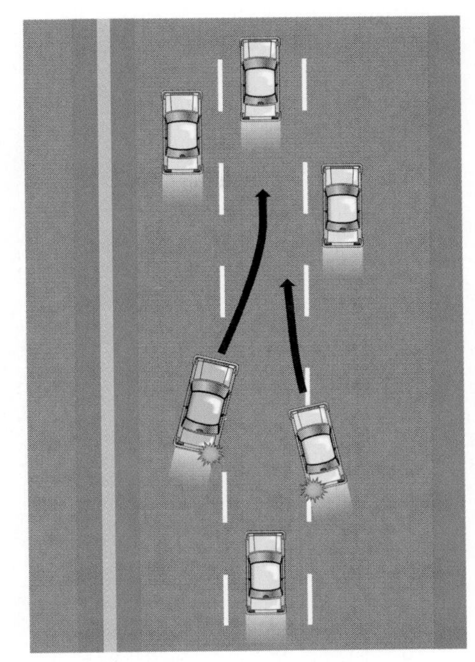

A conflict can occur when two drivers head for the same space at the same time.

The driver of the yellow car predicted a closed front zone and decided to change lanes.

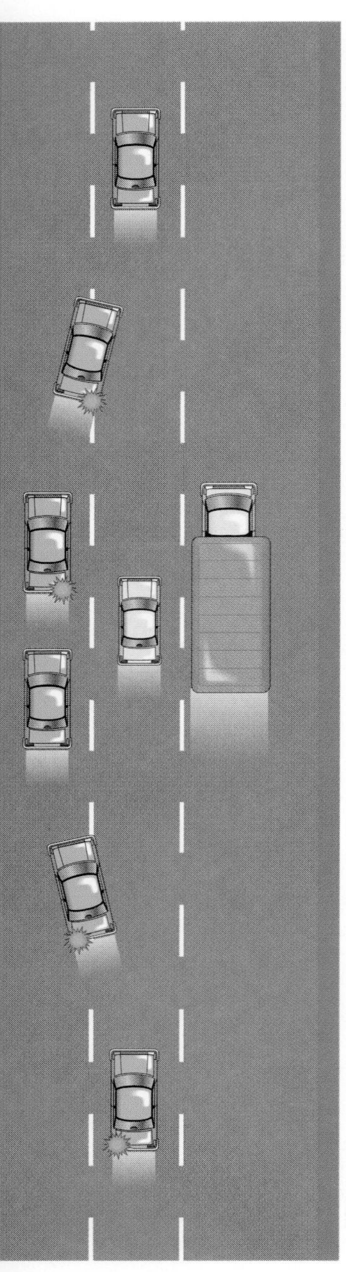

Use signals and constantly check traffic when passing on an expressway.

median as a driving lane when traffic is backed up. Drivers who drive illegally on the shoulder are also preventing emergency vehicles from having an open path of travel.

Passing and Being Passed

Passing other vehicles on an expressway usually is safer than passing on a two-lane highway. Because a median separates you from oncoming traffic on an expressway, a head-on collision is not a threat. However, expressway speeds and a high volume of traffic demand caution and concentration, along with the constant use of the IPDE Process, when passing. Always make sure conditions are safe for passing before you begin your maneuver.

Passing on the left is common on expressways. However, passing on the right is permitted if a slower driver is in the left lane.

When passing another vehicle, follow the procedure for making a lane change to the left. The yellow car in the picture is following the correct lane-change procedure to pass vehicles in the two right lanes.

After passing, return to your original lane by making a safe lane change.

Make these actions automatic when you pass:

- Evaluate the zone you are entering.
- Signal your lane change.
- Check blind-spot area by glancing over your shoulder to the left or right, as necessary.

When you are being passed, be aware of the position of the vehicle passing you. If you do not have enough space cushion to the side, move to lane position 2 or 3. Continue to check the vehicle that is passing you. Keep your speed steady and do not accelerate.

If you are continually being passed on the right, move to the lane on your right when it is safe to do so. When you are frequently being passed on both sides, you are in a potentially dangerous situation. You have reduced the space in your left and right zones and have greatly increased your degree of risk. Blending into the flow of traffic is just as important during passing as it is when entering or exiting an expressway.

Review It

1. How can using the IPDE Process help you maintain a safe path of travel on expressways?
2. When should following distances be increased for expressway driving?
3. What actions could you take when you are being tailgated?
4. What three actions should be automatic when changing lanes to pass on an expressway?

11.4

Exiting Expressways

Leaving an expressway safely requires planning and skill. Plan for your exit as early as possible. Scan signs to know which exit to take. When you see the sign for your exit, move into the lane designated by the sign. Most expressway exits provide a **deceleration lane,** an added lane in which to slow your vehicle without blocking the vehicles behind. Try not to decelerate until you are off the expressway and in the deceleration lane.

The deceleration lane leads into the **exit ramp,** the ramp leading off the expressway. Identify the sign that shows the exit-ramp speed. If you do not slow your vehicle enough in the deceleration lane, you might enter the exit ramp at too high a speed.

Many exit ramps lead into a sharp curve. The posted ramp speed limit indicates the top speed possible for negotiating the exit safely. Remember, if you miss the exit you want, go on to the next exit. *Never stop or back up if you go past your exit.*

Objectives

1. Explain how to apply the IPDE Process to exit an expressway.
2. List the steps for exiting an expressway.
3. Describe three possible exiting problems.

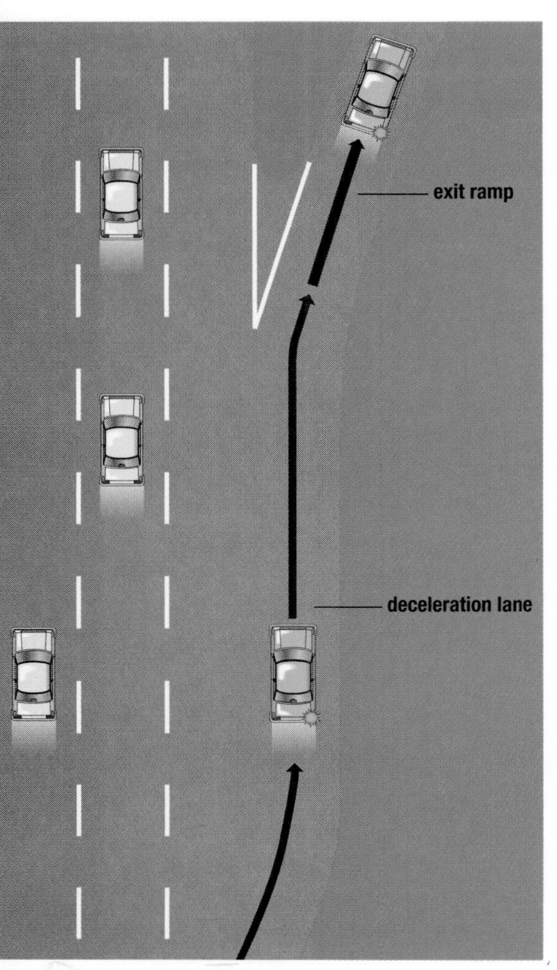

The parts of an expressway exit.

Applying the IPDE Process

Use the IPDE Process to plan your exit well in advance:

1. Identify the green expressway guide signs showing the distance to your exit.
2. Predict actions of other drivers who might be using the same exit.
3. Decide on the safe speed for exiting.
4. Execute your maneuver smoothly and blend with slower traffic.

Steps for Exiting

Follow these steps to exit an expressway:

1. At least one-half mile before the exit, check front and rear zones for traffic. Signal and move into lane position 3 in the lane that

Be in lane position 3 before you get to the deceleration lane.

Move into the deceleration lane.

Slow to the posted speed limit.

leads into the deceleration lane. This is shown in the first picture. Change only one lane at a time. Avoid last-second decisions and sudden moves. Do not reduce your speed until you are in the deceleration lane.

2. Move into the deceleration lane. Cancel your signal.
3. Flash your brake lights to warn drivers behind that you are slowing. Check your rear zones so you will know the speed of following traffic. Slow gradually and keep a safe space cushion ahead and behind you.
4. Identify the exit-ramp speed sign, as shown in the bottom picture. Check your own speed, and adjust to the posted speed limit. Predict a STOP or YIELD sign at the end of the exit ramp.

Be alert when entering traffic on a local highway or street after leaving the expressway. Expect two-way traffic, pedestrians, intersections, and the need for lower speeds. Check your speedometer frequently and be alert for the typical hazards of two-way streets and roads.

Possible Exiting Problems

Even though leaving an expressway should be a smooth operation, problems can occur. Be alert and ready to adjust to problem situations.

Crossing Paths On some expressways, like the one shown in the first picture on the next page, the same lane is used as both an entrance and an exit. Exiting traffic should merge behind entering traffic since entering traffic is accelerating.

Ramp Overflow Traffic can back up from an exit ramp onto the expressway, as the second picture shows. Rather than joining the overflow and risking a rear-end collision, go past the exit and use the next exit. Some drivers pull off on the shoulder out of the lane of traffic. This is both unsafe and illegal.

Start slowing early if you must use a backed-up exit. If you see vehicles backed up near the exit ramp, check your rear zone, flash your brake lights, and begin to slow. Check your rear zone again to make sure traffic is slowing. If traffic is not slowing, try to pass the exit area smoothly, and drive on to the next exit.

Short Deceleration Lane Slow more quickly if the deceleration lane is short. Evaluate your rear zones. This is critical in such situations. As you enter the deceleration lane

- judge the lane's length
- identify the exit-ramp speed
- check speed while braking
- check traffic in rear zones

Review It

1. How should you use the IPDE Process when planning an exit from an expressway?
2. What steps should you follow when exiting an expressway?
3. What are three possible exiting problems?

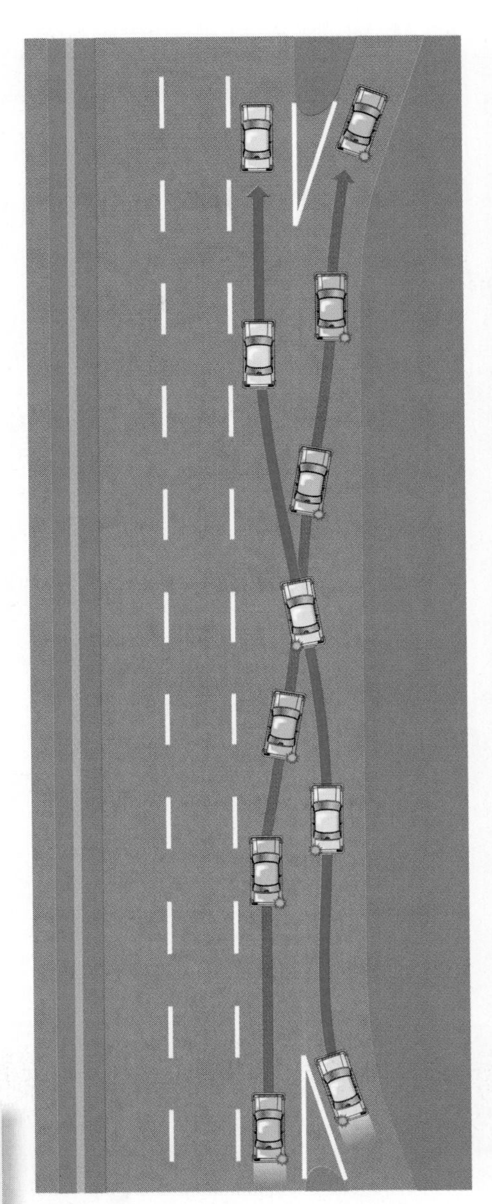

Driver's paths might cross when the same lane is used for entering and exiting.

What should drivers do when traffic is backed up near an exit ramp?

11.5 Special Expressway Problems

Objectives

1. Describe the cause of highway hypnosis and tell what actions to take to stay alert.
2. Explain what to do if your vehicle becomes disabled.
3. List three key factors that contribute to safe driving on expressways.

Expressways can provide the safest type of driving. Even so, problems can arise that present hazards and possible conflicts.

Driver Condition

Driving for long periods of time can affect drivers. Be alert for problems that can affect you and the other drivers on the road.

Highway Hypnosis

Staying alert can be a problem when you travel long distances on expressways. You may drive mile after mile at steady speeds with few hills, curves, or interchanges. You can be lulled into an inattentive, drowsy state known as **highway hypnosis.**

When you first notice that you are becoming drowsy or your attention is less focused, sit up straighter and open a window. Stop at the next exit and stretch or exercise. If you need more rest, stop at a safe place and take a brief nap.

Fall-Asleep Collisions

More than 100,000 collisions in the United States each year are caused by sleepiness. Fall-asleep collisions are twice as likely to involve fatalities as other types of collisions.

Sleepiness is a preventable cause of vehicle collisions. Drivers who fail to recognize their own fatigue and sleepiness, or even ignore it, pose a high-risk threat to themselves and to others on the roadway. All drivers are at risk for fall-asleep collisions.

Velocitation

Hours of driving can fool you into thinking your vehicle is traveling slower than it really is. You might then unconsciously drive too fast. This condition, called **velocitation,**

LEAVING EXPRESSWAYS Many drivers have difficulty adjusting to lower speeds after leaving an expressway. Some drivers fail to slow down to the posted speed limit and find themselves stopped by police officers. These drivers usually will be issued tickets for speed-limit violations.

can be especially hazardous when you exit an expressway.

The roadways you drive on after exiting usually have a lower speed limit than the expressway. If you are "velocitized," you might continue to drive at expressway speeds after making your exit. To prevent exceeding the local speed limit, check your speed often after exiting the expressway.

Roadway Conditions

Be aware of the characteristics of certain expressways in order to drive safely on them. Even under the safest conditions, roadway problems can still arise.

Expressways Through Cities

City expressways have more exit and entrance ramps than rural expressways. More ramps increase merging traffic conflicts and give indecisive drivers more opportunities for dangerous last-second decisions.

Remember the following points when driving on an expressway through a city, especially during rush hour:

- In most cases, drive in the center or left lane to avoid merging vehicles.
- Know well in advance where you want to exit. Get in the correct lane early. Fast-moving traffic can make lane changing difficult and dangerous.
- Search constantly for signs, signals, and roadway markings.
- Predict that other drivers are less alert and less aware than you are.

Disabled Vehicle

Take these steps with the first sign of trouble with your vehicle:

1. Check rear zones and signal. Pull as far as possible onto the shoulder or the median.
2. Turn on your hazard flashers. If the vehicle is not very far off the road, get everyone out and away from traffic.
3. When it is safe to do so, raise the hood and tie a white cloth to the antenna or door handle. If you have a cellular phone, call for help.
4. If you have emergency flares or reflectors, set them out at least 500 feet behind your vehicle when it is safe to do so.
5. Get back into your vehicle and lock all doors. Ask anyone who stops to assist you to go to a phone and call for help. Never get into a stranger's vehicle.
6. Do not stand in the expressway to direct traffic.

Roadway Repair

Be alert for roadway repair zones. Watch for orange construction signs and be prepared to slow as soon as you identify the first one. Early-warning construction signs with blinking lights indicate the construction-zone speed limit. Reduce your speed and follow the directions of the construction workers.

Rural Interstate Highways

Driving long distances on rural interstate highways can become monotonous. Check your speed frequently, and look as far ahead as possible into your target area.

If your vehicle becomes disabled, pull as far as possible onto the shoulder or median.

Fines are often doubled for speeding violations in construction zone areas.

Select your lane well in advance. Stay in that lane and have your money ready.

Try not to let larger vehicles tailgate you. Remember that they cannot stop as quickly as you can. Pass larger, slower-moving vehicles only when it is safe to do so.

Tollbooths

Tollbooth plazas are located along many expressways. You stop at a tollbooth and pay a fee, or toll, for driving on that expressway.

Rough sections of roadway, called *rumble strips,* are built into the approach lanes of some toll plazas. These strips warn you of the tollbooths ahead and remind you to check your speed.

When approaching a tollbooth plaza, look for a green light above a tollbooth. The green light indicates that the lane is open for traffic.

Many toll plazas have signs overhead in different colors, as the picture shows. These colors indicate the lanes for the tollbooths that are electronic, require exact change, or are attendant operated.

Toll plazas have at least three types of tollbooths. One type is automatic; the driver deposits coins into a machine. The second type is operated by an attendant for drivers without exact change and drivers of larger vehicles.

Another type of tollbooth is operated electronically. An electronic device is placed inside the driver's vehicle on the windshield or on the dashboard. As the driver approaches the designated toll lane, the device communicates electronically with a computer in the lane. The toll is then subtracted from a previously prepaid account.

Using Expressways Safely

Three key factors contribute to safe driving on expressways:

- cooperation among drivers
- concentration on the driving task
- use of the IPDE Process

Keeping these factors in mind as you gain expressway experience will enable you to contribute to low-risk expressway driving.

Review It

1. What are causes of highway hypnosis? What actions can you take to stay alert?
2. What should you do if your vehicle becomes disabled?
3. What are three key factors that can help you drive safely on expressways?

Chapter 11
Review

Reviewing Chapter Objectives

1. Characteristics of Expressway Driving

1. What are five reasons expressways have lower collision rates than other highways? (222)
2. What are four different types of expressway interchanges? (222–223)
3. What strategies can you follow for low-risk driving on expressways? (223–224)

2. Entering an Expressway

4. How do you properly enter an expressway? (225–226)
5. What are four possible problems you may have when entering an expressway? (227)
6. Why is entering an expressway from the left more hazardous than entering from the right? (228)

3. Strategies for Driving on Expressways

7. How can you use the IPDE Process to achieve a safe path of travel? (229–230)
8. When should following distances be increased for expressway driving? (232)

4. Exiting Expressways

9. How can you apply the IPDE Process to exit an expressway? (235)
10. What steps should you take when exiting an expressway? (235–236)
11. What are three possible exiting problems? (236–237)

5. Special Expressway Problems

12. How is highway hypnosis caused and what actions can you take to stay alert? (238)
13. What should you do if your vehicle becomes disabled on an expressway? (239)
14. What three key factors contribute to safe driving on expressways? (240)

Projects

Individuals

Observe Traffic As a passenger in a vehicle, observe vehicles that pass both the vehicle you are in and other vehicles. Record the number of vehicles you see passing in a five-minute period. Note the number of vehicles passing on the right and the number passing on the left. Also note whether the vehicles seem to be exceeding the speed limit. Discuss your observations in class.

Investigate Locate the interchanges on a map of your area and nearest city. Identify each as cloverleaf, diamond, trumpet, or all-directional. Discuss your findings in class.

Groups

Use Technology Use the Internet or other sources to research the use of tollbooth plazas in your state and neighboring states. Find out how many tollbooth plazas are being used. Find out whether the tollbooths operate with toll attendants, automatically, or electronically. Also find out how much money the booths collect annually and how the money is used. Write a group report based on your findings.

Demonstrate As a group, make an expressway model and label the various components. Present your model to the class. Group members should take turns explaining the purpose and potential problems related to each expressway component.

Chapter 11
Review

Chapter Test

Check Your Knowledge

Multiple Choice Copy the number of each sentence below on a sheet of paper. Choose the letter of the answer that best completes the statement or answers the question.

1. Expressways are safer than other types of roads because
(a) there is less traffic.
(b) there are no intersections or cross traffic.
(c) average speeds are higher.
(d) there is no barrier between opposing traffic lanes.

2. If traffic is backed up on the exit ramp you want to use, you should
(a) pass the ramp and use the next exit.
(b) stop on the expressway until the ramp is clear.
(c) pull onto the shoulder and wait.
(d) none of the above

3. Expressway collisions tend to be more serious than those on other types of roads, because expressways
(a) have median strips.
(b) have so many conflicts.
(c) have higher-speed travel.
(d) have more hazards.

Completion Copy the number of each sentence below. After each number, write the word or words that complete the sentence correctly.

4. You slow your vehicle without blocking those behind you when you are in the _____ lane.

5. A _____ interchange is used when a side road forms a T intersection with an expressway.

6. The right edge of the expressway should be marked with a _____ line.

Review Vocabulary

Copy the number of each definition in list A. Match the definition in list A with the term it defines in list B.

List A

7. group or formation of vehicles traveling on an expressway

8. speed used by most drivers on an expressway

9. condition of unconsciously driving too fast as a result of driving for long periods at high speeds

10. lane that permits drivers entering an expressway to accelerate to the speed of expressway traffic

11. stretch of roadway at the end of an acceleration lane where vehicles join the flow of traffic

List B

a. acceleration lane
b. velocitation
c. wolf pack
d. common speed
e. merging area

Think Critically

Write a paragraph to answer each question.

1. What are the pros and cons of higher-speed driving on an expressway?

2. How do you think wolf packs form on expressways?

Decision Making

1. The yellow car is about to enter the merge area. What should car 1 do? How can car 2 help? What should car 3 predict? What action should the driver of the yellow car be executing?

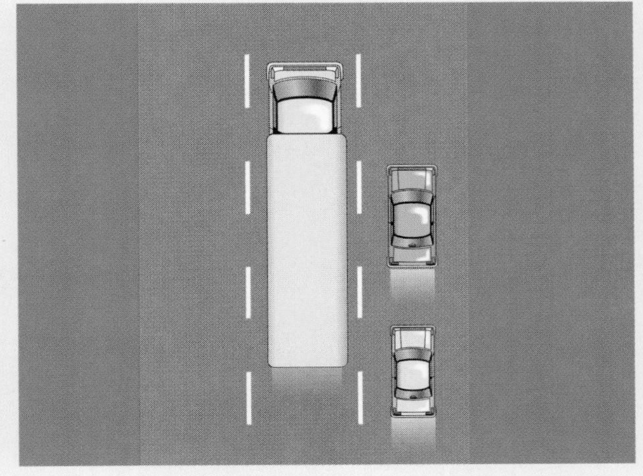

2. What unsafe practice is the driver of the yellow car following? What options does this driver have to improve the situation? How might the tailgater affect the yellow car driver's decision?

3. The driver of the yellow car plans to exit the expressway. The same lane is used for exiting and entering. What should the driver of the yellow car do? Why is this a wise decision?

4. What is the driver of the car required to do when driving through the construction zone?

THERMO KING
MACK

CHAPTER 12
Driving in Adverse Conditions

You Are the Driver!

Driving in traffic during good weather is difficult enough—but imagine driving in these snowy conditions! The unpredictable nature of other drivers makes this a high-risk situation. What will you predict others might do? How can you control your vehicle? Can you prepare for this ahead of time?

Extreme situations will raise many questions on how to drive safely. This chapter will help you answer those questions and show you how to better manage risk in these situations.

Go Online
PHSchool.com
For: Chapter 12 online activities
Visit: PHSchool.com
Web Code: cak-9999

12.1 Reduced Visibility

Objectives

1. Tell how to use the IPDE Process to manage risks in bad weather.
2. Explain what you can do to help others see you at dawn and dusk.
3. Describe the special techniques you can use for night driving.
4. Explain the procedure to use at night when an oncoming driver fails to use low-beam headlights.

Whenever visibility is reduced drivers need more time to use the IPDE Process. You can maintain a safe intended path of travel by

- slowing down to give yourself more time
- scanning in and around your path of travel to the target area to identify hazards early
- predicting others will make maneuvers into your intended path of travel
- deciding to position your vehicle ahead of time with an extra space cushion around it
- executing driving actions gently to maintain control so others know what you are doing

Your Vehicle Windows

The most important rule for your vehicle's glass is "keep it clean!" If dirty windows become a line-of-sight restriction, you will have a much harder time using the IPDE Process effectively.

A simple thing like moisture forming on the inside of your windshield can make the difference between safe, low-risk driving and colliding with another vehicle. Take these steps when the slightest amount of moisture builds up:

- Turn on your front-window defroster.
- Switch on your rear defogger.
- Use air conditioning and/or heater if it will help.
- Open windows as needed.

Clean all windows and lights ahead of time in bad weather. Keep a close check on any ice, snow, or dirt buildup, especially on headlights and taillights. Stop to clear them by hand.

Imagine what important things you don't see in the night.

Even in good weather, clean windows can be a problem. The plastics used in many vehicle interiors can give off vapors that coat the inside of windows over time. Cigarette smoke also can create a dirty-window problem. By keeping windows clear, you improve your ability to identify, especially at night.

Sun Glare

At times the sun can create severe and blinding glare conditions. Sun glasses and a sun visor can help, but try to avoid looking toward the sun.

By driving with low-beam headlights on all the time, you help other drivers see you. The brightest day will create the darkest shadows. With severe-glare situations and the sun behind you, be prepared for other drivers to miss seeing your signal or even seeing your vehicle.

Dawn and Dusk

Dawn and dusk driving situations can be very dangerous. The low visual contrast between moving vehicles and the driving scene can be deceiving. Again, by always driving with your headlights on low beam, you can help others to see you. How would you defend yourself if the oncoming driver in the top picture did not have headlights on?

Night

Low levels of light at night severely limit your ability to use the IPDE Process. Look at the picture on the left. Even with street lights, how do these nighttime conditions make driving more difficult? Would daylight make it easier? What things might you see during day-time driving that you would miss while driving at night?

Dawn driving without headlights on can set many traps.

Headlights Keep these points in mind when driving with your headlights on at night:

- Use high-beam headlights to see further down the road. Also, look beyond your headlights for important information. Only use your high-beam headlights when vehicles are more than one-half mile in front of you. Switch to low-beam headlights the instant you see the headlights of an oncoming vehicle, the taillights of a vehicle you are approaching, or the taillights of a vehicle that has just passed you. This prevents you from

Be ready to adjust to a new situation beyond the headlights.

To give yourself more time for the IPDE Process at night, look beyond the range of your headlights.

blinding the other driver with your headlights.

- Use low-beam lights in bad weather. In snow, heavy rain, or fog, high-beam headlights will reflect more light back into your eyes; as a result, you will see less.

Meeting Other Vehicles Take these actions if an oncoming driver fails to use low-beam headlights after you switch to low-beam headlights:

1. Is the oncoming driver far enough away to respond to you? Briefly flick your headlights from low to high to low to remind the oncoming driver to switch to low-beam headlights. Most new vehicles make this easy by having a flash-to-pass position on their high-beam control switch.
2. Is the oncoming driver still using high-beam headlights? Slow, move to lane position 3, and glance at the right edge of the road as shown here.
3. Could you be blinded by bright oncoming headlights? Look ahead with frequent quick glances to check oncoming traffic. *Do not stare directly into oncoming high-beam headlights.*
4. Is it possible you will encounter a hazard to the right after the oncoming vehicle? Be ready to adjust to a new situation beyond the oncoming headlights.

Overdriving Headlights The term **overdriving headlights** means driving at a speed that makes your stopping distance longer than the distance lighted by your headlights. Make sure you do not overdrive your headlights, especially in bad weather or on a slick road.

In normal driving conditions, use this 4-second stopping distance rule to see if you are driving within the range of your headlights.

1. Pick a fixed-checkpoint ahead the instant the checkpoint

appears in the area lit by your headlights as shown here.
2. Count off four seconds: "one-thousand-one, one-thousand-two, one-thousand-three, one-thousand-four."
3. Check your vehicle's position. When you have just reached your fixed checkpoint, you can assume your stopping distance on dry pavement is within the range of your headlights.

The stop sign is five seconds away. Are you overdriving your headlights?

Fog

When your headlights shine into fog, light is reflected back by water particles in the fog. This makes it harder for you to see. If you use high-beam headlights, your ability to see is reduced even further. Always use low-beam headlights in fog as shown below.

Fog also can reduce your ability to judge distances. Oncoming vehicles may be closer than you think. Avoid trouble by slowing and increasing the space cushion around your vehicle.

Thick fog, and in some situations heavy industrial smoke, can be very dangerous. Before entering fog, be prepared to slow or even park safely off the side of the road. Better yet, park in a rest area or parking lot.

In fog, oncoming traffic may be closer than the driver perceives.

If you stop at the side of the roadway, use your hazard lights to warn others that you are stopped.

Rain

Heavy rain reduces your ability to see and be seen. Keep your windshield clear by using your wipers and defroster on high. Make sure your low-beam headlights are already on as shown in the picture. Many states require low-beam headlights to be on when wipers are on. Reduce your speed. As with fog, if the rain is so heavy that you cannot see well, be prepared to pull off the road and sit out the storm in a safe location. Don't forget to use your hazard flashers.

Snow

Wind-driven snow can reduce your vision, cover roadway markings, and make steering more difficult. Be prepared to slow and steer carefully. Heavy snow can block your rear window, reducing visibility. Slush or ice also can build up on your windshield wipers. If snow, slush, or ice builds up, pull off the roadway and clean it off. Also clear your headlights, taillights, and other parts of your vehicle that need it.

By using headlights all the time, you won't have to remember to turn them on in the rain.

You Are the Driver!
What special actions should you be prepared to take in this heavy snow situation?

In blizzard conditions, the last thing you want is to be stranded in the middle of nowhere. If the weather is that bad, try to delay travel until roads and weather improve.

Use low-beam headlights when it snows, day or night. Reduce your speed to maintain control and to give others time to respond to you. If snow covers the road, closing your right-front zone, do not crowd the center of the road by moving to lane position 2. This action has the effect of narrowing the road and could lead to a head-on collision.

Review It

1. What actions should you take when using the IPDE Process in limited-visibility situations?
2. What steps can you take to help others see you at dawn and dusk?
3. When should you use low-beam headlights at night?
4. What steps should you take when an oncoming driver fails to use low-beam headlights?

12.2 Reduced Traction

Objectives

1. Describe what happens to traction during rain and snow.
2. List the steps you can take to avoid hydroplaning.
3. Describe how to correct a rear-wheel skid.
4. Tell how to use the controlled-braking technique.

As discussed in Chapter 5, traction allows your tires to grip the road so that you can control your vehicle. Rain, snow, ice, sand, and other materials can limit your traction. Reduced traction can create high-risk driving situations.

Wet Roadways

Rain-slick roads can create a problem for any driver. You can avoid trouble by knowing the right actions to take ahead of time.

When Rain Starts When rain starts to fall, it mixes with dust and oil on the road. This mix can make the road very slippery, until more rain washes it away.

Reduce speed to make better use of your limited traction on wet roads. You can get a little better traction by following the tire tracks left by the driver ahead.

Hydroplaning When a tire loses road contact by rising up on top of water and no longer has contact with the road, **hydroplaning** occurs. Hydroplaning is caused by a combination of standing water, speed, and tire condition. The deep tread of new, properly inflated tires will cut through the water and grip the road. But even with good tires, hydroplaning can occur at speeds of 35 mph, in water as little as 1/12-inch deep. Tires that are bald or underinflated can start to lose their grip and hydroplane at less than 35 mph. Slushy snow in standing water also increases the risk of hydroplaning.

If you must drive through standing water, take these steps to avoid hydroplaning:

- Reduce speed—especially if the water is deep enough to have raindrops "splash" on the water's surface.

You Are the Driver! What action should be taken to avoid hydroplaning before driving through the water?

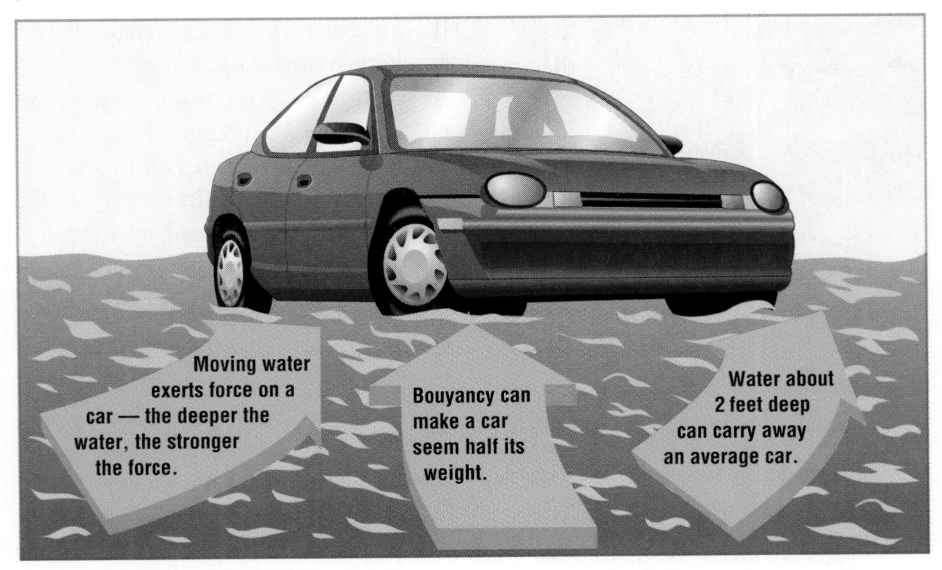

Deep water can be dangerous.

- Use properly inflated tires with good tread.

Deep Water When you don't know how deep the water ahead is, do not drive through it. Floods cause more deaths than any other weather condition, and 60 percent are vehicle related. If you must drive through deep water, use the following steps:

1. Estimate water depth by watching other vehicles and looking at objects such as fire hydrants, fence posts, and parked vehicles. *If there is even a possibility of the water coming up to the bottom of your vehicle—do not enter the water.*
2. If the water is just over the rims of your tires, drive slowly in low gear. Avoid driving on a soft shoulder. Try to drive on the higher, center of the road.
3. When driving at a low speed through water, apply a light brake pressure with your left foot to build friction and create heat on your brake pads. This heat will help dry your brakes and keep them working.
4. After leaving the water, squeeze your brake pedal lightly to see if your brakes are working normally. If your vehicle pulls to one side or does not slow, drive for a short distance while applying a light brake-pedal pressure with your left foot to help dry your brakes.

Snow

Different types of snow can produce different levels of traction. When fresh snow falls at low temperatures, traction can be fairly good. When traffic packs the snow at places like intersections, traction can be reduced. In subzero weather, even the moisture from vehicle exhaust can freeze into dangerous ice on the pavement.

Use gentle control actions to rock your vehicle.

Temperatures at or just below the freezing point (32°F or 0°C) can create dangerous traction situations. The combination of snow, slushy water, and ice can make for extremely slippery surfaces.

Driving Techniques for Snow Gentle acceleration, steering, and braking are the keys to vehicle control in snow. Put your vehicle in motion by gently squeezing the accelerator. If your drive wheels slip, release your accelerator and start again.

To improve traction on snow, use all-season tires. To improve traction even more, many states allow the use of tire chains at certain times. Chains are placed over the tread on the tires to increase traction.

Rocking a Vehicle Often you can move your vehicle out of deep snow, mud, or sand by driving forward a little and then back a little. By repeating this sequence, you can work your way out. This technique is called **rocking a vehicle.** Check your owner's manual to make sure this procedure will not hurt your transmission. If it is okay, follow these steps:

1. Straighten front wheels as the driver in the picture above has done.
2. Gently accelerate forward. *Do not spin your wheels.*
3. Let up on your accelerator. Pause just long enough to let the engine slow. Shift to REVERSE and gently move backwards. Let up on your

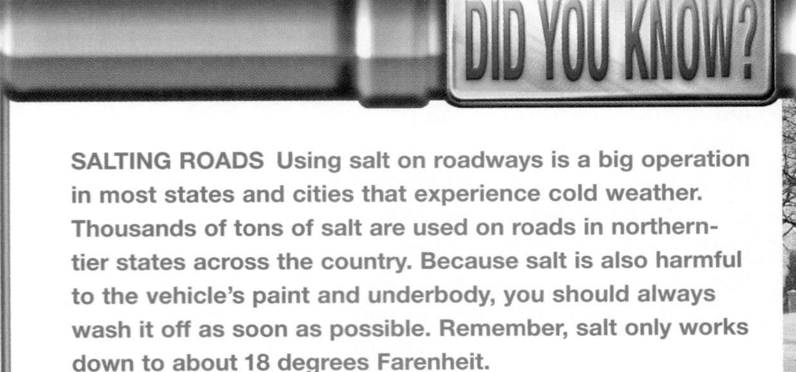

SALTING ROADS Using salt on roadways is a big operation in most states and cities that experience cold weather. Thousands of tons of salt are used on roads in northern-tier states across the country. Because salt is also harmful to the vehicle's paint and underbody, you should always wash it off as soon as possible. Remember, salt only works down to about 18 degrees Farenheit.

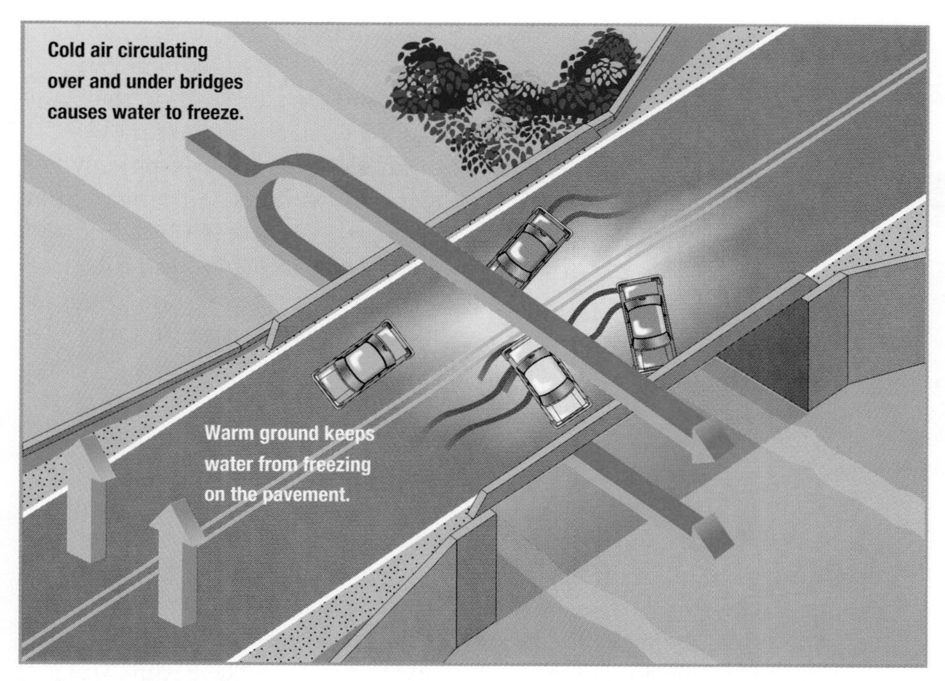

Ice forms on bridges first.

accelerator and shift to DRIVE to move forward.

4. Continue this backward-and-forward movement until your vehicle has cleared tracks that are long enough to drive out.

Ice

Be especially alert if temperatures drop below freezing and it is raining. These conditions are just right for snow, ice, and sleet. Predict the worst when ice begins to form.

Temperatures will change the amount of traction you will have on ice. If the temperature of ice warms from 0 degrees to 32 degrees Farenheit, your traction will be cut in half.

Squeeze your brakes lightly to check your traction in icy areas. Only do this at low speeds away from traffic. Slow gradually if your vehicle starts to slide.

Windows and windshield wipers can also ice up in severe weather. If your defroster cannot keep your windshield clear, pull out of traffic and clear it manually. It might be best not to drive at all.

If you must drive, be extra alert for these icy situations:

- **Ice on Bridges** Bridge roadways tend to freeze before other roadway surfaces. Cold air circulates above and below the roadway on bridges and overpasses as shown in the picture.
- **Black Ice** Be alert for "black ice" that forms in thin sheets. This can be extremely hard to see. Be extra careful for this type of ice in winter mountain situations.

Gravel on the road will affect your control.

- **Ice in Tire Tracks** Snow can pack down into ice in the normal driving tracks. Avoid these slippery tracks by moving a little to the right in lane position 3 to use the unpacked, less-slick portion of your lane.

Other Reduced-Traction Situations

Braking distance will always increase in low-traction situations. Slow early and then be ready to slow even more.

Gravel Roads Loose gravel on roads can act like marbles under your tires and cause skids. Well-packed wheel paths usually form on heavily traveled gravel roads. Drive in these paths for better traction and control. If you need to move out of the wheel paths, slow and hold your steering wheel firmly.

Leaves Wet leaves on the road can decrease traction and reduce your stopping and steering control. Slow ahead of time if you see wet leaves on the pavement.

Construction Areas Construction trucks and other equipment can leave mud, dirt, or sand on the road. Slow, steer gently, and obey workers' directions. Be especially careful for workers and construction drivers who do not see you. Use an extra space cushion to protect them. In many states, traffic fines double in construction zones.

Skidding

In Chapter 5 you learned how traction allows your vehicle to grip the road. You also learned what factors can reduce traction. In extreme reduced-traction situations, your tires may lose all or part of their grip on the road and **skid.** Skidding can happen on any surface while you are braking, accelerating, or steering.

In addition to slowing ahead of time, early detection is one of your best defenses to control skidding. What is the best way to detect a skid? Aim high to see your target

Respect the dangers around a construction site by lowering your speed and being ready to stop.

This set of photos shows two examples of a car skidding off target (the yellow circle). If your vehicle skids off target to the right, steer back toward your target area by turning the wheel to the left.

If your vehicle skids off target to the left, steer back toward your target area by turning the wheel to the right.

well down the road. The instant you see your vehicle is not traveling in your intended path of travel toward your target, you need to start correcting the skid. If you wait until you feel your vehicle skidding, you may not be able to correct the skid in time to avoid trouble.

These pages will show you how to correct most skidding situations.

In all these situations, remember:

1. A locked or spinning wheel provides no steering control.
2. Never give up trying to correct a skid.

Over-Power Skid If you apply too much power to your drive wheels, they may spin, thus causing a skid. To correct this, simply let off your accelerator.

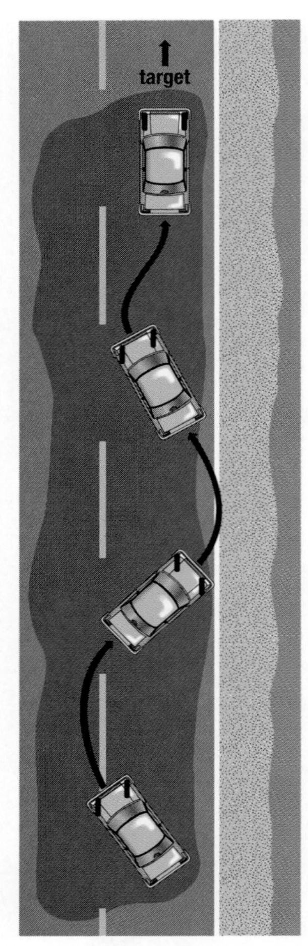

Correcting a fishtailing skid

Over-Braking Skid If your vehicle does not have an antilock braking system (ABS) and you over-brake, the wheels may stop while you are still moving. To correct this, release your brake pedal enough to get your wheels rolling. See the controlled braking section on the next page for more details.

Front-Wheel Skid You are in a front-wheel skid if you turn the steering wheel and your vehicle wants to slide straight ahead. Your vehicle responds less than you want it to. To correct this skid, you need to regain traction for steering. To do this, you need to

1. Release accelerator or brake pedal pressure.
2. Quickly apply and release the brake pedal to slow if your vehicle does not have ABS.
3. Continue to look and steer at the path of travel you want to follow.

Rear-Wheel Skid If you are steering straight and your vehicle starts to move off target to the left or right, you probably are just starting a rear wheel skid. This skid can be caused by using too much power or braking on slick surfaces. The instant this skid starts, do the following:

1. Release your accelerator or brake. With manual transmission, depress your clutch pedal.
2. Steer quickly and precisely in the direction your vehicle needs to go, as shown on page 257. On a straight road, steer for your target and intended path of travel. Be careful not to overcorrect for the skid by steering too much.
3. The rear end of your vehicle probably will continue to slide a little from side to side, or **fishtail,** after you have corrected the initial skid. Steer and countersteer in the direction your vehicle needs to go. As your speed drops, your control will increase.

Look at the illustration to the left to see how you can provide precise, smooth, continuous steering actions to correct a fishtail skid sequence.

Skidding in a Curve Slow ahead of time to avoid skidding in a curve. If you do skid in a curve, you probably are going to go off the road. If so, use the steps to correct a front-wheel or rear-wheel skid and steer for an off-road path of travel that is as safe as possible.

ABS enables you to steer and stop at the same time.

Controlled Braking

A panic stop can lock your wheels, causing a skid and loss of steering control.

Use **controlled braking** to reduce your speed as quickly as possible while maintaining steering control of your vehicle. Controlled braking is a technique of applying your brakes to slow or stop quickly without locking your wheels. Follow these steps to use controlled braking:

1. With the heel of your foot on the floor, let the ball of your foot press your brake pedal. You must press hard enough to slow your vehicle rapidly without locking your wheels.
2. If your wheels lock and your vehicle skids, ease up on your brake pedal just enough to let your wheels start rolling.
3. Keep using this squeeze-relax a little-squeeze process until you stop.

Using just the right amount of pressure is the hardest part in controlled braking situations. To overcome this problem, most new vehicles are equipped with an anti-lock braking system (ABS).

An ABS-equipped vehicle uses a computer to prevent its wheels from locking—even in an emergency stop. If your vehicle has an ABS, just press the brake pedal as hard as you can in an emergency. You may feel little pulses through the brake pedal or hear the ABS at work. Don't let up on the brake pedal; maintain firm pressure until you stop. Also remember, ABS vehicles will allow you to steer and brake at the same time as shown in the picture on the left. *They will not enable you to stop in a shorter distance.*

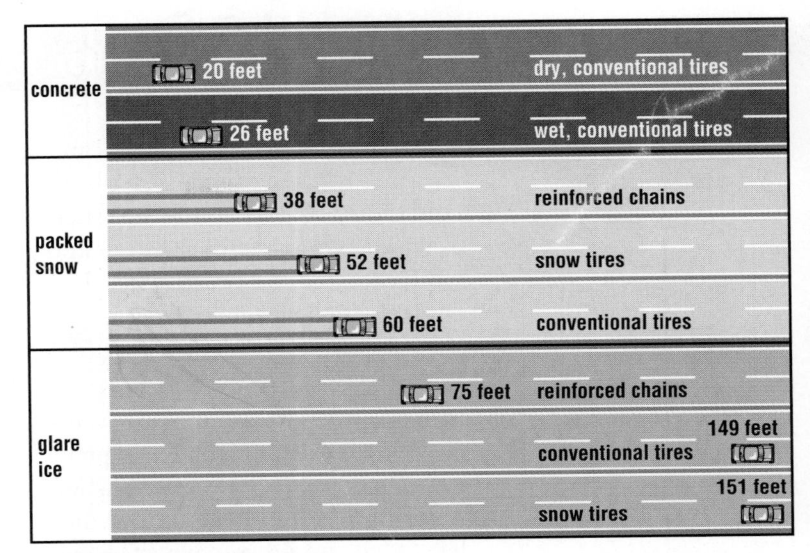

Braking Distances at 20 mph

The chart shows how long it takes to stop from 20 mph. Notice the difference that different tires and road surfaces can make.

Review It

1. What happens to traction during rain and snow?
2. What happens when a vehicle hydroplanes?
3. What are the steps you need to take to correct a rear-wheel skid?
4. What does controlled braking enable you to do?

12.3 Other Adverse Weather Conditions

Objectives

1. Explain how to control your vehicle in windy conditions.
2. List precautions for driving in extremely hot or cold weather.
3. Describe what to do to maintain vehicle control during winter driving.

Extreme weather conditions can make routine driving very difficult. Other adverse conditions such as wind, extreme temperatures, and winter weather may also affect the control you have while driving.

Wind

Strong winds can reduce your vehicle control. Imagine the truck pictured here is passing you on the left. A strong wind is blowing from the left. What should you expect? How can you maintain control?

Anticipate a strong blast of wind from the left after the truck passes. To maintain control, be ready to slow a little, move to lane position 3, and apply extra steering to the left just to keep moving in your intended path of travel.

You may experience this type of situation when driving out from under a bridge or from a tunnel. Just remember to keep a balanced grip on the steering wheel and be ready to make steering corrections for cross winds.

In the unlikely event you are in an area where tornadoes are spotted, be ready to act. The last place you want to be in a tornado is in a car. If you see a tornado and there is no place to take cover, stop, get out of your vehicle, and lay down in a ditch or under a bridge.

Expect the combination of a high cross wind and truck traffic to make driving tough.

In deep snow, make sure exhaust can get away from your vehicle.

Hot Weather

Your vehicle is designed to operate in a wide range of temperatures. It has a cooling system to help it warm up in winter and stay cool in the summer. But in extreme conditions, problems can develop.

Your temperature light or gauge indicates when your engine is too hot. When this happens, turn off your air conditioner. You may be uncomfortable, but you might also be able to cool your engine enough by turning on your heater. If the engine temperature warning light stays on, stop and park in a safe place to let the engine cool. Once cool, check your coolant level in your cooling-system surge tank. Never remove the radiator cap on a hot engine because the hot liquid inside can scald you. If needed, refill and repair your cooling system.

Cold Weather

Very cold weather creates problems. Be prepared by taking the following steps:

- **Be Alert for Exhaust Leaks** Carbon monoxide gas is created when your engine runs. This gas is colorless, odorless, and deadly. Even a small exhaust leak can be trouble. When driving, always have a source of fresh air coming into your vehicle—even if you have to open a window a little. If you are stuck in snow with your engine running, make sure your exhaust pipe is not blocked as this driver is doing.
- **Do Not Race a Cold Engine** Racing a cold engine will increase wear on it. Do not run a cold engine at high speeds.
- **Do Not Set Your Parking Brake** Ice or slush stuck to the underside of your vehicle can freeze your parking brake when you park your vehicle. In these conditions, use your automatic transmission park gear or reverse with a standard transmission.

Tips for Smooth Winter Driving

Winter driving will test the best of your IPDE driving skills. The extra

Clear snow off your roof, hood, and trunk so it will not blow off and block your vision.

effort you make to maintain an adequate line of sight and open zones is worth it. You can help smooth the way by following these tips:

- **Look and Listen for Traffic Reports** Be alert to television and radio reports about accidents, road repairs, and bad weather. You also can take advantage of Internet information sources.
- **Keep Windows Clear** Remove snow and ice before driving as this driver is doing. Don't forget your headlights and taillights. You want to see and be seen.
- **Respect Lower Speeds** Travel with the flow of traffic, but always maintain control of your vehicle.
- **Keep a Safe Following Distance** Allow six, seven, or more seconds of following distance just to make sure you have room.
- **Try to Keep Moving in Snow** If you must be out in a blizzard, be alert for drivers who are stalled, disabled, or moving extremely slowly. Try to avoid getting stuck behind them. Slow down and maneuver to avoid others and to keep moving. The energy of motion created by your moving vehicle can help carry you through snowy situations.
- **Use a Lower Gear on Slippery Roads** Use a lower gear to maintain control on ice or snow. Remember, keep moving to avoid getting stuck.
- **Avoid Cruise Control** Do not use cruise control on slippery roads. The system could cause you to lose control.

Review It

1. What actions must you take to maintain vehicle control in strong winds?
2. What can you do to cool an overheated engine?
3. Why should you try to keep moving at low speeds in heavy snow?

Chapter 12
Review

Reviewing Chapter Objectives

1. Reduced Visibility

1. How do you use the IPDE Process to manage risks in bad weather? (246)
2. What can you do to help others see you at dawn and dusk? (247)
3. What special techniques can you use for night driving? (247–249)

2. Reduced Traction

4. What happens to traction during rain and snow? (252)
5. What steps can you take to avoid hydroplaning? (252)
6. How do you correct a rear-wheel skid? (257)
7. How do you use the controlled-braking technique? (257–258)

3. Other Adverse Weather Conditions

8. How can you control your vehicle in windy conditions? (260)
9. What precautions can you take for driving in extremely hot or cold weather? (261)
10. What should you do to maintain vehicle control during winter driving? (262)

Projects

Individuals

Investigate Make a list of all the sources available to you to check on traffic conditions. Your list should include sources for local conditions as well as sources for conditions across the country.

Use Technology Use the Internet to check weather conditions throughout the United States. Identify places with weather conditions that could affect travel. Compare your findings with those of your classmates.

Groups

Demonstrate Using model vehicles, demonstrate to the class the various types of skids discussed in the text. Explain how the skids occur and how to correct for them.

Practice With the owners' permission, practice cleaning the outside windows of the vehicles parked in your school parking lot.

Chapter 12
Review

Chapter Test

Check Your Knowledge

Multiple Choice Copy the number of each sentence below on a sheet of paper. Choose the letter of the answer that best completes the sentence or answers the question.

1. When visibility is reduced, the first action to take is to
(a) maintain a steady speed. (b) stop.
(c) slow down.
(d) move closer to the windshield.

2. If traction conditions are hazardous, you should
(a) drive slowly. (b) not drive at all.
(c) drive close to other vehicles.
(d) use emergency flashers.

3. Traction on wet roads can be improved by driving
(a) toward the right edge of the roadway.
(b) at or near the posted speed limit.
(c) with reduced tire air pressure.
(d) in the tire tracks of the vehicle ahead.

4. When your temperature gauge indicates that your engine is too hot, you should
(a) turn on your heater.
(b) remove the radiator cap.
(c) turn on your air conditioner.
(d) none of the above

Completion Copy the number of each sentence below. After each number, write the word or words that complete the sentence correctly.

5. Wearing sun glasses and a sun visor helps you deal with blinding _____ conditions.

6. If it is snowing during the day or at night, you should always use _____ headlights.

7. _____ brakes allow you to steer and stop at the same time.

Review Vocabulary

Copy the number of each definition in List A. Match the definition in List A with the term it defines in List B.

List A

8. vehicle loses part or all of its grip on the road

9. repeating the sequence of driving forward a little and then back a little to move your vehicle out of deep snow, mud, or sand

10. reducing speed as quickly as possible while maintaining steering control of your vehicle

11. driving at a speed that makes your stopping distance longer than the distance lighted by your headlights

12. occurs when a tire loses road contact by rising up on top of water

List B

a. controlled braking
b. hydroplaning
c. rocking a vehicle
d. skid
e. overdriving headlights

Think Critically

Write a paragraph to answer each question.

1. Using the IPDE Process as your guide, explain how you can maintain a safe intended path of travel when visibility is reduced.

2. Which headlights (low-beam or high-beam) should you use when driving at night in adverse weather conditions? Explain your answer.

Decision Making

1. What actions should you take in this skidding situation?

2. In this winter situation, what precautions should you take when approaching the bridge?

3. As you approach this situation and see that the blue van has stopped, how would you use controlled braking?

4. What visual habit should you use to avoid being blinded by these oncoming high-beam headlights?

CHAPTER 13
Handling Emergencies

You Are the Driver!

Imagine that you are driving the blue car in this situation. The red car on your right pulls out in front of you. What should you do? What should you do if a collision occurs?

Vehicle malfunctions, driver errors, and roadway hazards can cause emergencies. In all cases, you must be prepared to act quickly to avoid or minimize a collision.

In this chapter you will learn how to handle many kinds of emergencies, and what steps to take if you are involved in a collision.

For: Chapter 13 online activities
Visit: PHSchool.com
Web Code: cak-9999

13.1
Vehicle Malfunctions

Objectives

1. List actions to take if a tire blows out.
2. List the proper steps to follow if the brakes fail.
3. Explain what to do if your accelerator sticks.
4. Describe what to do in case of steering failure.

Proper maintenance can prevent most vehicle malfunctions. When your vehicle gives you any warning signs, promptly make the necessary repairs.

Vehicle equipment sometimes will malfunction with no warning. A sudden malfunction can create an emergency. If prepared for an emergency, you will reduce your risk of serious trouble in traffic.

Tire Failure

Tires wear more quickly under unfavorable driving and poor maintenance conditions. Abrupt braking and sharp steering shorten tire life. Bumps, potholes, and poor roadway surfaces add to tire stress and can cause sudden damage to tires. Unbalanced wheels and poor alignment can cause tires to wear unevenly. Underinflation and overinflation are other causes of tire wear.

Blowout

A **blowout** occurs when a tire loses air pressure suddenly. A blowout might occur if the tire hits an object on the roadway or a pothole. Older, badly worn, or underinflated tires are more likely to blow out.

When a front tire blows out, the vehicle quickly pulls in the direction of the deflated tire. You must steer firmly against the pull of the vehicle. A left-front tire blowout is especially dangerous, since the vehicle will pull toward the lane of oncoming traffic.

When a rear tire blows out, the back of the vehicle can fishtail. When fishtailing occurs, the rear of the vehicle swerves back and forth. Handle a rear blowout like a skid.

Take the following actions when a tire blows out:

1. Grip the steering wheel firmly.
2. Ease up on the accelerator to slow the vehicle. *Do not brake.* Braking can cause the vehicle to swerve.
3. Check the traffic situation as you gain control of the vehicle.
4. Drive off the roadway slowly, braking gently.
5. Turn on hazard flashers. Drive slowly until you find a safe location to stop.

Changing a Tire

Even if you are an auto club member, you should know how to change a tire. Tire-changing instructions are included in the owner's manual for your vehicle. Practice changing a tire in a safe place.

To change a tire, you will need a **jack,** a hand-operated device used to lift and hold one corner or side of the vehicle. An elevated vehicle might slip off a jack. Never put yourself in a position where the vehicle could fall on you.

Follow these steps to change a tire:

1. Park on a level area away from traffic. Turn on the hazard flashers. Put the selector lever in PARK; use REVERSE in a stick-shift vehicle.

2. Set the parking brake.
3. Block the wheel that is diagonally opposite the flat tire. Carry two blocks of wood or two bricks in your trunk for this purpose. Place one block in front of the wheel and another block firmly behind the wheel. Blocking helps keep the vehicle from rolling once it is raised up by the jack.
4. Ask your passengers to get out of the vehicle and move to a safe place away from the roadway.
5. Take out the spare tire, jack, and lug wrench.
6. Assemble the jack. Position it under the vehicle.
7. Jack up the vehicle partway. The flat tire should touch the ground so that the wheel cannot turn.
8. Remove the wheel cover. Loosen the **lug nuts,** the devices that hold the wheel to the vehicle.
9. Jack up the vehicle until the tire completely clears the ground.
10. Use the lug wrench to remove the lug nuts. Place them in a safe place, such as your pocket.

If a left-front tire blows out, the vehicle might pull toward oncoming traffic.

11. Remove the wheel with the flat tire. Place the wheel to the side.
12. Mount the wheel with the spare tire. Rock it gently into position.
13. Replace and tighten the lug nuts.
14. Lower the vehicle slowly and remove the jack.
15. Use the lug wrench to tighten all the lug nuts again.
16. Leave the wheel cover off as a reminder to fix the flat. Put the wheel cover, flat tire, and tire changing equipment into the trunk. Remove the blocks.

Replace or repair the flat tire as soon as possible. If your spare tire is

Rock the spare tire into position as you mount it.

A quick look around your vehicle before driving may help you identify a worn tire, burned out light, or other problem—before a vehicle failure occurs.

a temporary or compact spare, drive on it only as necessary under the manufacturer's conditions of its use.

Brake Failure

Vehicles are required to have a two-part braking system. If one part fails, the other part still brakes two wheels. The brake warning light signals a brake failure. If both braking parts fail at the same time, your foot brake will have no braking power at all.

Total Brake Failure

Total brake failure rarely happens. When it does occur, the driver is usually braking hard for a stop.

Follow these steps immediately if your brakes fail:

1. Pump the brake pedal. Pumping might temporarily restore enough brake-fluid pressure to slow or stop your vehicle. You will know after three or four pumps if your brakes are going to hold.
2. Downshift to a lower gear. This uses the braking power of the engine to slow.
3. Pull and hold the parking-brake release lever out or hold the parking-brake button at "Off." Apply the parking brake. You can quickly release the parking brake for a moment if the vehicle begins to skid.
4. Search for an open zone. You can still steer. As a last resort, rub the wheels against a curb to reduce speed. If a collision is unavoidable, steer for a sideswipe rather than colliding head-on into something solid.

Power Brake Failure Brake "failure" with power or power-assisted brakes is usually the loss of power that helps you brake. The power stops if the engine stops, but the brakes have not failed. You must push the brake pedal harder.

Other Brake Failures

When brakes overheat, they can lose effectiveness. This condition, called **brake fade,** occurs after continuous hard braking. To regain full braking ability, stop the vehicle and let the brakes cool. Overheating can warp the rotors on disc brakes. As a result, braking becomes uneven, and the vehicle might surge forward as you brake. To restore smooth braking, you might need to have the rotors repaired.

Driving through water also can cause temporary brake failure. Gently brake after you leave the water. Friction can help generate heat to dry the brakes. Test them again to be sure they work properly.

If your brakes fail, apply the parking brake, but hold the button at "Off" or hold the release lever out.

Accelerator Malfunctions

You can lose control of your engine's speed when the accelerator malfunctions. Some problems can cause your vehicle to accelerate more than you intend, and other problems can keep your vehicle from accelerating.

Broken Spring

A broken accelerator spring is a serious problem. The accelerator pedal might be flat on the floor. You can no longer control engine speed with the accelerator.

If you have this problem, shift to NEUTRAL. Put on your hazard flashers, check traffic, and brake safely to the side of the road. Do not drive the vehicle until the spring is repaired.

Stuck Accelerator

The accelerator is stuck if the engine does not return to idling speed when you release the accelerator. One cause of a stuck accelerator is a wadded floor mat around the pedal.

A stuck accelerator is a critical emergency. While driving at a steady speed, you have no warning that the accelerator is stuck. You discover that there is a problem when you need to turn or stop.

Take these actions if your accelerator sticks:

1. Kick the side of the accelerator once to try to jar it free.
2. Apply the brakes.
3. Choose an escape path that leads to an open zone off the roadway. Continue braking.
4. If you are steering into a sharp curve or turn, shift to NEUTRAL. Depress the clutch in a stickshift vehicle. The engine will race, but power is removed from the wheels. You might damage the engine or transmission in an automatic transmission, but you might also avoid a collision.
5. Follow your escape path off the roadway.
6. Turn off the ignition once you are off the roadway.

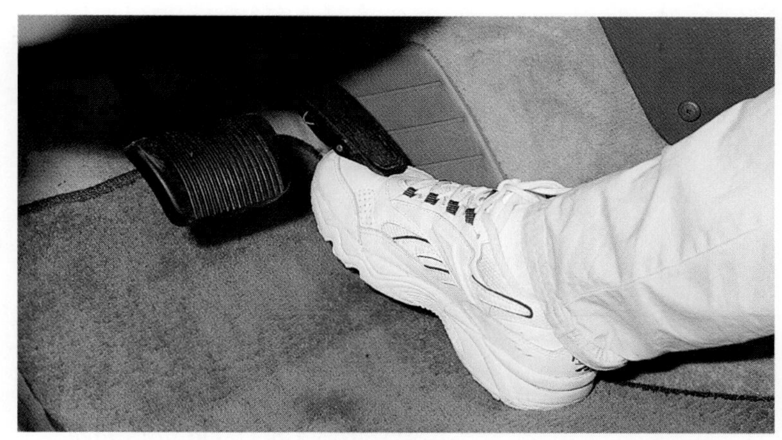

While stopped or driving in light traffic, you can try to free a stuck accelerator by putting your toe under it and lifting.

If you are in a light-traffic area, you might try to free a stuck accelerator while driving. Put your toe under the accelerator pedal and lift. *Never reach down with your hand to lift the pedal while driving.* You cannot see or drive safely from this position.

After stopping, take these actions:

- Remove any obstructions around, under, or over the accelerator.
- Tap the accelerator repeatedly.
- Put your toe or hand under the accelerator and lift.

After freeing the accelerator, test it before you drive. If a broken spring is the problem, do not drive until it is repaired.

Engine Failure

Usually you have very little warning that your engine is going to sputter or stop. With a stalled engine, you can still steer your vehicle. If you have power steering, you will have to steer harder.

Follow these steps if your engine stops suddenly:

1. Shift to NEUTRAL when the engine first sputters or stops.
2. Begin moving out of traffic to the nearest shoulder. Turn on the hazard flashers. Do not brake.
3. Try to restart the engine while you are moving. If the engine starts, shift into a forward gear and proceed. If it does not start, move onto the shoulder or to the curb, if possible. Steering will be harder when power is lost by engine failure. Try again to start the engine.
4. If the engine still fails to start, raise the hood and leave the hazard flashers on. Go for help. If you have a cellular phone, use it to secure assistance.

If your vehicle becomes disabled in risky locations, set flares or other warning devices to alert other roadway users.

If your engine fails, turn on the hazard flashers, move safely off the roadway, and raise the hood to signal you need help.

Flooded Engine

When too much fuel and not enough air reach the engine, it becomes flooded. You can flood the engine if you pump the accelerator when trying to start the vehicle.

Follow these steps to start a flooded engine:

1. Hold the accelerator pedal to the floor to let air in and to clear excess fuel from engine.
2. While holding the accelerator down, turn the ignition switch on steadily for five seconds. If the engine does not start, wait several minutes, and try again.
3. When the engine starts, release the accelerator gradually to help clear excess fuel from the engine.

Overheated Engine

Sometimes even a well maintained engine overheats in hot weather or in stop-and-go traffic. Driving up long hills with the air conditioner on also can cause overheating. The temperature light or gauge warns you if the engine overheats.

Take these steps if your engine overheats:

1. Turn off the air conditioner.
2. Turn on the heater to draw heat from the engine. You might be uncomfortable, but this will lower engine temperature.
3. During stops, shift to NEUTRAL. Press the accelerator gently to speed up the engine slightly.
4. If the temperature light stays on or if the gauge points to *hot*,

move to a safe place. Stop, turn off the engine, raise the hood, and let the engine cool. Do not add water to the radiator until the engine has cooled.

Steering Failure

Complete steering-system failure seldom occurs but is extremely serious.

Total Steering Failure

Take these actions if your steering fails completely:

1. Use your horn and hazard flashers to communicate your emergency.
2. Stop as quickly and safely as possible. Lift your foot from the accelerator. *Do not brake.* Braking could cause the vehicle to skid. Use the parking brake. Hold the parking brake release "Off" and use a quick on-off action.
3. Shift to a lower gear.

Power-Steering Failure

Power-steering failure occurs when the engine dies, when the power-steering fluid level is low, or when a drive belt slips or breaks. The steering mechanism still works, but you must exert more effort to steer.

Loss of Forward Vision

If you have lost forward vision, you must act promptly to regain your driving view. Slow and continue to drive in your path of travel.

The Hood Flies Up

This rare emergency usually occurs because the hood is not securely latched. Stop your vehicle if the hood is vibrating. Release the hood and secure it.

If your hood flies up, look through the space below the open hood and steer to a safe place.

Take these actions if the hood flies up while you are driving:

1. Slouch down in your seat to look through the crack below the open hood. Check the rear zone.
2. If you cannot see under the hood, roll down your window. Look in the direction that you are driving.
3. Turn on the hazard flashers. Pump the brakes gently to warn other drivers of your emergency.
4. Slow down, and drive out of the traffic flow to a safe location.

Headlights Fail

If you are driving at night and your headlights flicker, move quickly off the roadway to a safe place.

Follow these steps if your headlights fail entirely:

1. Turn on your right turn signal to light up an escape path to the right.
2. Immediately slow down and bring your vehicle to a safe stop.
3. Try the dimmer switch, parking lights, and hazard flashers. Some circuits might still work. If so, use

parking or hazard lights to help you drive off the roadway to a safe location.

4. Use the light from street lights, signs, buildings, or other vehicles to help you see. Move off the roadway to a safe location when the vehicle has slowed. Use a flashlight to check fuses or fuse clips. If necessary, replace or reseat the fuse before proceeding.

Splashed Windshield

Your windshield might be splashed with snow, slush, or mud. Immediately turn on your windshield wipers. Slow, and try to maintain your path of travel until you regain visibility. If you anticipate that your windshield will be splashed, turn on wipers before you lose vision.

Vehicle on Fire

A vehicle fire can be dangerous. The fire can involve fuel, oil, grease, ordinary combustibles, electrical equipment, or a combination of sources. Carry an A-B-C-type fire extinguisher that is designed to control such fires. Notify the fire department of any vehicle fires.

Do not open the hood if smoke is coming from under it.

Engine Compartment Fire

Most vehicle fires start in the engine compartment. Take these actions in case of fire:

1. Quickly steer the vehicle off the roadway to a safe, open area. Stay away from buildings and service stations. Turn off the ignition.
2. Have passengers move at least 100 feet away from the vehicle.
3. Estimate how serious the fire is. You might see flames and smoke around the hood. Do not try to put out the fire. Leave the hood closed. Move away from the vehicle while you wait for the fire department. The fuel tank could explode.

If you think that the fire is small enough to control and you have an A-B-C-type fire extinguisher, you should take these steps:

1. Use gloves or a rag to protect your hands. Turn your face away to protect yourself from the heat and flames. Carefully open the hood. Once the hood is up, the fire will burn freely.
2. Direct the extinguisher on the fire. Water will not put out oil and fuel fires and can spread the fire.
3. Never try to disconnect the battery or work with your hands under the hood while it is still hot.

Fire is possible in any collision where the engine compartment is smashed. Turn off the ignition, and

You Are the Driver!
Your car is stalled on the railroad tracks with a train approaching. What direction should you run when you abandon the car?

get passengers out and away from the vehicle.

Passenger Compartment Fire

A passenger compartment fire usually is caused by a carelessly handled match or burning tobacco product. Pull off the roadway. Use water or a fire extinguisher, and make sure the fire is completely out. Upholstery fires often restart.

Vehicle Stalls on Railroad Tracks

Weather, driver, or roadway conditions may cause a vehicle's engine to stall while crossing railroad tracks. Take these actions if your vehicle stalls on the tracks:

1. Check carefully to be sure no train is coming. Try to restart the vehicle. If the engine floods, hold the accelerator to the floor as you restart the engine.
2. If you cannot restart the engine, have passengers leave the vehicle. Have one passenger watch for trains, and ask others to help you.
3. Shift to NEUTRAL and push the vehicle off the tracks.
4. If a train is coming, abandon your vehicle. Move away from the tracks in the direction the train is approaching. This helps you avoid injury from flying fragments.

Review It

1. What actions should you take if a tire blows out?
2. What should you do if the brakes fail?
3. What actions should you take if the accelerator sticks?
4. What actions should you take if your steering fails?

13.2 Driver Errors

Objectives

1. Describe how to return to the roadway if your vehicle runs off the roadway.
2. Explain when to use an emergency swerve.

Driver errors cause many more emergencies than do vehicle malfunctions. Errors due to inexperience, lack of attention, or poor decisions often create driving emergencies. Any driver can be put in an emergency situation by the unpredictable act of another driver.

Developing automatic responses to emergencies is a critical part of the total driving task. Identifying an emergency, predicting its consequences, making correct decisions, and executing decisions quickly will help you avoid a collision.

Driving Off the Road

When a front wheel leaves the edge of the roadway, returning to the roadway can be easy if the shoulder is paved and in good condition. However, the shoulder is often not paved.

Many fatal one-vehicle collisions result when drivers brake and return suddenly to the roadway. In such a situation, the vehicle often rolls over. Other collisions can occur when drivers quickly return to the roadway and abruptly cross into other traffic.

Off-Road Recovery

Each different type of off-road situation requires a specific recovery technique. For example, if the drop-off is moderate and the shoulder of the road is not steeply sloped, follow these steps for a safe off-road recovery:

1. Hold the steering wheel firmly with both hands. The greater the drop-off between roadway and shoulder, the greater amount of steering control you need. Keep your vehicle heading straight toward your target.

IF YOU VEER OFF THE ROAD, DON'T TURN SHARPLY

If you veer off the road, turning the wheel sharply to try to get back onto the road can cause a roll-over crash. If you do veer off the road, you should brake gradually and steer straight. Try to come to a complete stop. Then, after confirming the road is clear of traffic, proceed at a very slow speed and steer the car slightly to get back onto the road.

2. Let up on the accelerator and brake gently to 5 or 10 mph. Avoid hard braking.
3. Position your vehicle so it straddles the roadway edge.
4. Select a place to return to the roadway where the shoulder is nearest the level of the roadway.
5. Check for traffic. Signal, check your blind spot, and return to the roadway.
6. Steer 1/8 to 1/4 of a turn toward the roadway to return. If the drop off is severe, you might need to slow more and turn very sharply to get back onto the pavement.
7. Countersteer sharply the instant the front tire touches the roadway. You **countersteer** when you steer in the opposite direction.
8. Center the vehicle in lane position 1 and reestablish your target. Cancel your signal. Accelerate to match the flow of traffic.

If traffic is heavy when you go off the roadway, drive entirely off the roadway. Stop and wait for a large gap in traffic before you reenter.

Sometimes an obstruction, such as a bridge or guardrail, might be on the shoulder ahead. In this case, you must make a quick recovery. Grip the steering wheel firmly. Countersteer *immediately* when the front wheel touches the roadway.

Emergency Swerving

Swerving is a last-second emergency means of avoiding a collision. Swerve only when you believe that braking will not prevent a collision. At speeds over 30 mph, you can usually swerve to a new path in less distance than the distance you needed to stop safely.

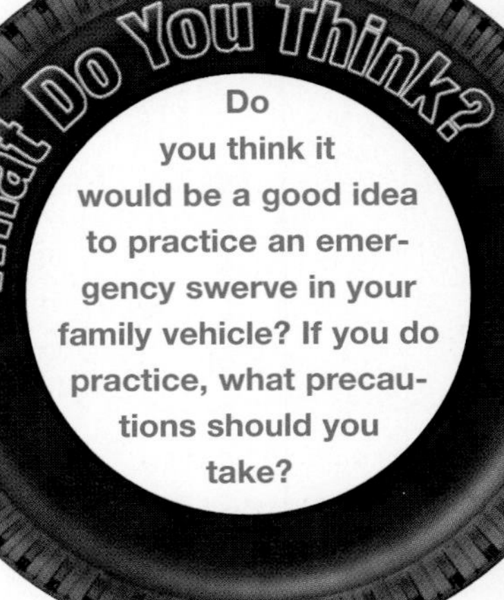

The Stop-Swerve Decision

The picture below shows a dangerous situation. The driver of the yellow vehicle might hit the brakes to stop. In some situations, this action will be the only choice. However, if the driver hits and locks the brakes, the vehicle might slide into the vehicle ahead. When moving at 30 mph or more, the traction created by the vehicle's tires can turn the vehicle sideways faster than braking traction can stop it.

When deciding whether to swerve around an object, be sure that no other vehicle is in the lane that you will enter.

Should the driver of the yellow car stop or swerve?

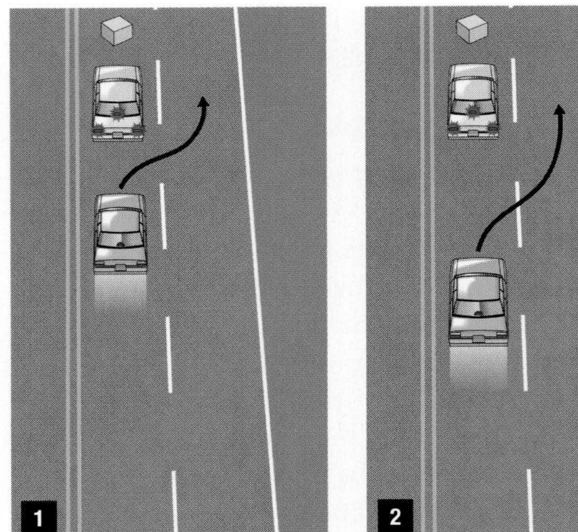

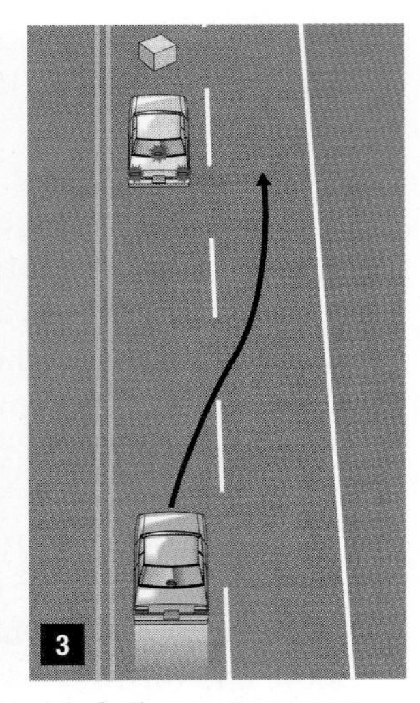

1. You must swerve sharply around a close object. 2. When the object is farther away, swerve less sharply. 3. The swerve is less sharp at a greater distance.

The stop-swerve decision is not an easy one to make. Any sudden action should be used only as a last resort. If a pedestrian steps in front of you, you might be forced to make a stop-swerve decision.

Use the IPDE Process and Zone Control System to protect yourself in stop-swerve situations. In addition, allow at least three seconds between yourself and the vehicle ahead.

Executing an Emergency Swerve

Follow these steps if you decide to swerve:

1. Identify the escape path.
2. Grip the steering wheel firmly and turn the wheel sharply in the direction of the swerve.
3. In the same rhythmic motion, countersteer to stabilize your vehicle. Straighten the wheel, and continue to steer in your path.

How Sharply to Swerve?

The amount of time available to swerve determines how sharply you must swerve. Consider two factors—distance and speed—when determining how much time is available. When the stopped vehicle is farther away, as shown above, the swerve will be less severe and easier to execute.

As speed increases, the less time you have to swerve. For example, you have about 2 seconds to swerve at 40 mph. You have just 1 second at 60 mph.

Review It

1. How should you return safely to the roadway if your vehicle runs off the roadway?
2. Under what conditions should you make an emergency swerve?

13.3

Roadway Hazards

Unusual and unexpected roadway hazards can cause you to lose control of your vehicle. Driving into deep water, sharp curves, and objects on the roadway can result in emergency situations.

Potholes in the Roadway

Potholes can develop as water collects in cracks in the roadway. The water can freeze and thaw, causing the cracks to expand. As vehicles drive over these water-filled cracks, they break up the roadway even more.

Potholes often have sharp edges which can severely damage tires. You can lose control of your vehicle—and severely damage it—if you hit a pothole at a fast speed.

Watch for potholes and avoid hitting them whenever possible. Drive carefully around or straddle a pothole. Stay in your own lane and check front zones as you try to avoid potholes in the roadway.

Drive slowly through potholes to prevent tire damage.

If you must drive through a pothole, slow down to prevent tire damage. By driving slowly, you can better keep control of your vehicle.

Sharp Curve

Driving around a curve fast is dangerous. Poor road conditions or crossing the center line might lead to a collision. The standard warning sign may not indicate exactly how sharp the curve is. Also, the warning sign might not have an advisory speed sign.

Take these actions if you enter a curve too fast:

1. Brake gently as soon as you realize your problem. If you are not yet in the curve, brake more firmly. If you are already in the curve, brake, but do not lock the wheels.
2. About halfway through the curve, look to your target and accelerate gently to help stabilize your vehicle.

Object on the Roadway

An object on the roadway creates a hazard, whether it is an object, leaves, an animal, or a person. A cardboard box in the street might not appear to be dangerous. Neither does a pile of leaves raked from a yard. However, avoid these and other objects on the roadway. You might not be able to identify the contents of the box. You cannot see a rake or other object in the leaf pile.

Objectives

1. Describe how to minimize vehicle damage caused by potholes.
2. Explain what to do if you enter a curve too fast.
3. Tell how to escape from a vehicle that is sinking in water.

You Are the Driver!
Should you steer around, brake, straddle, or drive over the object?

First check traffic, and then decide whether to steer around, brake, straddle, or drive over the object. Choose to straddle the object only if your vehicle can clear it and you cannot safely steer around it. Avoid swerving left across the center line because you could encounter other traffic. *Drive over an object only as a last resort.*

Vehicle in Deep Water

Do not attempt to drive through deep water on the roadway. Turn around or take another route.

Take these actions if your vehicle goes into deep water:

1. Open the window that is the most out of the water. Power windows might short circuit in water so open these windows immediately.
2. Unfasten your safety belt. Check your passengers, and have them unfasten their safety belts.
3. Exit promptly through the open window.

If the windows will not open, attempt to exit through a door. Do not panic if the door is slow to open. Pressure will equalize as water enters your vehicle. You then can open the door.

If your vehicle is totally submerged underwater, some air will be trapped for a brief time toward the highest point of the vehicle. Try to get a full breath or two of air while locating a window or door that is facing up. Open the window or door and leave your vehicle.

If you become trapped in your vehicle underwater, turn on your headlights. This can help rescuers find your vehicle more quickly.

Review It

1. What should you do if you see a pothole in your path of travel?
2. What actions should you take if you enter a curve too fast?
3. How should you escape a vehicle that is sinking in deep water?

13.4
Collisions

Most drivers are involved in a collision at some time during their lives. If you know in advance how to react, you can lessen the effects of a collision.

Minimizing Effects of a Collision

Suddenly, a vehicle emerges from a driveway and enters your path of travel. You know that you cannot avoid a collision. What should you do? If a collision is about to occur, act as follows:

- Above all, *do not give up*. Keep control of your vehicle. Any change of speed or direction that lessens the impact will help.
- Steer for something "soft" if you leave the roadway. Look for bushes or an open field.
- Avoid objects, such as trees and parked vehicles.
- Get yourself and passengers out and away from your vehicle if there is a chance of another vehicle colliding with yours.

Threat of a Head-on Collision

Because a head-on collision produces the greatest force of impact of any collision, serious injuries and/or death are more likely to occur. Take these steps if you are threatened with a head-on collision:

1. Maintain vehicle control. Brake hard, but do not lock the wheels. Slowing lessens the force of impact and gives the other driver space and time to recover control.
2. Blow the horn and flash the headlights. These actions might alert an impaired driver. Continue braking and move to the right if the driver does not heed your warning.
3. Steer right toward the shoulder. *Do not steer left*. The other driver likely will try to steer back into the proper lane. Prepare to drive entirely off the roadway to the right, if necessary.

Threat of a Side-Impact Collision

Take these steps to avoid or lessen the effect of a side-impact collision:

1. Brake or accelerate quickly. Do whichever seems more likely to lessen the collision impact.

Objectives

1. Explain how to avoid or minimize head-on, side-impact, and rear-end collisions.
2. List the immediate steps to take if a collision occurs.
3. Describe other follow-up steps needed after a collision.

Steer to the right if a head-on collision seems about to occur.

What can the driver of the white car do to minimize the effects of a second collision on the passengers?

Most states have what is known as a "Good Samaritan Law." These laws help protect people giving first aid at a collision scene.

2. Blow the horn to alert the other driver.
3. Change lanes or swerve away from the impact. Be aware of the constantly changing traffic situation around you.

The driver of the white car crossing the road in the picture above might find it difficult to avoid being hit from the side. However, by accelerating, the driver might avoid having the passenger compartment crushed. An impact to the passenger compartment often causes a second collision between passengers and the inside of the vehicle.

Threat of a Rear-End Collision

You are nearly defenseless against a rear-end collision when your vehicle is stopped. If your vehicle is in motion, you might not realize that a vehicle approaching from the rear is coming too fast and might not be able to avoid hitting your vehicle.

Take these actions if you are threatened with a rear-end collision:

1. Flash your brake lights early to alert the driver behind you.
2. As the vehicle nears, check your front zones for open space and move forward, if possible. This precaution gives the driver approaching from the rear more time and space to stop safely.
3. If the intersection is clear, accelerate to give the other driver more space to stop. If your path is not clear, turn right.
4. If a collision is unavoidable, release your brakes just before the collision occurs. This helps

What would you do if you saw this car approaching from the rear?

What procedures should you follow in a collision, even before help arrives?

soften the impact. Brake immediately after the collision to avoid sliding into another traffic lane.

Maintaining a 3-second following distance and stopping so that you see the tires of the vehicle ahead are good habits. These actions often can help you avoid being hit from behind.

If You Have a Collision

If you collide with another vehicle, a pedestrian, or someone's property, you are legally required to follow specific procedures.

Your First Steps

Each state has specific procedures that you must follow immediately when involved in a collision. All states require you to take these five steps.

1. Stop Immediately. Failure to stop is a serious offense. Move your vehicle to the side of the road. Do not leave your vehicle where it can block traffic unless it is so damaged it cannot be moved. Turn off ignition.

If you damage a parked vehicle even slightly, try to find the owner. If you cannot, write your name, address, and phone number on a note. Leave the note under a windshield wiper. Notify the police.

2. Aid the Injured. *Never move an injured person unless there is danger of fire or another collision.* Send for paramedics if anyone is seriously injured. Administer basic first aid for injuries such as severe bleeding, shock, and breathing stoppage only if you have completed a certified first-aid course.

DIALING 911 Dialing 911 to report emergencies is a relatively new system. As late as the mid-1980s, you had to call the full number for the service you wanted. As recent as the late 1960s, you may have called the local funeral home for ambulance service. Dialing 911 gets you fast, appropriate service when it is needed.

Exchange information with all drivers involved in a collision.

3. Prevent Further Damage. Warn oncoming traffic with flares or reflectors placed at least 100 feet ahead of and behind the collision site (500 feet away in high-speed traffic). If you do not have such devices, another person might stand in advance of the site and direct vehicles around the collision. Do not put yourself or others in danger while directing traffic.

4. Send for Police. You must call the police if anyone is injured or killed. Some states require you to call the police for any collision, even if no personal injuries are evident.

5. Exchange Information. Get and provide this following information from other drivers involved in the collision: names, addresses, driver's license numbers, license plate numbers, and insurance company names and addresses.

Note the names and addresses of passengers, the positions in which they were sitting, and the extent of their injuries. Getting and giving this information is your responsibility.

Additional Steps

Take these additional steps after a collision:

Record Witnesses' Names and Addresses Note the names and addresses of any witnesses to the collision. Make a sketch of the collision scene or take a photo. Record such facts as time, date, location, weather, and driving conditions. Note the name of the hospital to which any injured persons were taken. Note the name and badge number of the police officer at the collision scene.

Give Police the Facts Provide honest, accurate facts. Never argue about who was to blame, and never admit blame. Stay at the scene until all information has been recorded. Take your vehicle to a repair shop for any necessary repairs. You generally need two repair estimates for insurance purposes. Keep all bills.

File Necessary Reports Each state requires drivers involved in a collision to file a written report if someone was killed or injured, or if property damage exceeds a set amount. Some states require that a report be filed within 24 hours of the collision.

You must also produce proof of financial responsibility by showing a card that lists your current insurance coverage, or a bond card. Finally, notify your insurance agent promptly. If you fail to do this within the time specified in your policy, the company might refuse to pay your claim.

Review It

1. How can you minimize the impact of a head-on collision? a side-impact collision? a rear-end collision?
2. What steps should you take immediately if you are involved in a collision?
3. What additional steps should you take following a collision?

Chapter 13
Review

Reviewing Chapter Objectives

1. Vehicle Malfunctions

1. What actions should you take if a tire blows out? (268–269)
2. What are the proper steps to follow if the brakes fail? (270)
3. What should you do if your accelerator sticks? (271)
4. What should you do in case of steering failure? (273)

2. Driver Errors

5. If your vehicle runs off the roadway, how should you return it to the roadway? (276–277)
6. When should you use an emergency swerve? (277–278)

3. Roadway Hazards

7. How could you minimize vehicle damage caused by potholes? (279)
8. What should you do if you enter a curve too fast? (279)
9. How would you escape a vehicle that is sinking in water? (280)

4. Collisions

10. How do you avoid or minimize head-on, side-impact, and rear-end collisions? (281–282)
11. What are the immediate steps you should take if a collision occurs? (283–284)
12. What are the follow-up steps you should take after a collision? (284)

Projects

Individuals

Investigate Research the specific procedures you must follow when involved in a collision in your state. Write a report of your findings.

Observe As a passenger in a vehicle, look for hazards in the roadway for a week. Make a list of the hazards you see. Discuss the hazards with your class.

Interview Visit a local vehicle repair shop. Obtain the manager's permission to interview a mechanic. Ask the mechanic to explain the most common causes of engine failure. Report your results to the class.

Groups

Practice As a group, practice changing a tire on a vehicle provided by your instructor for this purpose. Group members should take turns performing the various steps.

Demonstrate List the possible vehicle malfunctions described in this chapter on separate pieces of paper. Each group member should draw one piece of paper, then explain to the group what should be done if faced with that malfunction.

Chapter 13
Review

Chapter Test

Check Your Knowledge

Multiple Choice Copy the number of each sentence below on a sheet of paper. Choose the letter that best completes the statement or answers the question.

1. If you have a blowout, which action should you avoid?
   (a) ease up on accelerator
   (b) pull off onto the shoulder slowly
   (c) brake hard
   (d) turn on hazard lights
2. Which action should you take first if the accelerator sticks while you are driving?
   (a) shift into a lower gear
   (b) turn off the ignition
   (c) apply the parking brake
   (d) kick the side of the accelerator
3. To avoid a side-impact collision, you should
   (a) lock your brakes. (b) brake or accelerate quickly.
   (c) steer to the left. (d) steer to the right.

Completion Copy the number of each sentence below. After each number, write the word or words that complete the sentence correctly.

4. An engine _____ when it has too much fuel and not enough air.
5. Vehicle fires generally start in the _____.
6. When water collects in roadway cracks, _____ can develop.
7. A _____ collision produces the greatest force of impact of any collision.

Review Vocabulary

Copy the number of each definition in List A. Match the definition in List A with the term it defines in List B.

List A

8. devices that hold the wheel to the vehicle
9. steer in the opposite direction
10. sudden loss of tire air pressure while driving
11. hand-operated device used to lift and hold one corner or side of the vehicle
12. loss of braking effectiveness caused by overheating of the brakes after long, continuous, hard braking
13. back and forth swerving of the rear of a vehicle

List B

a. jack
b. fishtailing
c. lug nuts
d. brake fade
e. countersteer
f. blowout

Think Critically

Write a paragraph to answer each question.

1. You are driving in a residential area and identify a vehicle in your right-front zone backing out of a driveway. You hit your brakes hard, but your vehicle does not slow or stop. What steps should you take?
2. You are involved in a collision on the freeway in a neighboring state. You are not hurt but are not sure about the driver of the other vehicle. What should you do?

Decision Making

1. This car just had a right-front tire blowout. What steps should the driver take to handle this emergency safely?

2. You are traveling at 30 mph. You brake for the stop ahead, but then realize that your brakes do not work. What should you do to stop the vehicle?

3. The driver cannot possibly stop in time to avoid hitting the bicyclist. What should the driver do?

4. You are driving the gray car. Both you and the driver in the white car are traveling 30 mph. The other driver is not aware of your car. What can you do to prevent a collision or keep the collision from being too serious?

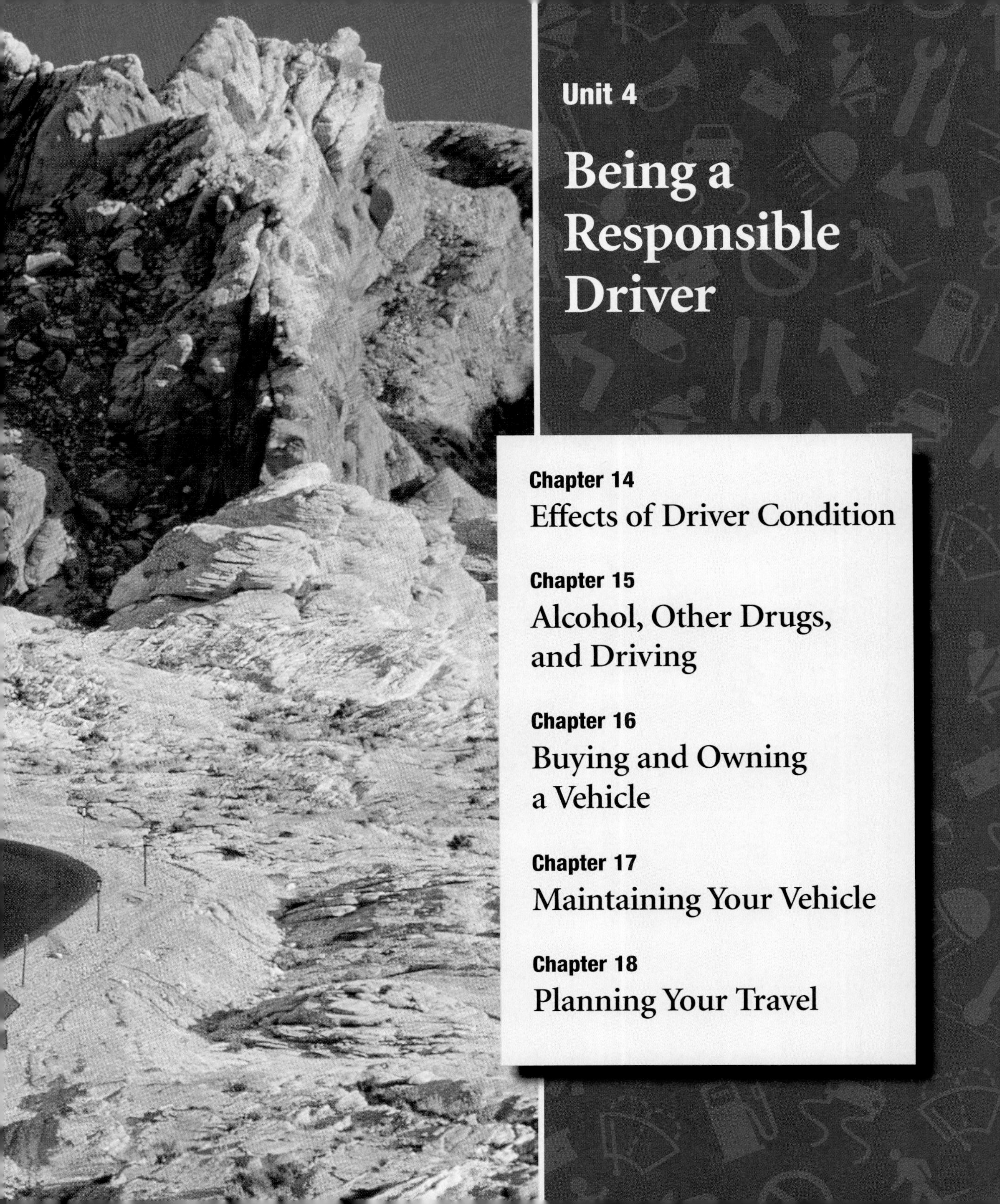

Unit 4

Being a Responsible Driver

CHAPTER 14
Effects of Driver Condition

You Are the Driver!

Imagine you have just been bicycle riding like these people. Every activity you do—including driving—involves some risk. You can keep your driving risks low if you are mentally alert, emotionally fit, and physically healthy. You must rely on your senses to help you stay on a safe, conflict-free path of travel.

This chapter discusses both your emotional and physical abilities as they relate to your driving. You will learn how your senses can help lower the risks involved in driving. You also will discover how a driver can compensate for physical disabilities that affect driving.

For: Chapter 14 online activities
Visit: PHSchool.com
Web Code: cak-9999

14.1 Emotions and Driving

Objectives

1. Tell how anger can affect your ability to drive.
2. Explain how passengers can help a driver.
3. Tell how you can manage your emotions while driving.
4. Describe the influence emotions have on your willingness to accept risk.

The word **emotion** is used to name a strong feeling. Anger, fear, and joy are examples of emotions. Emotions add a special flavor to life.

How Emotions Affect Driving

Emotions influence the way you think and act. When emotions affect your thoughts and actions, they can change the way you normally assess risk and make driving decisions. They can lead you to accept more or less risk than normal for the gain you receive. Emotions can be infectious; they can affect others in your vehicle and in vehicles around you.

A driver can minimize the effects of emotions by using courteous driving strategies. Using courtesy to influence the effects of emotions on others empowers you. In effect it can help keep you in control of yourself and others.

Mental Effects of Emotions

Strong emotions can interfere with your ability to think, reason, and make wise decisions. They can increase your chances of making a mistake. Emotions can affect the way you make judgments in a driving situation.

In some situations, a strong emotion can cause you to focus your attention on one event. You might miss other important events in a driving scene. In the picture, the driver in front has just cut over to the right lane and started to slow. This action could startle following drivers. It may cause them to become upset or angry. However, instead of becoming upset, they should increase the space between themselves and the vehicle ahead. Drivers need to reduce their own risk, rather than seek revenge or get even.

You Are the Driver!
How would you feel if this driver cut into your lane? What might the driver behind you think of your response?

Physical Effects of Emotions

Strong emotions also can cause changes in your bodily functions. Your body prepares itself for the stressful event. Your heartbeat increases, your breathing quickens, your digestion slows, and your muscles tighten.

Some emotional stress is needed to sustain life. However, continued emotional stress can exhaust you and contribute to adverse effects on the body such as heart disease and digestive disorders. The more tasks to be handled, the more complex and stressful the situation. Rush hour traffic can cause stress and fatigue in all drivers. Bumper-to-bumper driving situations in the city can also cause stress.

Anger While Driving

You usually rely upon a set of assumptions or expectations when driving. You assume that others will drive and act in a safe, responsible manner. You might be tempted to react angrily when you must change your expectations.

In normal driving situations, other drivers might interfere with your intended speed or path of travel. They might slow or change lanes improperly. They might not yield, may fail to signal, or may not move quickly enough when a traffic light changes. Sometimes you might think that other drivers are trying to irritate you. As a result, you might become angry.

Anger occurs more often to drivers than any other emotion. It can range from mild irritation to furious rage and can result in aggressive actions or even violent acts of "road rage."

In this picture, the driver is angry at the people who are talking and blocking his way. The driver is angry because he might be late for an appointment. If he cannot maintain emotional control, he might remain angry and react aggressively.

Anger can impair all of your driving skills. You might take risks

What Do You Think?

Some people believe that "road rage" is as dangerous as drunk driving. Do you agree? What makes you think that way?

The driver might remain angry long after the people have cleared his path.

Avoid situations that could evoke anger. Do not make emotional, last-second decisions when driving in heavy traffic.

you would not take if you were calm. You also might not see everything you should see and miss an important clue. You might force other drivers to stop or swerve abruptly. These last-second actions can cause conflicts and added stress not only for you, but for other drivers as well. Good drivers never surprise others.

What might you do when you become angry while driving—or confront other drivers who are? Think positively. Leave punishment to the police. Your acts of punishment may just aggravate the other drivers even more. Model good behavior. Consider that other drivers may have good reasons for their actions. Can you recall times when you have made similar decisions?

Other Emotions and Driving

Sorrow, depression, and anxiety are among other emotions that can adversely affect driving. These emotions can also slow body processes and reduce mental alertness.

Anxiety differs from anger. You might be anxious when driving in an unfamiliar, difficult situation. You might have trouble identifying hazards when you are confused. You might even feel panic-stricken. As a responsible driver, work to recognize difficult situations, and try your best to cope. It may mean delaying driving, but your risks will be reduced.

Excitement and happiness also can prevent you from fully concentrating on your driving task. A happy, excited driver can be just as impaired as an angry driver. After an intense event, such as a sports event, be sure that strong emotions do not impair your driving ability.

Emotions and the IPDE Process

The successful use of the IPDE Process requires total concentration on the driving task. You need time to use the IPDE Process. In a tight, high-stress situation, you need even more time to use the IPDE Process to keep from making wrong or late decisions.

You would need to have your emotions under control if you were driving into this situation.

Spirits might be high after winning a game, but drivers must remain in control.

Your emotional condition can drastically affect your driving ability.

Think how emotions could affect your driving if you were beside the truck pictured on the opposite page. The car ahead has been slowing and forcing you to slow. The truck driver has just decided to pass the car. You are not sure what the driver ahead is going to do. Another truck is behind the passing truck. As a result, the driver ahead and the truck drivers could cause you to make quick, irresponsible errors.

Passengers and Emotions

Peer pressure can be a very strong force, depending upon the situation. In a baseball game, team spirit can help win the game. In a vehicle, your passengers can strongly influence the way you drive.

In most group situations, one or more people need to assume responsibility and lead the group. When you are driving, you must be the leader and take control. You are responsible for the safety of your passengers.

In this picture, a championship soccer match has just ended. Everyone is going to celebrate. Emotions will be running high. The driver will be under special pressures to concentrate on the driving task. However, to make sure that nothing goes wrong, the driver must be the leader and maintain control of the situation.

Passengers can help the driver maintain control while driving. Here are actions you, as a passenger, can take to assist a driver:

- Avoid saying or doing anything that might distract or upset the driver. Refrain from heated discussions. Talk about positive events.
- Discourage the driver from taking reckless actions. Be prepared to intervene if the driver endangers others by reckless driving. Encourage the driver to let someone else drive, or refuse to ride in the same vehicle. Do what you must to protect yourself and others.

- Do not hesitate to compliment the driver for doing a good job of driving in a difficult situation. You might need the same support when you are the driver.

Effects on Risk Taking

Your emotions have a big influence on the amount of risk you are willing to take. You probably will be more likely to take risks if you are angry than if you are happy. When a driver cuts you off after passing, you might want to get even by taking chances that you would not normally take.

Mature, responsible drivers do not let their emotions make them take unnecessary risks. Taking a chance while driving can be deadly. You must be mature enough to adjust your behavior so that you do not drive into or create high-risk situations. You also must be mature enough to refuse to take part when other people suggest activities that could endanger you, your passengers, or other drivers.

Your emotions might cause you to take chances at different times on the same roadway. For example, if you were driving an injured friend to the hospital, your concern might cause you to drive fast, increasing the risks. An hour later, you probably would not drive home in the same manner. You then would drive more cautiously and courteously.

On the other hand, sometimes you might be so uninterested in your trip that you don't give your complete attention to the driving task. Driving the same route over and over may cause you to pay less attention to the driving task.

Even if you drive on the same street every day, always be aware of potential risks.

Controlling Emotions

During some performances, you are asked to hold your applause until a certain point. You must manage your emotions until the proper time. In driving, you must develop this same type of emotional discipline. You must strive to keep emotions from affecting your driving ability.

Coping with Emotions High-stress driving situations can cause emotions to surface. These techniques can help you manage your emotions while driving:

- Use the IPDE Process to drive in an organized manner. Learn and use correct driving procedures until they become habits. You then will be more likely to execute the proper action, even when under emotional stress.
- Anticipate emotion-producing situations, and adjust your expectations. Say to yourself, "I know there will be delays during rush hour, so I will allow more time to get home. I will not let the actions of others bother me."

AGGRESSIVE DRIVING Citizens Against Speeding and Aggressive Driving (CASAD) is a fairly new grassroots organization dedicated to making safer roads. CASAD members feel aggressive driving has become an epidemic. They believe it is socially unacceptable to speed and drive aggressively on any road under any circumstance.

- If you encounter an aggressive driver, do not challenge the driver. Avoid eye contact, ignore gestures, and remain calm. Adopt a "yield" attitude.
- Try to adjust your route to avoid irritating traffic situations.
- If you are tired, make a special effort to manage your emotions. A tired person can become upset more easily.
- Analyze your mistakes. Learn from them so that you are less likely to repeat the same mistakes.
- Keep courtesy as one of your personal rules of the road.

Goal of Emotional Control

Emotions are complicated and powerful forces. Learning about emotions and how to manage them is something most individuals work at all their lives. Maintaining an attitude of "I will always work to manage my emotions when driving" is a big step toward actually mastering your emotions. If you can manage your emotions and maintain your driving ability, those skills will help keep the risks of driving low as well as your stress level.

You can earn the respect of others if your emotions do not interfere with your driving ability.

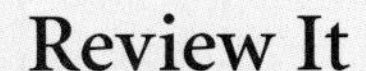

Review It

1. How can anger affect your ability to drive?
2. How can you help a driver when you are a passenger?
3. What can you do to manage your emotions while driving?
4. How can your emotions affect the risks of driving?

14.2
Physical Senses and Driving

Objectives
1. Define the parts of your field of vision.
2. Describe what you can do to compensate for poor depth perception.
3. Explain how your senses help you drive.

Your senses play a vital role in using the IPDE Process. You use your abilities to see, hear, smell, and detect motion to know what is occurring in and around your vehicle.

Driving, like other activities such as sports and mowing the lawn, exposes you to risks. As you drive, your senses help you stay alert and be aware of changing situations. If you know your physical abilities, you have a better chance of maintaining control over your vehicle and minimizing your driving risks.

Seeing

More than 90 percent of the information you gather while driving is received through your eyes. You must be able to clearly and quickly identify closing zones in your intended path of travel.

Your brain directs your eyes to focus on objects in and around your path of travel. Information is sent to your brain and combined with stored information. As a result, you can identify hazards, predict conflicts, decide to maintain or adjust your speed and position, and execute your decisions.

Visual Acuity

When driving you need the ability to see things clearly both near and far away. For example, you may need to read the gauges on your instrument panel in one instant, then identify oncoming traffic in the next. The ability to see things clearly is called **visual acuity.**

A person with normal visual acuity—called 20/20 vision—can read 11/32-inch letters on an eye chart from 20 feet away. If you have 20/20 vision, you should be able to read the term IPDE in the block on this page from 20 feet away.

You must pass a visual acuity test in order to obtain a learner's permit, and possibly again to get a driver's license. Most states require a minimum corrected visual acuity of 20/40 to drive. A person with 20/40 vision must be twice as close to an object to see it as clearly as a person with 20/20 vision must be. With 20/200, the person would have to be 10 times closer. If you must wear glasses or contact lenses to pass the vision test, then you must wear them whenever you drive.

IPDE

You have 20/20 vision in each eye if you can read these letters with each eye from 20 feet away.

Color Vision

Color vision is the ability to distinguish one color from another. Not being able to distinguish colors is called **color blindness.** Being able to see the colors red, green, and yellow is particularly important since these colors give the messages stop, go, and slow or caution. The most common type of color blindness is the difficulty to distinguish red and green.

A color-blind driver can compensate by

- remembering the order of the lights in a traffic signal. If the lights are vertical, the red light is at the top. If horizontal, the red light is on the left.
- knowing the meanings of traffic signs by their shapes
- reading all signs that appear with traffic signals
- checking all zones and 90 degrees to left and right before proceeding at traffic signals
- taking cues from other drivers

Field of Vision

Your field of vision is all the area that you can see around you while looking straight ahead. From this position, most people can see about 90 degrees to each side, or about a half circle. However, you can only see clearly in your area of central vision as shown in the pictures. This straight-ahead part of your field of vision is a small, 10-degree, cone-shaped area. As you drive, direct your central vision to your target area and 12–15 seconds ahead to identify zone changes.

Surrounding your central vision is peripheral vision. The farther from the central vision, the less clear the view. The part of your peripheral vision closest to your central vision

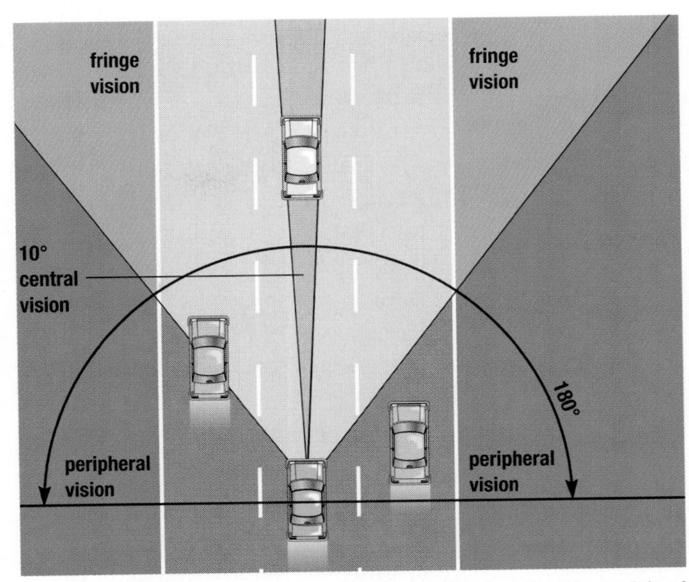

You see most clearly in the area of central vision, but the fringe vision is also important.

Use your central vision to check your target area and front zones. Use your fringe vision to check reference points and detect changes in your rearview mirror.

is called fringe vision. Side fringe vision is used to monitor a zone condition after it has been identified in central vision. The upper fringe vision is used to detect changes in the rear mirror. The lower fringe vision is used to monitor reference points for vehicle position.

Some people see less than a total of 180 degrees. A narrow field of vision—140 degrees or less—is called **tunnel vision.** A driver who has tunnel vision must compensate with more frequent head and eye movements.

Depth Perception

The ability to judge distance between yourself and other objects is **depth perception.** When driving you must judge the distance between your vehicle and other vehicles and other objects. Accurate judgment is more difficult when the other vehicle is moving.

A driver can compensate for poor depth perception by

- using a following distance greater than three seconds
- allowing for additional clear distance ahead before passing
- allowing greater distances at night than at daytime. (Darkness hides many guides you use in the daytime.)

Night Vision

The ability to see at night varies from person to person. Some people who see clearly in the daytime have poor night vision. Not being able to see well at night is called **night blindness.**

All people see less at night than in daylight. Colors are harder to identify. Details of objects do not appear as sharp as in daylight.

Your night vision is limited to the area lit by headlights, streetlights, and other lights. In rural areas, you might be in total darkness except for the area lit by your headlights.

At night you might not be able to see anything to the sides. You might be less able to read signs and roadway markings. Compare the two pictures that show the same situation.

You can see nearby objects and distant ones clearly in daylight.

Your ability to see objects and judge distance is limited at night.

You Are the Driver!
Some vehicles reflect sunlight into your eyes. How can you compensate?

The only difference is that one picture was taken during the day and the other one was taken at night. Notice that you cannot see as much at night. Your ability to judge distances accurately also decreases.

Glare

Glare occurs in the daytime when bright sunlight is reflected off shiny surfaces. Sunroofs and convertibles let in additional sunlight that can produce glare. At night, glare occurs when bright lights reflect off shiny surfaces. The term **glare resistance** describes the ability to continue seeing when looking at bright lights. Glare resistance varies from person to person. Some people are more sensitive to light than others.

Sudden glare can blind a person temporarily, especially at night. Headlights turn toward you at intersections. Bright lights appear from over hills and around curves. A vehicle using high-beam headlights approaches from behind. Your pupils open wide at night to let in all available light. When your eyes are suddenly exposed to bright lights, your pupils contract. You might be temporarily blinded before your pupils can adjust to the bright lights.

The term **glare recovery time** describes the time your eyes need to regain clear vision after being affected by glare. Your pupils can take 5–10 seconds to readjust. At 40 mph, you can travel more than the length of a football field while partially blinded.

Take these steps to avoid or recover from glare:

- Avoid looking directly at bright lights. Use the right edge of the roadway as a guide.
- Anticipate glare situations and glance away or squint.
- Use side fringe vision rather than central vision to check your lane position and the location of oncoming vehicles.
- If you are impaired by glare, slow until your vision clears.
- Wear sunglasses and use your vehicle's sun visor in bright sunlight.
- Adjust your rearview mirror for night use.

Vehicle Speed and Vision

As your vehicle's speed increases, your need for accurate vision also increases. Yet, at higher speeds, you have less time to see clearly. Your field of vision also is narrowed. At 55 mph, your clear side-vision area is less than half as wide as at 20 mph.

Objects off to your sides become blurred and distorted as your speed increases. This blur, or **speed smear,** as shown in the picture, has an effect much like tunnel vision. Your eyes tend to focus far ahead to where the roadway appears to come to a point. You see less and less of what is happening on the sides. Increase the frequency of your side glances when driving at highway speeds.

Other Senses and Driving

Sometimes you need to depend on other senses to identify threats to your path of travel. In complex driving situations, you may have to use more than one sense at a time.

Hearing

Your sense of hearing can alert you to the sounds of vehicle horns, train whistles, emergency-vehicle sirens, and engines and brakes of trucks and buses. You can also get early warning of mechanical problems by listening for unusual noises from your vehicle.

Drivers who have sounds blocked from them can be dangerous to themselves and to others. Driving with closed windows and with stereo or headsets on may make a driver unaware of critical traffic sounds. Using a cellular phone while driving creates a similar problem.

Drivers who are deaf know that they must compensate for what they cannot hear. They use their eyes more than drivers who have normal hearing.

Smell

Your sense of smell can identify an overheated engine or overheated brakes. Smelling exhaust fumes inside your vehicle can give you an

When you drive at higher speeds, your side vision is less clear.

early warning to the presence of deadly gases.

Sense of Motion

Certain sensations can give you clues to the movement of your vehicle. Your sense of balance tells you that you are veering right or left, changing speed, or going around a curve. A sudden vibration of the vehicle or jerk of the steering wheel might warn you of a mechanical problem, a flat tire, or a change in the roadway surface.

Risk Management

You increase or decrease your risk of becoming involved in a collision by changing the level of control you have over your vehicle. Impairment or inadequate use of senses of vision, hearing, smell, and motion will affect your ability to manage risks. Also, anything that distracts you from using your senses and concentrating on the driving task will increase your risk of a collision.

Distractions

A driver needs to focus on the driving task at all times. The driving scene can change quickly, and you need to be alert to changes so that you make decisions and act quickly.

An audio system in your vehicle can cause distractions, although it can be helpful if used safely. You need to keep the volume at a level that allows you to hear important traffic sounds such as sirens and horns. Also, do not wear headphones while driving. Headphones will block traffic sounds, and it is illegal in many states to wear them while driving. Avoid changing radio stations, tapes, and CDs while driving. You increase your risk of a collision any time you take your eyes off the road and a hand off the steering wheel.

Cellular phones can be helpful in a vehicle in emergencies, but they are dangerous to use while driving. Research studies have found that drivers talking on a cell phone were four times more likely to be involved in a collision. You should turn off your cell phone while driving. If you need to use the phone, pull off the road and stop the car.

Other distractions can come from people or pets in the vehicle. The driver is responsible for keeping passengers under control. Pets need to be placed in carriers or secured with special harnesses. The more distractions you can eliminate, the better you will be able to manage risks to avoid collisions while driving.

Review It

1. What is your field of vision? What part of your field of vision provides you with your clearest vision?
2. What can you do to compensate for poor depth perception?
3. How do your senses of seeing, hearing, smelling, and motion help you assess driving situations?

14.3
Physical Disabilities

Objectives

1. Tell what you can do to combat fatigue.
2. Explain what to do to avoid carbon monoxide exposure and how to deal with its effects.
3. Describe what drivers who have permanent disabilities can do to compensate.

Experienced drivers have learned to respond to temporary and permanent disabilities. Generally, driving is possible for people who have moderate to severe disabilities. However, a disability needs to be recognized before it can be overcome, whether temporary or permanent.

Temporary Disabilities

Sometimes you must drive even though you are not at your physical best. While you can compensate for some temporary disabilities, with others you should not drive until they no longer exist.

Fatigue

Mental or physical work, emotional stress, or loss of sleep can cause fatigue. Fatigue lessens your fitness to perform tasks, including driving. It dulls your senses and slows both mental and physical processes. If you are fatigued, you will need more time to use the IPDE Process.

Fatigue can also cause drowsiness. Drowsy driving is estimated to cause at least 100,000 collisions a year.

There are several danger signs of drowsiness:

- trouble keeping your head up
- drifting between lane positions
- wandering, disconnected thoughts
- inability to stop yawning
- eyes closing or going out of focus
- inability to concentrate on driving task

When are you about to fall asleep? That is hard to predict. Most people biologically prefer to sleep between 12:00 A.M. and 6:00 A.M., and again around 2:00 P.M. You may experience drowsiness during these times. Be cautious.

Drowsiness can interfere with a person's driving abilities.

Rest is the only safe remedy for fatigue. However, people often need to drive even when they are tired. If you are tired after work or school, take a break for a few minutes before you drive. You might also choose a quieter, less congested route home.

Take these actions to deal with fatigue on long drives:

- Rest before you start.
- Change drivers often.
- Stop every two hours. Walk, stretch, get a beverage or snack, or take a nap on long trips.
- Wear sunglasses in bright sunlight and to shield against snow glare.
- Use your orderly visual search pattern to keep your eyes moving.
- Be active—listen to the radio, sing, or talk with your passengers.
- Stop in a safe, well-lighted place if you feel drowsy. Lock the vehicle and take a nap.

If you feel tired often, check with your doctor. You may have a chronic illness or sleep disorder.

DROWSY DRIVERS According to a national poll, half of the people surveyed said they had driven while feeling drowsy. One in five admitted they had fallen asleep behind the wheel.

Temporary Illness or Injury

Any illness, even a cold, can impair driving to some extent. A temporary physical injury, such as a broken bone or a sprained ankle, also can impair your driving. These and other temporary conditions can cause discomfort and pain, limit physical movement, lessen endurance and strength, or dull your senses.

Effects of Medicines Many medicines have side effects that can interfere with your driving ability and risks. For example, medicine that reduces headache pain or relieves hay fever, might also cause drowsiness, dizziness, or reduced alertness.

If you take medicine, consider these points before you drive:

- Read the label to learn the possible side effects, as shown in the picture. Ask your physician or pharmacist about side effects.

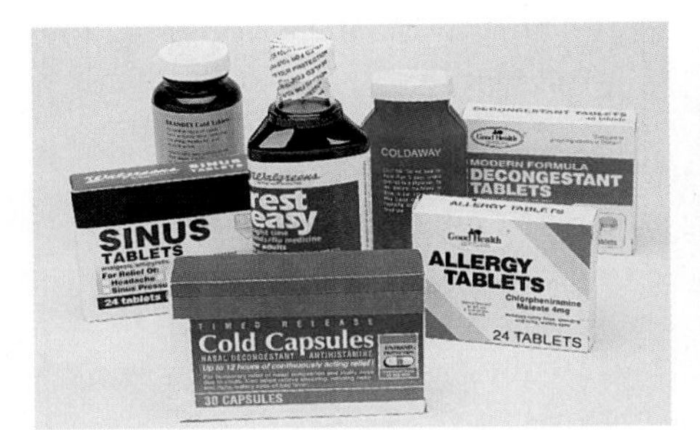

ALLERGY TABLETS

INDICATIONS FOR USE: provides relief from hay fever, upper respiratory allergy symptoms; sneezing; runny nose; itchy, watery eyes.
DOSAGE: Adults and children over 12; 1 tablet every 4 to 6 hours. Not to exceed 6 tablets in 24 hours. Children 6 through 11 years, ½ the adult dose (break tablet in half) every 4 to 6 hours. Not to exceed 3 whole tablets in 24 hours. For children under 6, consult a physician.
WARNING: Do not take this product if you have asthma, glaucoma, or difficulty in urination due to enlargement of the prostate gland, except under the advice and supervision of a physician.
CAUTION: Do not drive or operate heavy machinery as this preparation may cause drowsiness. Avoid alcoholic beverages while taking this product. May cause excitability, especially in children.
WARNING: Keep this and all drugs out of reach of children. In case of accidental overdose, contact a physician or poison control center immediately. As with any drug, if you are pregnant or nursing a baby, seek the advice of a health professional before using this product.
FORMULA: Each tablet contains Chlorpheniramine Maleate 4mg.
May also contain: Cellulose, Color, Croscarmelose Sodium, Dicalcium Phosphate, Lactose, Magnesium Stearate, Povidone, Sodium Starch Glycolate, Starch, Talc, and other ingredients.
Store at room temperature (59°-86°F)
Protect from excessive moisture.

Many commonly used medicines can affect your driving ability.

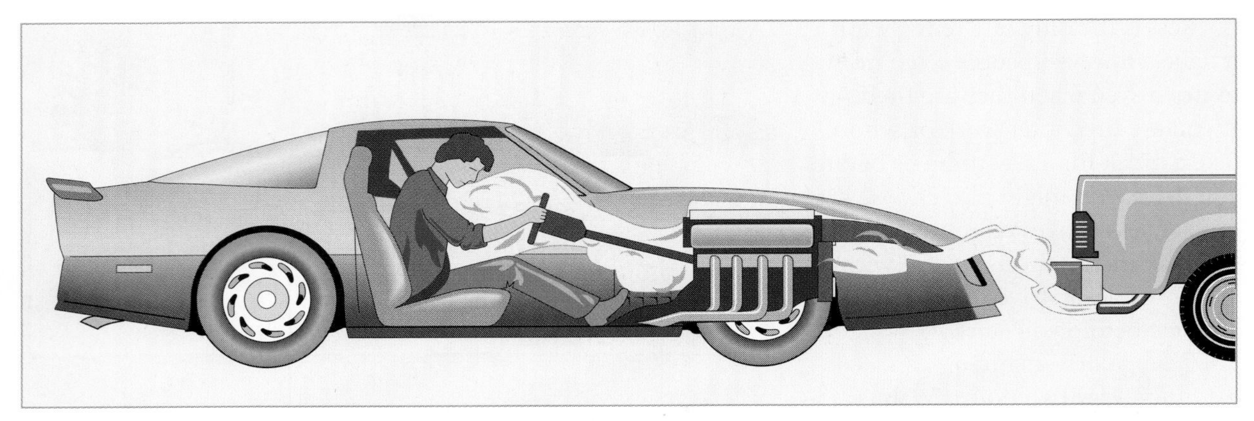

In heavy traffic, your intakes might draw in carbon monoxide from the exhaust of the car ahead.

- A medicine can affect you differently at different times.
- If possible, drive to your destination before taking the medicine.
- If you must drive after taking medicine, try to choose a quiet, less-congested route.

Effects of Carbon Monoxide Your vehicle's exhaust fumes contain **carbon monoxide,** a colorless, odorless, and tasteless gas. Carbon monoxide is present in all engine exhaust gases.

You can sometimes detect carbon monoxide in a vehicle because it is mixed with other exhaust fumes that do have an odor. However, you cannot tell how concentrated the carbon monoxide is by the odor of the exhaust fumes. If there is no odor, you cannot be sure there is no carbon monoxide.

Small amounts of carbon monoxide can cause drowsiness, headaches, muscular weakness, mental dullness, and nausea. Too much carbon monoxide can cause death.

Be alert for the danger of carbon monoxide in heavy traffic and in such enclosed areas as tunnels and underground parking facilities. Your heater or air conditioner vents might draw in exhaust fumes from the car ahead, as shown here. Leaving a rear window open might create a slight vacuum that pulls in exhaust fumes.

Take these actions to prevent carbon monoxide exposure and combat its effect:

- If your vehicle is parked in a garage at home, open the garage door before starting the engine.
- Avoid running the engine inside a garage. Move your vehicle outside after starting the engine.
- In stop-and-go traffic, keep a three-second following distance. Stop where you can see the tires of the vehicle ahead touching the pavement.
- In traffic jams, especially in enclosed areas, turn off the engine when possible.
- Check your exhaust system regularly.
- Do not drive with the rear windows open.

- Move a person who is overcome by carbon monoxide into fresh air. Seek medical help immediately.

Smoking Be aware that smoking while driving is dangerous. Smoking raises the carbon monoxide level in a person's blood. Smoke residue accumulates on windows and affects vision.

Discourage your passengers from smoking. Carbon monoxide from tobacco smoke can affect even non-smokers in an enclosed area such as a vehicle. If someone does smoke in your vehicle, open a window to provide fresh air.

Effects on Risk Taking

Temporary illness, such as a cold, can affect a driver's risk-taking decisions. Because they are temporary, many drivers do not recognize the illness's influence on their driving skills. They might be more willing to, and often do, take chances they would not take if they were well. Being tired or under the influence of medicines can increase your chances of being in a collision. Be aware of the side effects of medicines by reading the labels. Compensate for side effects of medicines and for illness by using an extra space cushion and taking even fewer chances.

Permanent and Physical Disabilities

Special vehicle equipment and controls can make it possible for many people with permanent disabilities to drive, as shown in the picture. Still others can control their disabilities with medication.

Older Drivers As a nation, we are healthier and living longer. As a result, more older drivers are using the roadways. One in six drivers is over age 65. Eighty percent of drivers over age 75

Vehicles are often adapted to help physically challenged people maintain independence.

Special parking areas and license plates help disabled drivers reach their destinations safely.

take prescribed medicines. Aging slows reflexes, dulls vision and concentration, can make muscles weaker and inflexible, and reduces depth perception and field of vision. Failure to yield the right of way is the main factor in collisions involving older drivers. However, drivers over 65 are still involved in fewer collisions per mile driven than those under 30.

Chronic Illnesses A chronic illness is an ailment that lasts over a period of years. Some chronic illnesses have little effect on driving. Other illnesses, such as heart disease, could seriously impair a person's ability to drive.

Some chronic illnesses require regular medications that can cause side effects that interfere with driving. Some people have diseases that cause sudden loss of consciousness or muscular control. Before these individuals can receive a driver's license, they must provide medical proof that their chronic illness is under control.

It is illegal to park in handicapped-designated parking spaces unless you have special identification.

Effects on Risk Taking

Most drivers with permanent disabilities do not take unnecessary chances with driving decisions influenced by their disabilities. These drivers often understand that the disability itself may put them at a higher level of risk. The solution is knowing that you have the disability, admitting you have it, and compensating for it.

Whatever the illness or disability, everyone who can perform the driving tasks safely and successfully earns the privilege of being licensed to drive when all other requirements are met. Sometimes they are required to take more frequent testing to maintain that privilege.

Some drivers with permanent disabilities have special license plates or window cards with the handicapped symbol. The symbol also appears on license plates or window cards of drivers who often transport handicapped people. Vehicles with these license plates can park in specially marked areas in parking lots and on streets.

Review It

1. How can you compensate for the effects of fatigue?
2. How can you avoid and combat exposure to carbon monoxide?
3. How can a permanent disability affect your driving?

Chapter 14
Review

Reviewing Chapter Objectives

1. Emotions and Driving

1. How can anger affect your ability to drive? (293–294)
2. How can you help a driver when you are a passenger? (295–296)
3. What can you do to manage your emotions while driving? (296–297)
4. How do emotions influence your willingness to accept risk? (296)

2. Physical Senses and Driving

5. What are the parts of your field of vision? (299–300)
6. What can you do to compensate for poor depth perception? (300)
7. How do your senses help you drive? (298–303)

3. Physical Disabilities

8. What can you do to combat fatigue? (304–305)
9. What can you do to avoid carbon monoxide exposure and deal with its effects? (306–307)
10. What can drivers who have permanent disabilities do to compensate? (307–308)

Projects

Individuals

Investigate Research newspaper articles about traffic collisions involving drivers who were fatigued. Write a report about a collision involving a driver who fell asleep at the wheel.

Observe Traffic Keep track of the sounds you hear for a week as a passenger in a vehicle. Make a list of each sound you hear, and count the number of times you hear that particular sound. (Focus on vehicle-related sounds and sounds coming from outside the vehicle. Do not include sounds made by the driver or passengers.) At the end of the week, compare your results with those of your classmates.

Groups

Demonstrate Prepare a short skit that takes place in a vehicle. Six students have just attended a football game at another school. They are on their way to a victory party. Demonstrate examples of good as well as unacceptable behaviors in the vehicle. Present the skit to your class.

Use Technology Prepare a spreadsheet that contains each group member's visual acuity score. (If you do not know your visual acuity score, you need to take a visual acuity test to find out.) List the different ratios in descending order.

Chapter 14

Review

Chapter Test

Check Your Knowledge

Multiple Choice Copy the number of each sentence below on a sheet of paper. Choose the letter of the answer that best completes the statement or answers the question.

1. Emotions influence driving because they
(a) cause you to drive fast.
(b) change the way you assess risk.
(c) change the way you make driving decisions.
(d) both b and c

2. A person who must be twice as close to an object to see it as clearly as a person with normal visual acuity has
(a) 20/20 vision.
(b) 20/40 vision.
(c) 20/60 vision.
(d) 20/200 vision.

3. The part of your peripheral vision closest to your central vision is called
(a) fringe vision.
(b) tunnel vision.
(c) depth perception.
(d) side perception.

4. The best way to prevent fatigue on long drives is to
(a) increase speed to shorten trip time.
(b) wear sunglasses.
(c) turn on the air conditioner.
(d) rest before you start.

Completion Copy the number of each sentence below. After each number, write the word or words that complete the sentence correctly.

5. While driving, drivers experience the emotion of _____ more often than any other.

6. Your _____ allows you to judge the distance between yourself and other objects.

7. Carbon monoxide gas is present in the _____ of a vehicle.

8. Most collisions involving older drivers are caused by failure to _____.

Review Vocabulary

Copy the number of each definition in list A. Match the definition in list A with the term it defines in list B.

List A

9. ability to continue seeing when looking at bright lights

10. occurs when objects off to your sides become blurred and distorted as your speed increases

11. ability to see things clearly both near and far away

12. time your eyes need to regain clear vision after being affected by glare

13. ability to judge distance between yourself and other objects

14. not being able to distinguish colors

15. not being able to see well at night

16. narrow field of vision of 140 degrees or less

List B

a. color blindness
b. speed smear
c. glare recovery time
d. visual acuity
e. night blindness
f. glare resistance
g. depth perception
h. tunnel vision

Think Critically

Write a paragraph to answer each question.

1. List and discuss the techniques you can use to control your emotions while driving.

2. Explain how you would prevent exposure to carbon monoxide poisoning in the vehicle you drive.

Decision Making

1. Where should you direct your clear central vision in the next few seconds of driving?

2. What is causing this driver to be impaired for a few seconds? What actions could the driver have taken to prevent this impairment? What can the driver do now to minimize the danger?

3. These people are having an argument. How could the argument affect the driver's ability to drive?

4. How are these passengers affecting the driver? What should they be doing to help?

MAINSTAGE
AT BUMBERSHOOT

CHAPTER 15
Alcohol, Other Drugs, and Driving

You Are the Driver!

These people are attending a music concert. They have been at the concert for several hours. Some of the adults drank a few alcoholic beverages. What driving abilities might be impaired when a person uses alcohol? What tests might drivers have to take if the police stop them? What can you do if you believe a person who had several drinks thinks it is safe to drive? This chapter discusses the effects of alcohol and other drugs. It will help you understand why you should never drink and drive.

For: Chapter 15 online activities
Visit: PHSchool.com
Web Code: cak-9999

15.1
Effects of Alcohol on Driving Safely

Objectives

1. Explain how alcohol affects mental and physical abilities needed for driving.
2. Define blood-alcohol concentration.
3. Explain factors that affect blood-alcohol concentration.
4. List five myths and truths about the use of alcohol.

Alcohol is the most commonly used drug in our society today. It is by far the most frequently found drug in fatally injured drivers.

Young people in their teens are among those in our society who use and abuse alcohol. Even though it is illegal for teens to drink, a significant percentage of them do drink. This segment of young people who drink alcohol presents a major problem for highway safety when they mix drinking with driving.

All states now enforce a minimum drinking age of 21. Laws against underage drinking and driving are more strictly and more vigorously enforced now than ever. Alcohol-related educational programs within schools, homes, and communities have increased. Nevertheless, alcohol-related collisions are still a major safety problem.

Alcohol Facts

Some people are not aware that alcohol is a drug. After all, it can be purchased legally. And commercial advertising depicts alcoholic beverage consumption as harmless fun.

The word *alcohol* is the commonly used term for the chemical substance ethanol, grain alcohol, or ethyl alcohol. Alcohol is the product of the fermentation of fruits, grains, or other plants. Alcohol is classified as a drug because of its effects on the body's central nervous system.

The effects of alcohol vary from person to person. However, everyone who uses alcohol is affected by it to some degree. One of the most serious problems of alcohol is the problem of the drinking driver. Drivers cannot afford to increase the risks of driving by having their abilities diminished by alcohol.

Alcohol is the most commonly found drug in fatally injured drivers.

Consider these facts about alcohol and driving:

- Young drinking drivers are involved in fatal crashes at twice the rate of drivers aged 21 and older.
- Drivers aged 16 through 20 are more likely to be alcohol-impaired than any other age group.
- Nearly half of those killed in alcohol-related collisions had not been drinking but were victims of drunk drivers.
- More than half of all fatalities during holidays are alcohol related.

Effects of Alcohol on Behavior

Number of drinks in one hour	BAC	Effects
1 serving	.02–.03%	Inhibitions are lessened. Judgment and reasoning begin to be affected.
3 servings	.05–.09%	Unable to think clearly. Judgment and reasoning are not reliable. Muscular coordination is impaired.
4 servings	.10–.12%	After four drinks, hearing, speech, vision, and balance are affected. Most behaviors are affected.

How Alcohol Affects Behavior

As soon as alcohol from a drink reaches the brain, it affects the way people think and behave. Just one drink can affect a person's behavior, both mentally and physically, regardless of the type of alcoholic drink. The same amount of alcohol does not affect all people the same way. Alcohol does not even affect the same person in the same way in all situations. The best way to avoid changes in behavior is to abstain from drinking.

Mental Abilities and Alcohol

Alcohol acts on the central nervous system like an anesthetic, slowing the activity of the brain. Alcohol is not digested. It is absorbed directly and quickly into the bloodstream through the walls and linings of the entire digestive tract.

Once alcohol enters the bloodstream, it quickly flows to the brain. Alcohol has the greatest effect on the parts of the brain that control judgment and reasoning—the two most critical mental skills needed by drivers. Physical abilities become impaired soon afterward.

Judgment and Reasoning A driver affected by alcohol has a decreased ability to reason clearly and make sound judgments. At the same time, the driver actually feels as though thinking and judging abilities are sharper, quicker, and more accurate than usual. In a way, alcohol puts sound judgment on hold.

A person in this condition can develop a false feeling of well-being. This feeling is known as **euphoria.** People in a euphoric state of mind may take chances they normally would not take. This behavior can be deadly when behind the wheel of a vehicle.

What Do You Think?

All states require a person to be 21 years old to purchase or consume alcoholic beverages. Should the minimum drinking age be lower than 21 years?

The IPDE Process is affected when judgment and reasoning abilities are reduced. An alcohol-impaired driver is less able to correctly interpret what he or she sees. Target areas may become unclear and scanning of zones may become erratic.

Because alcohol distorts vision, it reduces the effectiveness of the driver's orderly visual search pattern. A drinking driver's eyes are more likely to fixate in a stare, thus reducing the scanning and searching process. The driver is likely to look straight ahead or at any object that attracts attention. Staring usually results in the driver being unaware of vehicles to the sides as well as to the rear.

Inhibitions Alcohol weakens a person's **inhibitions,** the inner forces of personality that restrain or hold back one's impulsive behavior. As alcohol content in the body increases, a driver's inhibitions weaken. The person might drive too fast, take needless risks, or even drive into emergency situations without knowing or caring.

A driver who has been drinking would have difficulty seeing this pedestrian and reacting soon enough to stop.

Physical Abilities and Alcohol

As alcohol enters the bloodstream, the area of the brain that controls muscular movements, reflexes, and balance begins to slow down. The driver may recognize a dangerous situation, but the brain takes longer to process the information and react to the danger.

Reaction Time and Coordination
Alcohol slows reflexes and reaction time. Muscular coordination becomes slow and clumsy. A driver might oversteer, brake late, or accelerate suddenly. Alcohol especially affects the reflexes and reactions of beginning drivers.

Seeing and Speaking Abilities One of the most dangerous effects of alcohol is impaired vision. Impairment occurs in visual acuity, peripheral vision, night vision, color vision, and depth perception. Impaired vision combined with diminished judgment and slow reaction time can cause a driver who has been drinking to be in a conflict. For example, the driver in the picture might not identify the pedestrian in time to stop safely.

After only a few alcoholic drinks, the driver's visual acuity can become impaired. A person's ability to focus becomes fuzzy and unclear.

Alcohol also affects the reflex action of the eyes. At night, this impairment can be critical. As headlights of oncoming vehicles come closer, the pupils of the eyes normally become smaller to shut out excess light. This reflex keeps you from being blinded by the glare of the headlights. When the lights have passed, the pupils enlarge again to let in all available light.The ability of your eyes to make this change is extremely important.

After only a few drinks, this reflex action is impaired. The pupils do not become small rapidly as the bright lights approach, and they are slow to open after the bright lights pass. As a result, the driver can be blinded temporarily and may continue to have blurred vision for some time after meeting each vehicle.

After excessive drinking, a person might see multiple images. Each eye normally picks up a separate image of an object. These two images are coordinated by the brain so that the person sees only one image. After several drinks, however, coordination of the images becomes impaired. When driving, the person might see numerous images of a roadway center line, or of traffic signs, as the picture shows.

Alcohol also impairs depth perception. The drinking driver may misjudge the distance of oncoming or cross-traffic vehicles. A vehicle is perceived as being farther away than it actually is. In addition, drinking drivers cannot accurately determine the speed or distance of approaching vehicles. These drivers even lose the ability to judge their own speed or the distance they need for stopping.

Peripheral vision also is impaired by alcohol. When peripheral vision is narrowed, the driver must turn and look to the sides for potential problems. However, these drivers are usually not aware of this impairment so they do not make the effort to turn and look to the sides for potential conflicts. They often become a hazard themselves.

After several drinks, a driver may see multiple images of roadway signs.

Alcohol also can affect a person's speech. The speech pattern may become slurred and fuzzy, and spoken sentences may fail to convey meaning. With the lack of inhibitions, and with the feelings of euphoria, the drinking person often becomes more and more talkative with language that becomes less and less meaningful.

Other Physical Problems

As a person continues to drink, the center of the brain that controls breathing and heartbeat can become impaired. Death can occur if a large amount of alcohol is consumed over a short period of time. Usually, a person becomes unconscious and stops drinking before this point.

Amount of Alcohol in Standard Drinks

Drink volume		Percentage of alcohol		Amount of alcohol
12 ounces beer	×	5%	=	.60 ounces
5 ounces wine	×	12%	=	.60 ounces
$1\frac{1}{2}$ ounces whiskey (80 proof)	×	40%	=	.60 ounces

Long-Term Effects Long-term use of alcohol can lead to alcoholism, an addiction to alcohol. Alcoholism is a major problem in our society today. It has far-reaching effects, not only for the problem drinker, but for families and communities as well.

The seriousness as well as the number of collisions increases as the BAC increases.

Alcohol in the Body

The percentage of alcohol in a person's bloodstream can be determined by chemical tests. The amount of alcohol in the blood is called **blood-alcohol concentration (BAC).**

The level of intoxication is determined by the percent of alcohol in the bloodstream. Each drink adds about 0.02 to 0.03 percent to the person's BAC. The greater the BAC, the more dangerous driving becomes.

Amount of Alcohol in a Drink

Beer, wine, and liquor can all be thought of as "drinks." In standard sizes, drinks all have about the same amount of alcohol, as the chart shows.

The term "proof" describes the strength of liquor. Divide a liquor's proof number by two to determine its approximate percentage of alcohol. The chart shows that 80-proof whiskey is about 40 percent alcohol. A 100-proof liquor is about 50 percent alcohol.

Factors Affecting BAC The percentage of alcohol in the bloodstream depends on the following factors:

- **Amount of alcohol consumed** The more a person drinks, the higher the BAC.
- **Amount of time over which a given amount of alcohol is consumed** A person's BAC rises more rapidly if only short periods of time elapse between drinks.
- **Person's body weight** If other factors are equal, a heavier person may be affected less by the same amount of alcohol than a lighter person would be.

To a lesser degree, some types of food in the stomach may make a difference in the rate the alcohol is absorbed. However, even with food in the stomach, the absorption rate of alcohol into the bloodstream is

The Time It Takes for the Body to Rid Itself of Alcohol*		
Number of Drinks	BAC Range	Approximate Time to Eliminate Alcohol
1	.02–.03	1½ hours
2	.04–.06	3 hours
3	.06–.09	4 to 5 hours
4	.08–.12	5 to 7 hours

*The number will vary depending on the alcohol content of the drinks and rate of consumption.

rapid. When alcohol is mixed with carbonated beverages, the rate of absorption is even faster.

The safest decision a person can make about alcoholic beverages is the decision to abstain from drinking. At a social gathering, a person can choose a soft drink, set down an alcoholic drink and walk away from it, or say *no.*

Some people may decide they want to drink. Responsible friends can encourage them to limit their drinking by taking the following actions:

- Get them involved in other activities.
- Encourage them to decide on a limit of drinks in advance and stick to it.
- Ask them to avoid drinks with a high concentration of alcohol.
- Encourage them to sip a drink slowly. Suggest that they not drink more than one alcoholic beverage in an hour.
- Make them aware of their mental and physical behavior.

Controlling Impairment Alcohol is absorbed into the brain and the rest of the body very quickly, but it is very slow to leave. Alcohol continues to circulate throughout the body until it is oxidized and removed by the liver. The body rids itself of alcohol at a rate of about three-fourths of a standard drink an hour.

A person who has one drink needs about one and a half hours to rid the body of the alcohol in that drink. After consuming three drinks in an hour, a person needs more than four hours to oxidize and eliminate most of the alcohol. A person should not drive during those time periods. *Only time can reduce the body's BAC and that person's degree of impairment.* The chart shows the time needed for the body to rid itself of alcohol at the rate of about three-fourths of a drink in an hour.

You Are the Driver!
This man has had several drinks at a party. Which activity would lower his BAC so that he could drive home?

Myths and Truths About Alcohol

The following ideas about alcohol are *not* true. They are only myths.

- **I can sober up by drinking black coffee, taking a cold shower, or doing exercises.** The truth is that these activities do not reduce the BAC. The person may seem more alert, but the BAC is not reduced.
- **One little drink won't hurt me.** The truth is that taking one drink can make it easier to take the second and third drinks.
- **I will not be affected because I am only drinking beer.** The truth is that a 12-ounce can of beer contains as much alcohol as an average cocktail.
- **I can drive better after a few drinks.** The truth is that your driving abilities are diminished, not improved.
- **A young person cannot become a problem drinker.** The truth is that some young people become problem drinkers even as teens.

Reducing Driving Risk

As a responsible driver, you can help reduce the risk of drinking and driving. Always refuse to ride with drivers who have been drinking. Make every effort to keep others from driving when they have been drinking.

One way to reduce the risk involved with drinking and driving is to appoint a person to be the **designated driver.** That person decides ahead of time not to drink.

Review It

1. How does alcohol affect mental and physical abilities needed for driving?
2. What is meant by blood-alcohol concentration?
3. Describe factors that affect blood-alcohol concentration.
4. What are three myths about alcohol, and what is the truth about each myth?

15.2
Other Drugs and Driving

Besides alcohol, there are many other types of drugs that are both legal and illegal. When used properly, most legal drugs have a positive effect. However, even medicines designed for good can cause hazardous driving situations.

Types of Drugs

Most drugs are classified according to the effects they have on the central nervous system and bodily functions. Some drugs depress, or slow down, the central nervous system. Others stimulate it, or speed it up.

When legal drugs are taken in the prescribed amounts and for the right reasons, they are relatively safe. However, any drug can become dangerous if it is taken in excess, combined with other drugs, or otherwise misused or abused.

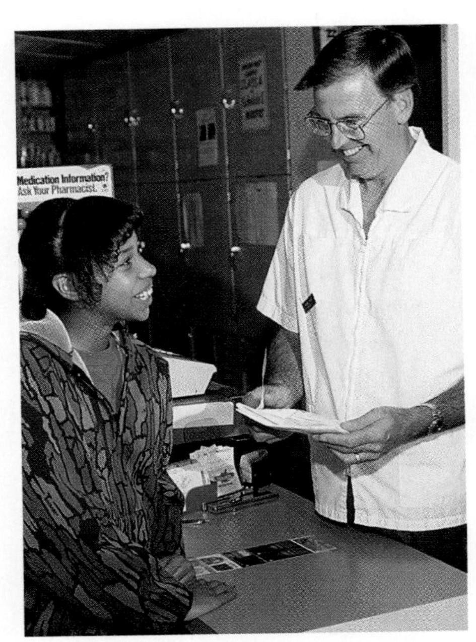

Learn about the side effects of a medicine by checking with the pharmacist.

Over-the-Counter Medicines

Drugs that can be obtained legally without a doctor's prescription are called **over-the-counter medicines,** or OTCs. Many over-the-counter medicines have side effects that can include drowsiness, dizziness, slowed reaction time, and poor judgment.

When buying any medicine, check the label for warnings of how it might affect driving performance. Check with the pharmacist, as the person in the picture is doing, if you are not sure of the labeling or of the possible side effects.

Prescription Medicines

A drug that can be purchased legally only when ordered by a doctor is called a **prescription medicine.** The law requires a prescription because the drug used can have very strong effects on the body.

Depressants

A **depressant** is a drug that can slow down, or depress, the central nervous system. Depressants such as barbiturates, sleeping pills, and tranquilizers are used to relieve tension, calm nerves, and treat high blood pressure.

A driver using depressants can become very relaxed, lose inhibitions, and have difficulty identifying,

Objectives

1. Explain the difference between the purchase of over-the-counter medicine and the purchase of prescription medicine.
2. Explain how depressants, stimulants, and hallucinogenic drugs can affect a driver.
3. Describe the effects of combining alcohol with other drugs.

MARIJUANA Chemicals in marijuana can remain in the body for weeks. Drivers can be given a test for drugs and can be issued a violation ticket if any trace of marijuana is found in the body. Traces of marijuana can be detected in the bloodstream even weeks after the person uses the drug.

predicting, deciding, and executing. Alcohol also is a depressant.

Stimulants

A **stimulant** is a drug that can speed up, or stimulate, the central nervous system. Amphetamines are a type of stimulant. When first taken, the user gets a feeling of high energy and alertness. Some people misuse these drugs to try to stay awake while driving long distances. However, the feeling of alertness soon wears off and the person becomes very tired very quickly, thus increasing driver-related risk.

Hallucinogens

Hallucinogens are unpredictable mind-altering drugs that can alter personality and cause panic or terror as they distort a person's sense of direction, distance, and time.

Marijuana Marijuana is a powerful mind-altering drug that affects the brain and other parts of the central nervous system. Marijuana can impair judgment, memory, depth perception, and coordination.

A marijuana user might feel that the effects have worn off, and it is safe to drive after a few hours. In reality, driving abilities remain impaired for a very long time.

Combining Drugs

You should not take more than one over-the-counter or prescription medicine without first consulting your doctor or a pharmacist.

Using alcohol while taking medicine is especially dangerous. If a person uses alcohol while taking an antihistamine for a cold, the nervous system can be slowed down much more than by using either drug alone. When other drugs are combined with alcohol, the effects of both drugs can be multiplied, rather than just added together. This is known as a synergistic effect.

Drug-alcohol combinations increase driving risks. Driving a vehicle after taking certain medications and drinking alcohol is neither wise nor legal.

Review It

1. How does the purchase of over-the-counter medicine differ from the purchase of prescription medicine?
2. How do depressants, stimulants, and hallucinogenic drugs affect a driver?
3. What is the effect of combining alcohol with other drugs?

15.3

Traffic Laws Governing the Use of Alcohol

All 50 states have become uniform in requiring a person to be 21 years of age to purchase or consume alcoholic beverages.

Alcohol-related vehicle collisions among teenagers dropped after states raised the drinking age to 21. Young drivers are less likely than adults to drive after drinking. However, the risk of collision is substantially higher when teenagers do drive after drinking.

Implied-Consent Law

Every state has an **implied-consent law** for drivers. Implied consent means that anyone who receives a driver's license automatically consents to be tested for BAC and other drugs if stopped for suspicion of drug use while driving.

If the driver does not cooperate with the officer and refuses to be tested for BAC, that driver's license can be suspended.

Levels of Intoxication

Because there is no "safe" amount of alcohol for drivers, all states have set a BAC level at which drivers could be charged with **driving while intoxicated (DWI).** In the past, that level was set at 0.10 percent or higher. However, research shows that the vast majority of drinking drivers are significantly impaired at 0.08 percent. The impairment primarily affects judgment and such critical driving tasks as braking, steering, and changing lanes.

In an effort to further reduce alcohol-related collisions, all states have set 0.08 BAC limits. For drivers over 21, if you drive with a BAC over 0.08, you are guilty of DWI.

In many states, a charge of **driving under the influence (DUI)** can be made if the driver's BAC is 0.05 or more. Other states make no distinction between DWI and DUI.

Penalties for Conviction

The penalties for conviction of driving while intoxicated and driving under the influence involve one or more of the following:

- suspension or revocation of driver's license
- payment of a fine
- serving a prison term

The most common penalty is suspension of the driver's license for a specified period of time.

Some states post the BAC level for intoxication on highways.

Objectives

1. Explain what is meant by the implied-consent law.
2. Describe zero-tolerance levels of intoxication, and tell how these levels can be measured.
3. Explain what a driver should do when stopped by a police officer.

Penalties are more severe if an intoxicated driver is involved in a collision. If a fatality results from the collision, the driver could be found guilty of manslaughter or even murder.

Drivers who are convicted of a second DWI or DUI offense usually receive much harsher penalties than for the first conviction. Licenses can be revoked for as long as three years. Prison terms can be longer and fines more costly.

Zero-Tolerance Law A **zero-tolerance law** makes it illegal for persons under the age of 21 to drive with any measurable amount of alcohol in the blood. All states have implemented zero-tolerance BAC levels for drivers under the age of 21. Most states have set the zero-tolerance BAC at 0.00 to 0.01 percent. Some states use a 0.01 or 0.02 BAC to define zero tolerance to allow for variations in alcohol testing instruments.

The intoxilyzer can show the person's BAC level.

If you are a driver under 21 and you have a BAC greater than 0.00–0.02 (depending on your state laws), you are guilty of DWI. Some states have also adopted a policy of "Zero tolerance means zero chances." In other words, drivers under the age of 21 receive harsh penalties for even their first offense.

Tests for Intoxication

Law enforcement agencies place a high priority on enforcing DUI and DWI laws. Several tests can be used to evaluate a person suspected of DUI or DWI. Tests can be given in the police station or on the roadside.

Chemical Testing

Chemical analysis of blood, urine, or breath can accurately determine BAC. The breath test is a widely used and simple analysis.

The breath-test machine most commonly used for determining BAC is an **intoxilyzer.** The person breathes into the intoxilyzer tube, as the man in the picture is doing. The intoxilyzer determines the BAC, which is then indicated on both the intoxilyzer screen and on a paper printout.

Field Sobriety Testing

Law officers in many states can give a **field sobriety test** when they suspect a driver of DUI or DWI. Field sobriety testing includes a series of on-the-spot, roadside tests that help an officer detect driver impairment. A variety of coordination tests and eye checks might be used.

One such test is the horizontal-gaze nystagmus test. The term **nystagmus** refers to the involuntary jerking of the eyes as the person gazes to the side. Most people show some nystagmus as their eyes track from straight ahead to the side. This test determines the point where the jerking begins. As the BAC increases, the jerking begins at an earlier point. Trained officers can estimate a person's BAC that will be accurate to within 0.02 percent of chemical test readings.

Other roadside tests demonstrate both physical and mental impairment. Balance, coordination, the ability to follow simple instructions, and the ability to perform two tasks at once may be tested. The inability to perform two tasks at once is called *divided-attention impairment.*

A simple divided-attention test might require the driver to walk heel to toe a certain number of steps, while at the same time giving an oral count of the number of steps taken. This procedure not only tests the person's ability to follow a set of instructions, but also tests both balance and counting abilities.

If You Are Stopped by a Police Officer

When a driver sees the flashing lights of a police vehicle in the rearview mirrors, it is usually a signal to pull over and stop. If you see such a signal, slow your vehicle until you are sure the officer is signaling for you. Pull over to the right and stop in a safe place, as the driver in the picture is doing. You might need to pull into a parking lot or a side street to be out of the way of moving traffic. Keep your hands visible as the officer approaches.

Stay in your vehicle and follow the instructions the officer gives you. You will be required to show your driver's license, and in states with mandatory insurance laws, you will need to show your certificate of insurance.

You Are the Driver!
What tests might you be required to take if the police officer suspects alcohol or drug impairment?

Review It

1. What is the implied-consent law for drivers?
2. What are zero-tolerance levels for intoxication, and how can they be measured?
3. What must a driver do when stopped by a police officer?

15.4 Coping with Peer Pressure

Objectives

1. Tell how peer pressure might affect one's decision about drinking and driving.
2. List five steps involved in making a responsible decision.
3. Explain what is meant by peer education.
4. Explain why everyone should share the responsibility of preventing friends from drinking and driving.

Many factors and influences have an impact on young people's decisions about how they want to live their lives. Pressure from other individuals and groups can cause conflicts or unsure feelings about decisions they will need to make.

Understanding Peer Pressure

The influence of others of a similar age is called **peer pressure.** Peers greatly influence each other because people naturally tend to want to belong to a group. Some of the strongest influences in a person's life are the attitudes and actions of friends and peers. Peer relationships are very powerful forces in shaping a person's future. Many decisions are made based on positive peer pressure or negative peer pressure.

Positive Peer Pressure

When peers exert a pressure on you in a positive way, they want to be helpful and encouraging. The students in the picture are demonstrating positive peer pressure as they cheer for their team to win the track meet.

Talking a friend out of drinking alcoholic beverages at a party or refusing to ride with someone who has been drinking are other examples of positive peer pressure. Exerting positive peer pressure on friends also can help strengthen positive decisions in young people, as they search for their own identity and struggle to fit in.

Negative Peer Pressure

Negative peer pressure occurs when others encourage you to do something that you believe is wrong or danger-

Cheering for friends to win a race is an example of positive peer pressure.

Steps for Making Responsible Decisions
1. Know when a decision is needed.
2. Consider the choices.
3. Consider the consequences and ask yourself these questions: ■ Is it legal? ■ Is it safe? ■ What would my parents and other family members think? ■ Does it show respect for myself and others?
4. Decide which choice is best.
5. Evaluate your decision to know if it was a responsible decision.

ous. When peers exert negative pressure, they do not have your best interests in mind. Because some people worry a great deal about what others think of them, negative pressure might result in them doing things that are against their beliefs and values. People who tell others that they can drive safely after drinking are exerting negative peer pressure.

Some people might also submit to indirect peer pressure. This type of pressure often occurs when a person *feels* pressure to use alcohol or other drugs just to fit in with the group.

Refusing to do things that you believe to be wrong and being able to say no without fear of losing friends indicates responsible behavior. Mature, independent thinking is especially important if you face peer pressure to use alcohol or other drugs when you will be driving.

Making Responsible Decisions

Learning how to make responsible decisions can help you be more in control of your life. Following the five steps listed in the decision-making chart will help you make responsible decisions.

Deciding About Drinking Each person must make his or her own decision whether or not to drink. The best decision a person can make is not to drink. Individuals who decide not to drink alcoholic beverages never need to worry about alcohol impairing their driving performance. However, nondrinkers must share general concern and care about people who do drink and then drive.

Peer Education

Underage drinking is a national problem with many causes and no simple solutions. Many schools have organized student programs for **peer education.** Peer education is a process in which young people help other young people make decisions and determine goals. Peer programs may be known by many other names, including peer counseling, peer men-

Peer leaders direct activities such as the "trust fall" to help others to develop trust.

toring, or peer helpers. Regardless of the name, the purposes and goals of such programs are the same.

Peer education programs help young people influence one another in a positive way. Many young people are more sensitive to the thoughts and opinions of their peers than to the thoughts and opinions of adults. Peer groups have properly trained peer leaders who can be more than a friend or a considerate listener. Peer leaders learn specific skills for helping others deal effectively with problems through activities that develop cooperation, trust, support, and confidence. The students in the picture are participating in such an activity.

Teachers, counselors, and other professionals supervise training of peer leaders. Peer leaders learn communication skills, referral skills, and problem-solving skills.

Actions You Can Take

The following activities can help peer groups get involved in school and community programs to help combat the underage drinking problem:

- Investigate the facts through local health departments, law enforcement officials, community recreation directors, doctors, and other youth.
- Get the word out. Work with your school to create and distribute flyers and newsletters about your program. Contact other community leaders and solicit their cooperation.
- Communicate your support of zero-tolerance laws to your governor, state legislature, and community officials.
- Work with local park district and summer recreation officials to expand summer recreation programs.

Many schools have developed programs, through the assistance of other organizations, to help influence people about the harmful effects of alcohol, as well as the problem of drinking and driving. Some of these organizations include Mothers Against Drunk Drivers (MADD), Alliance Against Intoxicated Motorists (AAIM), and Students Against Dangerous Decisions (SADD). Another program, sponsored by the National Highway Traffic Safety Administration, is a court program—Peer Justice and Youth Empowerment (PJYE). Teen drinking prevention plans can be implemented with the help of The United States Department of Health and Human Services.

FRIENDS DON'T LET FRIENDS DRIVE DRUNK

Responsibility to Others

When people are in situations where alcoholic drinks are served, their first responsibility is for their own actions. However, a person's responsibility increases when the situation involves drinking and driving.

To what extent should a person take responsibility for the actions of others? Some people hesitate to interfere in other people's lives. However, most people wisely realize that they are being caring friends when they prevent friends from driving after drinking. Just as the sign says, *Friends Don't Let Friends Drive Drunk.*

The drinker has the responsibility of not driving after drinking. However, everyone should accept the responsibility of trying to keep a drinker from driving. In some states, a person who serves alcohol is legally responsible if someone is injured or killed as a result of the actions of the drinking driver. A responsible host plans a party where no alcoholic beverages are served.

You must be able to recognize the signs of too much drinking in order to share the responsibility of friends who drink. If friends are drinking, look for these signs of impairment:

- walking unsteadily or stumbling
- demonstrating poor judgment in behavior
- slurred, unclear speech
- talking loudly
- losing track of time or day of week

Remember that peer pressure is a forceful reason for people to drink or not to drink. Some people will think that drinking helps them to be accepted by a certain group.

Problems can come into being when a person drinks as a part of a group. Group drinking can become competitive and one may be urged to drink to keep up.

Don't forget that only one drink can cause a person's BAC to reach 0.03 percent. Driving abilities can be impaired even at that BAC. The risk of collision increases greatly as drinking increases.

PLAN AHEAD Two-thirds of drivers involved in alcohol-related traffic fatalities have a BAC of 0.14 or higher. Help reduce this fatal injury rate by taking responsible actions toward friends who may drink at a party where alcoholic beverages are served. When you plan to ride with a friend to a party, make alternate plans ahead of time to ensure a safe trip home.

What You and Others Can Do

A nondrinker has decisions to make about keeping drinking friends from driving. A friend will help get a drinking friend home safely.

A nondrinker might also have to decide whether or not to ride with a drinking driver. There is only one safe decision. Find other transportation to get home safely. Stay overnight where you are, if necessary.

When friends plan parties, encourage them to refrain from serving alcoholic beverages. Also encourage them to invite nondrinkers. If you know that some people will bring alcoholic drinks, consider not attending the party.

The effects of alcohol can be very harmful, if not deadly, especially when operating a motor vehicle. Keeping unsafe drivers off the road is everyone's responsibility. Every driver has the additional responsibility of driving safely. Even though heavy drinkers are a major cause of alcohol-related injuries and fatalities, social drinkers share a great responsibility for alcohol-related collisions. Responsible drivers decide not to become a part of the drinking problem. Instead, they contribute to its solution.

Review It

1. How might peer pressure affect one's decision about drinking and driving?
2. What five steps are involved in making a responsible decision?
3. What is meant by peer education?
4. Why should everyone share the responsibility of preventing friends from drinking and driving?

Chapter 15

Review

Reviewing Chapter Objectives

1. Effects of Alcohol on Driving Safely

1. How does alcohol affect mental and physical abilities needed for driving? (315–317)
2. What is blood-alcohol concentration? (318)
3. What factors affect blood-alcohol concentration and how do they work? (318)
4. What are five myths about the use of alcohol and what is the truth about each myth? (320)

2. Other Drugs and Driving

5. How do purchasing over-the-counter medicine and prescription medicine differ? (321)
6. How do depressants, stimulants, and hallucinogenic drugs affect a driver? (321–322)
7. What is the effect of combining alcohol with other drugs? (322)

3. Traffic Laws Governing the Use of Alcohol

8. What is the implied-consent law? (323)
9. What are zero-tolerance levels of intoxication and how can these levels be measured? (324)
10. What should a driver do when stopped by a police officer? (325)

4. Coping with Peer Pressure

11. How might peer pressure affect one's decision about drinking and driving? (326–327)
12. What are the five steps involved in making a responsible decision? (327)
13. What is peer education? (327–328)
14. Why should everyone share the responsibility of preventing friends from drinking and driving? (329–330)

Projects

Individuals

Investigate Find out as much information as you can about collisions that occurred in your state last year involving underage drivers who were drinking. Use this information to write a persuasive argument about why teenagers should not drink and drive.

Use Technology Research the technology used in your state to determine blood-alcohol concentration. Find out how this technology works. Also find out the levels at which adults can be charged with *driving while intoxicated* or *driving under the influence* in your state. Share your results with the class.

Groups

Lobby Write letters to state and community officials communicating your support of zero-tolerance laws. Each student should address the letter to a different official. Share the letters with your class.

Debate Divide the class into two groups and debate the pros and cons of setting the drinking age at 21. Make a list of all reasons cited. Have one member from each group summarize the reasons and report them to the class.

Chapter 15
Review

Chapter Test

Check Your Knowledge

Multiple Choice Copy the number of each sentence below on a sheet of paper. Choose the letter of the answer that best completes the statement or answers the question.

1. All states enforce a minimum drinking age of
(a) 18. (b) 19. (c) 20. (d) 21.

2. Which of the following type of drugs slows down the central nervous system?
(a) stimulant (c) depressant
(b) hallucinogen (d) none of the above

3. The most common penalty for a first-time conviction of a DUI or DWI is
(a) driver's license suspension.
(b) prison term.
(c) payment of a fine.
(d) vehicle impoundment.

4. What advice should you give a social drinker planning to drive?
(a) Don't drink on an empty stomach.
(b) Appoint a designated driver.
(c) Be extra careful if you drink and drive.
(d) Wait one hour after drinking before driving.

Completion Copy the number of each sentence below. After each number, write the word or words that complete the sentence correctly.

5. The _____ law makes it illegal for persons under the age of 21 to drive with any measurable amount of alcohol in the blood.

6. In the process of _____, young people help other young people make decisions.

7. A person who decides ahead of time not to drink and is appointed to drive others who do drink is known as a _____.

Review Vocabulary

Copy the number of each definition in list A. Match the definition in list A with the term it defines in list B.

List A

8. drug that can slow down the central nervous system

9. drug that speeds up the central nervous system

10. amount of alcohol in the blood expressed as a percentage of alcohol in the bloodstream

11. drugs that can be obtained legally without a doctor's prescription

12. inner forces of personality that restrain or hold back one's impulsive behavior

13. involuntary jerking of the eyes as a person gazes to the side

List B

a. over-the-counter medicines
b. inhibitions
c. stimulant
d. depressant
e. nystagmus
f. blood-alcohol concentration

Think Critically

Write a paragraph to answer each question.

1. Using the framework of the IPDE Process, describe how alcohol impairs your ability to drive.

2. What strategies can you use to overcome negative peer pressure as it relates to drinking and driving?

Decision Making

1. This driver stopped for an hour on his way home from work. During that time he drank three beers. What effects might the beer have on the driver's abilities to drive safely?

2. This girl is about to purchase over-the-counter medicine to treat her cold. Why is it important that she read the label on the medicine bottle?

3. This driver has been stopped by police for suspicion of driving while intoxicated. What types of tests might he be requested to take? What can the tests detect and measure? What could happen if the driver refuses to take the tests?

4. Students can solicit support from community officials in an effort to combat the problem of underage drinking in their community. What type of activities might students and community leaders pursue in their endeavor?

CHAPTER 16
Buying and Owning a Vehicle

You Are the Driver!

There are many responsibilities that go along with vehicle ownership. What type of vehicle will best meet your needs? What features and options should you select? What can you afford? Should you buy or lease? What are the vehicle's operating costs? What is a fair price? What kinds and amounts of insurance will you need? What will the insurance cost? The choices can be overwhelming.

This chapter discusses various aspects of owning and operating a vehicle. It also covers vehicle insurance, environmental concerns, and personal responsibilities of owning and operating a vehicle.

For: Chapter 16 online activities
Visit: PHSchool.com
Web Code: cak-9999

16.1

Buying a Vehicle

Objectives

1. List the responsibilities of owning or leasing a vehicle.
2. List the various costs associated with owning and operating a vehicle.
3. Explain how to select a used vehicle.
4. Describe the options and steps in buying a vehicle.

Having your own vehicle gives you a lot of freedom and mobility. *It also carries a lot of responsibilities.* You will need to be able to afford the vehicle and to maintain it. If you are under the age of 18, you will likely share the responsibilities with your parents. You also will likely share the additional expenses for maintenance, repairs, insurance, and fuel.

Do You Need a Vehicle?

Are your driving needs great enough to justify owning a vehicle? Are there alternatives to buying a vehicle? The answers to these questions will help you decide whether your needs justify the expense of owning a vehicle.

Can You Afford to Own a Vehicle?

The cost of owning a vehicle can be more than you expect. Some of the major expenses of vehicle ownership are described below:

- **Purchase Price** The purchase price is the amount a person is charged and willing to pay for the vehicle. Consider what you can afford before selecting a specific type of vehicle. Shop around and compare prices of different makes and models. Newspaper ads and the Internet are good ways to compare prices.
- **Depreciation** A vehicle's value drops steadily over time, whether you use the vehicle a lot or very little. This decrease is called **depreciation.**
- **Financing** If you are able to purchase a vehicle by paying cash, you eliminate having to pay interest on a loan. Most people, however, obtain a loan when they purchase a vehicle. Make sure you shop around for the best loan rates available. Banks, credit unions, savings and loan associations, and car dealerships are often good sources.
- **Other Costs** Operating costs include fuel, oil, tires, repairs, and replacement parts. Licensing, registration, insurance, taxes, and loan interest also are costs to be considered. Costs also may include parking and toll fees.

Vehicle expenses can increase from year to year. Your annual operating costs will depend on how much you drive, where you drive, and your fuel economy. The more you drive, the greater the costs.

What Kind of Vehicle Should You Buy?

If you decide you absolutely need and can afford a vehicle, what type will you get? Examine your needs, wants, and budget. Ask yourself these questions:

- What will I use the vehicle for?
- Do I need certain passenger and cargo capacities? Will I need to tow anything?
- How many miles will I drive each year?
- Will I use the vehicle more for short trips or long trips?
- How long will I expect to keep the vehicle?

You need to consider many factors when determining what type of vehicle to buy. Consider all factors carefully before you go out and look at any vehicles.

Vehicle Size

Size is an important factor in buying a vehicle. What size vehicle will serve your needs? Consider these points:

- A smaller, lighter vehicle usually gets better gas mileage but does not offer as much protection in a collision as a larger, heavier vehicle.
- Smaller vehicles are easier to maneuver than larger vehicles, especially when parking.
- A larger vehicle provides a more comfortable ride but is usually more costly to operate than a smaller vehicle.
- A larger vehicle has a greater capacity for passengers and parcels than a smaller vehicle.

Engine Size and Types

Smaller engines usually are more fuel efficient than larger engines. However, a larger engine may be more feasible in a fully-equipped vehicle. Vehicles with larger engines typically cost more to maintain and repair.

Transmission

Most vehicles today are equipped with automatic transmissions that include automatic overdrive. This makes the vehicles nearly as fuel efficient as stickshift vehicles. Although the costs of repairs for an automatic transmission are usually higher, stickshifts may require repairs more often.

Optional Equipment

Decide what optional equipment you want, but be aware that options add to the cost of the vehicle. Technological advancements have resulted in "smarter" vehicles with options

Fuel efficient . . .

or sporty but expensive.

More room for passengers . . .

and more cargo capacity.

What Do You Think?

Some people prefer to lease a vehicle for a certain number of years. Why might leasing be more desirable than purchasing a vehicle?

designed for safety, comfort, and information.

Consider the potential for voice-activated controls for controlling the temperature inside the vehicle. Or, imagine a radar-like blind-spot warning device that helps you avoid backing into objects you can't see.

Know what safety options are included. Comfort options may make you feel good, but safety options can save lives, reduce injuries, and save you money. Ask your insurance agent about safety options that can save you money on insurance premiums.

Leasing a Vehicle

An alternative to purchasing a vehicle is **leasing.** In some ways, leasing is similar to owning a vehicle. You are responsible for monthly payments, fuel, and all the other types of operating costs you would incur if purchasing a vehicle.

The main difference is that after your lease contract expires, you do not own the vehicle. At the end of your lease, you must choose one of the following three options:

1. Return the vehicle and lease another vehicle.
2. Purchase the vehicle at a cost determined at the start of your lease.
3. Return the vehicle with no obligations to either lease another vehicle or purchase the vehicle you returned.

Lease payments are based on the difference of the value of the vehicle at the start of the lease, and the value at the end of the lease, plus interest. In contrast, when you take out a loan to purchase a vehicle, your monthly payments cover the entire cost of the vehicle over the term of the loan, plus loan interest.

Leasing is not for everyone. Most lease agreements limit how many miles you can put on the vehicle. Extra miles are likely to cost you an

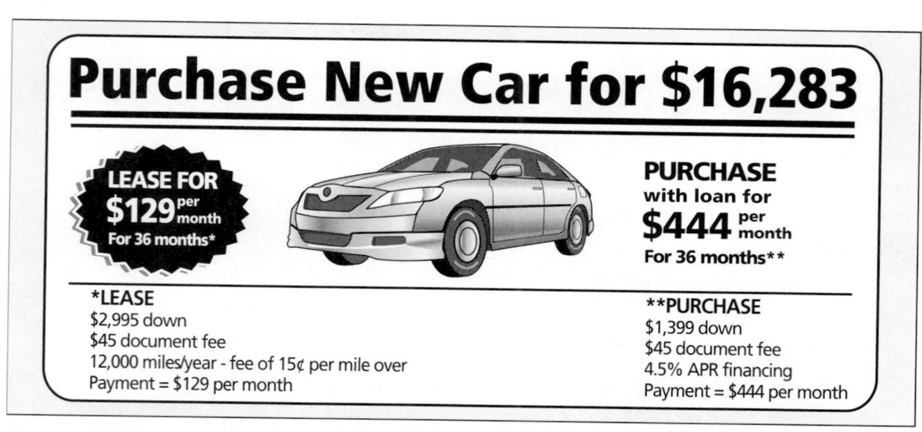

Compare the costs of leasing a vehicle to purchasing using a loan.

additional charge. Normal wear is considered, but any wear considered excessive will result in an extra charge. Make sure you understand all the terms of the contract before you sign a lease agreement.

Buying a Used Vehicle

You may decide to purchase a used vehicle if you cannot afford a new vehicle. Used vehicles can be purchased from a used-car dealer, a new-car dealer, or a private owner.

Buying a vehicle from a private owner may cost less. However, you need to consider the following:

- A private owner will seldom repair the vehicle or provide you with a **warranty.** A warranty is a written guarantee that the seller will make certain repairs for a stated period of time.
- In nearly all cases, a private sale is final.
- Used-car dealers usually have a large selection of vehicles available. Many used vehicles purchased from car dealerships carry a warranty.

Be aware that warranties do not cover everything. *Read the warranty carefully and know what is covered before you buy.*

How Much Should You Pay?

Publications like the *NADA Guide* (National Auto Dealers Association Guide) provide what are referred to as suggested **blue-book prices** for used vehicles. A blue-book price is the average market value for that model and age of vehicle. The value of a vehicle depends a great deal on the vehicle's condition. You can also use the Internet to compare prices of different makes and models of vehicles.

SHOPPING ON THE INTERNET More people use the Internet or special CD-ROM software each year when shopping for vehicles. This technology helps you review and compare vehicles and prices, apply for loans, and even purchase vehicles. Prices are often not negotiable and can be hundreds to thousands of dollars less than you would pay at a dealership.

Choosing a Used Vehicle

Selecting a good used vehicle takes time. When you find a vehicle you like, check it out.

- Besides looking good, make sure the vehicle is in good mechanical condition.
- Determine whether it was ever involved in a collision, or needs repairs.
- When possible, talk to the previous owner about the condition of the vehicle and previous maintenance service that was done on the vehicle.

Outside and Inside Checks

Walk around the vehicle to inspect it. Be sure to check

- doors and locks
- vehicle appearance
- fluid leaks
- evidence of collision damage

Enter the vehicle to check

- seats for comfort and condition
- lights and accessories
- mileage (odometer)
- pedals and steering wheel

Check the trunk to find

- evidence of damage
- spare tire
- tire jack

Open the hood to check

- signs of collision damage
- hoses and radiator for leaks
- condition of belts
- coolant level
- battery and cables

Test Drive Always take a vehicle you intend to purchase for a test drive. If the owner refuses to let you test drive the vehicle, look for another vehicle.

When you take a test drive, drive in areas and on roads with which you are familiar. Keep the following questions in mind as you test drive a vehicle:

- What do you hear and feel?
- Are the brakes in good condition?
- Is the steering firm?
- How is the suspension?
- Does the vehicle hesitate when you quickly accelerate?
- Is the vehicle comfortable?

Make these checks during the test drive:

- Turn the ignition switch on and check to see that all warning lights, signals, and headlights work.
- Start the engine. It should start easily. Warning lights should go out in a few seconds.
- Drive at low speeds and test the brakes several times. The vehicle should stop smoothly and straight.
- Make a number of right and left turns. There should not be any play in the wheel, and it should steer easily.
- Accelerate moderately. The vehicle should accelerate smoothly from 0–40 mph without hesitation.
- Test the brakes at various speeds. They should not grab or pull to one side. If equipped with antilock brakes, brake hard to ensure that the system works.

Carefully inspect the vehicle inside and out. Then have it inspected by a professional mechanic or technician.

Check under the hood when the engine is cool and running.

- Drive on a rough road at 25 mph, and turn off the radio. The vehicle should not rattle or feel unstable.
- Check oil pressure gauges and warning lights for low pressure, overheating, or any other malfunctions indicated by warning lights.

Have the Vehicle Inspected You have inspected the vehicle yourself—both inside and outside. Before you commit to buying it, you should have a trained technician also inspect it. It's an investment of time and money that may save you a lot in the long run.

Talk with the technician about possible needed maintenance or repairs. Obtain estimates on related costs for the repairs or maintenance. Problems with the transmission, brakes, gears, clutch, radiator, and exhaust system can be costly.

Before You Close the Deal

If the seller is going to make repairs, have the repairs written into the sales agreement. Make sure the vehicle includes an owner's manual and receipts of service repairs.

After you purchase the vehicle, read the owner's manual. The owner's manual is a valuable resource for learning about features of your new vehicle and the proper care and maintenance needs of the vehicle.

Review It

1. What are the responsibilities of owning or leasing a vehicle?
2. What are some of the costs of owning and operating a vehicle?
3. What procedures should you use to select a used vehicle?
4. What options and steps should you consider when buying a vehicle?

16.2

Insuring a Vehicle

Objectives

1. Explain what financial responsibility laws require.
2. Explain how auto insurance works.
3. Explain what different kinds of auto insurance cover.
4. List factors that affect the cost of insurance.

If you are involved in a collision, you may find that the largest expense of owning a vehicle is paying for damages you cause. Every state has a **financial responsibility law.** This law requires you to prove that you can pay for damages you cause that result in death, injury, or property damage.

What does your state say about financial responsibility? What type of penalties can be invoked for not complying with the financial responsibility laws in your state?

What Is Vehicle Insurance?

Insuring your vehicle is financial responsibility. You buy insurance from a company by paying a **premium,** a specified amount of money for coverage over a specified period of time, to the company. A policy is a written contract between you—the insured—and the insurance company. A policy includes the terms and conditions of insurance coverage.

Kinds of Insurance

There are many different types of insurance. Refer to the chart for a summary of various types of insurance and what each type covers.

Liability Insurance

Every state requires individuals to carry **liability insurance.** It is the most important insurance to have. Liability insurance protects the driver who caused the collision. It provides compensation for a harm or wrong to a third party for which the insured is legally obligated to pay. Liability insurance covers others when you are at fault.

Bodily-Injury Insurance One type of liability insurance, **bodily-injury insurance,** covers the driver who is at fault against claims. (*Claims* are formal requests for payments related to injuries to other people.) Most states require drivers to hold a specified minimum level of liability insurance.

Property-Damage Insurance Another type of liability insurance, **property-damage insurance,** protects the driver who is at fault against claims for damages to another person's property, up to specified limits. Make sure your level of coverage is adequate.

Medical Payment Insurance

This insurance pays medical and funeral expenses for bodily injuries sustained by occupants in an insured vehicle. It pays expenses up to stated amounts. This coverage does not depend on who was at fault in the accident.

No-Fault Insurance

Because of the backlog and long delays in litigation cases coming to a trial, some states have **no-fault insurance.** In such states, people involved in collisions recover losses and expenses associated with the

Car Insurance

Kind of Insurance	Coverage	Claim Includes	Minimum Amount	Notes
Bodily-injury liability	Pays claim against owner if someone is killed or injured and owner is at fault.	Hospital and doctor bills Legal fees Court costs Loss of wages	States normally specify minimum: $10,000–$30,000 for one person; $20,000–$100,000 for several persons.	Required in many states. Needed by all car owners. Minimum coverage required is generally too low.
Property-damage liability	Pays claim against owner if property of others is damaged and owner is at fault.	Other car and possessions in car. Damage to house, telephone pole, and traffic light.	States normally specify minimum: $5,000–$25,000	Required in many states. Needed by all car owners.
Uninsured-motorist* and underinsured-motorist	Pays for injuries to you and your passengers in case of hit-and-run collision, uninsured or underinsured motorist.	Hospital and doctor bills Legal fees Court costs Loss of wages (Does not cover property damage.)	Usually same as bodily-injury liability.	Required in many states. Needed by all car owners.
Collision	Pays cost of repairing or replacing owner's car when owner is at fault or when owner cannot collect from person at fault.	Repair or replacement of any car driven by owner or with owner's permission.	Insures for depreciated value of car. Owner decides on $100 to $500 (or more) deductible to reduce cost of premium.	Important for new or expensive car. Drop after 7–10 years of ownership or when value of car no longer justifies cost of coverages.
Comprehensive	Pays cost of repairing or replacing owner's car.	Fire, Earthquake Theft, Storm Flood, Riots Wind, Vandalism	Insures for depreciated value of car, usually with $100 to $500 (or more) deductible to reduce cost of premium.	Important for new or expensive car. Drop after 7 to 10 years of ownership.
Medical-payments	Pays medical costs for you and your passengers injured in any collision, regardless of fault.	Pays all immediate medical costs (generally in addition to other medical insurance).	Insures for $500 to $5,000 per person.	This insurance does not require a legal process to determine fault, while bodily-injury coverage usually does.
Towing	Pays cost of towing or minor repair to disabled car.	Dead battery Out of gas Flat tire Accident (regardless of cause or fault).	Usually pays amount validated by towing company.	Good to have. Not needed if owner belongs to automobile club with towing service.

*Note that uninsured-motorist insurance covers collision-related injuries only, not property damage. Some states now allow insurance companies to offer uninsured-motorist property damage insurance.

You should carry higher than minimum levels of bodily-injury liability insurance. The amounts of today's court settlements can be quite high.

collision directly from their own insurance company—regardless of who is at fault. However, coverage is limited as specified in the insurance policy. Details in how no-fault insurance is handled differs significantly from one state to another.

Collision Insurance

Collision insurance covers you if you are at fault in a collision, or not able to collect from the person who is at fault. Your collision insurance provides coverage to pay the costs of repair or replacement of your vehicle, less the **deductible** you have selected. A deductible is the amount you agree to pay towards the repair or replacement of the vehicle. Your insurance company agrees to cover the balance up to specified maximum limits. Know what the limit is with the company you choose.

You can select your deductible level. The higher the deductible you select, the greater the amount you are required to pay out of your pocket. However, the higher deductible you select, the lower your premium will be.

Comprehensive Insurance

What if your vehicle is damaged for some reason other than a collision? Your policy's **comprehensive insurance** can pay for replacement or repair of your vehicle. You also can select a deductible amount for comprehensive insurance. As with a collision deductible, the higher deductible you select, the more you agree to pay, and the lower your premium will be. Most insurance companies will only pay up to the estimated current value of the vehicle.

Damage caused by severe wind, hail, vandalism, or similar situations are typically included under comprehensive insurance. Most companies have restrictions on what causes qualify for comprehensive coverage. Check your policy to see what restrictions apply.

Uninsured and Underinsured Motorist Insurance

Uninsured motorist insurance protects you if you are struck by another vehicle whose driver has no insurance. Your company covers the costs of injuries to you and your passengers, up to a specified amount. Most states require insurance companies to provide this type of insurance.

If you have **underinsured motorist insurance** your insurance company will pay any costs that exceed what the other person's insurance company will pay as a result of a collision. Most states now require that companies offer this type of insurance to their customers.

Insurance Rates

A number of factors determine what you pay for insurance. Data on different factors are reviewed and statistics developed. Rates are then established based on the statistics. Factors upon which statistics are based and rates determined include:

- **Driving Record** Drivers with a certain number of convictions for moving violations and collisions pay higher premiums.

Insurance companies consider them greater risks to insure.

- **Age** Younger drivers have a proportionally higher number of collisions; thus, they have higher premiums. Older, more experienced drivers have fewer moving violations and are involved in comparatively fewer collisions. A principal driver is a person who will drive a certain vehicle most often. A person under the age of 25 listed as the principal driver of a vehicle could pay as much as four times more than an older driver.
- **Miles Driven** The more miles a vehicle is driven on a regular basis (usually annual), the greater the premium. This is because the vehicle is more exposed to the possibility of a collision.
- **Driver Gender** Male drivers tend to pay higher premiums. Historically, statistics have shown they drive more, have more collisions, and their crashes tend to be more severe than those involving young female drivers. However, the gap based on gender has narrowed.
- **Marital Status** Married drivers statistically have fewer collisions than unmarried drivers.
- **Type of Vehicle** Sports cars, some vans, and sport utility vehicles are very popular. They

INSURANCE Even though financial responsibility laws exist, a significant number of drivers do not have insurance. Without insurance people risk losing their life savings and can be forced to liquidate assets to cover required payments. Always comply with your state's financial responsibility laws.

Part of the procedure you should follow if you are involved in a collision is to exchange insurance information with the other drivers.

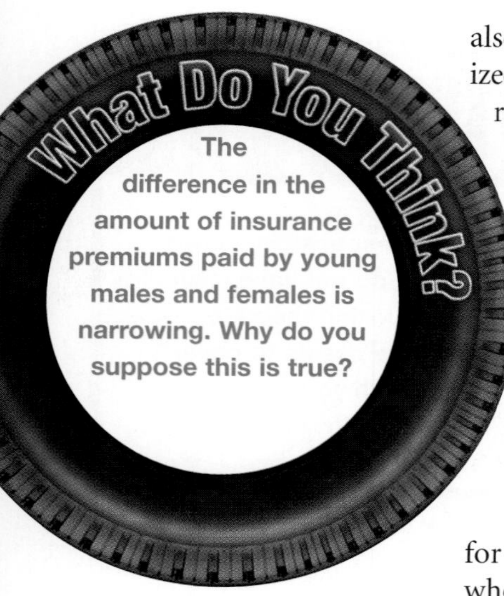

also tend to be stolen or vandalized more often and cost more to repair. Many larger vans, trucks, and sport utility vehicles tend to cause greater damage to vehicles they strike. Some insurance companies may charge higher rates to people who drive such vehicles.

- **Where the Driver Lives and Drives** Traffic density in urban areas increases the potential for collisions. Therefore, drivers who live in rural areas tend to pay less for insurance than those who live in larger metropolitan areas.
- **Driver's Claim Record** Higher and more frequent claims, especially for comprehensive and collision coverage, usually result in higher premiums.

Reduced Premiums

Most insurance companies reward low-risk drivers with reduced premiums. Premiums are often reduced for drivers who have

- maintained good grades in school, and in some cases, have successfully completed an approved driver education program
- had no claims or convictions for three years
- multiple vehicles insured under the same policy
- vehicles with certain safety features like airbags and anti-theft devices

Assigned-Risk Insurance

Some companies cancel an insurance policy if the driver or other insured drivers on the policy have been convicted of a drug- or alcohol-related violation. A driver who has several collisions or traffic convictions can be the cause for a company canceling a family's policy.

Drivers who have had their insurance canceled due to a poor driving record may not be eligible to obtain coverage at standard rates. Often times the only coverage these drivers can obtain is **assigned-risk insurance.** Assigned-risk insurance provides bodily injury and property damage liability coverage to high-risk drivers for a much higher premium. Assigned-risk drivers must drive violation-free several years before they can qualify for standard insurance.

Review It

1. What do financial responsibility laws require?
2. What is the purpose of auto insurance?
3. What are the different types of auto insurance?
4. What factors determine the premiums for auto insurance?

16.3

Environmental Concerns

Objectives

1. Describe how vehicle use adversely affects the environment.
2. Identify ways individuals can reduce the effects of vehicles on the environment.

Owning and driving a vehicle places many responsibilities on you. One is being aware of how vehicles affect our environment. Drivers must act responsibly to minimize the harm they may cause to the environment.

How Do Vehicles Affect the Environment?

All vehicle owners have a responsibility for ensuring that they do not harm the environment. This includes using more environmentally friendly products, and properly disposing vehicle parts, fluids, and components.

Almost every motor vehicle that uses gasoline or diesel fuel creates engine exhaust. Some exhaust gases contribute to air pollution.

Exhaust Gases

Over the years, improvements in the engineering of vehicles have resulted in smaller amounts of harmful exhaust emissions. Today's vehicles also get better gas mileage. However, each year drivers in the United States drive more vehicles more miles.

Carbon Dioxide Carbon dioxide (CO_2) is one of several gases in vehicle exhaust. Large amounts of this gas produce a "greenhouse effect," which warms the earth. Some scientists fear that too much warming will change the earth's climate.

Regularly maintaining your vehicle can help reduce the number of pollutants your vehicle emits. The less fuel your vehicle burns, the lower the levels of pollutants in its exhaust.

A number of states have implemented auto emissions inspection programs. These programs require owners to have their vehicle's emission levels periodically inspected. A vehicle must pass the inspection before its license can be renewed.

CFCs Until quite recently, most air conditioners contained freon gas, a chlorinated fluorocarbon (abbreviated CFC). Though effective in cooling air, when freon is released into the atmosphere, it breaks down the atmosphere's ozone layer.

The ozone layer shields the earth from the sun's ultraviolet rays, a known cause of skin cancer. If the earth's ozone layer continues to be reduced, it is likely rates of skin cancer will rise.

Does your state require vehicle testing at an auto emissions inspection center?

Refrigerant recovery systems are used on older vehicles to keep CFCs from escaping into the atmosphere.

All new vehicles use an alternative refrigerant in their air conditioning systems. Auto repair shops that service older vehicles whose air conditioners require freon are required to utilize refrigerant recovery systems. These systems capture any freon that escapes while the shop recharges a vehicle's air conditioning system.

Disposal of Vehicle Parts and Fluids

Vehicle batteries, oil filters, and fluids—oil, gasoline, transmission fluid, brake fluid, and antifreeze—contain hazardous substances. Never dump or dispose of these items in the garbage or down a drain. Collect these items and take them to the nearest hazardous waste collection center, or other appropriate collection location. Contact your local health department. They will probably know of appropriate drop-off locations for your hazardous wastes.

Other solid materials like tires, exhaust pipes, and mufflers also need to be disposed of properly. Piles of older tires placed out in the open are not only eyesores, they can become breeding grounds for insects and rodents that carry dangerous diseases.

Many vehicle parts can be recycled. Old tires now are being used to make floor mats and other rubber products. Glass and tires can be recycled into road-paving materials. Various plastics are being used to make other commonly used plastic products.

How Can Drivers Help the Environment?

Each person can utilize transportation and still help the environment. As technology increases, more and more alternatives are available.

Mass Transportation

Several forms of **mass transportation** (also called mass transit) are available throughout the United States. Mass transportation involves moving large numbers of people together from place to place.

Mass transportation is safe, efficient, and environmentally responsible. It includes small buses, city and suburban buses, and rail trams. It also includes urban mass transit systems common to some of our larger cities. Some rapid transit systems are already in place. Others are being developed. Using mass transit reduces the cost per passenger mile and decreases exhaust emissions.

Car and Van Pools

Other environmentally responsible systems include **car pooling** or **van pooling.** These are systems where several individuals share transportation to one or more destinations. As an incentive to car or van pooling, some highways have special lanes for use only by vehicles containing a certain number of passengers.

Many companies and government agencies provide vans and vehicles for use in a car or van pool. These systems help reduce the number of vehicles on the road, save fuel consumption, reduce overall amounts of exhaust, and decrease the amount of space needed for parking.

Alternative-Fueled Vehicles

Although many alternative-fueled vehicles are still in early stages of development, this is another option drivers have in reducing the harmful effects of driving on the environment. Many government agencies

Car or van pooling reduces the number of vehicles on the road, exhaust, and conserves the amount of gasoline consumed.

Hybrid vehicles use a combination of a gasoline-powered engine and electric motors, which reduces the amount of fuel used and harmful emissions.

have fleet vehicles that use cleaner burning fuels.

The worldwide supply of fossil fuels, including gasoline, continues to decrease. In an effort to reduce the dependence on gasoline, several alternative-fuel technologies are being explored. **Solar-powered vehicles** capture light energy from the sun and transform it into electricity. Other alternative-fuel technologies are hydrogen fuel cells and ethanol-burning engines. However, engineers have not completely addressed some of the problems associated with these technologies.

Another alternative technology is hybrid vehicles. Hybrid vehicles have both a gasoline-powered engine and one or more electric motors. Usually, the electricity that powers the electric motor is generated by the motion of the vehicle itself.

Most of these new alternative-energy technologies have two benefits. They use less gasoline while also reducing the emissions that harm our environment.

Hydrogen fuel cells provide energy by converting hydrogen into electricity.

Review It

1. What are some ways vehicles adversely affect the environment?
2. Name three ways individuals can reduce the harmful effects vehicles have on the environment.

Chapter 16
Review

Reviewing Chapter Objectives

1. Buying a Vehicle

1. What are the responsibilities of owning or leasing a vehicle? (336)
2. What are the various costs associated with owning and operating a vehicle? (336–337)
3. How would you select a used vehicle? (339–341)
4. What are the options you have and the steps you take when buying a vehicle? (337–341)

2. Insuring a Vehicle

5. What do financial responsibility laws require? (342)
6. How does auto insurance work? (342)
7. What do different kinds of auto insurance cover? (342–344)
8. What factors affect the cost of insurance? (344–346)

3. Environmental Concerns

9. How does vehicle use adversely affect the environment? (347–348)
10. In what ways can individuals reduce the effects of vehicles on the environment? (348–350)

Projects

Individuals

Use Technology Search the Internet for Web sites that deal with automobile sales. Choose one vehicle model. Compare options and prices for this model on several sites. Print out the pages that show these prices and bring them to class.

Investigate Go to the library (or search the Internet) to obtain a copy of the NADA Guide (or blue book). Look up the blue-book prices for the vehicles your family owns. Find out the original prices of the vehicles. Calculate how much each vehicle has depreciated.

Groups

Debate Form two teams. Debate the pros and cons of owning a large versus a small vehicle. Make a list of the reasons each team mentions. Compare your list with those of the other teams in your class.

Demonstrate Divide into groups of four or five. Each group member should obtain permission to inspect a vehicle in the school parking lot. Demonstrate to the group the steps you would take in inspecting the vehicle if you were considering buying it. Each group member should take notes on the others' inspections. Discuss whether you would buy the vehicles inspected.

Chapter 16
Review

Chapter Test

Check Your Knowledge

Multiple Choice Copy the number of each sentence below on a sheet of paper. Choose the letter of the answer that best completes the statement or answers the question.

1. The value of a vehicle drops steadily over time due to
(a) loan interest.
(b) depreciation.
(c) operating costs.
(d) insurance premiums.

2. If the used vehicle you are considering passes your tests, you should
(a) have a mechanic make a final check.
(b) buy it immediately.
(c) have a friend test drive the vehicle.
(d) buy it only if a warranty is offered.

3. Vehicle insurance that pays for damage caused by something other than a collision is called
(a) liability insurance.
(b) collision insurance.
(c) comprehensive insurance.
(d) uninsured motorist insurance.

4. Which of the following does nothing to help protect the environment?
(a) using mass transportation.
(b) driving alone in a vehicle.
(c) van pooling.
(d) using an alternative-fueled vehicle.

Completion Copy the number of each sentence below. After each number, write the word or words that complete the sentence correctly.

5. A driver whose insurance is canceled due to a poor driving record needs to obtain _____ insurance.

6. Large amounts of CO_2 in the atmosphere produce a _____, which warms the earth.

Review Vocabulary

Copy the number of each definition in list A. Match the definition in list A with the term it defines in list B.

List A

7. covers an insured's losses and expenses associated with a collision regardless of who is at fault
8. requires you to prove that you can pay for damages you cause that result in death, injury, or property damage
9. amount you agree to pay toward the repair or replacement of the vehicle
10. provides bodily injury and property damage liability coverage to high-risk drivers for a much higher premium
11. specified amount of money paid over a specified period of time paid for insurance coverage
12. covers the driver who is at fault against claims

List B

a. deductible
b. premium
c. no-fault insurance
d. bodily-injury insurance
e. assigned-risk insurance
f. financial responsibility law

Think Critically

Write a paragraph to answer each question.

1. List and discuss the advantages and disadvantages of leasing a vehicle.

2. How might you reduce premium rates for vehicle insurance?

Decision Making

1. You have a part-time job. What are the arguments for and against buying a vehicle?

2. You know the type of vehicle you want. You have found vehicles at a private seller, a used-car dealer, and a new-car dealer. How would you decide which vehicle to buy?

3. How should this person properly dispose of the used oil?

4. Your vehicle has been vandalized. What should you do? What type of insurance will cover the repairs?

CHAPTER 17
Maintaining Your Vehicle

You Are the Driver!

Imagine you own your own vehicle. Do you know how to check the oil level? Do you know what the tire pressure should be? What vehicle maintenance can you do? What maintenance should a mechanic or automotive technician do? Have you read the owner's manual for your vehicle?

The vehicles you drive are complex machines made up of many systems and parts. All vehicles need preventive maintenance and periodic repairs to help reduce operating costs. This chapter will familiarize you with the different systems of your vehicle and explain how to maintain your vehicle.

Go Online
PHSchool.com

For: Chapter 17 online activities
Visit: PHSchool.com
Web Code: cak-9999

17.1 Maintaining the Power Systems

Objectives

1. Identify the warning signs for needed repairs for the power and drive systems, ignition and electrical systems, lubrication and cooling systems, and fuel and exhaust systems.
2. Describe the steps to follow to start a vehicle that has a dead battery.

Your vehicle consists of many systems. Knowing about the different systems and the care they need can help you recognize and handle problems if they occur. Your owner's manual provides valuable information about how to maintain your vehicle and its various systems.

Power and Drive Systems

A vehicle's engine needs fuel to burn to create the power to move. The power generated from the **power-plant,** also known as the vehicle's engine or motor, is transmitted to a drive system that operates the front wheels, rear wheels, or all wheels in some vehicles. The powerplant is the source of energy that maintains a vehicle's movement.

New vehicles are powered by different types of internal combustion engines and a variety of electric motors or engine combinations. Selection of powerplant for a particular vehicle is based on its weight, usage, and government regulations.

Different drive-train systems are used for different vehicles. Some vehicles are rear-wheel drive, some front-wheel drive, and others all-wheel drive. The picture shows a front-wheel drive system.

Depending on the type of vehicle, the drive train has different components including

- powerplant (engine or motor)
- transmission
- clutch (in a stickshift)
- drive shaft or half shafts
- differential
- transaxle
- drive axles
- universal, or constant velocity joints

A vehicle's **transmission** houses different gears. The gears of the transmission enable the engine to deliver power to the drive wheels. Lower gears are for power and let the engine turn faster. Higher gears are for greater speed and let the engine turn more slowly and efficiently.

The **drive shaft** is a long metal tube in rear-wheel drive vehicles. The drive shaft carries power from the transmission to the **differential** in the rear of the vehicle. The differential has gears that allow one wheel to turn more slowly than the other when turning a corner.

In front-wheel drive vehicles, power is carried to the front wheels by two half shafts. A **transaxle** is

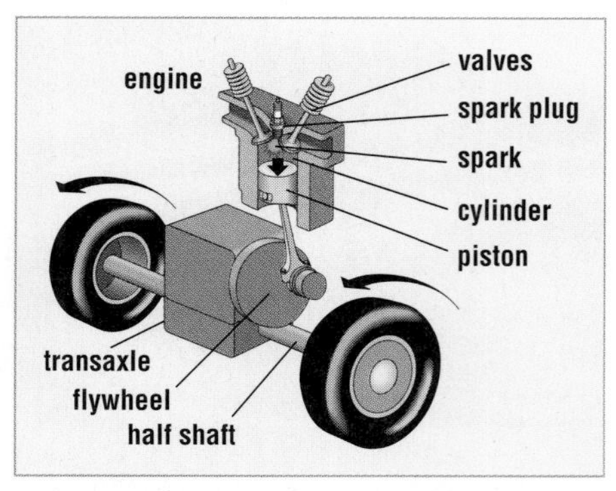

Transmitting power in a front-wheel drive vehicle

located between the two half shafts and replaces the transmission and differential.

Check your automatic transmission or transaxle fluid once a month. Jerky shifting, slipping in and out of gears while driving, or pauses before the vehicle starts to move are signs of a low transmission fluid level. Your owner's manual explains how to check the fluid level.

Ignition and Electrical Systems

The ignition system sets off combustion in your engine's cylinders. The electrical system is involved in the ignition process and also provides the electrical power needed to operate your vehicle's lights, controls, and accessories.

Alternator

When you turn your key in the ignition, an electrical current sent from the battery to the electric starter turns the engine. Once the engine is running, the **alternator** generates an electrical current that recharges the battery. A belt drives the alternator. Current from the battery continues to power the ignition system. This system delivers energy to each spark plug at the proper time to ignite the air–fuel mixture in each cylinder.

If the alternator light comes on while you are driving, or the battery gauge displays a strong discharge, the alternator is not working properly. It is not generating electricity. The problem could be as simple as a broken or loose belt, or as complicated as an internal electrical problem.

Battery

A vehicle's starter, lights, computer-assisted controls, and other electrical accessories depend on the electrical power stored in the battery.

Extreme cold or hot weather makes starting your vehicle difficult. A battery has less power when it is cold or overheated. Keep your battery charged to avoid failure. If the engine turns over very slowly when you try to start your vehicle, have the battery charged or replaced.

Keep battery cables tight and free of corrosion, especially where the terminals connect to the battery. Most batteries in today's vehicles are sealed and do not need to have their fluid levels checked. Read your owner's manual for maintenance information.

Always wear eye protection and gloves when working with, or around, a battery. A battery releases hydrogen gas, which is very explosive. Never expose a battery to an open flame or electrical spark. Never let

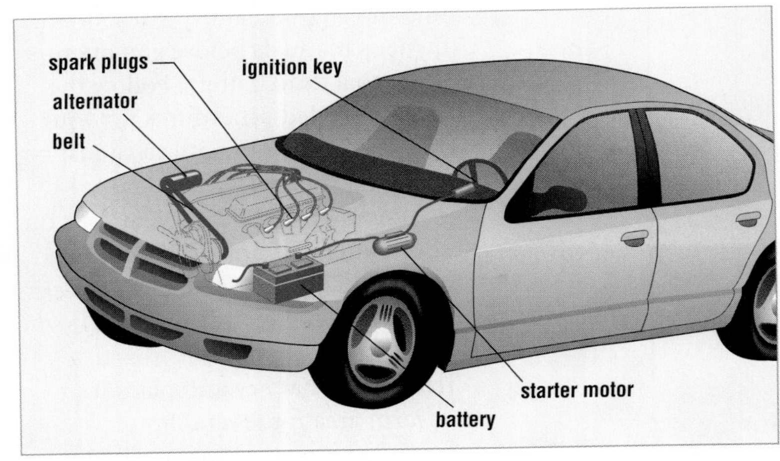

Ignition and electrical system

COMPUTERIZED SYSTEMS Many of today's vehicles are equipped with computerized engine-management systems. These systems control a vehicle's fuel, ignition, and emission systems. If a warning light comes on indicating your engine needs service, take it to a qualified technician who can service a computerized system.

battery fluid touch your eyes, skin, or clothing. The fluid is a strong acid that can cause severe injury.

Starting a Vehicle That Has a Dead Battery

If you turn the ignition key while in PARK or NEUTRAL and the starter makes no sound, it usually indicates a dead battery or bad battery connection. You may be able to jump-start your vehicle by using a jumper cable connected to another vehicle that has a good battery. Check both owner's manuals before you attempt to jump a dead battery. Follow the recommended procedures for your vehicle. *Note:* Both batteries must be the same voltage.

Remove any battery vent caps on your battery (if not a self-contained battery). *Do not jump a dead battery that has frozen cells; the battery might explode.* If the battery is frozen, remove the battery and place it in a warm area for several hours, away from direct heat, before trying to jump-start it.

Follow these steps when making a jumper cable connection:

1. Bring the two vehicles close together, but not touching. The jumper cables need to be able to reach both batteries and engines.
2. Turn off the engine of the vehicle with the good battery and all accessories on both vehicles. Shift the gears of each vehicle into NEUTRAL or PARK. Set the parking brakes.
3. Each battery has two terminals or posts. Each post should be marked with a plus (+) or minus (–) sign, or POS or NEG.
4. Securely clamp one end of the positive jumper cable (marked + or red) to the positive terminal of the good battery. Clamp the other end of the same cable to the positive terminal of the dead battery.
5. Clamp one end of the negative cable (marked − or black) to the negative terminal on the vehicle with the good battery. Note: Some owner's manuals may require the connection be to a negative ground somewhere on the engine away from moving parts.
6. Clamp the other end of the negative cable to a negative ground on the vehicle with the dead battery. A negative ground could be a large unpainted piece of metal away from moving engine parts and the battery. *Do not clamp the negative cable to the bad battery's negative post.*
7. Start the vehicle that has the good battery first. Let the vehicle idle for a few minutes. Then start the

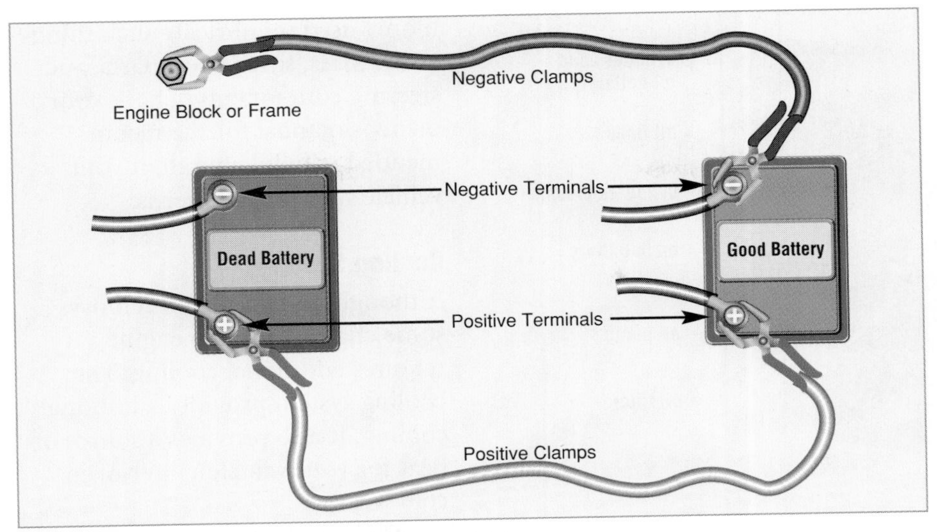

Jumper cable connections for jump-starting a vehicle

vehicle with the dead battery. Keep the vehicle with the dead battery running, but only at idle, until the jumper cables are removed.

8. Remove the cables in the opposite order from which they were attached. Store them in the trunk for future use.
9. Replace any vent caps. Throw away any cloth used to wipe the battery parts because the cloth may have acid on it.

Lights

Your lights not only help you see, but also help others see you. Defective lights and bulbs need to be replaced immediately. Check your headlights, taillights, backup lights, and turn signals often.

If a turn signal indicator on your instrument panel does not flash, but remains on, it is likely that the turn signal light is burnt out. Determine which signal light is out and replace it. Check your owner's manual for specific types of bulbs and lights for your vehicle.

Lubrication and Cooling Systems

Lubrication is the use of oil, grease, or other substances to reduce damage to moving parts from heat caused by friction. *Cooling* is a process of reducing heat that builds up in a vehicle's engine or transmission. Excessive heat can destroy the engine and other moving parts of the vehicle. Proper lubrication and cooling keeps the systems operating efficiently.

Lubrication System

Lubricants, such as oil, help the engine operate efficiently by reducing friction, carrying away engine heat, and cleansing engine parts.

The **oil pump** forces oil from the oil pan at the bottom of the

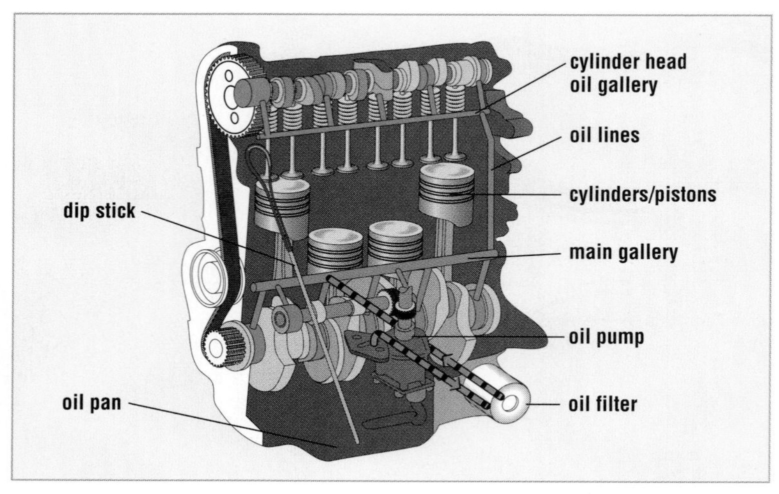

Lubrication system

engine through the oil filter. From the filter, the oil flows through oil lines to the engine's moving parts. Oil is returned to the oil pan, and the cycle is repeated.

All vehicles need to have the oil changed, either after a specific number of miles or months. Oil filters are typically replaced at the same time. If you make a lot of short trips, you may need to have your oil and filter changed more often than recommended.

If the oil-pressure warning light comes on while you are driving, it indicates oil is not going through your engine quickly enough to lubricate it. Pull over to the side of the road when it is safe to do so. Turn off your engine and wait a while before checking the oil level. If your oil level is not the problem, your vehicle needs service right away. Low oil pressure can damage an engine very quickly.

Your vehicle also needs to be greased periodically. Grease is commonly used to lubricate such things as the axles, suspension parts, and steering components. Check your owner's manual for the recommended schedule for all of your vehicle's lubrication needs.

Cooling System

Although lubricating oil removes some engine heat, the engine requires additional cooling. The cooling system provides additional cooling. It also provides a source of heat for your vehicle's interior in cold weather.

The cooling system includes a fan, fan belt or electric motor, radiator, water pump, coolant recovery (or surge) tank, thermostat, and hoses that connect the radiator to the engine. The **radiator** holds and cools the coolant, a mixture of water and antifreeze. The owner's manual indicates the correct mixture to use in your vehicle.

The **water pump** draws coolant from the radiator and forces it through the engine's cooling passages. The fan draws air through the radiator and helps cool the coolant.

The **thermostat** opens and shuts to control the flow of coolant to the radiator. When the temperature in the system rises to the correct level, the thermostat opens to let coolant flow to the radiator and maintain a stable temperature.

Overheating can damage your engine as a result of a low coolant level, blocked radiator airflow, frozen coolant in the system, or a faulty thermostat. Check your coolant level at least once a month. Check the coolant surge tank before you start the engine. If the coolant level is low, pour a 50/50 mixture of water and coolant into the surge tank to the prescribed level.

Check your radiator hoses every time you change your oil. Look for cracks and squeeze the hoses to feel for spongy spots. Replace hoses that are cracked, leaking, or have a spongy feel to them.

Many vehicle manufacturers suggest the cooling system be flushed and replenished with fresh coolant at least once every two years. Check your owner's manual for recommended service intervals for your vehicle.

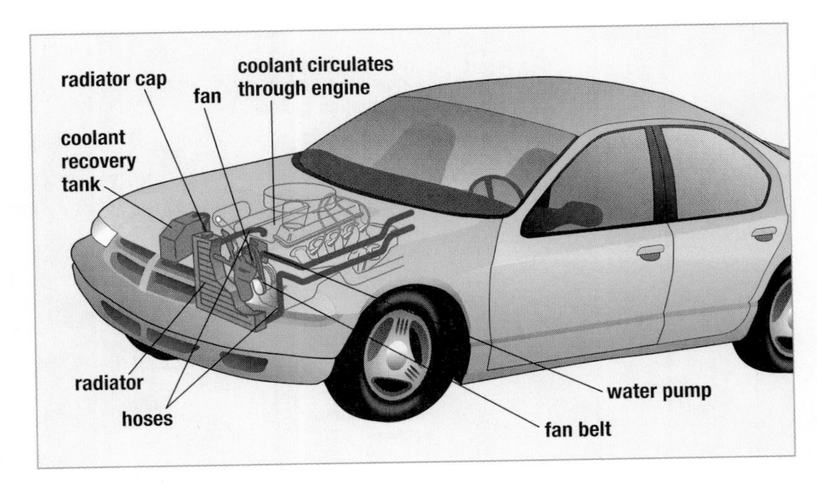

Cooling system

Fuel and Emission Systems

The purpose of the fuel system is to provide fuel needed for the creation of power to move a vehicle. The fuel system includes a fuel tank, fuel line, fuel pump, air cleaner, fuel filter, and carburetor or fuel-injection system.

The emission (or exhaust) system takes the exhaust created by the burning of fuel, and forces it through the exhaust system to the outside of the vehicle. The system includes the positive crankcase ventilation system (PCV), the exhaust gas recirculation system (EGR), the heat control valve, the catalytic converter, exhaust pipe, muffler, and tailpipe.

Fuel System

The fuel pump draws fuel from the fuel tank through the fuel line. Fuel is then pumped to the **carburetor** or **fuel-injection system.** Air is drawn through the air filter and mixes with the fuel. The fuel–air mixture becomes a fine mist for combustion in the cylinders of the engine.

Most new vehicles have electronic fuel-injection systems rather than carburetor systems. Fuel-injection systems deliver the exact amount of fuel to each of the engine's cylinders at the proper time to give maximum power and fuel efficiency. Fuel-injection systems also reduce the amount of pollution-causing gases.

If your vehicle hesitates or sputters while accelerating, or if the "service engine" light comes on, you may need to have your fuel system inspected.

Emission System

The combustion process creates exhaust. The emission system takes the exhaust and recirculates unburned fuel back into the combustion process for greater efficiency. The **catalytic converter** then converts harmful gases into less harmful gases and water. It also cuts down levels of nitrogen oxides, which the sun heats into smog.

Never add water alone to your cooling system. It will boil much faster causing the vehicle to overheat. Use an appropriate water–antifreeze mixture.

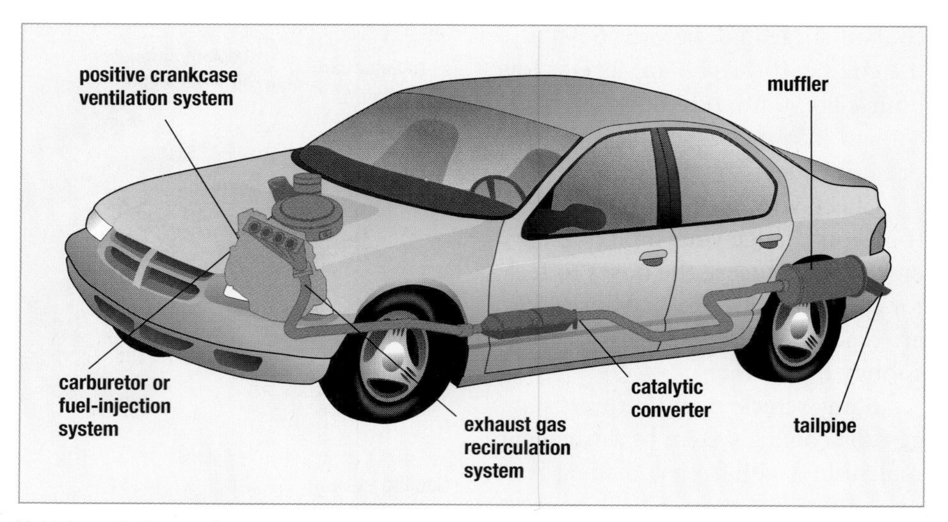

Vehicle emission system

The **muffler** reduces the noise from combustion sounds in the engine. Over time, holes develop in mufflers due to rust. If you notice that your vehicle's engine sounds louder and louder over time, it is likely you have a hole in your muffler.

After passing through the muffler, the exhaust leaves the exhaust system through the tailpipe at the rear of the vehicle.

Have your emission system checked periodically to ensure there are no leaks in the system. By doing this, you reduce your risk of carbon monoxide poisoning while driving.

Review It

1. Name at least one warning sign that indicates needed repairs for each of these systems: power, drive, ignition, electrical, lubrication, cooling, fuel, and exhaust.
2. What are the proper steps for starting a vehicle that has a dead battery?

17.2

Maintaining the Control Systems

Vital to the safe control of your vehicle are several different, but interrelated, systems and components. The steering, brake, and suspension systems are all part of your vehicle's traction-control system. Your tires are also components of your vehicle's traction-control system. All of these contribute to a vehicle's control, stability, and riding comfort.

Steering System

The steering system includes the steering wheel, steering column, steering gear, and the connections to the front wheels. The steering column transmits your steering input to move the front wheels of your vehicle in the direction you choose.

Most vehicles today have **power steering,** a system that uses a hydraulic pump and fluid to make steering easier for you. Avoid turning the steering wheel when the vehicle is not moving. This causes wear on the steering system.

Steering problems often develop gradually rather than suddenly. This may make them difficult to recognize. Any steering problem is serious and should be repaired immediately. Common indications of problems include

- "play" or excess movement in the steering wheel
- steering difficulty, even though the tires are properly inflated
- shimmying or wobbling, or shaking or pulling to one side under normal driving conditions
- squealing sounds when you make turns

Brake System

Good brakes are essential for the safe operation of a vehicle. The life expectancy and performance of your brakes depend on how you use and maintain them. A vehicle's brake system is composed of four individual brakes (one on each wheel), brake lines, brake fluid, wheel cylinders, and a master cylinder.

The brake system's **master cylinder** contains two parts. Each part controls two wheels. When a driver applies pressure on the brake pedal, brake fluid is forced from the master cylinder through the brake lines to each wheel's brake cylinder. The cylinder at each wheel forces the brake shoes or brake pads against a brake drum or disk. The pressure causes friction, which slows or stops the wheel.

Objectives

1. Identify the warning signs that might indicate the need for repair of the steering, brake, or suspension systems.
2. Identify ways to maintain tires for longer wear.

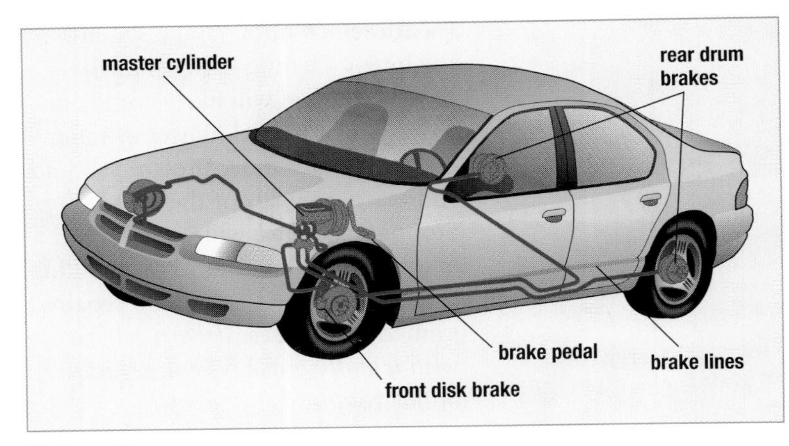

Brake system

DISK BRAKES AND DRUM BRAKES Many vehicles have a disk brake on each front wheel and a drum brake on each rear wheel. Some vehicles have disk brakes on all four wheels. A disk brake works as fluid pressure presses the pads against the sides of the rotating disk inside the wheel. A drum brake works as fluid pressure forces the brake shoes against the hollow cylinder drum inside the wheel. Each type of brake causes friction that slows or stops the turning wheels.

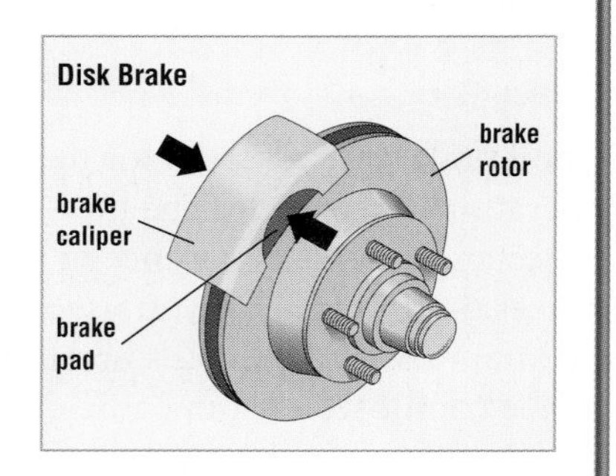

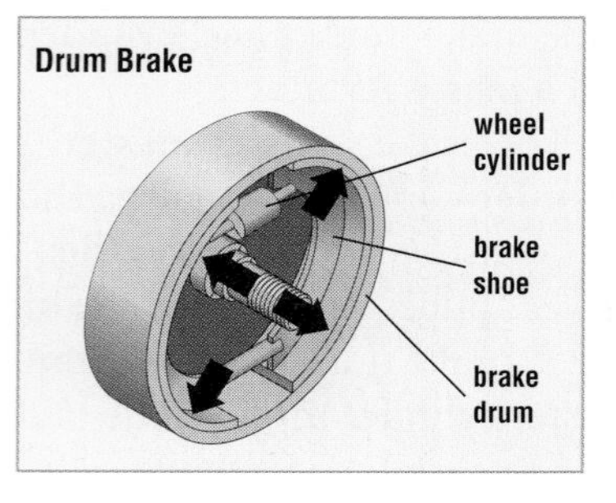

Most vehicles' brake systems are designed with fail-safe systems. If a leak develops in the brake system, the brake warning light on the instrument panel will likely come on. Because of the dual master cylinder, however, fluid under pressure should still reach one pair of the wheels. Stopping distance will increase and handling may be erratic. The braking system must be checked and repaired immediately. *Never drive a vehicle with a faulty brake system, regardless of the distance.*

A vehicle's disk and drum brakes self-adjust when braking in reverse. If you notice that the brake pedal goes closer than two inches to the floor when you press the brake pedal hard, adjust the brakes. To adjust the brakes, stop, back up, and brake firmly. Repeat this procedure several times. If the problem persists, have your brake system inspected.

If the brake or antilock brake warning light stays on after starting your vehicle or comes on while driving, these are indicators of possible brake problems. Some other indications of potential problems include

- "spongy" feel in the brake pedal
- pulling to one side when stopping with dry brakes
- grabbing or uneven brake action
- squealing or chattering noises in the brakes
- a need to push the brake harder than usual to stop the vehicle

The parking brake is a separate brake system. A steel cable connects the parking brake pedal or lever to a separate brake assembly on the rear wheels only. When properly adjusted and engaged, the parking brake should hold a vehicle on a hill. If the parking brake doesn't hold, have it repaired.

Keep the brake fluid in the master cylinder at the proper level. Use the brake fluid specified for your vehicle. Have your brakes checked on an annual basis, or as soon as you notice potential problems. Proper maintenance of your vehicle's brakes may not only save you money, but could save your life.

Suspension System

The suspension system includes a series of rods, bars, springs, and other components. This system keeps the wheels and tires pointed in the direction you are steering. The springs in the suspension system support the vehicle to allow a gentle up-and-down motion while driving. A shock absorber or strut assembly unit is located at each wheel to control hard bouncing and to keep the tires on the roadway.

If you notice your vehicle bouncing more than usual, or you find uneven tire wear, there may be a problem with its suspension. Check your owner's manual for the recommended intervals for servicing or replacing your vehicle's shocks, struts, and joints.

Tires: A Traction Control System

Your tires are your vehicle's lifelines to the roadway. It is important to understand your vehicle's tires and to ensure that your vehicle is equipped with tires that best meet your driving needs.

Tire Construction

A tire is made of rubber reinforced with layers of material under the tread. Each layer, called a *ply*, strengthens the tire and gives it shape.

A **belted tire** has special layers added to a bias-ply tire for improved strength, performance, and mileage. A **radial tire** has plies that run straight across under the tread, and strengthening belts of steel or other materials that circle the tire. Radial tires give improved tread mileage, traction, and fuel economy, compared to other tires.

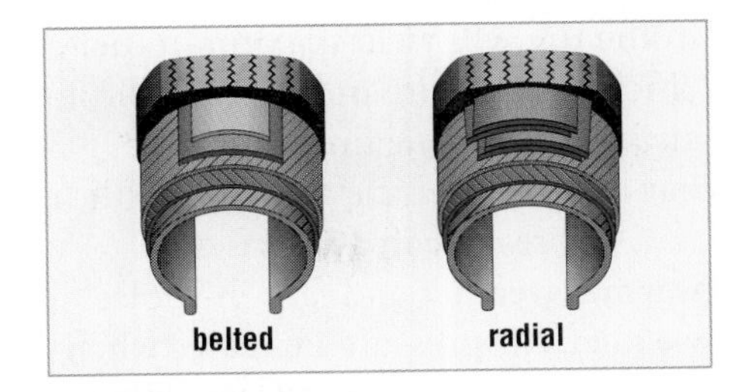

Tire construction

Information about the tire's construction, size, recommended inflation levels, and carrying capacity is clearly marked on the sidewall of the tire. New tires usually have a paper label attached with additional information.

Inflation and Tread

Maintain the manufacturer's recommended air pressure in the tires at all times. Keep a reliable tire gauge in your vehicle and use it regularly. Maintaining the proper air pressure

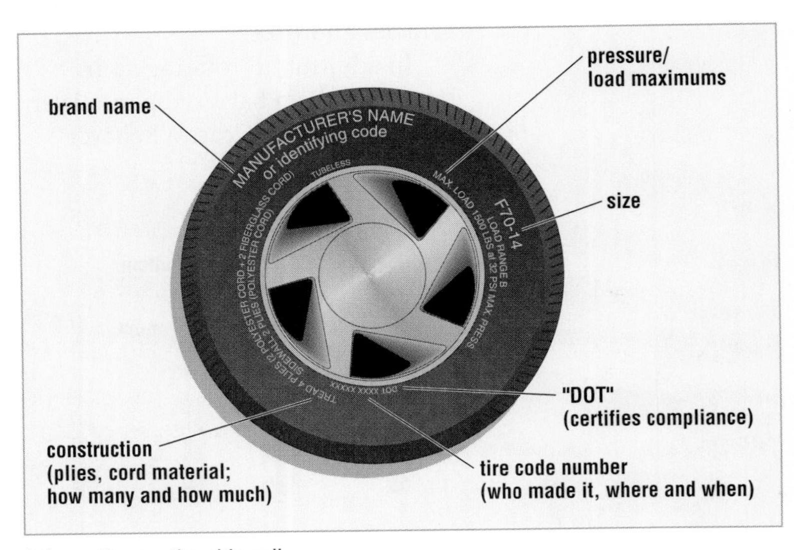

Information on the sidewall

in the tire will yield maximum fuel efficiency and tire mileage. Too little air in one of your tires can make handling the vehicle more difficult.

Air pressure in a tire rises in warmer weather and falls in cooler weather. Air pressure increases whenever the vehicle is driven, regardless of the distance of the trip. Don't let air out of a warm tire in an attempt to reduce the air pressure to the recommended level. The tire will be underinflated when it cools. Overall, cool tires will provide the most accurate and stable readings.

Rotation and Alignment

Rotate your tires regularly to promote longer tire life. Different rotation patterns are recommended for different vehicles and tires. See your owner's manual for the recommended pattern and schedule you should follow for your vehicle. The illustration shows different rotation patterns for different vehicles and tires.

In addition to rotating your tires, have them balanced periodically to promote even wear. Whenever you have your tires balanced, it is also a good idea to have your wheels aligned. Alignment is especially important on front-wheel drive vehicles. Proper wheel alignment also increases the life of the tires and reduces excessive and uneven wear.

Replacing Tires

Most tires have wear bars built into them. A smooth bar will appear across your tire when the tread has worn down. A worn tire has poor traction on wet roads and is more likely to fail. When you can see one or more wear bars on any tire, it is time to replace that tire.

Replacement tires should be the same size and type as the tires they are replacing. Never use radial tires with any other type of tire on the vehicle. Radial tires do not react the same as belted tires.

Tire Quality and Grading

All tires sold in the United States are rated on the Uniform Tire Quality Grading System, as seen in the chart.

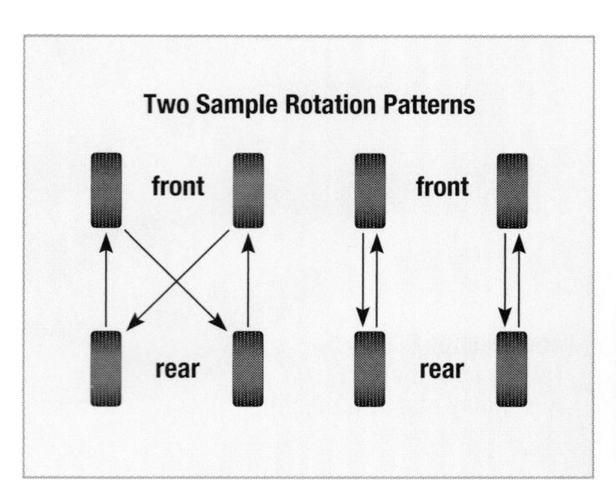

Tire rotation patterns

Notice the wear bar!

Grades of Tires

Tire Grading	Traction	Temperature	Treadwear
Highest	A	A	200 190 180 170 160
	B	B	150 140 130 120 110 100
Lowest	C	C	90 80 70 60 50

- A tire's traction is measured by its ability to stop a car in straight-ahead motion on a wet surface. An A-graded tire has the best traction performance.
- Temperature resistance indicates a tire's ability to withstand heat. A tire graded A is the most heat-resistant, and is the least likely to suffer a blowout under the same conditions as tires with grades of B or C.
- The higher the treadwear rating, the greater the mileage. A tire with a treadwear rating of 150 is expected to last 50 percent longer than one graded at 100.

A tire's performance is measured under ideal controlled conditions on specific test surfaces and over a special test route. They are rated by traction, temperature, and treadwear performance.

Keep safety in mind when you are in need of new tires. Compare and decide which type of tire offers the best value for the kind of driving you do. Check your owner's manual for recommendations on tires for your vehicle.

Review It

1. Identify at least one repair warning sign for the steering, brake, and suspension systems.
2. How can you maintain tires for longer wear?

17.3 Preventive Maintenance

Objectives

1. List preventive maintenance checks to make before and after starting the vehicle, while driving, and when fueling or servicing the vehicle.
2. Explain how to find a qualified mechanic or technician.

The routine care and attention you give your vehicle to avoid trouble later on is called **preventive maintenance.** This attention includes not only the day-to-day care, but also the periodic servicing recommended in your owner's manual.

The schedule of service for maintenance jobs is important. The manufacturer or dealer warranty may not stay in effect if maintenance schedules are not followed.

Routine Checks

You should make it a habit to pay attention to your vehicle's condition. Notice changes in its condition before driving and while you drive.

Before Starting the Engine

Before you enter the vehicle and start the engine, make a few quick inspections to avoid trouble while driving. Here are some examples:

- Look for signs of fluid leaks on the pavement under the vehicle. The color and location of the fluid can help you determine the type and source of the leak. The colors in the picture indicate the different types of fluids.
- Make sure your lights and horn work. When you turn the ignition on (without starting the engine) see that your warning lights come on. If one does not come on, check your fuses first. If the fuses are not the problem, then have the vehicle checked by a technician.

How to find leaks: At night, take light-colored paper and place it underneath your vehicle. In the morning, check the paper for fluid spots and their locations. Have any leaks repaired.

Colors indicate the type of fluid leaking out.

After Starting the Engine

After you start your engine, follow the steps and checks as described in Chapter 3. If you have any concerns, see your owner's manual.

While Driving

Follow the steps and procedures you learned in earlier chapters to measure your vehicle's performance. Notice any unusual instrument panel readings. Observe any out-of-the-ordinary sounds, odors, or vibrations of the vehicle.

At a Fuel Stop

Most drivers fill their own vehicle's fuel tanks at self-service stations. Turn off your engine before you begin refueling. Follow posted instructions for refueling. Smoking is *always prohibited* near fuel pumps.

Almost every gas station offers a selection of types and grades of fuel. Check your owner's manual for your vehicle's recommended octane rating.

Alternative fuels are becoming more common. One type of alternative fuel is gasohol. Gasohol is a blend of gasoline and either methyl or ethyl alcohol.

Whenever you stop for fuel, it's a good time to perform routine checks and service. Here are some examples:

- Check your oil level. Add oil if needed.
- Check the windshield washer fluid level. Add additional fluid to the reservoir, if needed.
- Clean your windshield, windows and headlights.
- Check your windshield wipers for cracks. Replace damaged blades.
- Check your tires. Do they look low? Is the tire pressure correct? Are there any visible cracks in the tire? Take care of crucial problems before you leave the gas station.

Selecting a Qualified Technician

Vehicles are complex machines. It is important that you find a reliable service and repair location staffed with trained and certified technicians and mechanics. Talk with people you know and respect. Ask your local better business bureau. If you are a member of a motor club, ask them for recommendations.

You could also visit different automotive repair shops. Find out if the technicians and mechanics are qualified and certified. Most major dealerships have highly skilled technicians and mechanics who have passed specialized tests to obtain their certifications.

Scheduled Service

Vehicles need periodic service. Your owner's manual shows the recommended maintenance intervals for you to follow. Save all of your service receipts. Keep a comprehensive maintenance history of your vehicle, especially for warranty-related repairs.

State Vehicle Inspections

Some states require periodic vehicle inspections. Inspections can detect safety-related problems before they become hazards. Owners are usually required to have all serious defects repaired before the vehicle can be licensed.

Review It

1. List some preventive maintenance checks you should make before and after starting the vehicle, while driving, and when stopping for fuel.
2. List the steps you can take to find a qualified technician or mechanic.

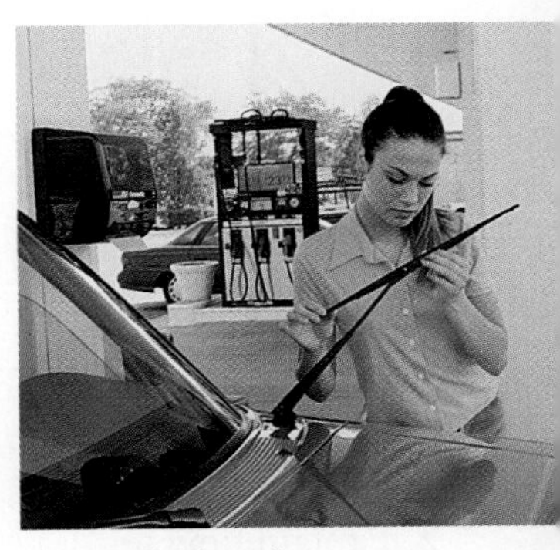

While refueling, clean your windows and check wiper blades for any damage or excessive wear.

17.4

Fuel-Saving and Recycling Strategies

Objectives

1. Identify ways you can improve a vehicle's fuel efficiency.
2. Explain how to calculate miles per gallon of fuel consumption.
3. Identify strategies for recycling automotive-related materials.

Advancements in design and technology have changed the ways our vehicles look and perform. Today's vehicles are designed and built for greater fuel efficiency. The way you drive can also improve fuel efficiency.

Facts About Fuel Efficiency

Even though vehicle designs and changes in the types of materials used in today's vehicles save fuel, drivers need to follow certain practices to help conserve resources.

Control Your Speed

Many newer vehicles have very fuel-efficient engines that achieve maximum fuel economy at speeds between 50–55 mph. However, strong winds can reduce an engine's fuel efficiency. While driving at speeds of more than 45 mph, keep your windows closed to cut wind resistance.

Higher speeds result in more fuel being used. For every 5 mph increase in speed above 55 mph, most cars get 1.5 fewer miles per gallon.

While driving in the city, coast to a stop when possible, and moderately accelerate to your desired speed. Very fast or very slow starts waste fuel.

Care for Your Engine

Use a vehicle with a warm engine, if you can. A warm engine is more fuel-efficient than a cold engine. The greatest fuel consumption is within the first few minutes after starting a cold engine. The most efficient way to warm up a cold engine is to drive it at moderate speeds for the first few miles. Avoid excessive idling to avoid wasting fuel and possibly damaging the engine.

Calculating Miles Per Gallon

Most drivers want to get the most miles from each gallon of fuel. Checking your fuel economy can warn you of potential mechanical problems. Follow these simple steps to calculate miles per gallon.

1. Fill the fuel tank. Record the odometer reading, or set the trip odometer at zero.
2. Drive normally until you have about a half tank of fuel.
3. Refill the tank. Record the number of gallons it took to refill the tank. Next, record the odometer or trip odometer reading.
4. Subtract the first odometer reading from the second. Then, divide the number of miles driven by the number of gallons of fuel it took to refill the tank. The result is the number of miles per gallon (mpg).

Vehicle Design

The designs of many vehicles have been streamlined to reduce wind resistance and help increase performance and fuel efficiency. Changes in the body shapes, wheel covers, bumpers, and headlights all have contributed to more fuel-efficient vehicles.

Notice how the newer vehicle is more aerodynamic.

In general, vehicles have become smaller and lighter over the years. Lighter-weight materials and plastics have replaced older, heavier steel and metal components. Smaller, lighter vehicles need less power to move. The result has been an increase in fuel efficiency.

Engine Improvements

Because of the types of materials used in manufacturing today's vehicles, smaller engines are common. Smaller engines are designed to provide adequate power for smaller and lighter vehicles. Smaller engines also provide better fuel efficiency.

Electronic ignitions and computerized **engine management systems** help vehicles' engines operate and use fuel efficiently. A computer monitors the fuel, ignition, and emission systems. The computer collects data about each system and automatically

Dispose of used fluids responsibly.

makes adjustments to the respective systems. These adjustments increase operational efficiency.

For example, the air–fuel mixture introduced into the cylinders is more precise and is burned more effectively as a result of the engine management systems. Less fuel is burned, and it is burned more efficiently. The result is greater fuel efficiency and fewer hazardous gases emitted into the atmosphere.

Recycling Strategies

Because of the concern over the environment, conservation of resources, and potential health hazards, many automotive materials are being recycled for reuse or turned into other consumer products.

Any materials meant to be used later, and not discarded, should be placed in sealed containers away from children and pets. Unused oil, gasoline, and antifreeze are just a few examples.

Make sure oil and antifreeze spills or puddles are promptly absorbed and cleaned from your driveway or garage. The sweet smell and taste of antifreeze could attract children and animals. If ingested, oil or antifreeze could poison and potentially cause death.

Many states have regulations for recycling oil and engine contaminants. Items that can be recycled, such as used motor oil, antifreeze, and batteries, should be taken to respective recycling centers, local drop-off locations, or hazardous waste collection locations.

If you have your vehicle serviced at an automotive service station or vehicle maintenance facility, you avoid the responsibility of having to handle or dispose of used parts, materials, and fluids. Businesses that service vehicles know how to properly deal with used automotive materials.

What Do You Think?

Many communities require quick-oil businesses to accept used motor oil and/or filters. Should this be a requirement? Why or why not?

Review It

1. What are some ways to improve the fuel efficiency of your vehicle?
2. Explain how to calculate miles-per-gallon of fuel consumption.
3. What are at least three examples of automotive-related items that can be recycled?

Chapter 17

Review

Reviewing Chapter Objectives

1. Maintaining the Power Systems

1. What are the signs that repairs are needed for the power and drive systems, lubrication and cooling systems, and fuel and exhaust systems? (356–362)
2. What steps should you follow to start a vehicle that has a dead battery? (358–359)

2. Maintaining the Control Systems

3. What are the signs that repairs are needed for the steering, brake, and suspension systems? (363–369)
4. How can you maintain tires for longer wear? (366)

3. Preventative Maintenance

5. What are the preventive maintenance checks to make before and after starting the vehicle, while driving, and when fueling or servicing the vehicle? (368–369)
6. How can you find a qualified mechanic or technician? (369)

4. Fuel-Saving and Recycling Strategies

7. In what ways can you improve a vehicle's fuel efficiency? (370)
8. How do you calculate miles per gallon of fuel consumption? (370)
9. What are the strategies for recycling automotive-related materials? (372)

Projects

Individuals

Interview Make a list of certified vehicle technicians and mechanics in your area. Interview three of them to find out what their qualifications are. Ask them how long they have been in business and what they like best about their job. Determine which one you would want to repair your vehicle.

Investigate Use the Internet to research ways that vehicle manufacturers recycle various components of their products. Write a report based on your research and share it with the class.

Groups

Use Technology Make a video about the preventive maintenance checks you should make on your vehicle. Each group member should explain a different aspect of preventive maintenance. Get an owner's permission to use an actual vehicle in your video. Present the video to your class.

Observe Each person in the group should check out the tires on ten vehicles in the school's parking lot. Note whether each tire is belted or radial. Note whether the tire is inflated properly and had adequate tread. Make a group spreadsheet based on each person's findings.

Chapter 17
Review

Chapter Test

Check Your Knowledge

Multiple Choice Copy the number of each sentence below on a sheet of paper. Choose the letter of the answer that best completes the statement or answers the question.

1. A vehicle's gears are housed in the
(a) powerplant. (c) drive shaft.
(b) transmission. (d) differential.

2. When jump starting a vehicle that has a dead battery
(a) make sure that both batteries are the same voltage.
(b) warm the battery up first if frozen.
(c) start the vehicle with the good battery first.
(d) all of the above

3. The master cylinder is found in a vehicle's
(a) steering system.
(b) suspension system.
(c) traction control system.
(d) brake system.

4. Preventive maintenance is
(a) caring for vehicle on an ongoing basis.
(b) caring for a vehicle once trouble begins.
(c) overhauling the engine.
(d) none of these

Completion Copy the number of each sentence below. After each number, write the word or words that complete the sentence correctly.

5. The _____ controls the flow of coolant to the radiator.

6. In rear-wheel vehicles, the _____ carries power to the differential.

7. A vehicle's catalytic converter converts harmful gases into less harmful gases and _____.

8. A power steering system uses a _____ pump and fluid to make steering easier.

Review Vocabulary

Copy the number of each definition in list A. Match the definition in list A with the term it defines in list B.

List A

9. engine part that mixes air and gasoline and sends it as a fine mist to the engine cylinders

10. tire that has special layers added to a bias-ply tire for improved strength, performance, and mileage

11. part of the cooling system that holds and cools the coolant

12. arrangement of gears at the rear of the vehicle allowing one wheel to revolve faster than the opposite wheel during turns

13. device that reduces the noise from combustion sounds in the engine

14. device that generates an electrical current needed to recharge the battery and operate electrical equipment in a vehicle

List B

a. radiator
b. differential
c. carburetor
d. belted tire
e. alternator
f. muffler

Think Critically

Write a paragraph to answer each question.

1. What happens if you fail to perform preventive maintenance on your vehicle?

2. Why is it important to recycle some of the automotive materials used to operate vehicles? How can you go about recycling these materials?

Decision Making

1. When the driver in the car applied his brakes, the car pulled to the right. What might this indicate about the braking system?

2. What is wrong with this car? What would you do to correct the problem?

3. These two people are attempting to make a jumper cable connection to start a car that has a dead battery. What steps should they take to properly complete the connection? Which vehicle has the dead battery?

4. This person is shopping for a new tire. He frequently drives long distances. What guidelines should he use in selecting a replacement tire?

CHAPTER 18
Planning Your Travel

You Are the Driver!

You are just about to arrive at your campsite to enjoy your family vacation. You have planned your trip thoroughly. You now know that safe, smooth, stress-free travel does not happen by chance. The better your planning and attention to detail, the better the trip.

In this chapter, you will learn how to plan local travel. You'll discover how to make long trips manageable—even though the planning can be complicated. Finally, you will have a chance to learn about special vehicles and trailers and how to drive them safely.

For: Chapter 18 online activities
Visit: PHSchool.com
Web Code: cak-9999

18.1
Local Travel

Objectives
1. State two questions you should ask yourself before making a short trip.
2. Name three things you can do to simplify a short trip.

Most of your driving will be short, local trips. Therefore, it is important to plan carefully for local travel. If you do, you will save yourself time, money, and fuel.

Short Trips

A short trip can be as simple as driving to a neighborhood store. Or it can mean driving to the other side of a large city. In any event, you want to arrive safely and on time. Before you start this kind of trip, ask yourself the following two questions.

Is This Trip Needed?

Since driving can be costly, you need to ask yourself if the trip is needed. If you can answer "yes," then ask yourself if there is a less expensive, more efficient way to make the trip. Could you use public transportation or share a ride with others? Simply driving around wastes money and fuel!

Another way to save yourself time, money, and fuel is to combine several small trips into one. You will also help yourself by extending the life of your vehicle. Short trips mean you will be driving a vehicle with a cold engine. Driving with a cold engine increases the wear on your vehicle and dramatically increases its fuel use.

Do I Have Enough Time?

If a trip is needed, will you have enough time for it? To be sure you do, make these smart decisions:

- **Allow Time** No matter how well you plan, if you don't leave on or

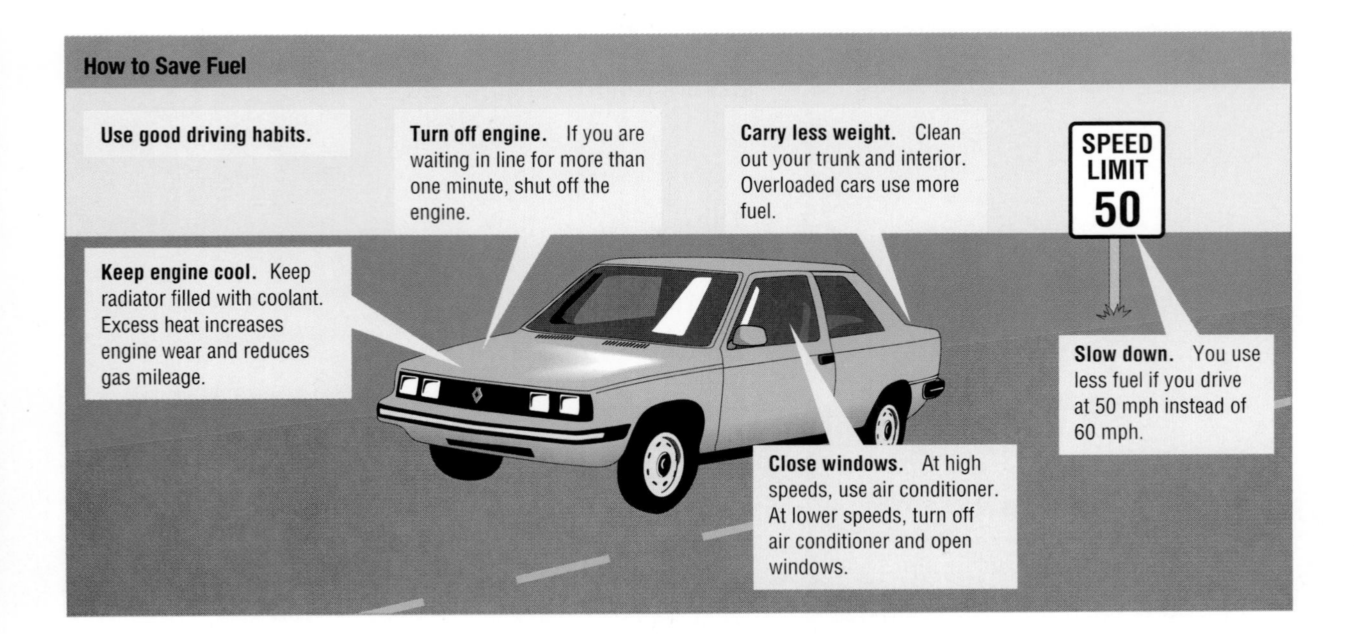

ahead of time, you will not reach your destination on time. It is very difficult and often dangerous to try to make up time as you drive. Allow extra time for delays caused by bad weather or heavy traffic.

- **Listen to Weather and Traffic Reports** Local weather and traffic reports are very useful for planning local travel.
- **Choose the Best Travel Time** In many cities, normal rush-hour traffic will test your patience and waste time and fuel. When possible, travel when traffic is light.

You can help plan the route as a passenger.

Planning Ahead

Have you ever watched skilled drivers? The reason they make driving look so smooth is that they think ahead. Following are three key ways you can make your travel smooth and stress free.

Vehicle Preparation Running out of windshield-washer fluid, driving on an underinflated tire, or having a turn-signal light fail might not sound like a big problem. However, each of these small problems could trigger a collision.

Be alert when you approach your vehicle. Before you drive, check your vehicle's tires, lights, and controls. If you detect the slightest problem, fix it before it becomes a bigger problem.

Each time you fill your vehicle's fuel tank, make a routine check of your oil, water, and windshield fluid levels. By following the points in the picture to the left, you can save fuel on every trip.

Route Selection Consider the travel time and the possible hazards when you select a route. In many cities, it is easier to drive a few more miles to take interstate expressways than it is to take local roads. You can save time and eliminate potential hazards by avoiding uncontrolled intersections and heavy traffic.

Know Your Route and Addresses Have you ever really been lost? It can be frightening, perhaps even dangerous. You can usually avoid this by planning your route ahead of time. Write down directions and have a map. If you have a passenger, let that person help to identify street names, directions, and addresses.

Review It

1. What two questions should you answer before starting a short trip?
2. What three things can you do to simplify a short trip?

18.2 Long-Distance Travel

Objectives

1. Describe how to prepare for a long-distance trip.
2. Tell what techniques you can use to stay alert while driving.
3. Describe four things you need to be alert for when driving a rental vehicle.

A well-planned trip can be a satisfying, memorable experience. There are many tools available to help you plan the details of your trip in advance.

Maps and Tour Books

The basic trip-planning tool is a road map. Maps are available at service stations, auto clubs, bookstores, and chambers of commerce. Make sure the map is the most current one available.

Good maps include a **legend** that explains the markings and symbols used on the map. For example, major highways and secondary roads are usually printed in different colors. Generally, major highways will allow you to reach your destination more quickly and directly. Travel on secondary roads might take more time, but it may allow you to visit interesting places along the way.

Another valuable trip-planning tool is a tour book. Tour books are published by auto clubs and other publishers. The books list hotels, motels, inns, restaurants, and popular places of interest, organized by city or town. By using a map in combination with a tour book, you can plan how many miles you will drive each day, what sites you will see, and where you will eat and sleep.

Internet Trip Planning

There are many Web sites that provide free trip-planning services. Some of the most useful services are sites that provide maps and directions from your starting point to your destination. These Web sites allow you to enter the address of where you are starting and where you wish to go. The software powering the Web site then maps out a route for your trip and provides step-by-step directions. You can print out the route map and directions and quickly be on your way. There are also trip-planning software packages that you can install on your computer that provide similar features.

When using Internet route-planning services or software, keep in mind that they don't always identify the most efficient routes and directions. It's always a good idea to confirm the directions on a road map or with a person who is familiar with the route.

In addition to route planning, the Internet can provide other information to help you plan your trip. You can learn more about your destination, make reservations, check the local weather forecast, and read reviews about attractions, hotels, and restaurants written by people who have used those services.

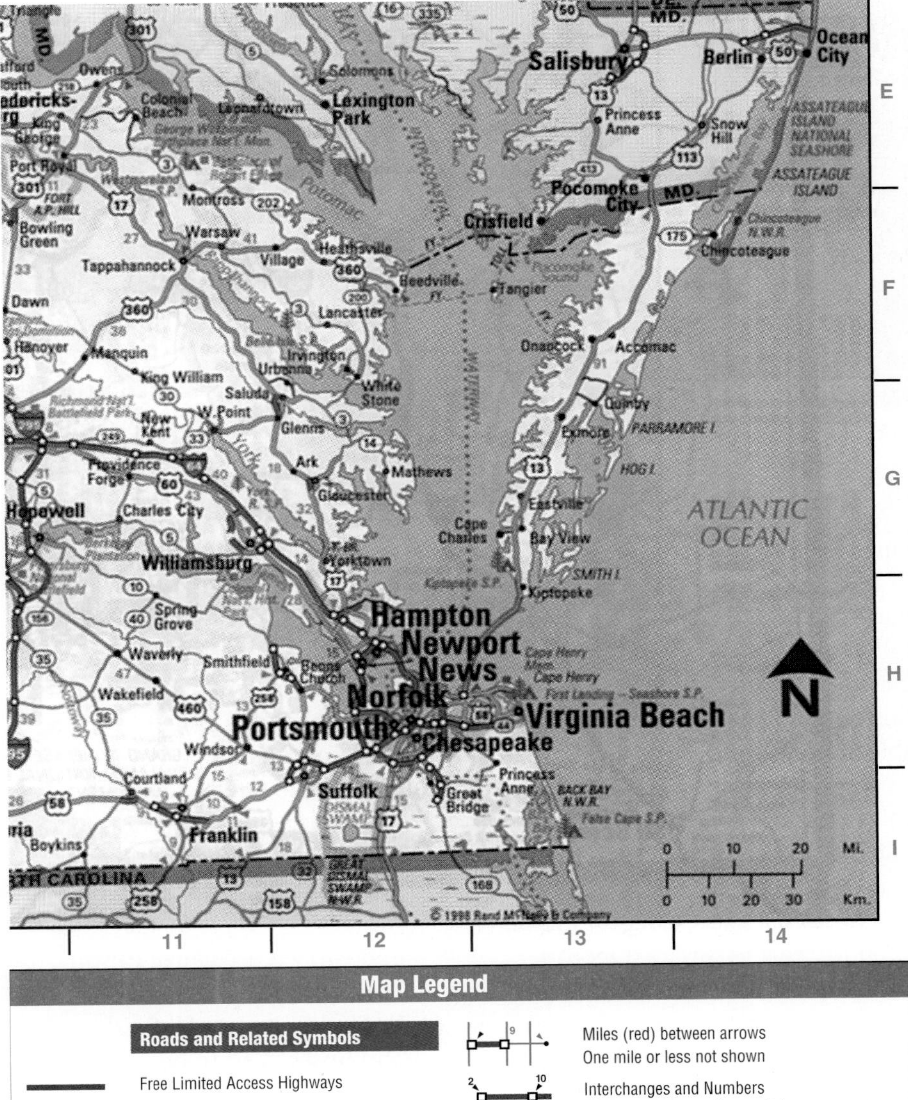

Map Legend

Roads and Related Symbols

Free Limited Access Highways

Under Construction

Toll Limited-Access Highways

Under Construction

Other Four-Lane Divided Highways

Principal Highways

Other Through Highways

Interstate Highways

U.S. Highways

State and Provincial Highways

Miles (red) between arrows
One mile or less not shown

Interchanges and Numbers
(For most states, mileages between interchanges may be determined by subtracting one number from the other)

Cities and Towns

Urbanized Areas

Separate cities within metro area

National Capital; State Capital

Cities, Towns and Recognized Places; County Seats; Neighborhoods (Size of type indicates relative population)

A map's legend explains the map's markings and symbols.

Virginia

Population: 6,216,568 (1990 Census)
Land Area: 39,598 sq. mi.
Capital: Richmond

Cities and Towns

GPS receivers can provide detailed driving directions to your destination.

There are numerous styles and manufacturers of GPS receivers. Before making a purchase, be sure to compare features, warrantees, and prices. In addition, there are Internet resources where you can read reviews and opinions from other consumers. These reviews can help you make an informed decision.

Global Positioning System (GPS)

Since 1994 there has been a network of navigation satellites orbiting Earth. This network of satellites is called the *Global Positioning System*. Originally launched by the military, this navigation network is now available to the general public.

The satellites transmit radio signals that can be received by devices called GPS receivers. Each GPS receiver is capable of using those radio signals to calculate its exact position on, or above, Earth's surface. Once the current position is calculated, the GPS receiver can then map out a route to the intended destination. GPS devices are available for automobiles, boats, and airplanes. There are even handheld devices ideal for hikers.

Some vehicles come equipped with factory-installed GPS receivers. Receivers can also be purchased as an accessory and installed in just about any vehicle.

GPS-equipped vehicles enable the driver to input a destination and receive real-time directions based on the vehicle's actual location at any point in time. If you make a wrong turn, or a detour appears unexpectedly, the GPS device automatically calculates a new route to your intended destination.

Preparing Your Vehicle

An important part of trip planning is making sure your vehicle is serviced before you take a long trip. Let the service technician know you will be driving a long distance. This can reduce the risk of service problems while traveling.

Here are the basic systems you should have checked:

- **Brake System** Make sure all parts are in good working order.
- **Exhaust System** There must be no leaks in this system.
- **Steering System** Wheels should be aligned. Shock absorbers should be ready for heavy loads. Tires should have ample tread and be properly inflated. Do not forget to check your spare tire and carry a tire gauge for on-road checks.
- **Engine Systems** All fluids, belts, and hoses need to be ready for heavy use. The engine should be tuned. Air-conditioning coolant also should be checked.

Special Equipment

Long-distance travel requires that you pack special equipment for use in emergencies or severe weather. This is equipment you may not normally carry.

Emergency Equipment

For emergency situations, you should consider packing the following items:

- cellular phone or CB radio to call for help (if available)
- containers of the right oil for your vehicle, antifreeze, and windshield-washer fluid
- A-B-C type fire extinguisher
- first-aid kit
- flashlight
- jumper cables
- spare fuses
- basic tools like an adjustable wrench, screwdriver, and pliers
- flares or reflectors

Winter Gear

If traveling in remote or mountain areas in winter weather, you will want to pack these additional items:

- blankets and additional warm clothing including gloves
- sleeping bags
- tire chains and/or snow tires
- high-energy food such as granola bars, nuts, and dried fruit
- window scraper and snow brush
- shovel
- tow line
- sand for extra traction

Personal Preparation

To complete your planning for the trip, make sure you have packed the following items:

- a variety of coins for tolls
- all maps and travel guides
- a spare set of vehicle keys
- all necessary medications
- telephone numbers for motor club, road emergencies, and anticipated stops
- traveler's checks, credit cards, and phone calling cards

Finally, set lights in your home on timers and stop regular deliveries. It is also a good idea to let a neighbor know when you are leaving, where you plan to be, and when you will return.

Vehicle Load

The best rule to keep in mind when traveling is to travel light. Added weight will increase your fuel consumption and affect the way your vehicle handles. If you do travel with a full load, follow these steps:

- Use the highest tire pressure listed in your owner's manual. However, do not overinflate the tires.
- Load the heaviest items on the bottom forward part of your trunk, if you are traveling in a car.
- Keep loose items in the trunk of your car.

Tire chains can make the difference in bad weather.

What Do You Think?

Statistics show that teens have more collisions per mile at night than older drivers. Why do you think teen drivers are at higher risk when driving at night?

Enjoying Your Travel

Over the years, experienced long-distance travelers have learned the subtle secrets that make traveling long distances enjoyable. Here are some tips that will help you enjoy your travel more.

Share Navigation Following a route by reading a map is called **navigating.** When you share driving, have your passenger navigate. Make sure you give each other directions well in advance. If you are alone, pull over to read maps, make calls, or ask directions at a service station.

Stay Alert Drowsy drivers are the cause of a great many collisions and near-misses. To stay alert, use a regular routine that includes the following:

- Drive only during the hours you are normally awake. Do not try to drive through the night. Avoid night driving when possible.
- Take regular breaks every two hours or so. Rotate drivers and get out of the vehicle to stretch.
- Keep fresh air circulating in the vehicle at all times.
- Drive with headlights on at all times, as shown here. This assures that you will always "see and be seen."
- Eat light.
- Maintain your focus on driving. Concentrate in heavy traffic or confusing situations.
- If your eyes are heavy and your concentration is not good, it is time to stop and rest.

Rental Vehicles

Many of your trips will be a combination of flying and driving. You will fly to your destination, and then rent a vehicle for transportation as shown on the opposite page. Use the same rules you would when shopping for any service as you look for a rental vehicle.

Decide these points before you rent a vehicle:

- What size and type of vehicle do you want? Compare prices.
- How long do you need it? A weekly rental may be cheaper than a daily rental.
- Will it be a round-trip or one-way rental? One-way rentals usually cost more.

Daytime headlight use makes for safer driving, especially with other drowsy drivers.

- How will you handle insurance? Your regular home, vehicle, or credit card insurance policy may provide part of the needed coverage.
- Will you fill the gas tank on return, or will you buy a full tank of gas with your rental agreement?
- Don't forget to bring a child seat if needed.

Also be aware that most companies will not rent a vehicle to individuals under age 21, and sometimes 25. But young drivers usually can become part of a rental plan for an added daily fee.

Rental companies can provide a range of services for customers. They will advise you on local laws and requirements, provide maps and directions, and give you the channel numbers of local radio stations that carry traffic reports. In addition, you should stick to these basics:

- Orient yourself to your vehicle before you drive out. Know where controls and devices are ahead of time. Make sure the jack and spare tire are in good shape. When driving in a strange area, keep your windows up and your doors locked.
- If you are bumped by another vehicle or asked to stop for advice or assistance, *don't stop.* Instead, drive to the nearest well-lit service area and ask for police assistance. If necessary, use your hazard flashers to signal a need for help.

Get oriented to your rental vehicle before you begin driving.

- Know the rental company's toll-free service number in case you need help with the vehicle.
- Store all valuables out of sight in the trunk or glove compartment. At night, take valuables with you.
- Park only in well-lit, secure areas.

Review It

1. How should you prepare in advance for a long-distance trip?
2. What steps can you take to stay alert while driving?
3. Name four things you should keep in mind when driving a rental vehicle.

18.3 Special Vehicles

Objectives

1. Describe some problems you might have while driving a large vehicle.
2. Explain some special steps you need to take when pulling a trailer.
3. Tell how to back a trailer.

Driving a recreational vehicle, using a rental truck, or pulling a trailer are three other ways you can travel. You will have to use additional precautions when driving these vehicles or pulling a trailer.

Large Vehicles

A vehicle used primarily for vacations and travel is called a *recreational vehicle.* A camper on a pickup truck or a large motor home are both examples of recreational vehicles.

Rental trucks are another type of large vehicle you might use. When renting one of these trucks, be aware that special insurance protection is needed.

As you drive large vehicles, you need to be alert to the following special performance aspects.

Seeing The minute you get behind the wheel of a large vehicle, you will see how difficult it is to get a full view of the driving scene. Your forward field of vision is open and easy to see. But your view to the sides and rear is severely limited. In short, your ability to use the IPDE Process to the front is better, but your ability to turn and back is restricted.

Look at the illustrations below. Notice how far ahead you can see over the tops of cars. Notice how hard it is to see to the rear left. It is just as difficult to see to the right and center rear. You can see how important it is for other drivers to give a large vehicle extra room to maneuver.

Backing Whenever possible, avoid backing. Instead, drive around the block or turn around in a large, open parking lot. When backing, get another person to stand beside and behind your vehicle to guide you.

Drivers of large vehicles can see more ahead but less to the rear.

You Are the Driver!
If you were driving this rental truck, how would you handle the situation?

Maneuvering Because your vehicle is large and heavy, it will not maneuver like a car. It will take longer to accelerate, brake, and turn.

Crosswinds The size of your vehicle will make it more difficult to control in high winds. If you encounter windy conditions of more than 30 mph, slow down or stop. Anticipate driving difficulty, and be ready to correct your steering. Under extremely windy conditions, some bridges or expressways may close temporarily.

Remember Your Size Hitting an overhead object like a roof at a drive-through restaurant is one of the most frequent collisions experienced. You must remember your large size when you project your path of travel, like the driver in the picture is doing.

Following Distance Because large vehicles are heavy, *your following distance must be four or more seconds.* This distance will allow more time for you to use the IPDE Process.

Fatigue It takes more effort to drive a large vehicle than a car. The ride can be rough and noisy. Plus, if driving a large vehicle is a new experience, it will require more concentration over a longer period of time. Plan frequent rest stops and change drivers when possible.

Trailers

Pulling a trailer will put an additional strain on your car. When pulling a trailer, you can count on

- doubling the time and space you need to accelerate, slow, and turn
- cutting your fuel economy almost in half

Making Sure You're Set Make these checks before pulling a trailer:

- Check your vehicle owner's manual to see how much weight you can tow.
- Check all fluids. Check your coolant level daily.
- Make sure all filters are clean.
- Inflate your rear tires to their maximum recommended level.
- Double-check all vehicle and trailer lights.
- Check your owner's manual to see if any special equipment is recommended.

Special Equipment To pull a trailer safely, you will need the appropriate size and strength trailer hitch, safety

Make sure safety chains are in place before moving.

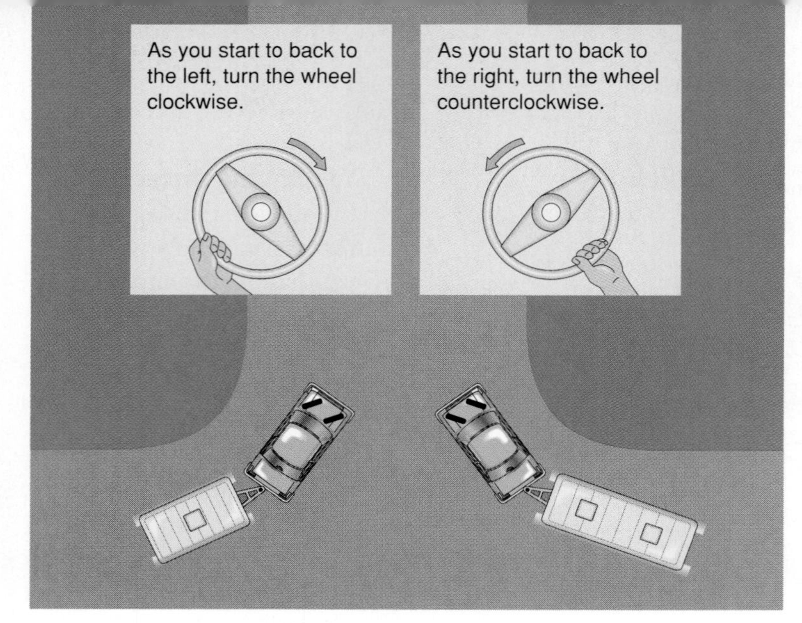

Take it slow and easy while backing a trailer.

chains, and extended mirrors on both sides of your vehicle. **Safety chains,** as shown in the picture on page 387, provide a backup link to your vehicle in case the hitch fails.

Load Check these points when loading your trailer:

- Place heavy items low over the trailer's axle.
- If your load is more than 1,000 pounds, you should get a trailer equipped with special brakes.
- Make sure that about 10 percent of the trailer's loaded weight is on the trailer's hitch.
- Secure the load with ropes.

Towing Techniques

When towing a trailer, remember, it will take you about twice as long to pass, stop, accelerate, and turn. Follow these rules when towing a trailer:

- Use a following distance of four or more seconds.
- Travel at the posted speed limit.
- Make turns slow and wide.
- If your trailer starts to sway or "fishtail," steer straight down the center of your lane, and let off the accelerator. Once the trailer stops swaying, use all brakes carefully.
- Allow twice as much distance to pass or stop.
- Shift to a lower gear before going up or down a steep hill.
- Be ready to slow or correct steering for crosswinds created by other vehicles.
- *Never carry passengers in a trailer.*
- If your vehicle overheats, turn off your air conditioner and turn on your heater.

Backing Look at the picture above to get an idea of what it's like to back a trailer. To back left, turn the wheel clockwise with your left hand. Turn the wheel counterclockwise to start your trailer backing right. Back slowly and make small steering corrections. If you cannot see out the back window, use your right and left mirrors. Always have a person outside your vehicle to help guide you.

Review It

1. What are three potential problems you might have while driving a large vehicle?
2. What steps should you follow when towing a trailer?
3. What procedure should you use when backing a trailer?

Chapter 18

Review

Reviewing Chapter Objectives

1. Local Travel

1. What two questions should you ask yourself before making a short trip? (378)
2. What three things can you do to simplify a short trip? (379)

2. Long-Distance Travel

3. What can you do to prepare for a long-distance trip? (380–382)
4. What techniques can you use to stay alert while driving? (384)
5. What four things should you be alert for when driving a rental vehicle? (384)

3. Special Vehicles

6. What potential problems might you have while driving a large vehicle? (386)
7. What special steps should you take when pulling a trailer? (387–388)
8. How do you back a trailer? (388)

Projects

Individuals

Observe Count the number of short vehicle trips all the drivers in your family make during a one-week period. Note which trips are necessary and which are optional. For the optional trips, list other ways in which the goal of the trip could have been accomplished.

Demonstrate Choose an out-of-state attraction at least 500 miles away from your school (theme park, national park, museum, etc.) Using a map and other travel information, determine the best way to reach this destination. Make a presentation to your class about how you would arrive at the destination. Include facts such as how many miles away it is, how much time it would take, and where you would stay overnight.

Groups

Use Technology Choose a destination at least 500 miles from your school. Each group member should use a different Internet search engine to find information about this destination. Write a group report that combines all the information found.

Practice Choose a destination within 20 to 40 miles of your school. Each group member should individually plan a route to this destination. Compare the routes. Which routes are quickest, easiest, and safest? (These will not necessarily be the same.)

Chapter 18
Review

Chapter Test

Check Your Knowledge

Multiple Choice Copy the number of each sentence below on a sheet of paper. Choose the letter of the answer that best completes the statement or answers the question.

1. Driving with a cold engine
(a) occurs on short trips.
(b) increases the wear on your vehicle.
(c) increases fuel use.
(d) all of the above

2. Routes mapped out by Web sites or software should always be
(a) reliable.
(b) confirmed.
(c) ignored.
(d) inaccurate.

3. For trips in winter weather, carry extra equipment, including
(a) a complete set of tools.
(b) flares or reflectors.
(c) sand for extra traction.
(d) a flashlight.

4. When driving a recreational vehicle, your blind spots are usually
(a) larger than with a car.
(b) only affected at night.
(c) the same as with a car.
(d) lower than with a car.

Completion Copy the number of each sentence below. After each number, write the word or words that complete the sentence correctly.

5. To avoid getting lost, plan your _____ ahead of time.

6. A _____ reads signals from navigation satellites.

7. When towing a trailer, it will take about _____ as long to pass, stop, or turn.

8. A large vehicle used primarily for vacations and travel is called a _____.

Review Vocabulary

Copy the number of each definition in list A. Match the definition in list A with the term it defines in list B.

List A

9. backup link used in case a trailer hitch fails
10. chart that explains the markings and symbols on a map
11. following a route by reading a map

List B

a. navigating
b. safety chain
c. legend

Think Critically

Write a paragraph to answer each question.

1. Why is it important to have a good reason for every short trip you make in your vehicle?

2. You are planning a ski trip in January with your friends. You will be driving your family's six-month-old sport utility vehicle. What should you do in advance to be prepared for the trip and for any emergencies that might occur?

3. Why is driving a large vehicle more difficult than driving a smaller vehicle?

Chapter 18 Review

Decision Making

1. What can you do to find out weather and traffic conditions before you begin a trip?

2. What main route would you take to go from Seattle to Redmond? What other routes are available?

3. What should you know about your rental car before driving it?

4. If you were pulling a trailer on this road and the trailer began to fishtail, what actions would you take?

Glossary

acceleration lane lane that permits drivers entering an expressway to accelerate to the speed of expressway traffic (225)

accelerator pedal controls the flow of fuel to the engine and regulates speed (43)

active restraint device restraint device that you have to engage (100)

advisory speed limit speed limit set for special conditions such as sharp curves (22)

alternator device that generates an electrical current needed to recharge the battery and operate electrical equipment in a vehicle (357)

alternator warning light light or gauge on the instrument panel warning that the battery is being drained (41)

angle parking parking the vehicle diagonally to the curb (120)

antilock braking system (ABS) computer-controlled braking system that keeps the wheels from locking if the driver brakes hard (41)

assigned-risk insurance provides minimum bodily injury and property damage liability coverage to high-risk drivers for a higher premium (346)

backup lights white lights at the rear of the vehicle that tell other drivers you are backing up (81)

banked curve curve higher on the outside than it is on the inside that helps overcome a vehicle's tendency to move to the outside of the curve (97)

basic speed law law stating that you may not drive faster than is safe and prudent for existing conditions, regardless of posted speed limits (22)

belted tire tire that has special layers added to a bias-ply tire for improved strength, performance, and mileage (365)

blind-spot area area that rearview mirrors cannot show (44)

blood-alcohol concentration (BAC) amount of alcohol in the blood expressed as a percentage of alcohol in the bloodstream (318)

blowout sudden loss of tire air pressure while driving (95, 268)

blue-book price average market value for a specific model and age of a used vehicle (339)

bodily-injury insurance covers the driver who is at fault against claims (342)

brake fade loss of braking effectiveness caused by the brakes overheating after long, continuous, hard braking (270)

braking distance distance your vehicle travels from the time you apply the brake until your vehicle stops (99)

car pooling several individuals sharing transportation to one or more destinations in a car (349)

carbon monoxide colorless, odorless, tasteless gas contained in the exhaust fumes of gasoline engines (261)

carburetor engine part that mixes air and gasoline in the proper proportion and sends it as a fine mist to the engine cylinders (361)

catalytic converter part of a vehicle's emission system that converts harmful gases into less harmful gases and water (361)

center of gravity point around which an object's weight is evenly distributed (92)

central vision cone-shaped area of up to 10 degrees in your field of vision in which you can see clearly while looking straight ahead (68)

closed zone space not open to you because of a restriction in your line of sight or intended path of travel (66)

clutch pedal pedal in a manual transmission vehicle that enables a driver to shift gears (43)

collision contact between two or more objects, as when two vehicles collide into each other (9)

collision insurance provides coverage to pay the costs of repair or replacement of your vehicle from a collision (344)

color-blindness inability to distinguish colors (298)

commentary driving system of thinking out loud as you practice the IPDE Process (83)

common speed speed used by most drivers on an expressway (231)

comprehensive insurance provides coverage for replacement or repair of your vehicle from damage other than from a collision (344)

compromise space reduce risk by giving as much space as possible to the greater of two or more hazards (79)

console compartment mounted between the front seats in a vehicle (42)

controlled-access highway highway that vehicles can enter and exit only at interchanges (222)

controlled braking reducing speed as quickly as possible while maintaining steering control of your vehicle (258)

controlled intersection intersection at which traffic signals or signs determine the right of way (134)

controlled railroad crossing railroad crossing controlled by flashing red lights and/or crossing gates (138)

countersteer steer in the opposite direction (277)

cover the brake take your foot off the accelerator and hold it over the brake pedal to be ready to brake quickly (184)

crossbuck large white X-shaped sign located beside an uncontrolled railroad crossing (141)

cruise control device that lets you maintain your desired speed without keeping your foot on the accelerator (42)

deceleration lane expressway lane used to slow your vehicle without blocking vehicles behind you (235)

decide third step of the IPDE Process in which the driver selects the best actions as well as when and where to take them to avoid conflicts (6)

deductible amount an insurance policyholder agrees to pay toward vehicle repair or replacement (344)

defensive driving protecting yourself and others from dangerous and unexpected driving situations (7)

delayed green light indicates that one side of an intersection has a green light while the light for the oncoming traffic remains red (137)

depreciation decrease in the value of a vehicle over time (336)

depressant drug that can slow down the central nervous system (321)

depth perception ability to judge distance between yourself and other objects (300)

designated driver person who decides ahead of time not to drink alcoholic beverages and is appointed to drive others who do drink (320)

differential arrangement of gears at the rear of the vehicle allowing one wheel to revolve faster than the opposite wheel during turns (356)

downshifting shifting from a higher to a lower gear (56)

drive shaft in rear-wheel vehicles, long metal tube turned by the transmission that carries power to the differential (356)

driving task all social, physical, and mental skills required to drive (6)

driving under the influence (DUI) an offense for which a driver can be charged in some states if the driver's blood-alcohol concentration is above 0.05 (323)

driving while intoxicated (DWI) an offense for which a driver can be charged in all states if the driver's blood-alcohol concentration is above a certain level (323)

emotion strong feeling such as anger, fear, and joy (292)

energy of motion kinetic energy or the energy an object has because it is moving (93)

engine-management system computerized system that monitors and adjusts the fuel, ignition, and emission systems (371)

entrance ramp ramp leading onto an expressway (225)

euphoria false sense of well-being developed as a result of alcohol or drug consumption (315)

execute fourth step of the IPDE Process in which a driver performs proper vehicle control responses to avoid possible conflicts (7)

exit ramp ramp leading off an expressway (235)

field of vision all the area a person can see while looking straight ahead (67)

field sobriety test series of on-the-spot, roadside tests that help an officer detect impairment of a driver suspected of DUI or DWI (324)

financial responsibility law law that requires you to prove that you can pay for collision damages you cause that result in death, injury, or property damage (342)

fishtail sliding of the rear of a vehicle from side to side (258)

flashing signal traffic signal that alerts drivers to dangerous conditions or tells them to stop (29)

force of impact force with which one moving object hits another object; varies according to speed, weight, and distance between impact and stop (100)

4–6 second range area where you will be traveling during the next 4 to 6 seconds, and where you get the final update of how you are controlling your intended path of travel (67)

fresh green light light that has just turned from red to green (136)

friction force that keeps each tire from sliding on the road (94)

friction point in shifting, the point at which you feel the engine take hold and the vehicle start to move (53)

fringe vision the part of your peripheral vision that is closest to your central vision and helps you monitor zone changes (300)

fuel-injection system fuel-combustion system (replacing a carburetor) in which vaporized fuel is pumped under pressure to the engine cylinders (361)

full stop a complete stop as required at a STOP sign or red light (20)

gap distance between vehicles (144)

glare recovery time time your eyes need to regain clear vision after being affected by glare (301)

glare resistance ability to continue seeing when looking at bright lights (301)

graduated driver licensing program program requiring young drivers to progress through a series of licensing stages with various restrictions (11)

gravity force that pulls all things to earth (92)

ground viewing making quick glances to the roadway in front of your vehicle (70)

guide sign sign that gives directions, distance, services, points of interest, and other information (25)

hallucinogen mind-altering drug that tends to distort a person's perceptions of direction, distance, and time (322)

hand-over-hand steering pulling the steering wheel down with one hand while the other hand crosses over to pull the wheel farther down (113)

hazard flasher device that flashes front turn-signal lights and taillights to warn others the vehicle is a hazard (44)

head restraints padded devices on the backs of front seats that help reduce whiplash injuries in a collision (44)

highway hypnosis drowsy or trancelike condition caused by concentration on the roadway ahead and monotony of driving (238)

highway transportation system (HTS) complex system made up of people, vehicles, and roadways (4)

hydroplaning occurs when a tire loses road contact by rising up on top of water (252)

identify first step in the IPDE Process in which the driver locates potential hazards (6)

ignition switch switch operated by a key which starts or stops the engine (42)

implied-consent law states that anyone who receives a driver's license automatically consents to be tested for blood-alcohol content and other drugs if stopped for suspicion of drug use while driving (323)

inhibitions inner forces of personality that restrain or hold back impulsive behavior (316)

international symbols symbols used on traffic signs that give a message without using words (26)

intoxilyzer breath-test machine most commonly used for determining blood-alcohol content (324)

IPDE Process organized process of seeing, thinking, and responding that includes the steps of identifying, predicting, deciding, and executing (6–7)

jack hand-operated device used to lift and hold one corner or side of the vehicle (268)

joining traffic turning right or left into lanes of other vehicles (144)

lane signal signal, usually overhead, that tells whether a lane can or cannot be used at a specific time (30)

leasing alternative to purchasing a vehicle (338)

legend chart that explains the markings and symbols used on a map (380)

liability insurance provides compensation for damages to a third party for which the insured is legally obligated to pay; covers others when you are at fault (342)

line of sight distance you can see ahead in the direction you are looking (65–66)

lug nuts devices that hold the wheel to the vehicle (269)

mass transportation involves moving large numbers of people together from place to place (349)

master cylinder device in the brake system from which brake fluid is forced to the wheel cylinders when a driver steps on the brake pedal (363)

median area of ground separating traffic moving in opposite directions (202)

merging area stretch of roadway at the end of an acceleration lane on an expressway where vehicles join the flow of traffic (225)

minimize a hazard reduce the possibility of conflict by putting more space between your vehicle and the hazard (78)

minimum speed limit speed limit to keep traffic moving safely by not allowing drivers to drive slower than a certain speed (22)

moped two-wheeled vehicle that can be driven with either a motor or pedal (160)

motor scooter low-powered, two-wheeled vehicle that is more powerful than a moped (161)

muffler device that reduces the noise from combustion sounds in the engine (362)

navigating following a route by reading a map (384)

night blindness not being able to see well at night (300)

no-fault insurance covers an insured's losses and expenses associated with a collision regardless of who is at fault (342)

no-zones large blind-spot areas where truck drivers cannot see other vehicles (168)

nystagmus involuntary jerking of the eyes as a person gazes to the side (325)

odometer device on the instrument panel indicating the total number of miles the vehicle has been driven (40)

oil pump device that forces oil from the oil pan to parts of the engine that need lubrication (359)

open zone space where you can drive without a restriction to your line of sight or intended path of travel (65)

orderly visual search pattern process of searching critical areas in a regular sequence (67)

overdriving headlights driving at a speed that makes your stopping distance longer than the distance lighted by your headlights (248)

oversteer turning the steering wheel too much (110)

overtake pass the vehicle ahead (186)

over-the-counter (OTC) medicine drug that can be obtained legally without a doctor's prescription (321)

parallel parking parking the vehicle parallel to the curb (121)

passive restraint device restraint device, such as an air bag or an automatic seat belt, that works automatically (100)

path of travel space your vehicle will occupy as you travel ahead (65)

pedestrian signal signal used at heavy traffic intersections that tells pedestrians whether they should walk or wait (30)

peer education process in which young people help other young people make decisions and determine goals (327)

peer pressure influence of others of a similar age (326)

perception distance distance your vehicle travels during perception time (98)

perception time length of time you take to identify, predict, and decide to slow for a hazard (98)

peripheral vision area a person can see to the left and right of central vision (68)

perpendicular parking parking the vehicle at a right angle to the curb (120)

personal reference point adapting the standard reference point to one's own vehicle (119)

point-of-no-return point beyond which a driver can no longer stop safely without entering the intersection (132)

powerplant vehicle's engine or motor that generates power (356)

power steering system that uses a hydraulic pump and fluid to make steering easier (363)

predict second step of the IPDE Process in which the driver anticipates possible conflicts (6)

premium specified amount of money paid to an insurance company for insurance coverage over a specified period of time (342)

prescription medicine drug that can be purchased legally only when ordered by a doctor (321)

preventive maintenance routine care and attention to your vehicle (368)

principal driver person who will drive a certain vehicle most often (345)

property-damage insurance protects the driver who is at fault against claims for damages to another person's property, up to specified limits (342)

protected left turn left turn made on a left-turn light, green arrow, or delayed green light while oncoming traffic is stopped (137)

protective equipment items a motorcyclist wears to protect head, eyes, and body (156)
pull-out area additional right lane on narrow mountain roadways for slower-moving vehicles (214)
push-pull steering pushing the steering wheel up with one hand and pulling it down with the other (113)

radial tire tire that has plies that run straight across under the tread and strengthening belts of steel or other materials that circle the tire (365)
radiator part of cooling system that holds and cools the coolant (360)
reaction distance distance your vehicle travels while you react (99)
reaction time length of time you take to execute your action (98)
recreational vehicle large vehicle such as a van, motor home, camper, travel trailer, pickup truck, or sport utility vehicle, used mainly for pleasure and travel (165)
reference point a part of the outside or inside of the vehicle, as viewed from the driver's seat, that relates to some part of the roadway (119)
regulatory sign sign that controls traffic (20)
restraint device any part of a vehicle that holds an occupant in the seat during a collision (100)
ride the brake resting your foot on the brake pedal while driving (184)
riding the clutch resting your foot on the clutch pedal while driving (54)
right of way privilege of having immediate use of a certain part of a roadway (21, 142)
right-turn-on-red turning right when the red signal is on unless specifically prohibited to turn (137)
risk in driving, possibility of having a conflict that results in a collision (4)
roadway marking marking that gives you a warning or direction (31)
roadway users people who use the HTS by walking, driving, or riding (4)
rocking a vehicle repeating the sequence of driving forward a little and then back a little to move your vehicle out of deep snow, mud, or sand (254)
rumble strips sections of rough pavement intended to alert drivers of approaching roadway construction, tollbooth plaza, or other traffic conditions (33)
runaway vehicle ramp place on mountain roads for vehicles to safely get out of traffic when their brakes are not effective (214)

safety chains backup link used in case a trailer hitch fails (388)
scanning glancing continually and quickly with very brief eye fixations through your orderly visual search pattern (68)
school zone portion of a street or highway near a school that is subject to special speed limits (24)
selector lever device in an automatic transmission vehicle used to select gears (42)
selective seeing identifying and selecting only those clues and events that restrict your line of sight or can change your intended path of travel (69)
separate the hazards process of adjusting the speed of a vehicle to handle one hazard at a time when two or more hazards threaten a driver (78)
shared left-turn lane lane on a busy street that helps drivers make safer mid-block left turns into business areas from a center lane (31, 115)
skid when tires lose part or all of their grip on the road (256)
slow-moving vehicle vehicle unable to travel at highway speed (209)
Smith System organized method designed to help drivers develop good seeing habits by using five rules for safe driving (7, 64)
solar-powered vehicle vehicle that captures light from the sun and transforms it into electrical power (350)
space cushion open area around a vehicle consisting of adequate following distance between it and the vehicles ahead and behind, plus swerve paths to left and right (76)
speed smear occurs when objects off to your sides become blurred and distorted as your speed increases (302)
stale green light light that has been green for a long time (136)
standard reference point point on the vehicle typical for most drivers (119)
stimulant drug that speeds up the central nervous system (322)
switchback turn in a road that bends sharply in the opposite direction (213)

tailgate to follow another vehicle too closely (180)

target stationary object that appears in the distance in the center of the path you intend to occupy (50)

target area section of roadway where the target is located and the area to the left and right of the target (66)

target area range space from your vehicle out to target area (66)

thermostat part of cooling system that opens and shuts to control the flow of coolant to the radiator (360)

total stopping distance distance your vehicle travels while you make a stop (98)

traction friction or gripping power between the tires and the roadway surface (74, 94)

tractor-semitrailer type of tractor-trailer that pulls one trailer; commonly called an "eighteen wheeler" (167)

tractor trailer truck that has a powerful tractor that pulls a separate trailer (167)

traffic circle intersection that forms when several roadways meet at a circle (130)

traffic signal any signal used to control the movement of traffic (27)

transaxle device in a front-wheel drive vehicle that carries power to the front wheels via two half-shafts (356)

transmission mechanism in a vehicle that delivers power from the engine to the drive wheels (356)

tread outer grooved surface of a tire that grips the road (94)

tunnel vision being able to see in a narrow field of vision of 140° or less (300)

turnabout maneuver for turning your vehicle around to go in the opposite direction (116)

12–15 second range area you will be traveling in during the next 12 to 15 seconds, and where you need to identify changes in your path of travel (66–67)

uncontrolled intersection intersection that has no signs or signals to regulate traffic (139)

uncontrolled railroad crossing railroad crossing that does not have flashing red lights or crossing gates (140)

underinsured motorist insurance covers costs that exceed what the other person's insurance company will pay as a result of a collision (344)

understeer not turning the steering wheel enough (110)

uninsured motorist insurance covers costs up to a certain amount if you are struck by another vehicle whose driver has no insurance (344)

unprotected left turn left turn made at a signal-controlled intersection without a special left-turn light (137)

van pooling several individuals sharing transportation to one or more destinations in a van (349)

vehicle code federal and state laws that regulate the HTS (5)

velocitation condition of unconsciously driving too fast as a result of driving for long periods at high speeds (238)

visual acuity ability to see things clearly both near and far away (298)

warning sign sign that alerts you to possible hazards and road conditions (23)

warranty written guarantee that the seller will make certain repairs for a stated period of time (339)

water pump part of cooling system that draws coolant from the radiator and forces it through the engine's cooling passages (360)

wolf pack group of vehicles traveling together in a bunch on an expressway (231)

yield to allow another vehicle or roadway user to proceed first (21, 142)

zero-tolerance law law stating it is illegal for persons under the age of 21 to drive with any measurable amount of alcohol in the blood (324)

zone one of six areas of space around a vehicle that is the width of a lane and extends as far as the driver can see (65)

Zone Control System organized method for managing the space—or six zones—around your vehicle (7, 64)

Index

Acknowledgments

Unless otherwise acknowledged, all photographs are the property of Prentice Hall. Page abbreviations are as follows: (t) top, (c) center, (b) bottom, (l) left, (r) right.

Cover David Epperson/Tony Stone Images; automobile console courtesy of Bredemann Ford, Glenview, IL
1 H. Abernathy/H.Armstrong Roberts, Inc.
2–3 David Young-Wolff/PhotoEdit
5 (br) Jonathan Naurok/PhotoEdit
5 (tr) Mark Burnett/Stock Boston
5 (l) Alan Carey/Image Works
10 Tony Freeman/PhotoEdit
17 (bl) Superstock, Inc.
18–19 Colin Young-Wolff/PhotoEdit
28 (t) Tony Freeman/PhotoEdit
37 Charles Feil/Stock Boston
38–39 Robert Llewellyn/Corbis
41 Courtesy, Jennings Chevrolet
42 Courtesy, Jennings Chevrolet
45 Courtesy, Jennings Chevrolet
48 Courtesy, Jennings Chevrolet
50 Courtesy, Bredemann Ford, Glenview, IL
60–61 Siri Schwartzman
70 Mark Richards/PhotoEdit
88–89 David R. Frazier Photolibrary
90–91 SuperStock, Inc./SuperStock
103 David J. Sams/Texas Imprint/Stock Boston
107 (tl) Courtesy, Bredemann Ford, Glenview, IL
113 Courtesy of American Driver and Traffic Safety Education Association
123 (all) Jim Brady
127 (r) SuperStock/Alamy
128–129 Mark Gibson
138 Frank Rossotto/Stock Market
148–149 Michael Newman/PhotoEdit
151 Ron Davis Photography
154 D. H. Hessel/Stock Boston
155 Motorcycle Safety Project/Courtesy, Northern Illinois University
160 (t) Robert Brenner/PhotoEdit
163 Ulrike Welsch/PhotoEdit
165 Gabe Palmer/Stock Market
166 Courtesy, Glenview, IL Fire Department
171 (bl) Courtesy, Glenview, IL Fire Department
172–173 SuperStock, Inc.
174–175 Neil Lukas/Dorling Kindersley
187 David Young-Wolff/PhotoEdit
193 (bl) Alex Segre/Alamy
194–195 Jeff Greenberg/PhotoEdit
202 Bill Horsman/Stock Boston
214 SPECTRUM EuroStock/Robertstock
215 Kent Knudson/Stock Boston
216 Tony Freeman/PhotoEdit
220–221 Tony Freeman/PhotoEdit
222 Alex MacLean/Landslides
223 (t) Alex MacLean/Landslides
223 (c) Alex MacLean/Landslides
223 (b) Alex MacLean/Landslides
231 Momatiuk & Eastcott/Stock Boston
238 Mark Burnett/Stock Boston
244–245 Chuck Keeler, Jr./Corbis
249 Mark C. Burnett/Stock Boston
250 Mulvehill/Image Works
251 Frank Siteman/Stock Boston
252 Robert W. Ginn/PhotoEdit
254 (b) Chris Sorensen/Stock Market
257 (tl) Jim Brady
257 (bl) Jim Brady
262 David Epperson/Tony Stone Images
266–267 Ingram Publishing/SuperStock
274 Jonathan Naurok/PhotoEdit
283 Bob Daemmrich/Stock Boston
288–289 A&L Sinibaldi/Tony Stone Images
290–291 Ron Chapple/PictureQuest
304 Cindy Charles/PhotoEdit
307 Felicia Martinez/PhotoEdit
308 John Neubauer/PhotoEdit
312–313 Park Street/PhotoEdit
314 (cap inset) Tony Freeman/PhotoEdit
321 Steve Skjold/PhotoEdit
326 Steve Skjold/PhotoEdit
333 (br) Cleve Bryant/PhotoEdit
334–335 Nick Vedros/SuperStock
337 (tl) Ron Kimball Stock Photography/Ron Kimball
337 (tr) Ron Kimball Stock Photography/Ron Kimball
337 (bl) Photo by Business Wire via Getty Images
337 (br) Carphotos/Alamy
347 Mark Burnett/Stock Boston
349 David Young-Wolff/PhotoEdit
350 (t) John Hillery/Reuters/Corbis
350 (b) Michael Klinec/Alamy
353 (tl) Vincent DeWitt/Stock Boston
353 (bl) Tony Freeman/PhotoEdit
353 (br) Tony Freeman/PhotoEdit
354–355 Tony Freeman/PhotoEdit
371 (t) Ron Perry/Transtock
371 (b) Donald Dietz/Stock Boston
375 (br) Rhoda Sidney/Image Works
375 (bl) David R. Frazier Photolibrary, Inc./Alamy
376–377 Jim Conaty/Omni-Photo Communications, Inc.
381 "Map © by Rand McNally R.L. #98-S-135"
382 allOver photography/Alamy
383 Charles Feil/Stock Boston
384 Spencer Grant/PhotoEdit
385 Michael Newman/PhotoEdit
391 (tl) Tony Freeman/PhotoEdit
391 (tr) Courtesy, Washington State Department of Transportation
391 (bl) Kathy Ferguson/PhotoEdit
391 (br) Bill Ross/H. Armstrong Roberts, Inc.